Patent Law
Essentials

Patent Law Essentials

A Concise Guide

THIRD EDITION

Alan L. Durham

Westport, Connecticut
London

Library of Congress Cataloging-in-Publication Data

Durham, Alan L., 1963-
  Patent law essentials : a concise guide / Alan Durham. – 3rd ed.
      p. cm.
  Includes bibliographical references and index.
  ISBN 978-0-313-35394-9 (alk. paper)
  1. Patent laws and legislation–United States. I. Title.
  KF3114.85.D87 2009
   346.7304'86–dc22   2008036354

British Library Cataloguing in Publication Data is available.

Library of Congress Catalog Card Number: 2008036354
ISBN: 978-0-313-35394-9

First published in 2009

Praeger Publishers, 88 Post Road West, Westport, CT 06881
An imprint of Greenwood Publishing Group, Inc.
www.praeger.com

Printed in the United States of America

The paper used in this book complies with the
Permanent Paper Standard issued by the National
Information Standards Organization (Z39.48–1984).

10   9   8   7   6   5   4   3   2   1

Contents

Preface

This book began with an expert witness. A preeminent authority in a specialized field of engineering, he had been hired to testify on the defendant's behalf in a high-stakes patent infringement case. Like many people who find themselves confronting the arcane system of patent law for the first time, he wanted know the "rules of the game." At the time there were expansive resources for lawyers, generally in many volumes, and study aids directed at law students, but no books I could recommend offering the right mixture of sophistication and simplicity. If there were such a book, I thought, I could use it myself. As an attorney in the field I knew the standard rules of patent law, but I did not always have at my fingertips recent authorities to support them. Those authorities had to be sought out in the multi-volume treatises or the indexed case reporters—a time-consuming chore simply because they included so much material. So I determined to write for myself a concise book on patent law that could serve either purpose. It would be accessible enough, I hoped, to introduce non-lawyers to the "rules of the game," while sophisticated enough to provide attorneys a useful desk reference—a starting place, at least, for further research. This is the result of that ambition, now in its third edition. I have been pleased to learn that not only attorneys and engineers have found it useful, but also business people, judges, patent examiners, professors, and law students—some of whom have contacted me with encouraging feedback. I thank them all.

As this edition goes to press, there are hints of change on the horizon. For years patent law seemed to grow irrepressibly. Through a series of landmark court decisions, computer software, biological organisms, and business methods all came within its expanding borders. Businesses found in their patent portfolios a new source of wealth, and disputes with corporate giants like Microsoft and Research In Motion made headlines. At the same time, the patent system seemed to lose some popular respect, as the idea caught on that "anything can be patented." Dubious patents, like the one for a method of exercising a cat using a laser pointer,[1] became the butt of humor. Yet now there are signs of contrary forces at work. The Supreme Court has rejected legalistic formulas to identify which inventions are patentably "non-obvious" in favor of plain common sense.[2] The Federal Circuit Court of Appeals has raised new questions about the patentability of abstract thought-based processes.[3] Meanwhile, Congress is considering dramatic patent law reforms that would make the U.S. system more like those of other nations, including enhanced opportunities for the public to oppose questionable patents.[4] What happens next is anyone's guess, but it is certain that patent law will remain, as it has always been, a dynamic and challenging field.

As before, I wish to thank my friends, colleagues, and students at the University of Alabama School of Law for their inspiration and encouragement. Dean Kenneth Randall and the Law School Foundation have supplied critical and much appreciated support for my research. I also thank my former colleagues at Morrison & Foerster and Brown & Bain (now Perkins Coie), whose understanding and flexibility made the first edition of this book a reality.

[1] U.S. Patent No. 5,443,036.
[2] KSR Int'l Co. v. Teleflex Inc., 127 S. Ct. 1727 (2007).
[3] In re Comiskey, 499 F.3d 1365 (Fed. Cir. 2007).
[4] See Section 12.5.

CHAPTER 1

Overview

1.1 ORIGINS

The historical antecedents of the United States patent system are often traced to seventeenth-century England. Then a "patent" might refer to nothing more than a legally sanctioned monopoly, granted to reward a loyal subject or sold to raise funds for the government. A merchant guild, for example, might purchase a patent for the exclusive right to sell playing cards. Freedom from competition allowed the patent owner to sell in larger volumes and at a higher price. Undoubtedly popular with the government and with the patent owners, these "odious monopolies" were a source of resentment to consumers and potential competitors. In 1624 the crown relented and the Statute of Monopolies, abolishing the general power of the monarch to grant exclusive rights, became law. Importantly, the statute ending the general practice of monopolies specifically exempted patents allowing inventors the exclusive right to their inventions.

The tradition of granting patents to inventors continued in colonial America and, in spite of some skepticism by influential thinkers such as Thomas Jefferson, it was incorporated in the laws of the United States. The framers of the Constitution provided to Congress, in Article I, Section 8, the power to "promote the Progress of Science and [the] useful Arts, by securing for limited Times to Authors and inventors the exclusive Right to their respective Writings and Discoveries." This brief language is the source of both patent law and copyright law in the United

States.[1] The specifics were left to Congress, whose last wholesale revision of the Patent Act occurred in 1952, and to the Patent and Trademark Office (also known as the Patent Office or PTO), a division of the Department of Commerce created in 1836. The federal courts too have played a significant role in interpreting, supplementing, and perhaps, on some occasions, rewriting the rules set down by Congress.

Although patent law has evolved in some ways, the theories behind it are much the same today as they were in the beginning. One theory, which still has an eighteenth-century flavor, is that inventors possess a natural right to their inventions that must be recognized by law. Creations are naturally the property of those who labored to create. The more common theory, and the one most clearly reflected in the Constitution, is that patents provide the encouragement necessary for industrial advancement. If a budding Edison feared that the rewards of his inventive efforts would be reaped by a copyist—who did not bear the costs of original research—he might abandon the laboratory for other pursuits. Society would then be denied the benefit of useful inventions. If an inventor can obtain a patent ensuring that only he will profit from his invention, he is more likely to invest the time, effort, skill and resources necessary to discover new technologies.[2]

Patents also benefit society by making available precise descriptions of new inventions. A patent is a public document published by the United States government. One requirement of a patent is that it describe the invention, in both words and drawings, in such detail that other persons in the field can understand the invention and practice it themselves. During the term of the patent, when only the patent owner and licensees have the legal right to practice the invention, this information may be of little interest. Yet patents remain in force only for a limited time, and when the patent expires the invention enters the public domain. The millions of patents that have already expired are a resource that may be freely exploited by anyone, and even an unexpired patent can provide inspiration for new and different approaches to technological problems.

The view that a patent is a kind of *bargain* between the inventor and the public, by which the inventor receives a limited monopoly in exchange for

---

[1] When the Constitution was drafted, "science" was used in a broader sense than it is today, and was generally synonymous with "knowledge." "Arts" also held a different meaning, and the term "useful arts" probably referred to what we would now call "technology." Although counterintuitive, the prevailing view of legal historians is that patent law promotes the "arts," while copyright law promotes "science."

[2] Another theory, popular with some legal scholars, is that patents make the exploitation of resources more efficient by putting a single entity—the owner of the patent—in charge. If multiple parties, without legal restriction, could race to exploit a newly discovered and valuable invention, much wasteful duplication of effort could occur. The costs of such waste are borne, ultimately, by society. Other scholars argue that the stimulating effects of competition counterbalance the waste of duplication.

disclosing the invention to the public, is of more than theoretical interest. Together with the overall constitutional goal of promoting the "useful arts," the bargain model of patents helps to shape the specific rules that determine whether a patent is valid or invalid. In particular, this model will resurface as we examine the concepts of enablement and best mode in Sections 8.6 and 8.7.

1.2 SUMMARY AND ROADMAP

A book about patent law is difficult to organize because an understanding of one principle is so often dependent on an understanding of other principles, ad infinitum. As a *New Yorker* article once observed, patent law is "apt to plunge all but the stoutest minds into dizzying swirls of logic."[3] What follows is a sort of roadmap to this book that may keep readers better oriented as they wind their way through the maze.

Chapter 1 (this chapter) introduces some of the history and theory underpinning patent law, and concludes with a brief discussion of the laws, judicial opinions, and other authorities that are cited throughout this book.

Chapter 2 distinguishes patents from other forms of intellectual property rights with which patents are often confused. Specifically, Chapter 2 briefly discusses copyrights, which protect works of authorship such as writings, musical compositions, and illustrations; trademarks, which protect corporate names and logos; and trade secrets, constituting confidential business information protected by law.

Chapter 3 leads the reader through a close examination of an actual United States patent found in Appendix A. This includes the patent drawings; the specification, which is a detailed prose description of the inventor's work; and the claims. The claims are the last portion of a patent, and they describe in careful terms exactly what the patented invention is.

Chapter 4 discusses the kinds of discoveries that can and cannot be patented, with sections devoted to abstract ideas, principles of nature, living organisms, artistic and literary creations, printed matter, and methods of doing business. Patent protection for computer software is a particularly thorny subject, and it is reserved for discussion with other specialized topics in Chapter 12.

Chapter 5 explains the process one goes through to obtain a patent from the United States Patent Office—a process known as patent prosecution. The complexities discussed include patent applications that spawn offspring, known as continuations, continuations-in-part, or divisional applications; interferences—procedures for determining which of two inventors having competing patents or patent applications actually invented first; and reissue and reexamination, both procedures allowing the Patent Office a second look at applications that have already issued as patents.

---

[3] John Seabrook, The Flash of Genius, THE NEW YORKER, January 11, 1993, at 40.

Chapter 6 examines the issue of inventorship—that is, who should or should not be credited as an inventor—and how an inventor can convey rights to a patented invention, either by assignment or by license. Chapter 6 also discusses how rights to a patented invention can be conveyed, intentionally or unintentionally, by an implied license.

Chapter 7 deals with the issue of interpreting patent claims. This is a difficult but extremely important issue, because deciding what a patent claim *means* is the starting point for determining if the patent is valid or infringed. Chapter 7 reviews some of the tools used to interpret patent claims, including the patent specification and the prosecution history. The latter is a record of the applicant's dealings with the Patent Office. Chapter 7 also discusses problems associated with certain specialized claim formats. Among these are "product-by-process" claims, which describe the invention in terms of the way it is made, and "means-plus-function" claims, which describe claim elements in terms of the functions they perform.

Chapter 8 is one of the longer chapters because it deals with the various conditions of patentability. If a patent application fails to meet any one of these conditions, it should be rejected by the Patent Office. If the application nevertheless slips through the Patent Office, the patent can be held invalid by a court. In fact, in most cases where a charge of infringement results in a lawsuit, the accused infringer argues that the patent is invalid.

Chapter 8 begins with a general discussion of the conditions of patentability, including the presumption that any patent is valid until proven otherwise. The specific topics covered in Chapter 8 include the utility requirement, which means that the patented invention must perform some useful function; the definiteness requirement, which means that the claims must be reasonably precise in identifying the patented invention; the enablement requirement, which means that the patent must include enough information so that others can practice the claimed invention without undue experimentation; the best mode requirement, which means that the inventor must have disclosed the best way he or she knew of practicing the invention at the time the application was filed; and the written description requirement, which means that the patent specification, as filed, must describe the invention ultimately claimed.

Chapter 8 then looks at the novelty requirement, which in many respects is the key to patentability. The claimed invention must be *new* and *non-obvious*, in comparison with the "prior art." Chapter 8 discusses the various kinds of prior art that may be relevant, including prior inventions, prior patents, and prior publications. Chapter 8 also discusses how the date of invention is determined, which can be a critical issue in deciding if another invention, or a patent or publication, is actually *prior* art.

Chapter 8 discusses both anticipation, which invalidates a claim covering an invention found in the prior art, and obviousness, which invalidates a claim covering subject matter that would have been obvious to a person of ordinary skill. If an invention is obvious, perhaps as an elaboration or a combination of prior inventions, it is not considered worthy of a patent. Obviousness is a difficult and subjective inquiry, invariably conducted in hindsight. Chapter 8 examines some of the "secondary considerations," such as commercial success, that are intended as more objective measures of whether an invention was obvious.

Chapter 8 continues with a discussion of the "statutory bars" that can invalidate a patent if the applicant was too slow in filing an application after the occurrence of a critical event—such as an offer to sell a product embodying the invention. Chapter 8 concludes with an examination of double patenting. Double patenting is a ground for invalidating a patent if the same inventor had already patented the invention. This prevents an inventor from obtaining multiple patents on the same thing, thereby extending the period of the patent monopoly beyond the intended span.

Chapter 9 examines two potential defenses to a charge of infringement that, if successful, result in a holding that a patent is "unenforceable." If a patent is unenforceable, a court will not use its powers to prevent that patent from being infringed. The first such defense discussed in Chapter 9 is inequitable conduct. Because only the applicant and the Patent Office are allowed to take part when an application is examined, it is important to hold applicants to a high standard of candor and fair dealing. Inequitable conduct occurs if an applicant intentionally deceives the Patent Office, or withholds critical information, during prosecution. The other unenforceability defense discussed in Chapter 9 is misuse. Misuse refers to attempts to leverage the patent monopoly beyond its intended scope—for example, by requiring that anyone practicing the patented invention purchase an *unpatented* product from the patent owner. This kind of "tying" and other forms of misuse may violate the federal antitrust laws, in addition to rendering a patent unenforceable.

Chapter 10 is another lengthy chapter because it deals with the subject of infringement. After a preliminary discussion covering the temporal and geographical limitations of a patent, Chapter 10 discusses "direct" and "indirect" infringement. Direct infringement includes making, using, selling, offering to sell, or importing into the United States something that falls within the scope of a patent claim. Indirect infringement means inducing or contributing to infringement—for example, by supplying a part that can be used only in a patented combination. An indirect infringer is liable in the same way that a direct infringer is liable.

Chapter 10 then discusses "literal infringement," which occurs if the infringing product or process includes every element required by a patent claim, exactly as described. Next is a discussion of the "doctrine of equivalents," which holds that a product or process can still infringe a claim even though it is *different* from what the claim literally requires, as long as the differences are insubstantial. This is a difficult concept, even for experts and judges, so it is covered in some detail. Chapter 10 discusses how the doctrine of equivalents has evolved, and it examines some of the tests used to determine if a product or process is or is not equivalent to a claimed invention. Chapter 10 also discusses limitations on the scope of equivalency imposed by the prosecution history, the patent disclosure, and the prior art. Chapter 10 further considers equivalency in the related context of means-plus-function claims, as well as the "reverse doctrine of equivalents," which holds that a product does not infringe, even though it is literally described by the patent claims, if it is sufficiently "changed in principle" from what the applicant actually invented. Finally, Chapter 10 discusses a little-used experimental use exception to infringement.

Chapter 11 introduces the subject of patent litigation. Specific topics discussed include jurisdiction and venue, which determine in what court a suit for infringement can be filed; actions for declaratory judgment, which permit an accused infringer to sue a patent owner rather than wait to be sued; burdens of proof, which determine who must prove what and how compelling the evidence must be; and the roles of judge and jury in deciding the various issues presented in a typical case. Chapter 11 also examines the kinds of relief that can be awarded in a suit for patent infringement. These include preliminary injunctions, which bar the continuance of the allegedly infringing activity during the pendency of the lawsuit; permanent injunctions, which permanently bar infringing activity if the patent owner prevails; and money damages, which compensate the patent owner for past infringement. The last award can take the form of lost profits or a reasonable royalty, and they can be increased as much as threefold if the infringement is found to have been willful. Chapter 11 also discusses defenses that can limit the recovery of damages, including the six-year statute of limitations, the patent owner's failure to properly mark products that it has sold, laches, and equitable estoppel. "Laches" refers to unreasonable delay in filing suit that somehow prejudices the accused infringer. "Equitable estoppel" refers to conduct by the patent owner that leads the accused infringer to believe that the patent owner will not pursue a claim.

Chapter 11 ends with a brief discussion of the International Trade Commission, an alternative forum for raising a claim of patent infringement if the accused products are imported into the United States from abroad.

Chapter 12 discusses several specialized topics, including design patents, plant patents, foreign patents, patents claiming computer programs, and the prospects for significant new legislation.

Appendices A and B provide, respectively, samples of actual utility and design patents issued by the United States Patent Office.

1.3 SOURCES OF LAW

Several important sources of patent law will be referenced throughout this book. One is the Patent Act, found at Title 35 of the United States Code. The Patent Act contains most of the legislation enacted by Congress that relates to patents. References to particular sections of the Act will generally be in the format "35 U.S.C. §____." Other important authorities are the Code of Federal Regulations (37 C.F.R.) and the Manual of Patent Examining Procedure (MPEP), which set forth detailed rules and regulations for obtaining a patent.

In addition to the statutes, rules, and regulations, one can find countless reported court decisions interpreting the patent laws. As in any field of federal law, the controlling precedents are those of the United States Supreme Court. However, the Supreme Court only rarely accepts appeals in patent cases, leaving most of the decision making to the lower courts. The most significant of these lower courts, at present, is the Federal Circuit Court of Appeals. Established in 1982, the Federal Circuit, based in Washington, D.C., hears all appeals of patent-related cases, regardless of the place where the suit was initially filed. Except on those occasions when the Supreme Court intervenes, the Federal Circuit is the ultimate authority on what patent laws mean, and all inferior courts, as well as the Patent Office, are bound by its interpretations.

Cases referred to in this book are accompanied by citations, generally in the footnotes. The standard citation format includes the name of the case, followed by the volume of the official reporter in which it appears, the abbreviated name of the official reporter, the relevant page numbers, and in parentheses an identification of the court and the date of the decision. For example, *Pfizer Inc. v. Apotex, Inc.*, 480 F.3d 1348, 1359–60 (Fed. Cir. 2007), refers to a case reported in Volume 480 of the *Federal Reporter* (Third Series) beginning at page 1348. The pages of particular interest are pages 1359–60, and the decision was rendered by the Federal Circuit Court of Appeals in 2007. These citations are provided in case the reader needs additional information or authority to support a particular proposition.

CHAPTER 2

Patents Distinguished from Other Rights

People sometimes confuse patents with copyrights or trademarks, saying, for example, that George Lucas has a "patent" on the name "Star Wars." Patents, copyrights, trademarks, and trade secrets are all legal means of protecting "intellectual property"—a term referring to the intangible creations of the human mind in which the law recognizes some form of ownership. However, patents, copyrights, trademarks, and trade secrets are each governed by a unique body of rules and requirements, and, in spite of some overlap, they are generally designed to protect different sorts of intellectual creations. Therefore, a good starting point for explaining what a patent *is* may be to explain what it is *not.*

2.1 COPYRIGHTS

Copyrights protect "works of authorship," broadly defined by statute to include writings in the conventional sense and, among other things, dramatic works, musical compositions, choreography, paintings, sculptures, photographs, motion pictures, audio recordings, and architecture. To some degree, any work of authorship has an aspect of creative "expression." Copyright protects this expression, not the underlying ideas. Although idea and expression can be difficult to sort out, one could, for example, borrow the information published in this book without violating its copyright. No matter what labor was expended to compile the information, it can be freely used.[1] On the other hand, duplicating the book's language or organization could tread on areas of expression—creative choices unique to the author and protected by copyright.

Copyrights do not apply to technological innovations or to the useful features of products. A new and more efficient spark plug design could not be copyrighted. Some useful products do have an aesthetic aspect that can be protected by copyright, but the artistic component of the design must be distinguishable from the utilitarian component. For example, a belt buckle might be copyrighted as a sculpture,[2] but the copyright cannot prevent the borrowing of some mechanical aspect of the design, such as an improved latching mechanism. In this respect a copyright is the antithesis of a patent, which is specifically intended to protect technological advancements. If one had both a copyright and a patent on the same belt buckle, the copyright would protect only the aesthetic appearance of the belt buckle, and the patent would protect only the mechanism by which it worked.[3]

As we will see in Section 8.9, an invention is patentable only if it is sufficiently new and different compared with prior inventions that persons skilled in the field would not have considered it obvious. In contrast, copyright law has no requirement of novelty. As long as the work of authorship is an original product of the author's imagination, a copyright cannot be denied simply because the work is similar to others that have gone before. This may be the case because of the difficulty of judging novelty or obviousness in relation to the kinds of creative works that are traditionally protected by copyright. Who can say whether the latest mystery novel is an obvious variation of the thousands that have gone before? By the same token, independent creation is a complete defense to infringement of copyright, regardless of the similarity of two works. If two songs are nearly identical to one another, but it can be shown that the second composer never had access to the first composition, the second composer committed no act of infringement.[4] Patent law is very different. One who innocently infringes a patent, perhaps not even knowing that the patent or the patented product exists, can still be held accountable in the courts.

One area in which patent and copyright converge is in the protection of computer software. Software blurs the boundaries between a work of authorship and a machine. From the perspective of a programmer, a computer program is a kind of writing. It is expressed in a language that resembles in some respects ordinary human languages, and the process of authorship involves some of the aesthetic choices and personal style associated with other forms of

---

[1] *See* Feist Publications, Inc. v. Rural Telephone Service Co., 499 U.S. 340, 347 (1991) (Facts are not copyrightable because they "do not owe their origin to an act of authorship.").

[2] *See* Kieselstein-Cord v. Accessories By Pearl, Inc., 632 F.2d 989 (2d Cir. 1980).

[3] Unless the patent was a "design patent," a special category of patent discussed in Section 12.1.

[4] Although the similarity of the two works could be considered evidence that the second composer did not, in fact, work independently.

writing. Copyright, rather than patent, would seem the proper vehicle for protecting this expression. On the other hand, a program is akin to a machine part when executed by a computer. The program controls the operation of the computer much as cogs and wheels controlled machines of an earlier era. From this perspective, a computer program seems outside of the subject matter protected by copyright and more suitable for protection by patent.

Courts and scholars have struggled for decades to determine the proper application of copyright and patent law to computer software. At present, both forms of protection are available, though each has its limitations. A computer program can be copyrighted, but this may not prevent someone else from extracting the functional aspects of the program to incorporate in a new program. The functional aspects of computer software can be patented as long as they meet the various requirements of patentability (such as novelty and non-obviousness) and as long as the patent steers clear of monopolizing an abstract idea, mathematical algorithm, or principle of nature. These special concerns are discussed in some detail in Section 12.4.

2.2 TRADEMARKS

Trademarks are governed by federal statutes, by state laws, and by common law. A trademark is a device, such as a word, phrase, or symbol, that is used to represent the origin of a product. A consumer who finds the word "Nike" on a shoe box, or the familiar Nike "swoosh" symbol, is entitled to conclude that the shoe sold in the box is the genuine article. The overriding purpose of trademark law is the protection of consumers, and disputes in this area are usually resolved by determining whether consumers would be confused by the use of a mark that is similar to the mark of another business. If another shoe manufacturer adopted the name "Nikke" for its line of products, the original Nike would doubtless challenge such use as unfair and confusing. Patents are granted only on inventions—not on labels, logos, or brand names. Trademarks, on the other hand, do not secure exclusive rights to the functional aspects of a product.[5]

2.3 TRADE SECRETS

Patents are not the only way that inventors can prevent others from taking advantage of their labors. Another option is to keep the invention a secret. An inventor cannot do both. As soon as a patent issues, the invention becomes public knowledge. This is a part of the bargain that the inventor strikes with the government in order to obtain the patent monopoly. However, the process of applying for a patent can be kept confidential. If an inventor applies for a

[5] Traffix Devices, Inc. v. Marketing Displays, Inc., 532 U.S. 23, 29 (2001).

patent, but the application is rejected, the inventor can abandon the attempt and still retain some protection by keeping the invention a secret.

Whether an inventor is better advised to patent an invention or simply keep it a secret may depend on the nature of the invention. If it is something that will be revealed as soon as products incorporating the invention are placed on the market, attempts to keep the invention secret may be self-defeating. On the other hand, certain inventions can be exploited without making them public. For example, an ordinary product, indistinguishable from any other, might be manufactured less expensively because of an innovative process. The process might be better protected through secrecy than through a patent, which would last only for a limited term.

If secret information is of the kind that gives one an advantage in business, it may be protectable under "trade secret" law. Trade secrets are largely governed by state laws, rather than federal law, so there is some geographic variation in the way the laws are organized and worded, and possibly in their scope of protection. However, nearly all states have adopted, in some form, a model statute known as the Uniform Trade Secrets Act. The definition of "trade secret" under the Uniform Act extends to various forms of information, including "a formula, pattern, compilation, program, device, method, technique or process."[6] Although such things as formulas, devices, and processes also fall within the realm of potentially patentable inventions,[7] trade secret law imposes a different set of requirements. To qualify as a protectable trade secret under the Uniform Act, the information must "derive independent economic value, actual or potential, from not being generally known to, and not being readily ascertainable by proper means by, other persons who can obtain economic value from its disclosure or use."[8] In other words, not only must the information be secret, it must also be *valuable*. In addition, the information must be "the subject of efforts that are reasonable under the circumstances to maintain its secrecy."[9] A company that is lax about security may be unable to resort to trade secret law to protect its information from use or disclosure. Patent law, in contrast, requires neither that an invention be economically valuable nor (under most circumstances) that it have been kept secret.[10]

While patent law bars "infringement," trade secret law forbids "misappropriation." Misappropriation includes unauthorized disclosure or use of

---

[6] Uniform Trade Secrets Act § 1(4).

[7] Trade secret law can also be used to protect certain kinds of business information that would not be patentable—for example, customer lists and marketing plans. As long as information is secret and valuable to a business, it can be protected as a trade secret, even though it is not an invention in the usual sense.

[8] Uniform Trade Secrets Act § 1(4)(i).

[9] Uniform Trade Secrets Act § 1(4)(ii).

[10] An exception arises if the invention was disclosed more than one year before a patent application was filed. See Section 8.10.

trade secret information by someone who has a duty to keep the information secret or to limit its use.[11] Employees, for example, are generally duty-bound to refrain from using or disclosing the trade secret information of their employers. So is anyone who has signed a contract or confidentiality agreement promising to protect the information. An employee of a soda company who publicized his employer's secret formula on the Internet, or who used the formula to devise a rival soda, would likely be held liable for trade secret misappropriation.

Misappropriation also includes (1) the use of information known to be derived from someone under a duty to keep it confidential and (2) acquisition of the secret information by "improper means."[12] A person who bribed a soda company employee to obtain its secret formula would likely be guilty of misappropriation. Finally, misappropriation can occur, under the Uniform Act, if trade secret information is used by persons who know that the information has come into their possession only because of a mistake. If a soda manufacturer received a fax from a competitor setting out a secret formula, and it was evident that the fax had been intended for someone else, the rival would probably not be permitted to keep the fax and use the formula.

Trade secret law differs from patent law in requiring either some connection with a duty, contractual or otherwise, to protect the confidential information; the use of improper means to acquire the information; or an evident mistake. If the information was acquired under other circumstances, it can be freely used. For example, the Uniform Act allows the acquisition of information by "reverse engineering." Reverse engineering means beginning with the finished product and analyzing it to determine the process by which it was developed or the principle of its operation. As long as the finished product was acquired legitimately—by purchase on the open market, for example—it is not a violation of trade secret law to reverse-engineer the product and use the resulting information in a competing product. Hence, if a rival soda manufacturer could analyze a beverage and determine the formula, trade secret law (applying the Uniform Act) would not prevent the rival from discovering and using that information. Patent law, in contrast, does not distinguish between information acquired legitimately or illegitimately. A product can still infringe a patent, even if it was the result of reverse engineering or independent development.

Trade secret law might seem at odds with patent law, which requires the public disclosure of information in exchange for exclusive rights. The Supreme Court, however, has ruled that the two bodies of law are not incompatible, and federal patent law does not preempt state trade secret laws.[13] One complements

---

[11] Uniform Trade Secrets Act § 1(2)(ii).

[12] *Id.*

[13] Kewanee Oil Co. v. Bicron Corp., 416 U.S. 470 (1974).

the other, and inventors have a choice of means to protect their inventions, the most appropriate of which will be determined by the circumstances.

2.4 PATENTS

Patents cover practical inventions in the "useful arts." Any technological advance, from a new microchip to an improved formula for bubble gum, can be the subject of a patent. A special form of patent known as a "design patent" can protect some forms of artistic expression (see Section 12.1), but the usual kind of patent–the "utility patent"–applies only to technological inventions. As a result, a patent cannot be granted for a painting, a novel, a song, a product name, or a company logo.

To obtain a patent, an inventor must file an application with the United States Patent and Trademark Office, and the application must describe the invention in such a way that persons skilled in the field could practice the invention. The application must conclude with numbered "claims" that describe in precise terms exactly what the patent is intended to cover. A patent can be granted, or if granted can be held valid in the courts, only if the claims describe an invention that is both *new* and *non-obvious.* Patent law thus includes a requirement of novelty that is absent from copyright and trademark law.

Once an application issues as a patent, the patent remains in force until 20 years after the date the application was filed. During that time, no one without the permission of the patent owner can (within the geographical limits of the United States) make, use, sell, offer to sell, or import the invention described by the patent claims. To do so is an infringement of the patent, regardless of whether the infringer copied the inventor's ideas or discovered them independently. In contrast to trademark law, which requires that the protected mark be *used* in business, a patent owner can choose to practice the claimed invention, license it to others, or prevent its practice altogether.[14]

---

[14] Until recently, a patent owner had unquestioned power to prevent anyone from practicing the claimed invention. However, since the Supreme Court's decision in *eBay Inc. v. MercExchange L.L.C.,* 547 U.S. 388 (2006), courts no longer issue injunctions automatically, even after a patent has been found valid and infringed. Particularly where the patent owner does not practice the claimed invention itself, a court may determine that the balance of hardships and the interests of the public counsel against entering a permanent injunction. Without an injunction, the patent owner is essentially forced to accept a compulsory license arrangement, where infringement cannot be stopped but the patent owner collects an ongoing royalty. See Section 11.8.

CHAPTER 3

Reading a Patent

Anyone interested in patent law should take the time to study an actual patent. Copies of three United States patents can be found in Appendix A of this book. The examples have been chosen for the sake of simplicity and brevity, and to show that inventors are still searching for a "better mousetrap."

The first patent claims a device for trapping a mouse with the help of a Ping-Pong ball. The mouse enters a tube, the tube tips forward as the mouse heads for the "smelly bait," and a Ping-Pong ball rolls down to block the mouse's escape. In the second patent, bait lures the mouse onto a bridge. Although the bridge appears to be secure, the weight of the mouse causes the bridge to spin sideways, sending the mouse plunging headlong into a bucket. The third patent claims a trap made from a soda can.

Although none of these inventions is complex, each patent includes the basic components found in patents awarded to the most sophisticated advancements. The first patent will be used as an example for most of the following discussion, but the reader should examine all three in order to get a feel for the way patents are organized.

3.1 GENERAL INFORMATION

Patents are officially known by their serial numbers, printed at the top right-hand corner of the patent.[1] For the sake of convenience patents are often referred to by the last name of the first listed inventor or by the last

---

[1] Serial numbers on recent patents are followed by a "kind code" indicating the type of document one is looking at. This code is typically either B2 (indicating an issued patent published before as an application) or B1 (indicating a patent not published as an application).

three digits of the patent's serial number. The first patent in Appendix A would be referred to as the Oviatt patent, or as the '918 patent. The date on which the patent issued appears directly below the serial number.

The title of the Oviatt patent appears at the top of the left-hand column: "Mousetrap for Catching Mice Live." The title of a patent has little official significance and can sometimes be misleading.[2] The description of the "Mousetrap for Catching Mice Live" suggests that the trap can be immersed in water and the rodent drowned. The name of the inventor, or inventors, appears directly below the title, together with the inventor's place of origin. Beneath the inventor's name is the name of any person or company to whom the inventor assigned rights in the patent, prior to the date of issue.[3] Since the Oviatt patent shows no assignee, ownership of the patent evidently was retained by the inventor. Patent rights can be assigned after the patent issues. When this is the case, the transfer of ownership will not be evident from the patent itself, but it may be recorded in the Patent Office's prosecution history file.

Moving down the left-hand column of the Oviatt patent, the next item to appear is the number of the original patent application.[4] The Patent Office assigns each patent application a serial number; it is not the same serial number ultimately assigned to the patent itself. Although this can result in some confusion, it allows reference to applications that never issued as patents. The Oviatt patent is the result of a single application, numbered 347,890. Often the situation is more complicated. The applicant may have filed an application that was rejected and abandoned in favor of a "continuation" or a "continuation-in-part" application.[5] Sometimes this happens several times, resulting in a chain of applications preceding the patent ultimately issued. In such cases, the patent will provide the "family history" as well as the serial number of the original application.

The Patent Office assigns each application to subject matter categories, which are sometimes narrowed to very particular fields. This is done so that the Patent Office (or anyone else for that matter) can conveniently search a given area and determine what has been patented so far. On the Oviatt patent, this classification information appears next to the bracketed numbers [51] and [52], the first part relating to international classification and the second to U.S. classification. Oviatt's mousetrap has been assigned to U.S. subject matter Class 43: "Fishing, Trapping and Vermin Destroying." It can

---

[2] *See* Pitney Bowes, Inc. v. Hewlett-Packard Co., 182 F.3d 1298, 1312 (Fed. Cir. 1999) ("[T]he purpose of the title is not to demarcate the precise boundaries of the claimed invention but rather to provide a useful reference tool for future classification purposes. . . . [W]e certainly will not read limitations into the claims from the patent title.").

[3] See Section 6.2.

[4] The next item on more recent patents is an indication of whether the patent term has been extended to account for delays during prosecution. See Section 10.1.

[5] See Sections 5.2 and 5.3.

be found specifically under subclasses 60 ("Traps: Imprisoning"), 61 ("Traps: Imprisoning: Swinging or Sliding Closure"), and 66 ("Traps: Self and Ever Set: Nonreturn Entrance: Victim-Opened").

As discussed in Section 5.1, part of the Patent Office's duty on receiving an application is to search its collection of prior patents to determine whether the application claims something new. The "Field of Search" area shows the categories that were reviewed by the Patent Office in its search for earlier patents. In the case of the Oviatt patent, the Patent Office searched the same subclasses noted above, with the addition of subclasses 58 ("Traps"), 67 ("Traps: Self and Ever Set: Nonreturn Entrance: Victim-Closed") and 75 ("Traps: Self-Reset: Smiting"). The search categories established by the Patent Office provide a brief catalog of modern technology. Class 43 is a testament to man's continuing war with the mouse, including subcategories for "impaling," "explosive," "choking or squeezing" and "electrocuting" traps, in addition to those that "smite."

Moving downward, the next section of the patent is a list of prior art references cited by the Patent Office during prosecution of the application. Prior art, discussed in Section 8.9.1, includes earlier patents and publications disclosing inventions similar to the one claimed by the patent applicant. The cited references are those that the Patent Office considered closest to the patented invention, though not so close as to prevent the patent from issuing. Looking once again to the Oviatt patent, the Patent Office cited three patents as prior art, two of them more than 75 years old: the Turnbo patent, issued in 1909; the Cushing patent, issued in 1917; and the Sackett patent, issued in 1988. All disclose some form of rat or mouse trap with a tilting mechanism to prevent the victim's escape.

Next to appear are the name of the patent examiner, or examiners, who reviewed the application for the Patent Office, and the name of the counsel or patent agent who represented the inventor during this process.

The paragraph entitled "Abstract" provides a summary of the invention.[6] This is the place to look for the gist of the invention, before tackling the detailed description that follows the drawings. The abstract typically includes a brief description of how the invention works and why it is useful.

3.2 DRAWINGS

After the abstract appear the patent drawings. These are often far more helpful in understanding the invention than a written description alone would be. Although drawings are not required for every patent, nearly all

---

[6] I use the term "invention" here to refer loosely to the technological advancement described in the patent disclosure. In a specific sense, the "invention" is defined by the patent claims. See Section 3.4.

include some form of illustration. The Oviatt patent, like most patents, shows the invention from a variety of views so that all details are readily visible. Figures 3 and 8 show the invention before the mouse has sprung the trap. Figure 9 shows the movement of the Ping-Pong ball and the appearance of the trap after it has tipped forward on its pivot. Figure 2 is a "mouse eye view." Patents sometimes include exploded views, cross sections, or views of individual components when those views are helpful in explaining the invention. Some patents include graphs or flow charts.

Patent drawings are generally surrounded by numbers and arrows, as are the drawings in the Oviatt patent. These are reference numbers corresponding to the written description of the invention found in the body of the patent. For example, the Oviatt patent identifies sphere 9 as the Ping-Pong ball, lump 10 as the bait, and rodent M as the mouse.[7] Patent drawings sometimes depict different embodiments of the invention. Figure 1 of the Oviatt patent shows the trap set up on a stand made of wire, whereas Figure 5 shows the trap resting on the edge of a plastic ring. The inclusion of alternative embodiments shows that the inventor's ideas were not limited to a particular implementation of the invention.

3.3 SPECIFICATION

After the drawings comes the section of the patent referred to as the "specification." The specification describes the invention, or technology related to the invention, in words rather than pictures. Often the specification begins with a "Background of the Invention" section discussing the technology as it existed before the patented invention was made. This allows the inventor to point out the shortcomings of what has gone before and highlight the advantages of the patented invention. The Oviatt patent begins in typical fashion by describing the health menace posed by mice and the disadvantages of typical traps that kill the mouse, where it is left to decompose, smell, and endanger children and pets. Oviatt then explains that his own invention avoids these problems by trapping the mouse alive.

Many specifications include a "Summary of the Invention" section, which is used to list the objectives of the patented invention. Oviatt states that the "main object" of his invention is to "trap a mouse alive." Other, subsidiary objectives are to provide an inexpensive trap, a trap that can be immersed in water to drown the mouse, and a trap that is reusable.

The next section of the Oviatt patent is, again in typical fashion, a "Brief Description of the Drawings." This portion of the patent explains in the most general way what is depicted in the drawings: Figure 1 is a top view, Figure 3 is a cross section, Figure 5 is an alternative embodiment.

---

[7] Note that the numbers used in labeling a patent drawing need not be consecutive. The Oviatt patent uses numbers 90 and 100, but there is no 89 or 99.

The next section of the Oviatt patent is entitled "Description of the Preferred Embodiment." Almost every patent has a similar section where the inventor describes the "preferred embodiment" in great detail, identifying in the process all of the components visible in the drawings. The preferred embodiment is the inventor's favored implementation of the invention. Inventions are usually general concepts that, at a detailed level, could be implemented in any number of ways. In the Oviatt patent, the tilting tube and the rolling ball are general concepts that characterize the invention. Oviatt might be entitled to claim any mousetrap that shares those features. But in the specification, we learn of the inventor's preference for a Ping-Pong ball, and we are given two possible designs for the fulcrum on which the trap teeters—one a stand preferably made of wire, and the other a plastic ring with one flat edge.

Disclosure at this level of detail satisfies two requirements of the patent laws: that inventors provide in the specification sufficient information to allow persons skilled in the field to practice the invention, and that inventors disclose the *best* way they know of to practice the invention. These requirements, known respectively as the "enablement" and "best mode" requirements, are discussed in Sections 8.6 and 8.7. The details discussed in the specification *do not*, under most circumstances, limit what the patent covers. Even though the specification describes a Ping-Pong ball, the patent might still cover a similar mousetrap that used a rubber ball.

In fact, the Oviatt specification includes warnings to that effect. Just before the numbered claims, we find the following caveat:

> Although the present invention has been described with reference to preferred embodiments, numerous modifications and variations can be made and still the result will come within the scope of the invention. No limitation with respect to the specific embodiments disclosed herein is intended or should be inferred.

3.4 CLAIMS

The last and most important section of a patent consists of the numbered "claims." The claims, not the drawings or the specification, define what the patent "covers" and what will infringe. In the Oviatt patent we find eight claims.

Claims come in two forms—independent claims and dependent claims. An independent claim stands by itself, whereas a dependent claim explicitly refers to another claim and incorporates its terms by reference.[8] Claim 1 of

---

[8] *See* Monsanto Co. v. Syngenta Seeds, Inc., 503 F.3d 1352, 1357 (Fed. Cir. 2007). One cannot infringe a dependent claim without also infringing the independent claim to which it refers. *Id.* at 1359. A dependent claim is invalid if, through some error of drafting, it somehow fails to incorporate all of the elements of the independent claim. Pfizer, Inc. v. Ranbaxy Labs. Ltd., 457 F.3d 1284, 1291-92 (Fed. Cir. 2006).

the Oviatt patent is an independent claim. Claim 2 is a dependent claim because it refers to "The mousetrap of claim 1 wherein . . ." Claim 2 is read as though it incorporates all of the language of Claim 1, plus the additional language of Claim 2. Claim 3 is another dependent claim, which this time refers to Claim 2 ("The mousetrap of claim 2 wherein . . ."). Since Claim 2 depends from Claim 1, the effect of Claim 3 is to incorporate *all* of the language of Claims 1, 2, and 3.

Claims generally begin with a "preamble" that establishes the context of the invention. As discussed in Section 7.6, the preamble is sometimes treated as a claim limitation and sometimes as introductory language that has no legal effect. This can have important consequences. Claim 1 of the Oviatt patent begins with the preamble "A mousetrap comprising . . ." If this were the last reference in the claim to a mouse, the effect given to the preamble would determine whether the claim covered an otherwise identical squirrel trap. The preamble usually ends with the term "consisting of" or "comprising."[9]

The indented paragraphs following the preamble are the claim "elements" or claim "limitations." Almost all patent claims cover a combination of elements or limitations. Looking at Claim 1 of the Oviatt patent, we find the following combination set forth:

1. A mousetrap comprising:

   a main tube having a central fulcrum means, a bait end, and a ball end;

   a base stand having a means to support the main tube at the fulcrum;

   said bait end further comprising mouse bait and a main tube closure;

   said ball end further comprising a ball and a main tube closure;

   an entrance tube depending down from the main tube at the central fulcrum means, and angled toward the ball end;

   said entrance tube having a mouse entrance adjacent a supporting surface for the base stand; and

   said main tube having a horizontal load position where said ball rests at the ball end, wherein a mouse enters the mouse entrance, walks toward the base up the entrance tube, and passes the fulcrum means, thereby causing the main tube to teeter down at the bait end, and cause the ball to roll down the main tube and then down the entrance tube, functioning to block an egress of the mouse out the mouse entrance.

Claim 1 of the Oviatt patent would cover any mousetrap that included each of the elements described. If a mousetrap did not incorporate one or more of the described elements, it would fall outside the scope of the claim. Hence if a mousetrap did not tip like the Oviatt mousetrap, but instead

---

[9] See Section 7.6.

relied on a spring-loaded mechanism to shoot a Ping-Pong ball down the tube to trap the mouse, that trap would lack the "fulcrum means" required by Claim 1, and it would fall outside the literal scope of the claim.[10]

The language used in patent claims is generally more formal and technical, and sometimes more obscure, than everyday language. Claim 1 of the Oviatt patent is not a particularly bad example, but it does include terms such as "fulcrum means," "supporting surface," "horizontal load position" and "egress," which might seem more grandiose than the invention requires. Claim drafters, whether inventors or attorneys, resort to such technical or pseudo-technical language because of the importance of the words to the legal effect of the patent. Insofar as possible, the claim language must describe exactly what the patent covers. Claim drafters therefore must be precise in their description of the invention but must not limit themselves by the choice of language to something narrower than the inventor intends to claim.

The Oviatt patent has three independent claims—Claims 1, 6, and 8—and five dependent claims. A patent generally can have as many claims as the inventor desires, although more claims can mean paying the Patent Office an additional fee. Each claim can be treated in some respects as if it were a separate patent. Although people often speak of a patent being infringed, it is really a claim, or a series of claims, that is infringed. A device may infringe one claim of a patent but not another, perhaps because of a minor variation in language. An inventor who describes the invention through more than one claim decreases the chance that a potentially infringing product will escape because of some small difference. Using more than one claim is also a hedge against the possibility that a claim will be held invalid by the courts. One claim may be held invalid, while another, with slightly different language, survives.[11]

Note how the Oviatt patent describes the same concept, in slightly different terms, in Claims 1, 6, and 8. Claim 1 speaks of a pair of tubes—a "main tube" and an "entrance tube." Claim 8, on the other hand, speaks of a "'Y' shaped tube." The Oviatt patent also illustrates how dependent claims are often used to include details described in the specification but omitted from the broader claims. For example, Claim 4 specifically limits the "ball" of Claim 1 to a "ping-pong ball." If it proved to be the case that a mousetrap had been invented prior to Oviatt's that used a rubber ball, the broader claim might be held invalid while the narrow claim might not.

---

[10] See Section 10.5. As discussed in Section 10.6, a product that differs from what the claim literally requires may still infringe, under the "doctrine of equivalents," if the differences are insubstantial.

[11] *See* 35 U.S.C. § 282 ("Each claim of a patent . . . shall be presumed valid independently of the validity of other claims. . . .").

CHAPTER 4

Patentable Subject Matter

The Supreme Court has observed that the realm of patents embraces "anything under the sun that is made by man,"[1] but this is not literally true. First, the Constitution limits the power of Congress to the promotion of the "useful arts." These are generally understood to include technological endeavors rather than, for example, artistic or social endeavors.[2] The types of creations that can be patented are further limited by the language of the Patent Act. Section 101 of the Patent Act (35 U.S.C. § 101) provides as follows:

> Whoever invents or discovers any new and useful process, machine, manufacture, or composition of matter, or any new and useful improvement thereof, may obtain a patent therefor, subject to the conditions and requirements of this title.[3]

In order to be patented, an invention must fall within one of the statutory categories of "process, machine, manufacture, or composition of matter."[4]

---

[1] Diamond v. Chakrabarty, 447 U.S. 303, 309 (1980).

[2] *See* In re Comiskey, 499 F.3d 1365, 1374–75 (Fed. Cir. 2007) (the Constitution limits patentable subject matter to the "useful arts"). In a recent *en banc* decision, the Federal Circuit noted that a "technological arts" test of patentability would be unclear due to the uncertain meaning of the term "technology," and declined the opportunity to adopt such a test explicitly. In re Bilski, 2008 U.S. App. LEXIS 22497, *41 (Fed. Cir. 2008) (*en banc*). Nevertheless, it may be that the Constitution demands such a limitation.

[3] "Manufacture" is an abbreviated term for an article produced by a manufacturing process. In re Nuitjen, 500 F.3d 1346, 1356 (Fed. Cir. 2007). "Composition of matter" is a broad term that is most often applied to chemical compounds and the like, but that could literally refer to any agglomeration of physical substances. *See* Diamond v. Chakrabarty, 447 U.S. 303, 308 (1980).

[4] *See Nuitjen*, 500 F.3d at 1353 (claims to transitory electromagnetic signals are unpatentable because they fall within none of the categories enumerated in § 101).

Since these terms are deliberately broad, this is seldom an obstacle. Yet certain categories of invention or discovery have been held to exceed the statutory boundaries of patentable subject matter, or are sufficiently close to those boundaries as to generate controversy. The most important of these fall under the rubric of abstract ideas, thought processes, principles of nature, living organisms, literary or artistic creations, printed matter, methods of doing business, or computer programs.

4.1 ABSTRACT IDEAS

The most general category of unpatentable subject matter, and perhaps the hardest to define, is "abstract ideas."[5] Obviously, one can patent an idea if it is in the form of a new process, machine, manufacture, or composition of matter. On the other hand, one cannot patent an idea that is without a material form or a practical application.[6] For example, one probably could not patent the idea of "renewable energy resources." The idea is a useful one, but to be patentable it should take the form of a particular kind of renewable energy resource. Patents are intended to reward and encourage those who make tangible contributions to the useful arts. If patents were awarded to abstract ideas, rather than to practical applications of those ideas, the effect might be to discourage advancements in those arts.

4.2 THOUGHT PROCESSES

Whether one can patent a thought process is a question with a complicated history. The term "process," as found in § 101 of the Patent Act, does not exclude the possibility. Although in some contexts courts have described a patentable process as one that transforms a physical material into "a different state or thing,"[7] it was not necessarily their intention to *limit* the term "process" to those situations alone.[8] On the other hand, courts have sometimes held it self-evident that thought processes are unpatentable.[9] Some cases discuss a patentability exception for *purely* mental processes, as opposed to processes that might also be performed by a machine.[10] A machine might calculate a number, but it could not select the right drapes for the living room.[11] Other cases suggest that a "mental steps doctrine" is unnecessary; the real issue is whether the claimed process falls within the

---

[5] *See* In re Comiskey, 499 F.3d 1365, 1376 (Fed. Cir. 2007).

[6] *See Id.* at 1376–77.

[7] Cochrane v. Deener, 94 U.S. 780, 788 (1876).

[8] *See* In re Prater, 415 F.2d 1393, 1403 (C.C.P.A. 1969).

[9] In re Abrams, 188 F.2d 165, 168 (C.C.P.A. 1951).

[10] *See id.* at 1401–02; In re Yuan, 188 F.2d 377, 380 (C.C.P.A. 1951).

[11] *See* In re Musgrave, 431 F.2d 882, 889 n.4 (C.C.P.A. 1970) (discussing methods requiring the exercise of "peculiarly human" values).

"useful arts."[12] Supreme Court cases addressing other issues continued to list mental process, together with abstract ideas and principles of nature, among the kinds of unpatentable invention,[13] but the Federal Circuit's emphasis on useful results, rather than physicality,[14] began to give the "mental steps" exception to patentable subject matter the character of a historical curiosity.

This changed abruptly in 2007 with *In re Comiskey*.[15] Here the Federal Circuit, addressing a patent application for a system of legal arbitration, held that "mental processes—or processes of human thinking—standing alone are not patentable even if they have practical application."[16] In order to be patentable, a thought process must be tied to something physical; the exercise of human intelligence alone is a matter beyond the scope of the patent laws.[17] Together with other recent Federal Circuit opinions,[18] *Comiskey* seems to mark the end of an era in which the bounds of patentable subject matter were ever expanding.

4.3 PRINCIPLES OF NATURE

Although the Patent Act defines "invention" as meaning "invention *or discovery*,"[19] the courts have long held that the truths of nature cannot be patented, even by the people who discover those truths. The clearest examples can be found in the formulas of mathematics or the physical sciences. Pythagoras may have been the first to appreciate that the sums of the squares of the two sides of a right triangle are equal to the square of the hypotenuse, but such insights do not qualify as patentable inventions.[20] Similarly, Einstein could not have patented the relationship of mass to energy in the form of the equation $E = mc^2$.[21] On the other hand, one could patent a novel apparatus, method or composition of matter that puts a principle of nature to practical application—for example, a new surveying instrument that makes use of the Pythagorean theorem, or a nuclear reactor based on

---

[12] *Id.* at 893. This development, according to Justice Stevens, "effectively disposed of any vestiges of the mental-steps doctrine." Diamond v. Diehr, 450 U.S. 175, 200 (1981) (Stevens, J., dissenting).

[13] *See* Gottschalk v. Benson, 409 U.S. 63, 67 (1972).

[14] *See* State Street Bank & Trust Co. v. Signature Financial Gp., 149 F.3d 1368 (Fed. Cir. 1998) (holding patentable under § 101 a system of organizing a family of mutual funds).

[15] 499 F.3d 1365 (Fed. Cir. 2007).

[16] *Id.* at 1377.

[17] *Id.* at 1378–79. In the *Bilski* case, the Federal Circuit adopted a "machine-or-transformation test" for patentable processes that seems to exclude any process consisting entirely of mental steps. The test holds that a patentable process must be tied to a particular machine or it must transform an article "into a different state or thing." *See* In re Bilski, 2008 U.S. App. LEXIS 22497, *43–44 (Fed. Cir. 2008) (*en banc*).

[18] *See, e.g.*, In re Nuitjen, 500 F.3d 1346 (Fed. Cir. 2007) ("signals" are too intangible to fall within any recognized category of patentable subject matter).

[19] 35 U.S.C. § 100.

[20] *See* Parker v. Flook, 437 U.S. 584, 590 (1978).

[21] *See* Diamond v. Chakrabarty, 447 U.S. 303, 309 (1980) ("Einstein could not patent his celebrated law").

Einstein's discovery.[22] Because the formulas of science and mathematics are generalized descriptions of the universe, any invention, at some level, can be described by those formulas.[23] As long as the invention is not the formula itself but instead a useful application or embodiment of the formula, it is potentially patentable.

The rule against patenting a principle of nature has been applied to materials discovered in nature, as well as to abstract relationships and physical laws. The discovery of a new mineral in the earth would not entitle the discoverer to patent it.[24] On the other hand, one who discovers a specific *use* for a natural material, such as the treatment of a disease, can patent that method of use, so long as it is new and non-obvious.[25] If others discover further uses for the material, those also are potentially patentable. Some problems can be avoided through careful claim drafting. The Patent Office denied one inventor a patent on a shrimp that was beheaded and cleaned, but still protected by its shell.[26] Although the shrimp was no longer whole, that which remained was still a "product of nature" and in its original state. Had the inventor instead claimed a *method* of preparing a shrimp, he would more likely have met the qualification for patentable subject matter.

It might be argued that investigation into the principles of nature is a pursuit just as valuable as the development of technology, and that awarding patents to significant discoveries would encourage such investigation. Why, then, are patents unobtainable on newly discovered natural laws? One argument is that a patent on a principle of nature would be too broad. A principle may lead to a vast spectrum of practical applications, many of which could not have been foreseen by the discoverer of the principle. However, as we will see in Section 10.6.5, even inventions of the ordinary kind (such as machines, processes, and compositions of matter) may be applied after their invention in ways that the inventor could not have predicted. This is particularly true of "pioneering" inventions, often regarded as those *most* worthy of a patent. Another, perhaps sounder argument is that patent law should not take from the public that which it has already possessed. New inventions take nothing from the public because, by definition, the inventions did not exist before. On the other hand, principles of nature exist even before they are discovered, and the public may, in some sense, have used these principles before they were appreciated. One patentee discovered that omitting antioxidants from vitamin

---

[22] *See* Mackay Radio & Telegraph Co. v. RCA, 306 U.S. 86, 94 (1939) ("While a scientific truth, or the mathematical expression of it, is not a patentable invention, a novel and useful structure created with the aid of knowledge of scientific truth may be.").

[23] *See* Dickey-John Corp. v. Int'l Tapetronics Corp., 710 F.2d 329, 348 n.9 (7th Cir. 1983) ("all inventions that work can be explained in terms of basic truths").

[24] Diamond v. Chakrabarty, 447 U.S. 303, 309 (1980).

[25] Similarly, a new use for an existing artificial compound can be patented, though the discoverer of the new use is not entitled to a patent on the compound itself. *See* In re Schoenwald, 964 F.2d 1122, 1124 (Fed. Cir. 1992).

[26] Ex parte Grayson, 51 U.S.P.Q. 413 (Pat. Off. Bd. App. 1941).

supplements ensured the effectiveness of other ingredients. Yet the Federal Circuit found no patentable invention in this discovery. Vitamin supplements without antioxidants had already been available to the public, even if the benefits of omitting the antioxidants had never been fully appreciated. [27]

A recent case of interest is *Laboratory Corp. v. Metabolite Labs., Inc.,*[28] where the patented invention was a method of diagnosing a vitamin deficiency by observing the level of a certain amino acid in a patient's blood. The Supreme Court decided to hear the case, but then changed its mind and dismissed the appeal. Justice Breyer, joined by two other justices, objected to the dismissal and wrote an opinion with some noteworthy observations on patentable subject matter. Justice Breyer argued that too much patent protection can impede the advancement of the useful arts.[29] In this case, he said, infringement required nothing more than observing a natural phenomenon and thinking about it, which crossed the line of patentable subject matter.[30] Interestingly, Justice Breyer disowned the Federal Circuit's frequent pronouncement that a process producing a "useful, concrete, and tangible result" is always within the scope of § 101.[31] Justice Breyer's views are not necessarily those of the majority of the Supreme Court, but like *In re Comiskey,*[32] his *Lab Corp.* opinion seems to mark a push-back against the expansionism of recent years.

4.4 LIVING ORGANISMS

Advances in technology sometimes compel a reassessment of the scope of protection available through the patent laws. Until recently, the idea of patenting a living animal might have seemed absurd. Even when an explorer discovered a species that was previously unknown, the explorer could not claim to have invented the species; the explorer merely discovered what was already there.[33] The situation has changed with the development of techniques allowing scientists to rearrange the genetic codes of existing species. Now biologists can truly claim to have invented a form of life that did not exist before. Still, the notion that a person or a company can claim a property interest in a life form is one that is unsettling to many people.

The Supreme Court, in *Diamond v. Chakrabarty,*[34] addressed the question of whether a genetically engineered bacterium devised to break down crude

---

[27] Upsher-Smith Lab., Inc. v. Pamlan, L.L.C., 412 F.2d 1319, 1323 (Fed. Cir. 2005).

[28] 548 U.S. 124 (2006).

[29] *Id.* at 127–28.

[30] *Id.* at 136.

[31] *Id.* at 136–37.

[32] See Section 4.2.

[33] A breeder might stake a stronger claim to invention, but the idea of patenting an improved cow or chicken seems never to have been seriously entertained before the era of genetic engineering.

[34] 447 U.S. 303 (1980).

oil could be patented. The bacterium was undeniably useful, since it could be used to treat oil spills. It was also new. No naturally occurring bacteria possessed the same ability to break down all of the components found in crude oil. The Patent Office rejected Chakrabarty's patent application on the ground that a living organism cannot be patented. The majority of the Supreme Court disagreed, holding that Congress had established a broad scope of patentability, and that if Congress wished to exclude genetically engineered life forms it would have to do so explicitly. The court also observed that the most important inventions may be those least foreseeable to the legislature. Literally speaking, new bacteria are "manufactures" and "compositions of matter," and are patentable as such.

The principles of *Chakrabarty* have since been extended to multicellular organisms. In 1988 Harvard University obtained a celebrated patent on a genetically engineered mouse. The mouse is useful in laboratory studies because it is particularly susceptible to cancer. The PTO Board of Appeals and Interferences[35] has also held patentable a genetically altered oyster that can be enjoyed year-round, in contrast to naturally occurring oysters, which must be avoided during the summer months.[36] The Patent Office has announced that it will not permit a patent on a human being, though certain activists, so far unsuccessfully, have pressed claims to "human-animal chimeras" genetically combining the attributes of humans and those of other species.

Although a special kind of patent, discussed in Section 12.2, is available for plant life, the Supreme Court has held that plant life is also appropriate subject matter for a utility patent.[37] This is a natural extension of *Chakrabarty*, although if Congress saw fit to create a specific set of rules governing plants, one might infer that plants were outside the scope of the preexisting statute.

4.5 ARTISTIC AND LITERARY CREATIONS

Generally speaking, the proper vehicle for protecting artistic and literary creations is the copyright.[38] Utility patents are intended to protect, as the name implies, *useful* inventions. In this context, "useful" is meant in the narrow sense of a practical advancement in a technological art.[39] Design patents are available for ornamental designs as applied to utilitarian objects, but they are a different kind of patent subject to a different set of rules.[40] If

[35] See Section 5.1.
[36] Ex parte Allen, 2 U.S.P.Q.2d 1425 (PTO Bd. App. & Int. 1987).
[37] J.E.M. AG Supply, Inc. v. Pioneer Hi-Bred Int'l, Inc., 534 U.S. 124 (2001).
[38] See Section 2.1.
[39] *See* In re Comiskey, 499 F.3d 1365, 1374–75 (Fed. Cir. 2007).
[40] See Section 12.1.

an inventor applies for a utility patent on what is essentially an ornamental feature, the invention may be held outside of the subject matter permitted under § 101.[41]

4.6 PRINTED MATTER

Another exception to patentability concerns "printed matter." Generally speaking, a manufactured article or composition of matter is not patentable if the only thing that distinguishes it from prior inventions is the presence of pictures or writing. One could not, for example, obtain a utility patent for a baseball cap merely because it bears a new team logo, even though the cap is new and useful, and caps, as such, are articles of manufacture.

On the other hand, an invention that involves printed matter may be patentable, as long as the invention as a whole calls for a new structure, or the printed matter bears a novel functional relationship to the "substrate"— that is, the physical object on which the matter is printed. In one instance, an inventor applied for a patent on a scheme for deliberately mislabeling a measuring cup to solve the problem of measuring when making less than a full recipe. A cook who wishes to prepare, for example, one-third of the amount specified in a recipe may be left with the difficult task of measuring quantities such as 1/3 of 2/3 of a cup. The inventor conceived of a measuring cup for fractional portions. The cook who wishes to make a 1/3 recipe simply selects the 1/3 recipe cup, and when he fills the cup to the 2/3 cup mark, he actually has the desired 2/9 cup. Although the markings were the only difference between the inventor's measuring cups and other measuring cups, the useful relationship between the markings and the cups was enough to place the invention within the scope of patentable subject matter.[42]

A similar issue can arise in the case of computer storage media, which function to store information, though not in printed form. Is a computer disk patentable merely because it contains new information? The answer may depend on the nature of the information. Under its current guidelines, the Patent Office will presume that a computer-readable storage medium that can be used to direct a computer to operate in a particular manner is an "article of manufacture" and falls within the scope of patentable subject matter. A CD-ROM, for example, that contains a new computer program will presumptively qualify as patentable subject matter. However, a known storage

---

[41] *See, e.g.*, Levi Strauss & Co. v. Golden Trade S.r.L., 1995 U.S. Dist. LEXIS 4899 (S.D.N.Y. 1995) (garments treated to produce a "stone-washed" pattern, but which did not differ from their predecessors in any manner affecting utility, were not patentable subject matter).

[42] Application of Miller, 418 F.2d 1392 (C.C.P.A. 1969).

medium encoding data representing "creative or artistic expression," such as a work of art, literature or music, will be considered unpatentable.[43]

4.7 METHODS OF DOING BUSINESS

Business methods were long thought to be unpatentable, perhaps because they exceed the scope of the technology-oriented "useful arts." Accounting techniques and the like may be too remote from the disciplines of science and engineering to be suitable for the patent system.[44] On the other hand, an *apparatus* used in business—such as a cash register—would usually be considered patentable subject matter. An apparatus is a technological means to an end.

The Federal Circuit bucked tradition in 1998, when in *State Street Bank & Trust Co. v. Signature Financial Gp.*[45] it rejected the business method exception to patentability as "ill-conceived" and thinly supported. Business methods, the court held, are subject to the same standards of patentability as any other method. The patented invention in *State Street* involved a system for organizing a group of mutual funds under the common ownership of a partnership, an arrangement that produced economies of scale and tax advantages. The claims described a system and method for performing the necessary accounting, though in such broad terms that anyone creating such a fund and using a computer would necessarily infringe. The court found that the claims did not describe an unpatentably abstract algorithm[46] because the computerized manipulation of data representing money is a "useful, concrete and tangible result."[47] Whether the invention represented an advancement in the "useful arts" the court did not say, perhaps assuming that any claim to a computerized "system" must qualify automatically.

Predictably, *State Street* opened the door to numerous patent applications claiming business methods. But in 2007 *In re Comiskey*[48] suggested a change of

---

[43] MPEP § 2106. The Federal Circuit has stated that the "printed matter" cases have no relevance where the "matter" is to be processed not by a human mind, but by a computer. In re Lowry, 32 F.3d 1579, 1583 (Fed. Cir. 1994). However, if the distinguishing feature of the invention consists of stored information rather than revised structure, whether in the form of printing on paper or data on a computer disk, the same concerns can be raised about the suitability of the invention for patent protection. The Patent Office has embarked on a reasonable course by attempting to distinguish between a computer program that causes a computer to function in a particular way, and stored data that merely represents a musical, literary, or artistic creation. Still, future court decisions will likely be necessary to sort out when a computer disk with stored data is patentable and when it is not.

[44] *See* Ex parte Murray, 9 U.S.P.Q.2d 1819 (PTO Bd. Pat. App. & Int. 1988) (holding unpatentable an accounting method allowing users to enter, categorize, and total expenditures, and display the results in an expense analysis report).

[45] 149 F.3d 1368 (Fed. Cir. 1998).

[46] See Section 12.4.

[47] *State Street,* 149 F.3d at 1373.

[48] 499 F.3d 1365 (Fed. Cir. 2007).

course. First, the Federal Circuit held explicitly that patentable subject matter is limited to advancements in the "useful arts,"[49] perhaps excluding business methods not associated with technological innovations. Second, the court revived the "mental steps" doctrine, which forbids patents to thought processes.[50] Although many business methods will be implemented by computers, some may require nothing more than human thought. That was the case for Comiskey, whose method of legal arbitration could be conducted without the assistance of a machine. Finally, inventions combining mental process with computers may be patentable subject matter, but "[t]he routine addition of modern electronics to an otherwise unpatentable invention typically creates a prima facie case of obviousness."[51] In the subsequent *Bilski* decision, the Federal Circuit disavowed the "useful, concrete and tangible result" language of *State Street* as inadequate. Rather, a patentable process must be tied to a particular apparatus or it must transform an article "into a different state or thing." If a business method meets neither qualification, it is not patentable subject matter.[52] In *Bilski*, the court continued to deny that business methods are *always* unpatentable, yet many of the abstract business innovations that seemed patentable after *State Street* now seem ineligible. Although *Comiskey* did not overrule *State Street*, it marks a significant change of emphasis.

As methods of doing business become increasingly dependent on computers, questions regarding the patentability of business methods are often subsumed within the larger question of when computer programs can be patented. This complex question is reserved for discussion in Section 12.4.

---

[49] *Id.* at 1374.

[50] *Id.* at 1377–79.

[51] *Id.* at 1380. A "prima facie" case means a case that must be rebutted with contrary evidence. Section 8.9.6 discusses obviousness, a separate ground for invalidating a patent or denying a patent application.

[52] In re Bilski, 2008 U.S. App. LEXIS 22497, *38–42 (Fed. Cir. 2008) (*en banc*).

CHAPTER 5

Patent Prosecution

5.1 EXAMINATION

The process of applying for a patent, also known as patent "prosecution," begins when the inventor, on his own or through his agent or attorney, files an application with the Patent Office for "examination." The application includes essentially the same things that a patent would include—a specification describing the invention in detail, drawings, and claims.[1] The Patent Office assigns the application to a "patent examiner" who has expert knowledge in the field of the invention. Since the Patent Office requires a filing fee, an issue fee, and various other fees, obtaining a patent can easily cost several thousand dollars, exclusive of any fees paid to a patent attorney or agent.[2]

The patent examiner searches for "prior art" patents already granted on similar inventions in order to determine if the invention claimed in the application is new and non-obvious.[3] The examiner also reviews the application to determine if it meets the other requirements of a valid patent, such as having claims that are sufficiently definite.[4] After reviewing the application and searching for prior art, the examiner prepares a written "Office Action" to tell the applicant which claims are "allowed" or rejected and to explain any problems with the application. In many cases the examiner will reject the

---

[1] As discussed below, a "provisional application" may omit the claims.
[2] Reduced fees are available to individuals and "small entities" (see MPEP § 509.02), but the costs are still considerable. A current fee schedule can be obtained by visiting the PTO website at http://www.uspto.gov.
[3] See Section 8.9.
[4] See Section 8.5.

claims as originally filed on grounds that the invention is already disclosed in, or obvious in light of, prior patents.

Following such a rejection, the applicant is permitted to file a written response. Sometimes the response is to argue the point with the examiner and attempt to explain, on legal or technical grounds, why the claims should be allowed after all. Often, however, the response is to amend the claims in an effort to distinguish the invention from what has gone before. It is also possible to cancel claims or add new claims. When claims are amended, or new claims added, the applicant should explain why the changes overcome the problems found by the examiner.[5]

After a response from the applicant, the examiner prepares another Office Action, which may allow the claims or reject them once again. This process continues until the claims are allowed or until the examiner announces that the rejection is "final," which generally occurs after the second rejection.[6] A final rejection can be appealed to the Patent Office Board of Appeals and Interferences, and from there to the Federal Circuit Court of Appeals.[7] If the situation appears hopeless, the application can be abandoned.

Although patent prosecution resembles a court proceeding in some respects—applicants are typically represented by attorneys who present legal arguments to the examiner "judge"—the situation differs in a very significant respect. In a typical court proceeding, the judge hears argument and evidence presented by adversaries having opposing points of view. Patent prosecution, on the other hand, is "ex parte," meaning that there is no adversary present. A company that might infringe the patent has no opportunity to argue to the examiner that the patent should not issue. In fact, a potential infringer may have no way of knowing that the application is under consideration. It is the job of the examiner to represent the interests of the public and ensure that no patent issues unless it meets all of the legal requirements. Yet the opportunity to present unrebutted arguments provides applicants with a great advantage, and that advantage is magnified in litigation by the presumption that all issued patents are valid.[8]

Because patent prosecution is ex parte, the individuals involved are held to a higher standard of candor and fair dealing than is typical of court

---

[5] Although the claims can be amended, the specification cannot be changed to add "new matter." 37 C.F.R. § 1.118. "New matter" can be added only by filing a continuation-in-part. See Section 5.2.

[6] Recent legislation permits applicants to extend examination of disputed claims on payment of a fee, without the need to resort to the filing of a "continuation" of the kind discussed in Section 5.2. 35 U.S.C. § 132(b). A request under the new legislation is known as a Request for Continued Examination, or RCE.

[7] See 35 U.S.C. § 141. Alternatively, an applicant disappointed with the decision of the PTO Board may file a civil action in the United States District Court for the District of Columbia, from which any further appeal would be, again, to the Federal Circuit. See 35 U.S.C. § 145.

[8] See Section 8.2.

proceedings. If, for example, the applicant is aware of information that might call into question whether the patent should issue—such as a close prior art reference—the applicant must bring that to the attention of the examiner. If the applicant, or the applicant's attorney, fails in that duty of candor, the patent may later be held "unenforceable" by a court.[9]

In some other countries, patent applications are made public or "laid open" after an initial examination by the patent office, to allow the interested public to oppose the application. This lessens the likelihood that a patent will be granted simply because the patent office failed to discover the most pertinent prior art. The United States, which long conducted examinations in secret, recently enacted legislation requiring the publication of patent applications[10] 18 months after they are filed, or sooner at the request of the applicant.[11] Applicants may request swift publication because of the opportunity to obtain "provisional rights" before the patent issues.[12] On the other hand, an applicant can avoid publication by certifying that the invention has not and will not be the subject of an application in another country that *already* requires publication 18 months after filing.[13] Moreover, the law forbids, without the consent of the applicant, any form of third-party opposition or protest following the publication of the pending application.[14] While the new rules may advantage patent applicants under some circumstances, they offer marginal benefits to potential challengers, and prosecution remains ex parte.

The Patent Act also allows "provisional applications."[15] A provisional application includes a specification and drawings, but it need not include any claim.[16] Within 12 months, the applicant must file an ordinary application, or the provisional application will be deemed abandoned.[17] The advantage of a provisional application is that it allows an inventor to file an application, and obtain a priority date,[18] before the applicant is ready to formulate a claim.[19] In addition, while the applicant enjoys the benefits of the provisional application's early filing date, the resulting patent does not expire until 20 years after the filing date of the ordinary application.[20] Nevertheless, applicants should approach this option with caution. The

---

[9] See Section 9.1.
[10] This applies to utility patents, not design patents. *See* 35 U.S.C. § 1222(b)(A)(iv). Design patents are discussed in Section 12.1.
[11] 35 U.S.C. § 122(b).
[12] See Section 10.1.
[13] 35 U.S.C. § 122(B)(i).
[14] 35 U.S.C. § 122(c).
[15] *See* 35 U.S.C. § 111(b).
[16] 35 U.S.C. § 111(b)(2).
[17] 35 U.S.C. § 111(b)(5).
[18] See Section 8.9.3.
[19] See 35 U.S.C. § 119(e)(1).
[20] See Section 10.1.

benefit of the earlier filing date can be obtained only if the disclosures of the provisional application satisfy the requirements of Section 112, Paragraph 1, of the Patent Act, including the enablement,[21] best mode,[22] and written description[23] requirements. Since satisfaction of those requirements ultimately depends on what is *claimed*, preparing one's disclosure before one is ready to formulate a claim may be a hazardous affair.[24]

Prosecution is a slow process and may take years. All of the documents filed by the applicant or by the examiner become part of the "prosecution history" of the patent. The prosecution history (also known as the "file history" or "file wrapper") becomes available to the public if the patent issues, and it is an important resource for interpreting what the claims mean. If in response to a rejection the applicant argues in favor of a narrow claim interpretation, that same interpretation is likely to be adopted by a court in any subsequent litigation.[25]

5.2 CONTINUATIONS AND CONTINUATIONS-IN-PART

In some instances, an applicant may choose to start over, in a sense, by filing a "continuation." A continuation is an application that has the same disclosure as the prior application (i.e., the same specification) but new claims.[26] As long as the continuation is filed before the original application is abandoned, and as long as the continuation includes an explicit reference to the original application, the continuation, and any patent claims that issue from it, will be treated as though filed on the date that the original application was filed.[27] As in the case of reliance on a provisional application,[28] the earlier filing date may be important in determining the priority of the invention as compared to other inventions or references.[29] The original

---

[21] See Section 8.6.

[22] See Section 8.7.

[23] See Section 8.8.

[24] *See* New Railhead Mfg., L.L.C., v. Vermeer Mfg. Co., 298 F.3d 1290 (Fed. Cir. 2002) (The disclosure of a provisional application did not adequately describe the later-claimed invention; consequently, the patentee could not obtain the early filing date necessary to avoid invalidation of the patent based on a public use bar (see Section 8.10.2).).

[25] See Section 7.3.

[26] *See* Transco Prods. Inc. v. Performance Contracting, Inc., 38 F.3d 551, 555 (Fed. Cir. 1994); MPEP § 201.07. One reason to file a continuation is to permit the amendment of claims that have already been subject to a "final" rejection. *See Transco*, 38 F.3d at 559. Hence the availability of extended examination (35 U.S.C. § 132(b)) reduces the need for continuations.

[27] *See* Mendenhall v. Cedarapids, Inc., 5 F.3d 1557, 1565 (Fed. Cir. 1993); 35 U.S.C. § 120; MPEP § 201.11. If the original application names more than one joint inventor, the continuation must name the same inventors, or a subset of them. 35 U.S.C. § 120; In re Chu, 66 F.3d 292, 297 (Fed. Cir. 1995).

[28] See Section 5.1.

[29] See Section 8.9.2.

application may be abandoned after the continuation is filed, or prosecution of the two applications may continue in parallel.

The second application may lead to another, and a "chain" of applications can be created in this way.[30] The application that comes last on the chain will receive the benefit of the first application's filing date, as long as each link in the chain meets the requirements of continuity—that is, each application includes the same disclosure as the one preceding it, and each was filed before the preceding application was abandoned. Related applications are often referred to using a family tree analogy, in which case an earlier application may be referred to as the "parent" or "grandparent" of a later application.

On other occasions, an applicant may choose to file a "continuation-in-part." A continuation-in-part is like a continuation, but it includes *additional disclosure* in the specification.[31] A continuation-in-part might be filed if the applicant discovers an improvement on the basic invention disclosed in the original application and desires a patent claim to match. The important difference between a continuation and a continuation-in-part is that the latter is entitled to the filing date of the original application *only* as to claims supported by the disclosure of the original application.[32] Any claim supported by newly added material (referred to as "new matter") is entitled only to the filing date of the continuation-in-part application.[33]

Suppose, for example, that an inventor filed an application for a basic mousetrap on January 1, 2001. The application disclosed and claimed the combination of a spring, a latch, and a trigger that releases the spring when disturbed by a mouse. Later that month, the inventor discovered a new kind of trigger less likely to release the spring prematurely. Because the original application was still in prosecution, the inventor filed, on February 1, 2001, a continuation-in-part disclosing both the basic mousetrap design of the first application and the improved trigger. If the second application includes a claim having nothing to do with the new trigger, and the claim is fully supported by the disclosure of the original application, that claim will receive the benefit of the January 1 filing date. However, a claim that does refer to the new trigger is entitled only to the

---

[30] PTO rules intended to limit the number of continuations available to applicants were recently held to exceed the PTO's rulemaking authority. *See* Tafas v. Dudas, 2008 U.S. Dist. LEXIS 26086 (E.D. Va. 2008). Excessive delay through the unnecessary filing of continuation after continuation may give rise to "prosecution laches," barring the patentee from relief. *See* Symbol Techs., Inc. v. Lemelson Medical, Education & Research Found., LP, 422 F.3d 1378, 1385 (Fed. Cir. 2005).

[31] *See Transco*, 38 F.3d at 555; MPEP § 201.08.

[32] The support must be adequate to satisfy the written description requirement of 35 U.S.C. § 112. See Section 8.8.

[33] *See* Augustine Medical, Inc. v. Gaymar Indus., Inc., 181 F.3d 1291, 1302 (Fed. Cir. 1999); Waldemar Link GmbH v. Osteonics Corp., 32 F.3d 556, 558 (Fed. Cir. 1994).

February 1 filing date. If another inventor filed an application on a mouse-trap trigger on January 15, 2001, the difference could be significant in determining priority.[34]

An exception to the rules just described arises if the matter newly added to the continuation-in-part application is *inherent* in the original application, even though not explicitly disclosed. Suppose that the inventor of the mousetrap realized that the design disclosed in the original application was more compact than most, so that the trap could be slipped into a smaller space. The inventor might decide to file a second application, styled as a continuation-in-part, explicitly pointing out this newly discovered advantage, and a claim might be drafted that referred explicitly to the trap's dimensions. As long as this characteristic was inherent in the design originally disclosed, even though not discussed, the claim would be entitled to the filing date of the original application.[35]

5.3 DIVISIONAL APPLICATIONS

Another complication in a patent "family tree" arises when, in the view of the examiner, the application claims more than one distinct invention. For example, the same application might claim both a new mousetrap design and a new "artificial cheese" to be used as bait, either of which could be used without the other. The examiner might determine that each was a separate invention, which should be claimed in its own application subject to its own fees and prior art search. When this occurs, the examiner issues a "restriction requirement" compelling the applicant to choose which of the two inventions to pursue. The other invention can then be made the subject of a "divisional" application. The divisional application includes the pertinent part of the original disclosure, and it is entitled to the same filing date.[36]

5.4 INTERFERENCES

One responsibility of a patent examiner is to search for other patent applications that claim the same invention as the application under consideration. Since it is not uncommon for an invention to occur to two inventors at nearly the same time, it is also not uncommon for two patent applications to claim essentially the same thing. If such an application is discovered, the

---

[34] See Section 8.9.2.

[35] *See* Therma-Tru Corp. v. Peachtree Doors Inc., 44 F.3d 988, 992–93 (Fed. Cir. 1995); Kennecott Corp. v. Kyocera Int'l, Inc., 835 F.2d 1419, 1421–23 (Fed. Cir. 1987).

[36] *See* 35 U.S.C. § 121; MPEP § 201.06; Transco Prods. Inc. v. Performance Contracting, Inc., 38 F.3d 551, 555 (Fed. Cir. 1994).

Patent Office will conduct an "interference" proceeding to determine which of the applications deserves priority.[37] Interference proceedings are conducted by the Board of Patent Appeals and Interferences, and examination of the interfering applications is generally halted until the interference is resolved. In contrast to the usual course of patent prosecution, an interference is a trial-like adversarial proceeding in which each applicant has an opportunity to present evidence and argument in favor of its position.[38] An interference is time-consuming and can delay issue of a patent for years.

Although interferences are generally a contest between two or more pending applications, occasionally an interference occurs between an application and a patent that has already issued. In this case, the interference may occur at the instigation of the applicant, but the applicant must claim entitlement to an interference no more than one year after the patent has issued.[39]

Even if two applicants describe essentially the same invention, they are likely to use different language in their claims. In order to clarify what the disputed invention is, the Patent Office devises its own claims, known as "counts," to describe the subject matter of the interference. A count may be identical to a claim submitted by one of the applicants, or it may be a new description of the invention. The purpose of the interference is to decide if both applications support a claim to the invention described by the count, and, if so, which applicant invented first. Although an applicant may be able to avoid an interference by denying any intention to claim the subject matter described by the count, the denial will prevent the applicant from afterward obtaining a patent on that invention.[40]

In an interference, the applicant who was first to file is known as the "senior party" and other applicants are known as "junior parties." The senior party is presumed to have invented first, but that presumption can be overcome by evidence presented by a junior party.[41] Ultimately, the issue of

---

[37] *See* 35 U.S.C. § 135; Case v. CPC Int'l, Inc., 730 F.2d 745, 748 (Fed. Cir. 1984). Two applications claim the "same invention" if the invention of one is the same as, or obvious in light of, the invention of the other. 37 C.F.R. § 1.601(i), (n); *see also* Medichem, S.A. v. Rolabo, S.L., 437 F.3d 1157, 1161 (Fed. Cir. 2006) ("two-way" test requiring that invention A would anticipate or render obvious invention B if it came first, and vice versa). A patent on a species will prevent the later patenting of a genus that includes that species. The species always anticipates the genus. On the other hand, a patent on a genus (e.g., all A plus B) will not prevent the later patenting of a species within that genus (e.g., A plus B *plus C*), so long as the species is a non-obvious variation. *See* Eli Lilly & Co. v. Bd. of Regents of the Univ. of Washington, 334 F.3d 1264, 1270 (Fed. Cir. 2003). Consequently, overlapping genus and species patents can sometimes co-exist.

[38] Note that similar contests over priority can arise in the course of infringement litigation. See Section 8.9.1.3.

[39] 35 U.S.C. § 135(b). An interference can occur between *two* issued patents, but in this case the Patent Office has no jurisdiction. An interference between two issued patents must be conducted by a federal court. *See* 35 U.S.C. § 291.

[40] *See* 37 C.F.R. § 1.605(a).

[41] *See* Brown v. Barbacid, 276 F.3d 1327, 1332–33 (Fed. Cir. 2002).

which applicant was first to invent turns on questions of conception, reduction to practice, and diligence, all of which are discussed in Section 8.9.2. The victor in an interference can proceed with patent prosecution. The loser, barring an appeal,[42] must abandon his application or pursue claims to a different invention.

5.5 REISSUE

Apart from an interference, there are two instances in which an already issued patent may return to the Patent Office to undergo further proceedings. They are known as "reissue" and "reexamination." Reissue is a means for applicants to correct errors in a patent. The error may be a defect in the specification or drawings, or the applicant's claims may have been too broad or too narrow in comparison to what the applicant could rightfully claim.[43] If the claims are too narrow, they may fail to protect the full measure of the invention; if too broad, they may run afoul of the prior art.[44]

The reissue application cannot add "new matter" to the original application,[45] and the patentee can wait no more than two years to seek claims through reissue that would broaden the scope of the original claims.[46] If the PTO allows the reissue, the applicant must "surrender" the original patent in

---

[42] An appeal can be taken either to the Federal Circuit Court of Appeals or to a federal district court. *See* 35 U.S.C. § 146.

[43] *See* 35 U.S.C. § 251. Minor errors of a clerical or typographical nature can be rectified without further examination by a "certificate of correction." *See* 35 U.S.C. §§ 254, 255; Central Admixture Pharmacy Services, Inc. v. Advanced Cardiac Solutions, P.C., 482 F.3d 1347, 1353 (Fed. Cir. 2007). If correcting the error would mean broadening the claim, the error (*and* how to correct it) must be clearly evident to persons examining the original document. *See Central Admixture*, 482 F.3d at 1353; Arthrocare Corp. v. Smith & Nephew, Inc., 406 F.3d 1365, 1374–75 (Fed. Cir. 2005). Note that the PTO examines *all* claims of a patent during reissue proceedings, including those that are unchanged from the original patent. A patentee who initiates a reissue proceeding therefore runs some risk that a claim already issued will be held invalid when looked at again. *See* Hewlett-Packard Co. v. Bausch & Lomb Inc., 882 F.2d 1556, 1563 (Fed. Cir. 1989).

[44] See Section 8.9.

[45] See Section 5.2. Furthermore, the reissued patent must claim the same invention *disclosed*, if not adequately claimed, in the original patent. *See* Hester Indus., Inc. v. Stein, Inc., 142 F.3d 1472, 1484 (Fed. Cir. 1998). This is similar to the "written description" requirement, discussed in Section 8.8.

[46] 35 U.S.C. § 251. This rule is strictly interpreted. If there is any conceivable device or method that would infringe the new claims but would not have infringed the original claims, the new claims are "broader" and cannot be obtained more than two years after the patent issued. *See* Tillotson, Ltd. v. Walbro Corp., 831 F.2d 1033, 1037 n.2 (Fed. Cir. 1987). On the other hand, an original claim and a reissue claim may be identical in scope, even if they do not use precisely the same words (e.g., one could refer to "12 inches" where the other refers to "one foot"). *See* Anderson v. International Eng'g & Mfg., Inc., 160 F.3d 1345, 1349 (Fed. Cir. 1998).

favor of the revised version.[47] The latter is enforced from its own date of issue, and it expires when the original patent would have expired.[48] Any claims carried forward in substantially identical form are enforceable as though they had been in effect from the issue date of the original patent. In other words, a court can assess damages for infringement after and *before* the reissue, even though the patentee "surrendered" the original claims.[49]

When applying for a reissue, the applicant must file a declaration identifying an error requiring correction and affirming that any errors occurred without deceptive intent.[50] What constitutes "error" can be a difficult issue. An applicant's deliberate choice to cancel a broad claim in favor of a narrow one in order to avoid prior art is not an "error" that can be corrected by reissue, even if the applicant has second thoughts.[51] On the other hand, a patent attorney's "failure to appreciate the full scope of the invention" generally is recognized as an "error" justifying reissue with broadened claims.[52]

Although patent claims can be broadened by reissue, Congress foresaw the potential unfairness to anyone who steered clear of the original narrow claims, but not the new, broader ones. To protect such persons, the law recognizes "intervening rights."[53] If, prior to the reissue, a person or corporation made, used, purchased, imported, or offered to sell a product that did not infringe the original narrow claims, that person or corporation may continue to use that product, or may sell it to someone else or offer it for sale, even if doing so would infringe the broadened claims.[54] If, for example, a business had in its inventory items manufactured before the reissue that

---

[47] 35 U.S.C. §§ 251, 252.

[48] 35 U.S.C. § 251. Reissued patents have a serial number beginning with "Re" or ending with "E."

[49] *See* 35 U.S.C. § 252; Laitram Corp. v. NEC Corp., 952 F.2d 1357, 1360–61 (Fed. Cir. 1991).

[50] *See* 37 C.F.R. § 1.175; Medrad, Inc. v. Tyco Healthcare Gp. LP, 466 F.3d 1047, 1052 (Fed. Cir. 2006).

[51] *See* In re Serenkin, 479 F.3d 1359, 1362 (Fed. Cir. 2007) ("the deliberate action of an inventor or attorney during prosecution generally fails to qualify as a correctable error"); Medtronic, Inc. v. Guidant Corp., 465 F.3d 1360, 1372–73 (Fed. Cir. 2006) (discussing the "recapture rule" that forbids regaining, through reissue, claim coverage deliberately surrendered during prosecution). "Error under the reissue statute does not include a deliberate decision to surrender specific subject matter in order to overcome prior art, a decision which in light of subsequent developments in the marketplace might be regretted. It is precisely because the patentee amended his claims to overcome prior art that a member of the public is entitled to occupy the space abandoned by the patent applicant." Mentor Corp. v. Coloplast, Inc., 998 F.2d 992, 994–95 (Fed. Cir. 1993); *see also Hewlett-Packard*, 882 F.2d at 1565 ("error" must involve "inadvertence, accident, or mistake"). The rationale for the "recapture rule" is also relevant to prosecution history estoppel, discussed in Section 10.6.8.

[52] *See Medtronic*, 465 F.3d at 1372; *Hester*, 142 F.3d at 1479–80. The error need not have been unavoidable or undiscoverable. *Medtronic*, 465 F.3d at 1372.

[53] *See* 35 U.S.C. § 252.

[54] *See* 35 U.S.C. § 252; Shockley v. Arcan, Inc., 248 F.3d 1349, 1360 (Fed. Cir. 2001). These absolute rights apply only to items that existed before the reissue, not to additional items of the same type. *Id.*

would infringe only the modified claims, that business would have the absolute right to sell those products after the reissue without incurring liability. Moreover, a court may allow additional items of the same nature to be made, used, or sold after the date of the reissue if "substantial preparation" to do so occurred before the reissue, and the court deems such measures equitable in light of the investments made and businesses commenced before the reissue.[55] A business that had invested in a factory to manufacture the newly infringing item would likely be allowed to continue producing and selling the item even after the reissue. Naturally, these rights do not extend to anyone who made no investments in an infringing activity until after the date of reissue.

5.6 REEXAMINATION

"Reexamination" allows the Patent Office to reconsider the validity of already issued claims in light of newly discovered prior art patents or printed publications. The purpose of reexamination is to provide a quicker and less expensive alternative to litigation when, for one reason or another, the Patent Office failed to consider important prior art during the initial prosecution, and as a result the validity of the patent is in doubt. Reexamination differs from most Patent Office proceedings in one important respect. Although third parties generally have no role in patent prosecution, reexamination can be requested by anyone, including a licensee, an accused infringer, or a government agency.[56] All that is necessary to begin (besides the money to pay the reexamination fee) is knowledge of a prior patent or printed publication that casts doubt on the validity of some or all of the patent claims.[57]

The party requesting the reexamination must submit to the Patent Office a list of prior art and a statement explaining why it is pertinent.[58] The Patent Office forwards a copy of the request to the patent owner. Within three months, the Patent Office must decide whether the request raises "a substantial new question of patentability."[59] If the answer is no, the decision is final and unappealable. If the answer is yes, the Patent Office orders a reexamination. At that point the patent owner may file a

---

[55] *See* 35 U.S.C. § 252; *Shockley,* 248 F.3d at 1360–61.

[56] *See* 35 U.S.C. § 302; In re Freeman, 30 F.3d 1459, 1468 (Fed. Cir. 1994); Syntex (U.S.A.) Inc. v. U.S. PTO, 882 F.2d 1570, 1573 (Fed. Cir. 1989).

[57] Reexamination can be based only on prior patents or printed publications, not, for example, on a claim of invalidity based on sales of the patented product prior to the application's "critical date." See Section 8.10.1. This limitation helps to keep reexamination proceedings comparatively simple and expedient.

[58] *See* 35 U.S.C. § 302.

[59] 35 U.S.C. § 303. The "new question" may be based on prior art already considered by the Patent Office. 35 U.S.C. § 303(a).

statement, including any proposed changes to the claims, and the party requesting the reexamination may file a reply.[60]

If the traditional procedures are followed, from that point onward reexamination proceeds by the rules devised for ordinary patent prosecution, and the party requesting reexamination has no further involvement.[61] Recently, Congress created an alternative "inter partes" procedure allowing the requesting party much greater participation, including the opportunity to comment upon and rebut arguments made by the patent owner throughout the reexamination.[62] However, the party requesting inter partes reexamination cannot raise any invalidity arguments in subsequent litigation that were or *could have been* raised during the reexamination[63]–a drawback that may lead some to choose the traditional procedure.

If necessary, claims can be *narrowed* during reexamination so that they avoid the newly discovered prior art.[64] The patentee is not allowed to enlarge the scope of the claims.[65] When the reexamination is concluded, the examiner issues a certificate canceling any claims held invalid, confirming any claims held patentable, and incorporating into the patent any new or revised claims.[66]

Although one would expect reexamination to be requested by someone wishing to attack the patent, sometimes it is requested by the patentee, as a way of *strengthening* a patent that might be held invalid in litigation. If the Patent Office finds that the claims are valid in spite of the additional prior art, a court is unlikely to hold otherwise. On the other hand, if the prior art is so close that the claims must be modified, reexamination provides an opportunity to do so. Thus, while a request for reexamination may signal doubts as to the validity of the patent, if the patent survives the process it is likely to be stronger than ever.

---

[60] 35 U.S.C. § 304. If the request for reexamination is made by someone other than the patentee, the patentee has no opportunity to make its views known until *after* the Patent Office has decided whether there is a "substantial new question of patentability." *See* 37 C.F.R. § 1.530(a); Platlex Corp. v. Mossinghoff, 771 F.2d 480, 483–84 (Fed. Cir. 1985).

[61] *See* In re Opprecht, 868 F.2d 1264, 1265 (Fed. Cir. 1989).

[62] *See* 35 U.S.C. §§ 311–318.

[63] 35 U.S.C. § 315(c).

[64] However, "[u]nless a claim granted or conferred upon reexamination is identical to an original claim, the patent can not be enforced against infringing activity that occurred before issuance of the reexamination certificate. 'Identical' does not mean verbatim, but means at most without substantive change." Bloom Eng'g Co. v. North American Mfg. Co., 129 F.3d 1247, 1250 (Fed. Cir. 1997).

[65] 35 U.S.C. § 305.

[66] 35 U.S.C. § 307.

CHAPTER 6

Ownership and Other Rights

6.1 INVENTORSHIP

The right to obtain a patent initially belongs to the inventor.[1] When a patent application is filed it is important to designate the proper inventor of the subject matter claimed. A patent can name a single inventor, or it can name two or more joint inventors.[2] It is often in the latter case that questions arise regarding who should or should not receive credit.

An inventor is anyone who participated in the mental act of *conceiving* the invention.[3] If two people work together on a project and both contribute to a

---

[1] *See* 35 U.S.C. §§ 111, 115, 116; Beech Aircraft Corp. v. EDO Corp., 990 F.2d 1237, 1248 (Fed. Cir. 1993). The inventors named on the patent are presumed to be correctly named. *See* Cook Biotech Inc. v. Acell, Inc., 460 F.3d 1365, 1381 (Fed. Cir. 2006); Caterpillar Inc. v. Sturman Indus., Inc., 387 F.3d 1358, 1377 (Fed. Cir. 2004). That presumption can be overcome only by "clear and convincing evidence." *Caterpillar,* 387 F.3d at 1377; Linear Technology Corp. v. Impala Linear Corp., 379 F.3d 1311, 1318–19 (Fed. Cir. 2004).

[2] Each joint inventor named on an application need not have contributed to every claim. 35 U.S.C. § 116; Stern v. Trustees of Columbia University, 434 F.3d 1375, 1378 (Fed. Cir. 2006) ("a contribution to one claim is sufficient to be a co-inventor"); Ethicon, Inc. v. United States Surgical Corp., 135 F.3d 1456, 1460 (Fed. Cir. 1998). If an application names A, B, and C as joint inventors, some claims may represent the work of A and B alone, or B and C alone, or A alone, or B alone, and so forth. Absent an agreement to the contrary, each inventor owns "a pro rata undivided interest in the entire patent, no matter what their respective contributions." *Id.* at 1465. This is true even if an inventor contributed to the subject matter of only one claim in a patent having many claims. *Id.* at 1466.

[3] *See Stern,* 434 F.3d at 1378 (conception is the "'touchstone of inventorship'"); Board of Educ. v. American Bioscience, Inc., 333 F.3d 1330, 1337 (Fed. Cir. 2003). The contribution should be to the *claimed* invention, not to peripheral matters that may have been discussed in the patent specification. *See Caterpillar,* 387 F.3d at 1378.

patentable idea, both can be named on the application as joint inventors. This is true whether the specific contribution of each is difficult to identify, as may be the case when an idea arises from collaborative "brainstorming,"[4] or whether the contribution of each inventor is a discrete component of the whole.

Not all contributions rise to the level of invention. Someone who had supervisory responsibility for a project but added nothing to the conception of the invention would not properly be considered an inventor. Similarly, someone who built or tested the completed invention, but did not contribute to its conception, could not be considered an inventor, no matter how important that person's contribution to the project as a whole.[5] Even someone who identifies a problem is not considered a co-inventor of the solution, in spite of the fact that identifying the problem is often a significant step. As one court observed, "[i]t is one thing to suggest that a better mousetrap ought to be built; it is another thing to build it."[6]

Deciding who should be credited as an inventor can be a difficult task, as illustrated by the case of *Hess v. Advanced Cardiovascular Sys., Inc.*[7] The invention was a balloon angioplasty catheter—a device that can be threaded through a narrowed artery and then inflated in order to reduce the blockage. The doctors responsible for the invention had tried various materials without success, when they were referred to Mr. Hess, an engineer with Raychem who was familiar with their line of heat-shrinkable plastics. Hess identified specific materials that would provide the doctors with what they needed. The materials worked, the doctors obtained a patent, and the invention was a commercial success.

Eventually, Hess claimed that he should have been named on the patent as a co-inventor because the invention would not have succeeded without his contribution. The Federal Circuit disagreed. The court compared Hess's contribution to that of a scientific treatise or a product catalog; he merely provided information regarding existing technology. "The principles [Hess] explained to [the doctors] were well known and found in textbooks. Mr. Hess did no more than a skilled salesman would do in explaining how his employer's product could be used to meet a customer's

---

[4] *See* Canon Computer Sys., Inc. v. Nu-Kote Int'l, Inc., 134 F.3d 1085, 1088 (Fed. Cir. 1998) ("As any member of a large discussion group well knows, it is often difficult to remember who first said what.").

[5] *See Board of Educ.*, 333 F.3d at 1338 ("One does not qualify as a joint inventor merely by assisting the actual inventor."); *Ethicon*, 135 F.3d at 1460 ("[O]ne of ordinary skill in the art who simply reduced the inventor's idea to practice is not necessarily a joint inventor, even if the specification discloses that embodiment to satisfy the best mode requirement."); Sewell v. Walters, 21 F.3d 411, 416–17 (Fed. Cir. 1994). Although attorneys often assist inventors in preparing a patent application, they generally should not be considered joint inventors. *See* Solomon v. Kimberly-Clark Corp., 216 F.3d 1372, 1382 (Fed. Cir. 2000) ("An attorney performing that role should not be a competitor of the client, asserting inventorship as a result of representing his client.").

[6] *See* Buildex Inc. v. Kason Indus. Inc., 4 U.S.P.Q.2d 1803, 1805–06 (E.D.N.Y. 1987).

[7] 106 F.3d 976 (Fed. Cir. 1997).

requirements."[8] Still, one can understand why Hess felt that identifying the right materials for the new application added more to the inventive idea than the passive contributions of a textbook author.

For two or more persons to be named as joint inventors, they must have *collaborated* in some way.[9] Two inventors who were unaware of each other's work could not be considered joint inventors, even if their efforts overlapped and even if the two inventors were employed by the same company.[10] Similarly, if inventor B simply builds on the published work of inventor A, the result is the sole invention of inventor B, not the joint invention of A and B. On the other hand, joint inventors need not have physically worked together at the same time, nor is it necessary that the contribution of each be equivalent in type or amount.[11] If inventor A partially completed an invention, then passed it along to inventor B with the intention that inventor B continue, A and B could be considered joint inventors of the finished invention. There are no distinctions drawn between co-inventors based on the significance, ingenuity, or timing of their contributions.[12]

If an application names the wrong inventors (as can easily happen, given the ambiguities in defining the role of "inventor"), the application, or issued patent, can be corrected to name the proper inventors without affecting the validity of the patent.[13] The incorrect naming of the inventors must, however, have occurred through error and without deceptive intent.[14]

---

[8] *Id.* at 981; *see also Board of Educ.,* 333 F.3d at 1342 ("teaching skills or general methods that somehow facilitate a later invention, without more, does not render one a coinventor").

[9] Burroughs Wellcome Co. v. Barr Labs., Inc., 40 F.3d 1223, 1227 (Fed. Cir. 1994) ("A joint invention is the product of a collaboration between two or more persons working together to solve the problem addressed."); Credle v. Bond, 25 F.3d 1566, 1574 (Fed. Cir. 1994). Accordingly, co-inventors should have had an "open line of communication" during the relevant period. *Cook Biotech,* 460 F.3d at 1373.

[10] Kimberly-Clark Corp. v. Procter & Gamble Dist. Co., 973 F.2d 911, 916 (Fed. Cir. 1992).

[11] 35 U.S.C. § 116; *Burroughs,* 40 F.3d at 1227.

[12] The contribution of an inventor cannot, however, be so minor as to be "insignificant." *See Cook Biotech,* 460 F.3d at 1373; *Caterpillar,* 387 F.3d at 1377; Acromed Corp. v. Sofamor Danek Gp., Inc., 253 F.3d 1371, 1379 (Fed. Cir. 2001) ("[A] purported inventor must show that he made 'a contribution to the claimed invention that is not insignificant in quality, when that contribution is measured against the dimension of the full invention, and [did] more than merely explain to the real inventors well-known concepts and/or the current state of the art'."). The contribution of a joint inventor must have been more than "merely exercising ordinary skill in the art," which includes explaining concepts already well known. *Caterpillar,* 387 F.3d at 1377.

[13] *See* 35 U.S.C. §§ 116 (correction of inventorship for a pending application), 256 (correction of inventorship for an issued patent). If the inventors are incorrectly named, and the patent is not saved by correction, the patent can be considered invalid under § 102(f), discussed in Section 8.9.7. *See Solomon,* 216 F.3d at 1381; Pannu v. Iolab Corp., 155 F.3d 1344, 1349–50 (Fed. Cir. 1998). If the problem *is* corrected, the validity of the patent is restored even for the period before the correction. Vikase Corp. v. American National Can Co., 261 F.3d 1316, 1329 (Fed. Cir. 2001). This is a rare example of a kind of "conditional invalidity."

[14] 35 U.S.C. §§ 116, 256.

6.2 ASSIGNMENTS

Although the right to apply for a patent belongs to the inventor, and an application must be filed on the inventor's behalf,[15] often someone other than the inventor *owns* the patent. A transfer of rights of ownership is known as an "assignment." An assignment might include all rights in the patent, or a more limited interest such as the exclusive right to a geographical area.[16] The assignee may file a document with the Patent Office recording the fact of the assignment.[17] An assignee who receives all rights to the patent by assignment is henceforth the party with the power to sue for infringement.[18]

A common element of an employment contract, particularly in the case of engineers and scientists, is that any patentable inventions made by the employee in the course of employment must be assigned to the employer. Even if the employment contract is silent, an obligation to assign is likely implied if invention falls within the natural scope of the employee's duties.[19] Thus, while patents bear the name of individual inventors (the "Smith patent" or the "Jones patent"), often a corporate assignee owns the rights. In fact, a corporate assignee can prosecute a patent in the name of the inventor and ultimately obtain rights to the invention, even if the inventor refuses to cooperate.[20]

6.3 LICENSES

A patent license is a more limited transfer of rights than an assignment. A licensor retains ownership of the patent but grants the licensee the right to practice the claimed invention, usually in exchange for some sort of royalty.

---

[15] *See* 35 U.S.C. §§ 115–16.

[16] 35 U.S.C. § 261. Courts usually characterize assignments of less than an entire interest as "licenses" rather than assignments. The Federal Circuit has called the borderline between assignments and licenses "impressionistic," urging that one focus less on labels than on the characteristics of the transferred rights, which, as we will see, can affect the transferee's ability to file suit. International Gamco, Inc. v. Multimedia Games, Inc., 504 F.3d 1273, 1279 (Fed. Cir. 2007).

[17] 35 U.S.C. § 261. Failing to record the transfer may cause problems if another party, without notice of the assignment, subsequently purchases an overlapping interest. *See id.* (assignment void against a subsequent purchaser without notice, unless recorded before that purchase or within three months of the date of the patent).

[18] *See* Rite-Hite Corp. v. Kelley Co., 56 F.3d 1538, 1551 (Fed. Cir. 1995) (right to sue belongs to the patentee or the patentee's successors).

[19] *See* Teets v. Chromalloy Gas Turbine Corp., 83 F.3d 403, 407 (Fed. Cir. 1996). Even if no agreement to assign is express or implied, if the inventor used company time or materials, or if the employee introduced the practice of the invention into the employer's business, a court is likely to recognize a "shop right" benefiting the employer. A shop right is a non-exclusive, non-transferable right allowing the employer to practice the invention, royalty-free, even if the employee is allowed to patent the invention as an individual. *See* McElmurry v. Arkansas Power & Light Co., 995 F.2d 1576, 1580–82 (Fed. Cir. 1993).

[20] *See* 37 C.F.R. § 1.47.

A license can be exclusive or non-exclusive. If it is exclusive, there is only one licensee, and only that licensee has the right to practice the claimed invention. Sometimes, but not always, a licensee obtains the right to "sub-license" others.

An exclusive licensee may file suit against an infringer in order to pre-serve its exclusivity. Whether the owner of the patent must join in that suit, and be bound by the result, depends on the nature of the license. The issue turns on whether the license divides rights to the patent in such a way that a potential infringer might be subject to multiple claims. If the licensee owns "all substantial rights" to the patent, making the transfer an assignment in all but name, the licensee may sue on its own behalf.[21] The same is true if the licensee received an exclusive license to practice the patent in a geographi-cal area.[22] On the other hand, an exclusive "field of use" license does not give the licensee standing to sue on its own. In *International Gamco*, the licensee received exclusive New York rights to use a computerized gaming system in the field of "lottery games." Because one could debate the mean-ing of "lottery games," a potential infringer in New York might have been subject to competing claims for royalties. Consequently, the licensee could not sue in its own name but had to involve the patent owner as co-plaintiff.[23] A *non*-exclusive licensee cannot sue at all and must rely on the patent owner to protect its interests.[24]

Some patent owners practice the claimed invention themselves, while others profit by licensing others to do so.[25] Patent owners have no obligation to license.[26] Although this might give the patent owner the power to reap monopoly profits, such is the reward for discovering patentable innova-tions.[27] On the other hand, the Supreme Court recently held that injunctions barring future infringement may be refused even after an infringer has been

---

[21] *See* International Gamco, Inc. v. Multimedia Games, Inc., 504 F.3d 1273, 1276 (Fed. Cir. 2007).

[22] *Id.* at 1276.

[23] *Id.* at 1277–80. If a patentee refuses to cooperate as co-plaintiff, an exclusive licensee may join the patentee as a defendant. *See* Rite-Hite Corp. v. Kelley Co., 56 F.3d 1538, 1552 (Fed. Cir. 1995).

[24] *See Rite-Hite,* 56 F.3d at 1552.

[25] On occasion patent owners "cross-license" their patents, each patent owner granting to the other the right to practice some or all of the inventions in its patent portfolio. Where two or more companies hold basic patents in the same field of technology, this can be an expedient way to ensure that mutually destructive litigation does not take the place of competition in the marketplace.

[26] *See* 35 U.S.C. § 271(d)(4).

[27] Whether a patent really confers that kind of power depends on the availability of alternatives that easily substitute for the patented invention. If one has patented a mousetrap, but other mousetraps work just is well, there is no leverage for demanding more than a competitive profit. In the end, consumer demands in the marketplace decide the financial reward for any patentable advancement.

successfully sued.[28] If the court finds that the adequacy of monetary relief and other factors counsel against entering a permanent injunction, the result is, in effect, a compulsory license to the infringer with royalties determined by the court.[29]

6.3.1 Implied Licenses

Sometimes patent licenses are not express but implied.[30] An implied license is a reflection of the shared expectations of parties who have had dealings with one another, even if those expectations were not made explicit.[31] An implied license, like an express license, is a defense to a claim of infringement.[32]

6.3.1.1 "First Sale"

Because a patent owner has, among other rights, the exclusive right to "use" the patented invention, a patent owner might sell a patented article, only to forbid its use by the purchaser. Needless to say, most purchasers expect to use the things they buy. In order to fulfill this expectation and similar ones, whenever a patented article is purchased from the patent owner, without any express restriction or reservation of rights, the law recognizes an implied license allowing the purchaser to use the article, repair it,[33] or sell it to someone else. As stated in one Federal Circuit opinion, "an authorized sale of a patented product places that product beyond the reach of the patent. . . . The patent owner's rights with respect to the product end with its sale."[34] A patent owner who intends otherwise must make those intentions explicit.[35]

The "first sale" of a patented article, without restrictions, is said to "exhaust" the rights of the patent owner.[36] In other words, whatever compensation the

---

[28] eBay Inc. v. MercExchange, L.L.C., 547 U.S. 388, 391–94 (2006).

[29] *See* Paice LLC v. Toyota Motor Corp., 504 F.3d 1293, 1314–15 (Fed. Cir. 2007).

[30] Carborundum Co. v. Molten Metal Equipment Innovations, Inc., 72 F.3d 872, 878 (Fed. Cir. 1995).

[31] *See Carborundum,* 72 F.3d at 878; McCoy v. Mitsuboshi Cutlery, Inc., 67 F.3d 917, 920 (Fed. Cir. 1995) (implied license arises from "entire course of conduct" between the parties).

[32] *Carborundum,* 72 F.3d at 878.

[33] Unless the repairs are so extensive that they are really a "reconstruction" of the patented invention. See Section 10.4.

[34] Intel Corp. v. ULSI Sys. Tech., Inc., 995 F.2d 1566, 1568 (Fed. Cir. 1993); *see also* Hewlett-Packard Co. v. Repeat-O-Type Stencil Mfg. Corp., 123 F.3d 1445, 1451 (Fed. Cir. 1997).

[35] Explicit restrictions *are* possible. For example, one could sell a patented item with the requirement that it be used only once. Reuse of that item by the purchaser would be considered patent infringement. *See* Mallinckrodt, Inc. v. Medipart, Inc., 976 F.2d 700 (Fed. Cir. 1992).

[36] *See* Quanta Computer Inc. v. LG Electronics Inc., 128 S. Ct. 2109, 2115 (2008); Monsanto Co. v. Scruggs, 459 F.3d 1328, 1335–36 (Fed. Cir. 2006); Anton/Bauer Inc. v. PAG Ltd., 329 F.3d 1343, 1349 (Fed. Cir. 2003).

patent owner receives from the "first sale" is all the patent owner can expect, even if the article is sold and resold, used and reused, many times.[37] The same result follows a "first sale" by a licensee of the patent owner; the licensee may owe royalties to the patent owner, but the article sold is afterward "free of the patent."[38]

A similar rule applies where a patent claims a method and the patent owner sells an apparatus used in that method.[39] For example, a patent might claim a "method of catching mice," and the apparatus sold might be a kind of mousetrap. Anyone who purchases a mousetrap expects to use it for catching mice, and if the only method of using the mousetrap is the same one claimed in the patent, the purchaser reasonably expects to use that method. Such expectations lead to the following rule: an unrestricted sale of an apparatus by the patent owner confers an implied license to use that apparatus to practice a patented method, if the apparatus has no non-infringing uses.[40] On the other hand, if the apparatus does have other uses, one cannot infer a license to the patented method.[41]

6.3.1.2 Legal Estoppel

Another situation in which a patent license can be implied falls under the heading of "legal estoppel." Simply put, legal estoppel is a doctrine that prevents a patent owner from licensing one patent, only to make that license worthless by enforcing another.[42] Suppose that an inventor obtained two patents—one a broad patent covering a new mousetrap design, and the other a narrow patent covering a particular variation of that design. A mousetrap

---

[37] The "first sale" must be an authorized sale by the patent owner or a licensee of the patent owner. If the product originated with an infringer, downstream purchasers can be held to infringe by using or reselling the product. *See Intel,* 995 F.2d at 1572–73 (Plager, J., dissenting). However, if the infringer was sued and compelled to pay money damages to the patentee, that payment amounts to a "first sale," and the infringing goods are subsequently beyond the reach of the patent. *See* King Instrument Corp. v. Otari Corp., 814 F.2d 1560, 1564 (Fed. Cir. 1987).

[38] *See* Unidisco, Inc. v. Schattner, 824 F.2d 965, 968 (Fed. Cir. 1987).

[39] *See Quanta,* 128 S. Ct. at 2117 ("methods . . . may be 'embodied' in a product, the sale of which exhausts the patent rights").

[40] *See Quanta,* 128 S. Ct. at 2119; Met-Coil Sys. Corp. v. Korners Unlimited, Inc., 803 F.2d 684, 686 (Fed. Cir. 1986). There is no ongoing right to practice the method after the apparatus is worn out. *See* Carborundum Co. v. Molten Metal Equipment Innovations, Inc., 72 F.3d 872, 878 (Fed. Cir. 1995).

[41] *See* Bandag, Inc. v. Al Bolser's Tire Stores, Inc., 750 F.2d 903, 924 (Fed. Cir. 1984). The alternative use need not be optimal, but it should be "reasonable." *See* Glass Equipment Development, Inc. v. Besten, Inc., 174 F.3d 1337, 1343 (Fed. Cir. 1999).

[42] *See* Spindelfabrik Suessen-Schurr Stahlecker & Grill GmbH v. Schubert & Salzer Maschinenfabrik Atiengesellschaft, 829 F.2d 1075, 1080 (Fed. Cir. 1987). "The rationale . . . is to estop the grantor from taking back that for which he received consideration." *Id.*

within the scope of the narrower patent would necessarily fall within the scope of the broader patent as well. Anyone who received an express license to the second patent would likely receive an implied license to the first under the principle of legal estoppel. Otherwise the patent owner could prevent the licensee from taking any benefit from the license it obtained.

6.3.1.3 *Industry Standards*

The preceding are merely common examples of implied licenses. Any conduct by a patentee that could lead one to infer a waiver or an abandonment of the patentee's rights may have similar effects.[43] An increasingly common example involves the adoption of a patented technology as an "industry standard." Many industries, such as the computer and telecommunications industries, depend on such standards to ensure that equipment from different manufacturers can work together. Once such a standard is adopted, companies in the industry are virtually compelled to conform. If the industry standard is covered by a patent, should all companies in the industry be forced to pay a royalty? In some cases the answer is yes, but if the patent owner promoted the adoption of the technology as a standard and gave the impression that the standard could be practiced free of obligations, the circumstances could establish an implied license.[44] Otherwise an industry could be lured into adopting a standard, only later to be faced with claims of infringement.

---

[43] *See* Wang Labs., Inc. v. Mitsubishi Electronics America, Inc., 103 F.3d 1571, 1580 (Fed. Cir. 1997).

[44] *See Wang,* 103 F.2d at 1575, 1581–82.

CHAPTER 7

Interpreting Patent Claims

The claims are the most important part of any patent. They define what the patented invention is.[1] Hence, the first step in determining whether a patent is valid or infringed is to analyze the claims and determine precisely what they mean.[2] This analysis is known as "claim construction" or "claim interpretation."[3]

Claims are written in the English language, but they often employ an obscure technical vocabulary. The following is an example of patent claim language:

1. An aqueous cosmetic emulsion comprising:
   i) an isoparaffin;
   ii) a C8-C22 alkyl phosphate salt;
   wherein the isoparaffin and alkyl phosphate salt are present in a respective weight ratio of from about 40:1 to about 1:1, and said emulsion having a viscosity ranging

---

[1] Phillips v. AWH Corp., 415 F.3d 1303, 1312 (Fed. Cir. 2005) (*en banc*); Computer Docking Station Corp. v. Dell, Inc., 519 F.3d 1366, 1373 (Fed. Cir. 2008).

[2] In the rare instance that the parties do not dispute the meaning of the claims, a formal step of claim construction may be unnecessary. *See* Hakim v. Cannon Avent Gp., PLC, 479 F.3d 1313, 1318 (Fed. Cir. 2007).

[3] The Patent Office during prosecution will give claims their "broadest reasonable interpretation." In re Bigio, 381 F.3d 1320, 1324 (Fed. Cir. 2004). This provides extra insurance that newly issued claims do not encroach on the prior art. If the applicant did not intend the broader interpretation, the applicant can amend the claim language to make that clear. Once the patent has issued, courts no longer apply the broadest reasonable interpretation if the evidence better supports a narrow construction. *See* Atlantic Thermoplastics Co. v. Faytex Corp., 970 F.2d 834, 846 (Fed. Cir. 1992). In most other respects, the claim interpretation rules applied by the courts and the Patent Office are the same.

from about 35 to about 90 Brookfield units as measured with a Brookfield
Viscometer Model LTV using a #4 spindle rotating at 60 rpm at 25° C.[4]

The claim is for a hand lotion.

The opacity of claim language can be traced to two sources. First, because
patents are awarded to technological advancements, a technical vocabulary is
often best suited to describe what the invention is. The language of the preceding example would be meaningful to the chemist who invented the lotion
and to other chemists who are likely to be reading the patent. Second, because
of its legal significance, claim language must describe the invention precisely.
If a claim employs a narrow term instead of a more accurate, broader term,
the patent may exclude a product legitimately within the scope of the applicant's invention. If the preceding example had used the term "hand lotion"
instead of "cosmetic emulsion," the claim might have been too narrow to
cover a face cream that consisted of the same combination of materials. On
the other hand, if claim language is too broad, the patent may be anticipated
by a prior art reference and made invalid.[5] The specific measure of viscosity
in the preceding example may have been all that distinguished the invention
from other lotions. So everyday language that would serve as a casual description of an invention will not do for a patent claim. Finding the right words to
describe an invention, from both a technical and a legal viewpoint, is one of
the most important tasks faced by a patent attorney.

Patent claims should be interpreted from the perspective of their intended
audience—persons skilled in the field of the invention at the time the patent
application was filed.[6] In deciding what a patent claim means, guidance can
be found in the following sources:

- The "ordinary meaning" of a word
- The specification
- The prosecution history
- Other claims

Although patentees sometimes testify as to what they *intended* a claim to
mean, such subjective, post hoc testimony carries little weight.[7] Indeed, even if
what the claim says is clearly *not* what the applicant intended, a court will not

---

[4] Conopco, Inc. v. May Dep't Stores Co., 46 F.3d 1556, 1560 (Fed. Cir. 1994).

[5] See Section 8.9.5.

[6] *See Phillips,* 415 F.3d at 1312–13; *Computer Docking Station,* 519 F.3d at 1373; Ortho-McNeil
Pharmaceutical, Inc. v. Caraco Pharmaceutical Labs., Ltd., 476 F.3d 1321, 1326 (Fed. Cir.
2007); Dayco Products, Inc. v. Total Containment, Inc., 258 F.3d 1317, 1324 (Fed. Cir. 2001)
("If an argument offered in support of a particular claim construction is so convoluted and
artificial that it would not be apparent to a skilled artisan reading the patent and the prosecution history, the argument is simply unhelpful to the performance of our task.").

[7] *See* Solomon v. Kimberly-Clark Corp., 216 F.3d 1372, 1379 (Fed. Cir. 2000); Senmed, Inc. v.
Richard-Allan Medical Indus., Inc., 888 F.2d 815, 819 (Fed. Cir. 1989).

overlook unambiguous claim language. In *Chef America, Inc. v. Lamb-Weston, Inc.*,[8] the claim required that dough be heated in an oven to a temperature of 400 to 800 degrees Fahrenheit, a temperature that would give one's frozen pizza the consistency of a charcoal briquette. The patentee meant that the *oven* should be that hot, not the dough itself. The court refused to ignore the language of the claim, in spite of the absurd result: "we construe the claim as written, not as the patentees wish they had written it."[9]

Sometimes it is difficult to reconcile conflicting evidence on how claim language should be interpreted. For example, in *Vitronics Corp. v. Conceptronic, Inc,*[10] the critical term "solder reflow temperature" could have meant the temperature at which solder began to melt, or the higher temperature at which it flowed freely. The standard literature in the field supported the former meaning, but the examples discussed in the patent seemed consistent only with the latter. The court had to choose, because infringement depended on the proper definition.

On various occasions, the Federal Circuit has discussed procedures for weighing conflicting evidence. In *Vitronics*, the court emphasized "intrinsic" evidence—evidence, that is, found in the patent itself or in the prosecution history.[11] It approved resort to "extrinsic" evidence, such as technical dictionaries, only in the rare case that the intrinsic evidence was ambiguous.[12] On the other hand, some later cases—most notably *Texas Digital Systems, Inc. v. Telegenix, Inc.*[13]—emphasized the "plain meaning" of claim language, best exemplified by neutral sources such as dictionaries.[14] Following *Texas Digital,* one might begin the process of claim interpretation with just the kind of extrinsic evidence dismissed in *Vitronics.*

In 2005 the Federal Circuit, in *Phillips v. AWH Corp.*,[15] addressed these contradictions through a hearing *en banc.* Although the court found the recent emphasis on dictionaries overdone, it refrained from introducing a rigid hierarchy excluding extrinsic evidence in all but the rarest of cases. It admitted that there is "no magic formula or catechism" for construing claim

---

[8] 358 F.3d 1371 (Fed. Cir. 2004).

[9] *Id.* at 1374. Mistakes can be corrected through other procedures. See Section 5.5.

[10] 90 F.3d 1576 (Fed. Cir. 1996).

[11] *Id.* at 1583.

[12] *See id.* ("In most situations, an analysis of the intrinsic evidence alone will resolve any ambiguity in a disputed claim term. In such circumstances, it is improper to rely on extrinsic evidence."). The emphasis on intrinsic evidence reflects the idea that patents must provide fair warning to the public. *See id.* ("The claims, specification, and file history, rather than extrinsic evidence, constitute the public record of the patentee's claim, a record on which the public is entitled to rely.").

[13] 308 F.3d 1193 (Fed. Cir. 2002).

[14] *See id.* at 1202–03 ("Dictionaries, encyclopedias and treatises, publicly available at the time the patent is issued, . . . are unbiased reflections of common understanding."); Interactive Gift Express, Inc. v. CompuServe Inc., 231 F.3d 859, 866 (Fed. Cir. 2000) ("Dictionaries, which are a form of extrinsic evidence, hold a special place. . . .").

[15] 415 F.3d 1303 (Fed. Cir. 2005) (*en banc*).

language, and no particular sequence of steps that a court must invariably apply. Rather, one must interpret claim language as it would be understood by persons in the field of the invention, which includes proper regard for what the patent itself has to say. Extrinsic evidence can be illuminating, but if the patent is perfectly clear, one cannot contradict its meaning by resort to other sources of information.[16] In that respect, the court reaffirmed *Vitronics* at the expense of *Texas Digital.* With that general guidance in mind, one can still usefully apply the rules discussed in the remainder of this chapter to the challenging task of claim interpretation.

7.1 "ORDINARY MEANING"

A natural place to begin one's claim interpretation is with the "ordinary meaning" of the terms in question.[17] Many cases speak of a "heavy presumption" that claim terminology should be given its ordinary or customary meaning.[18] On occasion, the ordinary meaning of a term may be apparent even to a layman.[19] Or, if the term is not a technical one, its ordinary meaning may be found in a general-purpose dictionary.[20] Often the terms used in patent claims are technical terms with specialized meaning to persons skilled in the art of the invention.[21] On those occasions, a court may also look to technical dictionaries and similar references for assistance.[22] Of course, the

---

[16] *See id.* at 1324.

[17] *See* Phillips v. AWH Corp., 415 F.3d 1303, 1312 (Fed. Cir. 2005) (*en banc*) ("We have frequently stated that the words of a claim 'are generally given their ordinary and customary meaning.'"); Computer Docking Station Corp. v. Dell, Inc., 519 F.3d 1366, 1373 (Fed. Cir. 2008).

[18] *See* Elbex Video, Ltd. v. Sensormatic Electronics Corp., 508 F.3d 1366, 1371 (Fed. Cir. 2007); Leibel-Flarsheim Co. v. Medrad Inc., 358 F.3d 898, 913 (Fed. Cir. 2004); CCS Fitness, Inc. v. Brunswick Corp., 288 F.3d 1359, 1366 (Fed. Cir. 2002).

[19] *See Phillips,* 415 F.3d at 1314; C.R. Bard, Inc. v. U.S. Surgical Corp., 388 F.3d 858, 863 (Fed. Cir. 2004) (questioning the need to consult references when the terms were as commonplace as "conformable" and "pliable").

[20] *See Phillips,* 415 F.3d. at 1314 (for non-technical vocabulary "general purpose dictionaries may be helpful"); Greenberg v. Ethicon Endo-Surgery, Inc., 91 F.3d 1580, 1583 (Fed. Cir. 1996).

[21] Even terms that have non-technical meanings may have to be placed in an appropriate technological context. *See* TAP Pharmaceutical Prods., Inc. v. Owl Pharmaceuticals, L.L.C., 419 F.3d 1346, 1354 (Fed. Cir. 2005). If the patentee uses a term that means *nothing* in the field of the invention, a court must look entirely to intrinsic evidence to construe it. *See* Network Commerce, Inc. v. Microsoft Corp., 422 F.3d 1353, 1359–60 (Fed. Cir. 2005) (the term "download component" had no "commonly understood meaning reflected in general dictionaries" nor any "specialized meaning in the relevant art"); Irdeto Access, Inc. v. Echostar Satellite Corp., 383 F.3d 1295, 1300 (Fed. Cir. 2004).

[22] *See Phillips,* 415 F.3d at 1314 ("Because dictionaries, and especially technical dictionaries, attempt to collect accepted meanings of terms used in various fields of science and technology . . . [they] can assist the court in determining the meaning of particular terminology to those of skill in the art of the invention."); MIT v. Abacus Software, 462 F.3d 1344, 1351 (Fed. Cir. 2006) (where the specification provided no definition, explicit or implicit, of the term "scanner," the court could look to definitions from technical and general-purpose dictionaries).

claims are not to be read through the use of a dictionary alone, as though one were translating a Russian novel word by word; instead, one must read the claims, as a person skilled in the art would, in the context of the entire patent document.[23]

Even expert testimony may be admitted "to clarify the patented technology and to explain its meaning through the eyes of experience."[24] On the other hand, courts are well aware that the opinions of experts maybe colored by hindsight and the interests of the litigants who employ them. Hence courts treat expert testimony with appropriate skepticism; unsupported assertions may be ignored and expert testimony discounted if it is "at odds with the claim construction mandated by . . . the written record of the patent."[25]

7.2 SPECIFICATION

If a word has an "ordinary" or "plain meaning," one might suppose that its interpretation would be uncontroversial, yet words as simple as "on" and "a" have been the subjects of intense debate in the context of infringement litigation.[26] One reason is that a patent applicant can be "his own lexicographer"—which is to say, an applicant can devise his own vocabulary to describe the invention.[27] Words can be used in ways that differ from their ordinary sense, or new words can be invented. Nevertheless, if the applicant uses words in a specialized or unusual sense, that sense must be made clear in the patent specification.[28]

---

[23] *See Phillips*, 415 at 1313; Atofina v. Great Lakes Chemical Corp., 441 F.3d 991, 996 (Fed. Cir. 2006) (court can choose from dictionary definitions as directed by intrinsic evidence); Free Motion Fitness, Inc. v. Cybex Int'l, Inc., 423 F.3d 1343, 1349 (Fed. Cir. 2005).

[24] Aqua-Aerobic Sys., Inc v. Aerators Inc., 211 F.3d 1241, 1245 (Fed. Cir. 2000); *see also Philips*, 415 F.3d at 1318 (Expert testimony may be admitted "to provide background on the technology at issue, to explain how an invention works, to ensure that the court's understanding of the technical aspects of the patent is consistent with that of a person of skill in the art, or to establish that a particular term in the patent or the prior art has a particular meaning in the pertinent field."); Serio-US Indus., Inc. v. Plastic Recovery Techs. Corp., 459 F.3d 1311, 1319 (Fed. Cir. 2006).

[25] *Phillips*, 415 F.3d at 1318; *Network Commerce*, 422 F.3d at 1361.

[26] Senmed, Inc. v. Richard-Allan Medical Indus., Inc., 888 F.2d 815, 819 (Fed. Cir. 1989); North American Vaccine, Inc. v. American Cyanamid Co., 7 F.3d 1571, 1575–76 (Fed. Cir. 1993).

[27] *See* Phillips v. AWH Corp., 415 F.3d 1303, 1316 (Fed. Cir. 2005) (*en banc*); Sinorgchem Co. v. Int'l Trade Comm'n, 511 F.3d 1132, 1136 (Fed. Cir. 2007); Honeywell Int'l, Inc. v. Universal Avionics Sys. Corp., 493 F.3d 1358, 1361 (Fed. Cir. 2007) ("When a patentee defines a claim term, the patentee's definition governs, even if it is contrary to the conventional meaning of the term.").

[28] *See* Merck & Co. v. Teva Pharmaceuticals USA, Inc., 395 F.3d 1364, 1370 (Fed. Cir. 2005); Bell Atlantic Network Services, Inc. v. Covad Communications Gp., Inc., 262 F.2d 1258, 1268 (Fed. Cir. 2001). The specification "must clearly redefine a claim term 'so as to put a reasonable competitor or one reasonably skilled in the art on notice that the patentee intended to so redefine that claim term.'" Elekta Instrument S.A. v. O.U.R. Scientific Int'l Inc., 214 F.3d 1302, 1307 (Fed. Cir. 2000).

The patent specification is a place for the applicant to elaborate on the invention, and it serves as a "dictionary" to define, expressly or by implication, any specialized meaning to be given terms used in the claims. Accordingly, the specification is "the single best guide to the meaning of a disputed term."[29] In all cases it is highly relevant, and in many it is dispositive.[30] If the specification clearly shows that the applicant did not use a term in its ordinary sense, the specification takes precedence.[31]

Although the specification is an indispensable tool for claim interpretation, there is always a danger that it will be used not to *define* a term used in a claim, but to *add limitations* that do not appear in the claim at all. A specification must describe specific examples, or "preferred embodiments," that fall within the scope of the patent claims but are not co-extensive with them.[32] The details of these preferred embodiments do not limit the scope of the claims, unless the claims say so.[33]

Consider, for example, the claims in *In re Paulsen*,[34] which described a "portable computer" with a hinged case allowing the display screen to be latched in an upright position during use. The patentee argued that the term "portable computer" did not include a calculator. If the claims did cover a calculator, they would be found invalid because of a prior Japanese patent. The patentee pointed out that the specific "portable computer" disclosed in the specification incorporated a sophisticated display, advanced data processing capability, communications ports, and other attributes that are characteristic of a laptop personal computer rather than a calculator.

---

[29] *Phillips*, 415 F.3d at 1321; Kim v. Conagra Foods, Inc., 465 F.3d 1312, 1318 (Fed. Cir. 2006); Vitronics Corp. v. Conceptronic, Inc., 90 F.3d 1576, 1582 (Fed. Cir. 1996).

[30] *Phillips,* 415 F.3d at 1315; Computer Docking Station Corp. v. Dell, Inc., 519 F.3d 1366, 1374 (Fed. Cir. 2008); *Vitronics*, 90 F.3d at 1582.

[31] *Phillips*, 415 F.3d at 1316.

[32] See Section 3.3. It is seldom correct to interpret claim language to *exclude* the patentee's own preferred embodiments. *See* Oatey Co. v. IPS Corp., 514 F.3d 1271, 1277 (Fed. Cir. 2008); Chimie v. PPG Indus., Inc., 402 F.3d 1371, 1377 (Fed. Cir. 2005); *Vitronics*, 90 F.3d at 1583 ("[s]uch an interpretation is rarely, if ever, correct and would require highly persuasive evidentiary support"). But on occasion no other reading of the claim language is possible. *See Elekta*, 214 F.3d at 1308 ("in light of the prosecution history and the unambiguous language of the amended claim, we conclude that this is the rare case in which such an interpretation is compelled").

[33] *See Phillips*, 415 F.3d at 1323 ("although the specification often describes very specific embodiments of the invention, we have repeatedly warned against confining the claims to those embodiments"); *Computer Docking Station*, 519 F.3d at 1374; Ventana Medical Sys., Inc. v. Biogenix Labs., Inc., 473 F.3d 1173, 1181 (Fed. Cir. 2006); Teleflex, Inc. v. Ficosa North America Corp., 299 F.3d 1313, 1326 (Fed. Cir. 2002) ("the claims must be read in view of the specification . . . but limitations from the specification are not to be read into the claims"). Even if the specification describes only one embodiment, the claims will not be limited to that embodiment without "expressions of manifest exclusion or restriction." Gemstar-TV Guide Int'l, Inc. v. Int'l Trade Comm'n, 383 F.3d 1352, 1366 (Fed. Cir. 2004).

[34] 30 F.3d 1475 (Fed. Cir. 1994).

Nevertheless, the court found that none of these things were required by the claims. Since the claims merely said "portable computer," and the court found that a calculator was a kind of "portable computer" as that term is generally understood, the claims were broad enough to include a calculator.[35]

Sometimes, as in *Paulsen*, the patentee tries to "read into" the claims limitations found in the specification, in order to narrow the claims sufficiently to avoid the prior art. In other cases, it is the accused infringer who seeks to read in those limitations in order to narrow the claim and avoid infringement. In neither case is the practice allowed. Note that there is sometimes a fine line between "reading in" a limitation absent from the claims and using the specification to *interpret* the claims in a particular fashion.[36] The patentee in *Paulsen*, for example, might have argued that "computer" is a term with various meanings and that reading the claim language *in light of* the specification would suggest the narrower meaning.[37]

There is one important exception to the rule that limitations found only in the specification cannot be read into the claims. This exception applies to claims drafted in the "means-plus-function" format provided for in Paragraph 6 of 35 U.S.C. § 112. Claims of this type are discussed in Section 7.7.4.

7.3 PROSECUTION HISTORY

Another resource for interpreting claim language is the prosecution history. This is (ideally) a complete record of the proceedings before the Patent Office.[38] It includes both the prior art cited during examination and any remarks or representations that may have been made by the applicant

---

[35] *Id.* at 1479–80.

[36] *See Phillips*, 415 F.3d at 1323; Liebel-Flarsheim Co. v. Medrad Inc., 358 F.3d 898, 904 (Fed. Cir. 2004).

[37] Resolving the tension between interpreting claim language in light of the specification and reading into the claim limitations found *only* in the specification depends upon "how the specification characterizes the claimed invention." Alloc, Inc. v. International Trade Comm'n, 342 F.3d 1361, 1370 (Fed. Cir. 2003). The specification may "refer[] to a limitation only as a part of less than all possible embodiments," or it may "suggest[] that the very character of the invention requires [that] the limitation be a part of every embodiment." *Id.* If "the specification makes clear at various points that the claimed invention is narrower than the claim language might imply, it is entirely permissible and proper to limit the claims." *Id.* If, for example, the specification strongly discourages a particular approach, the claims may be interpreted to exclude that approach. *See* Honeywell Int'l, Inc. v. ITT Indus., Inc., 452 F.3d 1312, 1320 (Fed. Cir. 2006) ("Repeated derogatory statements concerning one type of material" served as a disavowal of the subject matter: "If the written description could talk, it would say, 'Do not use carbon fibers.'").

[38] Sometimes matters are decided in a telephone conference, of which there is often an inadequate record.

concerning the proper interpretation of the claims.[39] The prosecution history may be more ambiguous than the specification because it documents ongoing discussion between the patent applicant and the examiner. Nevertheless, the prosecution history can "demonstrat[e] how the inventor understood the invention and whether the inventor limited the invention . . . making the claim scope narrower than it would otherwise be."[40]

Claims must be interpreted in the same way in litigation as they were in the Patent Office. Otherwise applicants could treat their claims as the proverbial "nose of wax" to be twisted one direction in prosecution (perhaps to avoid a close prior art reference) and another direction in litigation (perhaps to encompass an accused product similar to that reference).[41] Such inconsistency in interpretation would pervert the process of examination, and it would hinder potential competitors who should be entitled to rely on the public record in judging the scope of the patentee's claims.[42]

During prosecution, an applicant may *disavow* a claim interpretation that would otherwise have been plausible based on the ordinary meaning of the term.[43] The surrender must be "clear and unmistakable" from the perspective of a person of ordinary skill reviewing the prosecution history.[44] Occasionally, a court will overlook what was obviously a *mistaken* charac-

---

[39] *See* Phillips v. AWH Corp., 415 F.3d 1303, 1317 (Fed. Cir. 2005) (*en banc*).

[40] *Id.*; *see also* Regents of the Univ. of California v. Dakocytomation California, Inc., 517 F.3d 1364, 1372–73 (Fed. Cir. 2008); Seachange Int'l, Inc. v. C-Core, Inc., 413 F.3d 1361, 1372 (Fed. Cir. 2005).

[41] *See* Vitronics Corp. v. Conceptronic, Inc., 90 F.3d 1576, 1583 (Fed. Cir. 1996); Southwall Techs., Inc. v. Cardinal IG Co., 54 F.3d 1570, 1578 (Fed. Cir. 1995).

[42] *See* Springs Window Fashions LP v. Novo Indus., L.P., 323 F.3d 989, 995 (Fed. Cir. 2003) ("The public notice function of a patent and its prosecution history requires that a patentee be held to what he declares during the prosecution of his patent. A patentee may not state during prosecution that the claims do not cover a particular device and then change position and later sue a party who makes that same device for infringement.").

[43] *See* Elbex Video, Ltd. v. Sensormatic Electronics Corp., 508 F.3d 1366, 1371 (Fed. Cir. 2007); Golight Inc. v. Wal-Mart Stores Inc., 355 F.3d 1327, 1333 (Fed. Cir. 2004); Omega Eng'g, Inc. v. Raytek Corp., 334 F.3d 1314, 1324 (Fed. Cir. 2003) ("[W]here the patentee has unequivocally disavowed a certain meaning to obtain his patent, the doctrine of prosecution disclaimer attaches and narrows the ordinary meaning of the claim congruent with the scope of the surrender."). A disclaimer may occur "where an applicant argues that a claim possesses a feature that the prior art does not possess in order to overcome a prior art rejection." *Seachange*, 413 F.3d at 1372–73.

[44] *Elbex*, 508 F.3d at 1371; *Seachange*, 413 F.3d at 1373 ("A disclaimer must be clear and unambiguous."); Cordis Corp. v. Medtronic AVE, Inc., 339 F.3d 1352, 1363 (Fed. Cir. 2003).

terization of the invention by the applicant during prosecution.[45] This is appropriate, however, only when the error is so apparent that a reasonable person would not be misled.[46]

7.4 OTHER CLAIMS

Comparing different claims can assist in determining their meaning.[47] This particularly occurs in the context of the "doctrine of claim differentiation," which holds that each claim should be presumed to differ in scope from every other claim.[48] For example, if a dependent claim adds a limitation to an independent claim, one should presume that the same limitation is not present, implicitly, in both claims.[49] The assumption is that an applicant would not intentionally draft two claims that covered, in different words, precisely the same subject matter. The doctrine of claim differentiation is not absolute, however.[50] Sometimes the only reasonable interpretation of a claim is one that makes it redundant.

---

[45] *See, e.g.,* Intervet America, Inc. v. Kee-Vet Labs., Inc., 887 F.2d 1050, 1053–54 (Fed. Cir. 1989).

[46] *See* Biotec Biologische Naturverpackungen GmbH v. Biocorp, Inc., 249 F.3d 1341, 1348 (Fed. Cir. 2001) ("An error in the prosecution record must be viewed as errors are in documents in general; that is, would it have been apparent to the interested reader that an error was made, such that it would be unfair to enforce the error."); Hockerson-Halberstadt, Inc. v. Avia Gp. Int'l, Inc., 222 F.3d 951, 957 (Fed. Cir. 2000) (distinguishing *Intervet* and denying the patentee the requested "mulligan that would erase from the prosecution history the inventor's disavowal of a particular aspect of a claim term's meaning").

[47] *See* Phillips v. AWH Corp., 415 F.3d 1303, 1314 (Fed. Cir. 2005) (*en banc*) ("Because claim terms are normally used consistently throughout the patent, the usage of a term in one claim can often illuminate the meaning of the same term in other claims. . . . Differences among claims can also be a useful guide in understanding the meaning of particular claim terms.").

[48] *See* Curtiss-Wright Flow Control Corp. v. Velan, Inc., 438 F.3d 1374, 1380 (Fed. Cir. 2006); Kraft Foods, Inc. v. International Trading Co., 203 F.3d 1362, 1366 (Fed. Cir. 2000) ("two claims of a patent are presumptively of different scope"); Beachcombers, Int'l, Inc. v. Wildwood Creative Prods., Inc., 31 F.3d 1154, 1162 (Fed. Cir. 1994) (an interpretation that would render a claim superfluous is "presumptively unreasonable").

[49] *See Phillips,* 415 F.3d at 1315; *Curtiss-Wright,* 438 F.3d at 1380; SunRace Roots Enterprise Co. v. SRAM Corp., 336 F.3d 1298, 1303 (Fed. Cir. 2003) (the "presumption is especially strong when the limitation in dispute is the only meaningful difference between an independent and dependent claim, and one party is urging that the limitation in the dependent claim should be read into the independent claim").

[50] *See* Regents of the Univ. of California v. Dakocytomation California, Inc., 517 F.3d 1364, 1375 (Fed. Cir. 2008); *Curtiss-Wright,* 438 F.3d at 1380–81; *Kraft Foods,* 203 F.3d at 1368 (claim differentiation "is 'not a hard and fast rule'").

7.5 VALIDITY

Another basic principle of claim interpretation is that claims should, if possible, be read in a manner that preserves their validity.[51] The source of this rule is obscure, but perhaps the underlying assumption is that the interpretation supporting validity must be the interpretation the Patent Office had in mind. Like the doctrine of claim differentiation, this principle does not justify a claim interpretation that is unreasonable or unsupported by the evidence.[52]

In any case, a claim must be interpreted in the same way when the issue is infringement as it is when the issue is validity.[53] If a claim is interpreted in a narrow fashion to avoid a potentially invalidating prior art reference, that same narrow interpretation must be applied in comparing the claim to the accused product. The meaning of a claim cannot change to suit the convenience of the patent owner.[54]

7.6 PREAMBLES

A peculiar rule of claim interpretation involves the "preamble"–the first paragraph of a patent claim, typically ending with the word "comprising." In the claim set out at the beginning of this chapter, the preamble language is "An aqueous cosmetic emulsion comprising . . ." The preamble often characterizes the category of invention or its intended use–e.g., a mousetrap or a "cosmetic emulsion"–but it does not in itself recite the checklist of claim

---

[51] Liebel-Flarsheim Co. v. Medrad Inc., 358 F.3d 898, 911 (Fed. Cir. 2004); Tate Access Floors, Inc. v. Interface Architectural Resources, Inc., 279 F.3d 1357, 1367 (Fed. Cir. 2002); Apple Computer, Inc. v. Articulate Sys., Inc., 234 F.3d 14, 24 (Fed. Cir. 2000) ("'claims should be read in a way that avoids ensnaring the prior art if it is possible to do so'"). The axiom applies, however, only if the meaning of the claim remains ambiguous in spite of the normal procedures of claim interpretation. *Liebel-Flarsheim*, 358 F.3d at 911.

[52] *See* Nazomi Communications, Inc. v. ARM Holdings, PLC, 403 F.3d 1364, 1368 (Fed. Cir. 2005) (interpretation preserving validity adopted only "if practicable"; courts "should not re-write claims to preserve their validity"); *Apple Computer*, 324 F.3d at 24; Quantum Corp. v. Rodime, PLC, 65 F.3d 1577, 1584 (Fed. Cir. 1995) ("Although [courts] construe claims, if possible, so as to sustain their validity . . . it is well settled that no matter how great the temptations of fairness or policy making, courts do not redraft claims."). Claim construction should not *begin* with preserving the validity of the claim; when it does, "the construing court has put the validity cart before the claim construction horse." *Nazomi*, 403 F.3d at 1369.

[53] Kim v. Conagra Foods, Inc., 465 F.3d 1312, 1324 (Fed. Cir. 2006); Amgen, Inc. v. Hoechst Marion Roussel, Inc., 314 F.3d 1313, 1330 (Fed. Cir. 2003); Amazon.com, Inc. v. Barnesandnoble.com, Inc., 239 F.3d 1343, 1351 (Fed. Cir. 2001).

[54] A disadvantage borne by patent owners in litigation is that they must find a single claim interpretation that supports a finding of *both* validity and infringement. An accused infringer, on the other hand, can be satisfied with an interpretation that renders the claim invalid *or* a different interpretation that renders the claim not infringed. Which interpretation the court chooses may be a matter of indifference to the accused infringer.

elements that defines the patented invention. In such cases the preamble is not considered a claim limitation, and this can have important consequences. Imagine a product identical to the "cosmetic emulsion" described in the example but used as an industrial lubricant. If the preamble were disregarded, the lubricant would infringe the claim.

Courts treat a preamble as a claim limitation only if it "'recites essential structure or steps, or if it is necessary to give life, meaning, and vitality to the claim.'"[55] This is a nebulous distinction. On occasion the preamble must be counted because the "body" of the claim that follows includes references to language found there. The body of the claim used as an example refers to "said emulsion," so it is likely that a court would consider the "aqueous cosmetic emulsion" language a claim limitation.[56] On other occasions, preamble language is "essential" because the applicant relied upon it to distinguish the invention from the prior art.[57] On the other hand, if the preamble states an intended use or environment for the invention, but the remainder of the claim by itself describes what the invention *is*, then the preamble will not be treated as a part of the claim.[58]

If the claim read without the preamble leaves one guessing what the invention is, the preamble cannot be ignored. In *Diversitech Corp. v. Century Steps, Inc.*,[59] for example, the claim referred to an equipment-supporting base

---

[55] NTP, Inc. v. Research in Motion, Ltd., 418 F.3d 1282, 1305 (Fed. Cir. 2005); *see also* Bicon, Inc. v. Straumann Co., 441 F.3d 945, 952 (Fed. Cir. 2006); Catalina Mktg. Int'l, Inc. v. Coolsavings.com, Inc., 289 F.3d 801, 808 (Fed. Cir. 2002). Yet there is no "litmus test" for deciding if a preamble should be considered a claim limitation. *Bicon*, 441 F.3d at 952. "To say that a preamble is a limitation if it gives 'meaning to the claim' may merely state the problem rather than lead one to the answer." Corning Glass Works v. Sumitomo Electric U.S.A., Inc., 868 F.2d 1251, 1257 (Fed. Cir. 1989). The decision must be made in the context of the entire patent, which may establish "'what the inventors actually invented and intended to encompass by the claim.'" *Catalina*, 289 F.3d at 808. Specifically, structure or steps recited in the preamble and "underscored as important by the specification" are more likely to be considered claim limitations. *Id.*

[56] *See Bicon*, 441 F.3d at 952 ("when the limitations in the body of the claim 'rely upon and derive antecedent basis from the preamble, then the preamble may act as a necessary component of the claimed invention'"); *NTP*, 418 F.3d at 1306.

[57] *See* In re Cruciferous Sprout Litigation, 301 F.3d 1343, 1347 (Fed. Cir. 2002); *Catalina*, 289 F.3d at 808.

[58] "[A] preamble is not limiting 'where a patentee defines a structurally complete invention in the claim body and uses the preamble only to state a purpose or intended use for the invention.'" *Catalina*, 289 F.3d at 808; *see also Bicon*, 441 F.3d at 952. "[P]reamble language merely extolling benefits or features of the claimed invention does not limit the claim scope without clear reliance on those benefits or features as patentably significant." *Catalina*, 289 F.3d at 809. Similar rules apply to "whereby clauses." If a method claim describes a step "whereby" the invention accomplishes some task, the clause will be overlooked if it does no more than recite the intended result. On the other hand, if the whereby clause "states a condition that is material to patentability, it cannot be ignored in order to change the substance of the invention." Hoffer v. Microsoft Corp., 405 F.3d 1326, 1329 (Fed. Cir. 2005).

[59] 850 F.2d 675, 677–78 (Fed. Cir. 1988).

comprising a foam core and a cementitious coating. Without the preamble, the claim would have referred to the core and the coating, but one would have no idea what the invention really was. In *Diversitech* the court found the preamble necessary to define the invention. In contrast, in *STX LLC v. Brine, Inc.*,[60] the preamble boasted that the patented lacrosse stick would provide "improved handling and playing characteristics." Because the remainder of the claim stood alone as a structurally complete description of the stick, the court did not find that the preamble language limited the claim.[61]

On the subject of preambles, it is important to note the difference between "comprising" and "consisting of," the two phrases that typically conclude a claim preamble. "Comprising" is a term of art, meaning that the invention consists of the following combination of claim elements, by themselves or in combination with additional elements.[62] In *Gillette Co. v. Energizer Holdings, Inc.*,[63] the court found that claims to a razor "comprising" three blades could be applied to four-blade razors too. A four-blade razor has three blades—plus one more. "Consisting of," on the other hand, means "the following elements *and no others.*"[64] "Comprising" is the broader and generally more useful term. If the preamble ends with "consisting essentially of," the claim allows additional, unrecited ingredients, but only if they do not change the basic characteristics of the combination.[65]

7.7 SPECIAL CLAIM FORMATS

Several specialized claim formats are available to inventors who wish to use them.

7.7.1 Jepson Claims

One specialized claim format is known as a "Jepson claim."[66] A Jepson claim covers an improvement to an existing product. The Jepson format includes a recitation of the pre-existing components in the preamble, and the improvement in the body of the claim.[67] For example:

In an instrument marker pen body including an ink reservoir and means for receiving a writing tip, *the improvement comprising* a pen arm

---

[60] 211 F.3d 588 (Fed. Cir. 2000).

[61] *Id.* at 591.

[62] *See* Carl Zeiss Stiftung v. Renishaw PLC, 945 F.2d 1173, 1178 (Fed. Cir. 1991); Water Techs. Corp. v. Calco, Ltd., 850 F.2d 660, 666 (Fed. Cir. 1988).

[63] 405 F.3d 1367 (Fed. Cir. 2005).

[64] *See* CIAS, Inc. v. Alliance Gaming Corp., 504 F.3d 1356, 1361 (Fed. Cir. 2007).

[65] *See Water Techs.*, 850 F.2d at 666.

[66] Named after Ex parte Jepson, 243 O.G. 525 (Ass't Comm'r Pat. 1917), the case that first approved the format.

[67] *See* Ethicon Endo-Surgery, Inc. v. U.S. Surgical Corp., 93 F.3d 1572, 1577 (Fed. Cir. 1996).

holding means consisting of an integrally molded hinged member adapted to fold against a surface of the pen body and to be locked against said surface by engageable locking means and to receive and secure in place against said surface a pen arm when said hinged member is in its folded and locked position.[68]

The words "In [a pre-existing device], the improvement comprising" are typical of a Jepson claim. The significance of a Jepson claim is that the elements recited in the preamble are claim limitations, and the patent applicant, by implication, admits that those elements exist in the prior art.[69]

7.7.2 Markush Claims

Another specialized claim format is the "Markush claim," generally used to describe chemical and biological inventions. A Markush claim includes a claim element selected from a group of possibilities—for example, "a sugar selected from the group consisting of sucrose, fructose, and lactose."[70] "Markush groups" are used when there is no generic term that conveniently describes the desired claim element.[71]

7.7.3 Product-by-Process Claims

While most patent claims can be characterized as process, apparatus, or composition of matter claims, a so-called product-by-process claim straddles the usual categories. A product-by-process claim, as the name suggests, describes a product made by a specific process. Traditionally, product-by-process claims have been used when the invention is best described in terms of how it is made rather than what it is.[72] Consider how an omelet could be described to someone who had never seen one. One might attempt to describe an omelet in physical or chemical terms, but a better approach would be to provide the recipe. At one time product-by-process claims were allowed only when the invention could not be described except through the "recipe"—for example, when the precise physical characteristics of the product could not be determined. Now they are allowed even if they are not strictly necessary.

There has been much debate about the role to be given the process in interpreting a product-by-process claim. In *Scripps Clinic & Research Found. v. Genentech, Inc.*,[73] the Federal Circuit held that the process described in a

---

[68] Pentec, Inc. v. Graphic Controls Corp., 776 F.2d 309, 312 (Fed. Cir. 1985) (emphasis added).

[69] *Id.* at 315.

[70] For an example of a Markush claim, *see* Merck & Co., Inc. v. Mylan Pharmaceuticals, Inc., 190 F.3d 1335, 1339 (Fed. Cir. 1999).

[71] *See* Application of Weber, 580 F.2d 455, 457 n.4 (C.C.P.A. 1978).

[72] *See* In re Thorpe, 777 F.2d 695, 697 (Fed. Cir. 1985).

[73] 927 F.2d 1565 (Fed. Cir. 1991).

product-by-process claim could be ignored in determining the scope of the claim. In other words, if the claim recited the product of process X, an *identical product* made by a *different process* would still infringe.[74] According to this way of thinking, the process recited in a product-by-process claim simply defines the product in a roundabout manner. The subject matter of the claim is still the omelet, not the recipe. This interpretation of the law follows the practice of the Patent Office in determining if a product-by-process claim should issue. The Patent Office will not issue a product-by-process claim unless it finds that the product, not just the process, is something new.[75]

However, in *Atlantic Thermoplastics Co. v. Faytex Corp.*,[76] a different panel of Federal Circuit judges rejected the earlier interpretation and held that the process set forth in a product-by-process claim does limit the claim, at least in litigation, so an identical product made by a different process does not infringe.[77] According to this court, the *Scripps Clinic* rule was contrary to Supreme Court authority and the hornbook principle of patent law that all elements of a claim are essential in determining infringement. Although it acknowledged that different standards are applied in patent prosecution, the court noted that this discrepancy is not unique. For example, the Patent Office will give claims their "broadest reasonable interpretation," whereas no such rule applies in litigation.[78]

Conflict in the Federal Circuit can be resolved through a procedure allowing an expanded, or *en banc*, panel of all the judges on the Federal Circuit to review the case and decide collectively how the conflict will be settled. Unfortunately, the procedure was not followed in this instance, and the conflict between *Scripps Clinic* and *Atlantic Thermoplastics* remains. As a rule, if two decisions of the Federal Circuit conflict, the earlier one (i.e., *Scripps Clinic*) takes precedence.[79] Yet if *Scripps Clinic* really was contrary to Supreme Court precedent (a matter on which the Federal Circuit judges disagree), then the Supreme Court authority would control.[80] More

[74] "[T]he correct reading of product-by-process claims is that they are not limited to product[s] prepared by the process set forth in the claims." Scripps Clinic & Research Found. v. Genentech, Inc., 927 F.2d 1565, 1583 (Fed. Cir. 1991).

[75] *See Thorpe,* 777 F.2d at 697.

[76] 970 F.2d 834 (Fed. Cir. 1992).

[77] *Id.* at 847.

[78] *Id.* at 846. The court suggested, but did not clearly state, that a product-by-process claim involving a new process but an old product would be held valid in litigation, even though it would be (or should be) rejected by the Patent Office. If this were not true, it would violate the principle that claims must be given the same interpretation for infringement as for validity.

[79] Newell Co. v. Kenney Mfg. Co., 846 F.2d 787, 765 (Fed. Cir. 1988). Relying on this principle, some lower courts have rejected the reasoning of *Atlantic Thermoplastics* in favor of *Scripps Clinic. See, e.g.,* Trustees of Columbia Univ. v. Roche Diagnostics GmbH, 126 F. Supp. 2d 16, 32 (D. Mass. 2000).

[80] Some lower courts have adopted this approach. *See, e.g.,* Lupin Ltd. v. Abbott Labs., 491 F. Supp. 2d 563, 567–68 (E.D. Va. 2007).

than a decade later, it is still impossible for anyone to say precisely what the law is.[81]

7.7.4 "Means-Plus-Function" Claims

One form of specialized claim format that has become extremely common is the "means-plus-function" format authorized by 35 U.S.C. § 112, Paragraph 6. At one time, courts held that a claim to an apparatus must describe the features of the apparatus in precise physical terms rather than in terms of the functions they perform. So, for example, a claim to a mousetrap could properly refer to a "steel spring" but could not refer simply to a "means for snapping the trap shut." The latter claim would literally cover a mousetrap with a steel spring, a plastic spring, a rubber band, or any other mechanism that might close the trap. Such a claim would not adequately define the invention, since it could cover many things that the patentee had not invented or disclosed.

Permitting a patentee to describe a feature of the invention in terms of its function does have certain advantages, however. In the prior example, the inventor might have in mind the steel spring, the plastic spring, the rubber band, and dozens of other means for snapping the trap shut, and the choice of which to use might have little to do with the essence of the invention. A person skilled in designing mousetraps who read the patent might also realize that various forms of springs and elastic bands could be used. In this situation, it would seem pointless to require the inventor to provide a long list of every variety of spring, rubber band, or similar device that the inventor could imagine. Moreover, it might be too easy for a competitor to avoid the patent simply by coming up with a closing mechanism that the patentee had neglected to list.

The result of this tension between convenience and the need for specificity in claim drafting was legislative compromise, embodied in § 112, ¶ 6, which states:

> An element in a claim for a combination may be expressed as a means or step for performing a specified function without the recital of structure, material or acts in support thereof, and such claim shall be construed to cover the corresponding structure, material or acts described in the specification and equivalents thereof.

Thus, an inventor can choose to describe an element of the invention as a physical structure (i.e., "steel spring") or as a "means" for performing a specified function (i.e., "means for snapping the trap shut"), leaving it to the specification to describe the physical structure that performs the function. If the inventor chooses the latter option, the claim will cover the

---

[81] In SmithKline Beecham Corp. v. Apotex Corp., 439 F.3d 1312, 1316–17 (Fed. Cir. 2006), the Federal Circuit noted the long-standing conflict but declined to address it.

specific structure disclosed in the specification and "equivalents" of that structure (i.e., a mousetrap with a steel spring or the equivalent of a steel spring).[82] Deciding just what is "equivalent" is a matter discussed in Section 10.7.

Although any claim element including the word "means" is *presumed* to be a means-plus-function element construed in accordance with § 112, ¶ 6,[83] that presumption can be rebutted if the claim element, contrary to the language of § 112, ¶ 6, *does* recite structure.[84] For example, in *Envirco Corp. v. Clestra Cleanroom, Inc.*,[85] the Federal Circuit held that a claim element calling for a "second baffle means" was not a means-plus-function element because the claim recited structural information concerning the location and formation of the baffle.[86] The difference is significant; when a claim element is construed as a means-

---

[82] For an inventor to take advantage of § 112 ¶ 6, the patent or prosecution history must provide a clear association between the means element and corresponding structure in the specification. Default Proof Credit Card Sys., Inc. v. Home Depot U.S.A., Inc., 412 F.3d 1291, 1298 (Fed. Cir. 2005). If multiple structures described in the specification perform the specified function, the means element reads on each of them and their equivalents. *See* Linear Tech. Corp. v. Impala Linear Corp., 379 F.3d 1311, 1322 (Fed. Cir. 2004); TI Gp. Automotive Sys., Inc. v. VDO North America, L.L.C., 375 F.3d 1126, 1137 (Fed. Cir. 2004). If *no* embodiment described in the specification provides structure to support the means-plus-function element, then the claim is invalid on grounds of indefiniteness. Biomedino, LLC v. Waters Techs. Corp., 490 F.3d 946, 950 (Fed. Cir. 2007); Intellectual Property Development Inc. v. UA-Columbia Cablevision of Westchester Inc., 336 F.3d 1308, 1319 (Fed. Cir. 2003). When a patent claims a computer-implemented invention in means-plus-function format, its disclosure of structure must be more than a reference to a general-purpose computer or microprocessor. Aristocrat Techs. Australia PTY Ltd. v. Int'l Game Tech., 521 F.3d 1328, 1333 (Fed. Cir. 2008). However, reference to a specific program algorithm can supply the missing "structure," because a programmed general-purpose computer is, in effect, a special-purpose machine. *Id.*

[83] *Biomedino*, 490 F.3d at 950; Lighting World, Inc. v. Birchwood Lighting, Inc., 382 F.3d 1354, 1358 (Fed. Cir. 2004).

[84] *See Biomedino*, 490 F.3d at 950 ("'This presumption can be rebutted when the claim, in addition to the functional language, recites structure sufficient to perform the claimed function in its entirety.'"); *TI Gp.*, 375 F.3d at 1135; Micro Chemical, Inc. v. Great Plains Chemical Co., 194 F.3d 1250, 1257 (Fed. Cir. 1999). The presumption also fails if the claim element recites no function for the "means" to perform. *See* Allen Eng'g Corp. v. Bartell Indus., Inc., 299 F.3d 1336, 1347 (Fed. Cir. 2002). An element that does *not* use the word "means" is presumed *not* to be a "means-plus-function" element. Depuy Spine, Inc. v. Medtronic Sofamor Danek, Inc., 469 F.3d 1005, 1023 (Fed. Cir. 2006) (describing the presumption as "'a strong one that is not easily overcome'"); MIT v. Abacus Software, 462 F.3d 1344, 1353 (Fed. Cir. 2006). However, the presumption will be rebutted and § 112, ¶ 6 applied if, even in the absence of "means" vocabulary, the element employs functional language and omits an adequate disclosure of structure. *See MIT*, 462 F.3d at 1353–54 ("colorant selection mechanism" interpreted as a means-plus-function element because the word "mechanism" does not describe any specific structure); *but cf. Lighting World*, 382 F.3d at 1358–61 (although the term "connector" does not bring to mind any specific structure, it is still a structural term; it is not a nonce word like "widget" or "ram-a-fram").

[85] 209 F.3d 1360 (Fed. Cir. 2000).

[86] *Id.* at 1365.

plus-function element, the patent owner is put to the additional burden of demonstrating that the structures of the accused product are identical or equivalent to the structures disclosed in the patent specification. Some patent applicants seem to overuse the "means" format, perhaps not appreciating the risks.[87]

Note that § 112, ¶ 6 applies only to a "claim for a combination." A "single means claim" is still considered invalid.[88] One could not claim, for example, just "a means for catching a mouse" and leave it at that. The "means-plus-function" format can be used only when the claim breaks down the invention into specific components.

7.7.5 "Step-Plus-Function" Claims

The language of § 112, ¶ 6 also provides for a "step-plus-function" claim—in other words, a process claim in which a step of the process is described solely in terms of the "function" performed by that step, without the recital of a specific "act." Such a claim would cover the "act" described in the specification and its equivalents.[89] While it is comparatively easy to distinguish between a *function* and a *structure*, it is much more difficult to distinguish between a *function* and an *act*. Returning to the mousetrap example, a claim element that referred to a "means for snapping the trap shut" would clearly be a means-plus-function claim element, because, other than the generic term "means," the language describes the physical structure solely in terms of the function it performs. Imagine, however, a mouse-trapping process claim, one element of which is "closing the trap to imprison the mouse." Is "closing the trap" (or for that matter "imprisoning the mouse") a "function" or an "act"? Does it describe the step itself or only the result of the step?

According to the Federal Circuit, a "function" refers to "'*what* a claim element ultimately accomplishes.'"[90] An "act" corresponds to "'*how* the function is accomplished.'"[91] This would suggest that "imprisoning the mouse" is a function, and "closing the trap" is an act. However, it is difficult to maintain the supposed distinction. In *Masco Corp v. United States*, the court held that "transmitting a force" was an "act" because "transmitting" described *how* the force was conveyed through mechanical parts.[92] Yet "transmitting a force"

---

[87] *See Allen Eng'g*, 299 F.3d at 1348 (patent applicant was "clearly enamored of the word 'means,'" using it repeatedly where, due to the recitation of structure, such use did not trigger § 112, ¶ 6).

[88] *See* In re Hyatt, 708 F.2d 712, 714 (Fed. Cir. 1983).

[89] The term "step for" suggests an intention to invoke § 112, ¶ 6, though the term "steps of" does not. Masco Corp. v. United States, 303 F.3d 1316, 1327 (Fed. Cir. 2002).

[90] *Id.* (emphasis in original).

[91] *Id.* (emphasis in original); *see also* Seal-Flex, Inc. v. Athletic Track and Court Construction, 172 F.3d 836, 849–50 (Fed. Cir. 1999) (Rader, J., concurring).

[92] *Masco*, 303 F.3d at 1328; *see also* O.I. Corp. v. Tamar Co., 115 F.3d 1576 (Fed. Cir. 1997) ("the step[] of . . . passing the [material] through a passage" construed as an "act" rather than a function).

could be understood as a necessary result, accomplished by the action of any number of mechanical contrivances—more of a *what* than a *how*.

The Federal Circuit seems reluctant to construe any claim as a step-plus-function claim—which is understandable given the difficulties. It has observed that "[i]f we were to construe every process claim containing steps described by an 'ing' verb, such as passing, heating, reacting, transferring, etc. into a step-plus-function limitation, we would be limiting process claims in a manner never intended by Congress."[93] Unless patentees find the step-plus-function option indispensable, which is unlikely considering how seldom courts hold it to apply, perhaps the best solution would be legislation removing the problematic language from § 112, ¶ 6.

---

[93] *O.I. Corp.*, 115 F.3d at 1583; *see also* Cardiac Pacemakers, Inc. v. St. Jude Medical, Inc., 381 F.3d 1371, 1382 (Fed. Cir. 2004) ("Method claims necessarily recite the steps of the method, and the preamble words that 'the method comprises the steps of' do not automatically convert each ensuing step into the form of § 112 ¶ 6."). Claims that use the term "step for" are *not* presumed to be drafted with §112 ¶ 6 in mind; however, claims that *omit* the words "step for" are presumed to be ordinary method claims. *Id.* at 1382–83.

CHAPTER 8

Conditions of Patentability

8.1 EXAMINATION VERSUS LITIGATION

Before a patent issues, the application must go through a process of "examination" by the Patent Office.[1] The purpose of the examination is to ensure that the application meets various requirements imposed by law. These requirements, which are explained in some detail in the pages that follow, include the following:

- The invention must have *utility*.
- The claims must be *definite*.
- The specification must *enable* the practice of the invention and must disclose the inventor's *best mode* of practicing the invention.
- The claimed invention must be *novel*–that is, it must be new and *non-obvious* in comparison to the prior art.

In spite of the examination process, patents sometimes issue that fail to meet these fundamental requirements. This is not always the fault of the Patent Office. For example, the Patent Office cannot judge whether a claim is novel in comparison to an earlier product if, as not infrequently occurs, the Patent Office is not even aware of the earlier product. Moreover, patent examination is not a practical forum for inquiring into certain questions, such as whether the information disclosed in a specification really reflects the applicant's "best mode." Questions like these can be explored effectively only in an adversarial proceeding. For all of these reasons, courts have the

[1] See Section 5.1.

power to find an issued patent invalid,[2] and invalidity is a complete defense to infringement.[3]

The patentability requirements discussed in this chapter are relevant in the examination process, where they can be grounds for rejecting an application, and in the litigation context, where they can be grounds for holding an already issued patent invalid. There are some procedural differences in the way these requirements are enforced in the Patent Office and in the courts. For example, when judging whether a claim is novel, the Patent Office will give the claim its "broadest reasonable construction."[4] A court will not.[5] Nevertheless, the rules and precedent that apply in one context generally apply in the other context as well.

8.2 PRESUMPTION OF VALIDITY

Although courts have the power to hold an issued patent invalid, they do not discount the work of the Patent Office entirely. All patents are presumed valid, and the burden of overcoming that presumption rests with the accused infringer.[6] The presumption can be overcome only by "clear and convincing evidence" of invalidity.[7] This standard of proof is something less than the "beyond a reasonable doubt" standard of criminal law, but it requires more than just a preponderance of the evidence.[8] The presumption of validity applies only after a patent has issued; there is no presumption in the Patent Office in favor of the applicant.[9]

---

[2] *See* Pfizer, Inc. v. Apotex, Inc., 480 F.3d 1348, 1359 (Fed. Cir. 2007) ("a court is never bound by an examiner's finding in an ex parte patent application proceeding"); Quad Environmental Technologies Corp. v. Union Sanitary Dist., 946 F.2d 870, 876 (Fed. Cir. 1991) ("The courts are the final arbiter of patent validity and, although courts may take cognizance of, and benefit from, the proceedings before the patent examiner, the question is ultimately for the courts to decide, without deference to the rulings of the patent examiner.").

[3] Lough v. Brunswick Corp., 86 F.3d 1113, 1123 (Fed. Cir. 1996).

[4] Phillips v. AWH Corp., 415 F.3d 1303, 1316 (Fed. Cir. 2005) (*en banc*); In re Icon Health & Fitness, Inc., 496 F.3d 1374, 1379 (Fed. Cir. 2007); In re Morris, 127 F.3d 1048, 1054 (Fed. Cir. 1997).

[5] *See* Atlantic Thermoplastics Co. v. Faytex Corp., 970 F.2d 834, 846 (Fed. Cir. 1992).

[6] 35 U.S.C. § 282; Pfizer, Inc. v. Apotex, Inc., 480 F.3d 1348, 1359 (Fed. Cir. 2007); Apotex USA, Inc. v. Merck & Co., 254 F.3d 1031, 1036 (Fed. Cir. 2001); Budde v. Harley-Davidson, Inc., 250 F.3d 1369, 1376 (Fed. Cir. 2001). The presumption is "related to the presumption that the PTO does its job properly." Superior Fireplace Co. v. Majestic Prods. Co., 270 F.3d 1358, 1367 n.1 (Fed. Cir. 2001).

[7] *Pfizer*, 480 F.3d at 1359; Intellectual Property Development Inc. v. UA-Columbia Cablevision of Westchester Inc., 336 F.3d 1308, 1319 (Fed. Cir. 2003); *Budde*, 250 F.3d at 1376.

[8] *Pfizer*, 480 F.3d at 1359 n.5 ("The 'clear and convincing' standard is an intermediate standard which lies somewhere in between the 'beyond a reasonable doubt' and the 'preponderance of the evidence' standards of proof."). The evidence must produce an "abiding conviction" that the facts are "highly probable." *Id.*

[9] In re Morris, 127 F.3d 1048, 1054 (Fed. Cir. 1997).

Some older cases found a weakened presumption of validity where the challenger relied on grounds that were not considered by the Patent Office. The Federal Circuit maintains that the presumption of validity is ever present and unchanging, no matter what grounds of invalidity may be asserted.[10] It admits, however, that the presumption is easier to overcome when the grounds are new, since the court is not put in the position of contradicting an expert examiner.[11]

The presumption of validity applies separately to each claim of a patent.[12] Even if Claim 1 has been proven invalid by clear and convincing evidence, Claim 2 is unaffected until a challenger proves that it, too, is invalid. Generally, a patentee's goal in litigation is to prove infringement of at least one valid claim.

8.3 ASSIGNOR ESTOPPEL

"Assignor estoppel" is a doctrine that prevents one who assigns patent rights from arguing when convenient that the same patent is invalid. Consider the following scenario. An inventor obtains a patent on a new apparatus and then assigns all rights to his employer.[13] The inventor receives valuable consideration for the assignment—perhaps a bonus. Afterward the inventor leaves his employer to form his own company and produces a product covered by the patent. The former employer accuses the inventor of infringing what is now its patent. The inventor can argue about the scope of the patent, but cannot assert an invalidity defense such as anticipation or obviousness.[14]

---

[10] *Pfizer*, 480 F.3d at 1359–60; Hybritech Inc. v. Monoclonal Antibodies, Inc., 802 F.2d 1367, 1375 (Fed. Cir. 1986) ("the presumption remains intact and on the challenger throughout the litigation, and the clear and convincing evidence standard does not change").

[11] Ultra-Tex Surfaces, Inc. v. Hill Bros. Chemical Co., 204 F.3d 1360, 1367 (Fed. Cir. 2000) (describing the "additional burden" faced by the challenger who relies on "the very same references that were before the examiner"); *Hybritech*, 802 F.2d at 1375 ("the introduction of prior art not before the examiner may facilitate the challenger's meeting [its] burden of proof").

[12] 35 U.S.C. § 282 ("Each claim of a patent . . . shall be presumed valid independently of the validity of other claims; dependent or multiple dependent claims shall be presumed valid even though dependent upon an invalid claim."). There is one very specialized exception involving obviousness challenges to claims describing substances produced by biotechnological processes. *See* 35 U.S.C. §§ 282, 103(b)(1).

[13] See Section 6.2.

[14] *See* Pandrol USA, LP v. Airboss Railway Prods., Inc., 424 F.3d 1161, 1166 (Fed. Cir. 2005); Mentor Graphics Corp. v. Quickturn Design Sys., Inc., 150 F.3d 1374, 1378 (Fed. Cir. 1998) ("Without exceptional circumstances (such as an express reservation by the assignor of the right to challenge the validity of the patent or an express waiver of the assignee of the right to assert assignor estoppel), one who assigns a patent surrenders with that assignment the right to later challenge the validity of the assigned patent.").

Anyone who assigns patent rights to another in exchange for valuable consideration[15] implicitly acknowledges the validity of the patent and gives up the right to challenge that validity later on. In fairness, "an assignor should not be permitted to sell something and later assert that what was sold is worthless, all to the detriment of the assignee."[16] The rule applies to the individual who assigned the patent, and it may apply to others with whom that individual is involved. For example, if the defendant company is not owned by the inventor/assignor, but it employs him in a position of responsibility, the company may still be barred from contesting the validity of the patent.[17]

8.4 UTILITY

Section 101 of the Patent Act states that a patent may be granted to the discoverer of a "new and useful" invention. Article 1, Section 8 of the Constitution also speaks of promoting the "useful" arts. From these sources, courts have derived the rule, known as the utility requirement, that an invention must be useful before it can be patented.[18]

A patentable invention must have a "specific and substantial utility"– meaning a practical or "real-world" application.[19] Incremental achievements in basic research, important to researchers as *steps* toward practical advancements, still lack the immediate benefit needed to satisfy the utility requirement.[20] Similarly, the discovery of a new substance, or a process for making a substance, does not warrant a patent unless a use for that substance has been identified.[21] In these cases a patent might only impede the further research required to produce genuinely useful discoveries.[22] Accordingly, an application must describe the utility of the claimed invention in terms that are specific, not speculative or nebulous.[23] One cannot,

---

[15] The "valuable consideration" need not be a separate payment or bonus. Where the inventor/assignor is an employee of a corporation, that employee's regular salary is likely to be considered adequate consideration, at least if the invention was within the scope of the inventor/assignor's employment. *See* Diamond Scientific Co. v. Ambico, Inc., 848 F.2d 1220, 1225 (Fed. Cir. 1988).

[16] *Diamond Scientific*, 848 F.2d at 1224; *see also Pandrol*, 424 F.3d at 1166–67 (assignor estoppel prevents "unfairness and injustice").

[17] *See* Shamrock Techs., Inc. v. Medical Sterilization, Inc., 903 F.2d 789, 793 (Fed. Cir. 1990).

[18] *See* Stiftung v. Renishaw PLC, 945 F.2d 1173, 1180 (Fed. Cir. 1991). The utility requirement does not apply to design patents, discussed in Section 12.1.

[19] In re Fischer, 421 F.3d 1365, 1371 (Fed. Cir. 2005).

[20] *See id.* at 1375.

[21] *See* In re Ziegler, 992 F.2d 1197, 1201–03 (Fed. Cir. 1993) (that a compound can produce a "film" is an inadequate statement of utility, if the usefulness of the film itself is unclear).

[22] Although the unavailability of patents for basic scientific research may discourage endeavors that would ultimately prove of great benefit, courts have concluded as a matter of policy that it is more important to leave scientific knowledge unencumbered until it reaches the stage of practical application. *See* Brenner v. Manson, 383 U.S 519, 534 (1966).

[23] *Fischer*, 421 F.3d at 1371.

for example, merely argue that the substance one has discovered holds promise as a research tool.[24]

New pharmaceuticals present a special problem because years of testing may be required to demonstrate that they are safe and effective. In *In re Brana*,[25] the Federal Circuit held that animal studies could provide sufficient evidence of utility, even though FDA approval would require further testing.[26] The court explained that if full FDA approval were required before a patent could be granted, the costs would discourage some companies from patenting, and perhaps from developing, potentially important discoveries.

Inventions that serve a relatively trivial purpose still have utility. One can find many patents claiming toys, novelties, and the like. If they serve their purpose, they are useful enough to receive a patent.[27] The only kinds of practical invention categorically excluded from patentability on grounds of non-utility are those whose purpose is deemed illegal or "immoral." Until 1977, gambling machines were held to lack utility.[28] The exclusion still applies to any invention useful only in committing a crime or fraud—such as a method of counterfeiting currency.[29]

One of the more curious utility cases of recent years is *Juicy Whip, Inc. v. Orange Bang, Inc.*,[30] where the invention was a beverage dispenser like those one might see at the concession stand of a movie theater. The dispenser *appeared* to dispense the beverage from a supply in a glass bowl. In fact, the machine mixed the beverage elsewhere as it was dispensed—more practical option,

---

[24] Because other countries have different requirements regarding such disclosures, *see* Cross v. Iizuka, 753 F.2d 1040 (Fed. Cir. 1985), these problems often arise when the applicant attempts to rely on a foreign application in order to establish priority. See Section 12.3.

[25] 51 F.3d 1560 (Fed. Cir. 1995).

[26] "Usefulness in patent law, and in particular in the context of pharmaceutical inventions, necessarily includes the expectation of further research and development. The stage at which an invention in this field becomes useful is well before it is ready to be administered to humans." *Brana*, 51 F.3d at 1568.

[27] "The threshold of utility is not high: An invention is 'useful' under section 101 if it is capable of providing some identifiable benefit." Juicy Whip, Inc. v. Orange Bang, Inc., 185 F.3d 1364, 1366 (Fed. Cir. 1999). One patent demonstrating the potential breadth of the concept of utility is U.S. Patent No. 5,457,821, entitled "Hat Simulating a Fried Egg." According to the specification, "[t]he hat finds utility, for example, as an attention-getting item in connection with promotional activities at trade shows, conventions, and the like. Further the hat is useful in connection with egg sale promotions in the egg industry." Perhaps a design patent would have been more appropriate. See Section 12.1.

[28] *See* Tol-O-Matic, Inc. v. Proma Produkt-Und Marketing Gesellschaft M.b.H, 945 F.2d 1546, 1552 (Fed. Cir. 1991).

[29] "'All that the law requires is that the invention should not be frivolous, or injurious to the well-being, good policy, or good morals of society. The word *useful* therefore is incorporated into the act in contradistinction to mischievous or immoral.'" *Id.*, 945 F.2d at 1553. Even the exception for inventions with immoral or illegal purposes "has not been applied broadly in recent years." *Juicy Whip*, 185 F.3d at 1366–67.

[30] 185 F.3d 1364 (Fed. Cir. 1999).

but somehow less tempting to purchasers.[31] Although the purpose of the invention was to mislead consumers, the court found that the invention had utility. As the court observed, "[i]t is not at all unusual for a product to be designed to appear to viewers to be something it is not," examples including imitation diamonds and simulated leather.[32] It is the task of other government agencies, not the Patent Office, to protect consumers from potential deception.[33]

It might be argued that an invention is useful only if it is an improvement over the prior art. However, an invention can still be patented even if it is inferior to, or no better than, existing devices or methods.[34] As the Federal Circuit has observed, "An invention need not be the best or the only way to accomplish a certain result, and it need only be useful to some extent and in certain applications."[35] It would be difficult, and perhaps pointless, for the Patent Office to attempt to assess in every case whether the claimed invention is really an improvement. An invention inferior to its predecessors in some respects may be superior in others. In many cases, the advantages of a particular invention cannot be fully appreciated until long after it is patented. In the end, the Patent Office is not in the business of judging whether one invention is better than another. This is one reason the popular conception of a patent as an award for technological achievement is misguided. In spite of the frequent attempts of advertisers to imply that a product is "so good it's patented," patents are a reflection of novelty, not of merit.

Inventions must achieve a minimum level of operability, since an invention that fails to work at all cannot be said to have utility.[36] In most cases, the Patent Office accepts the applicant's representation that the invention works.[37] The Patent Office is not equipped to perform experiments. But

---

[31] "The display bowl is said to stimulate impulse buying by providing the consumer with a visual beverage display. A pre-mix display bowl, however, has a limited capacity and is subject to contamination by bacteria." *Id.* at 1365.

[32] *Id.* at 1367. The comparison may be a bit unfair. Imitation goods may *substitute* for the real thing without, necessarily, *fooling* anyone. The purpose of the beverage dispenser seems to have been only to mislead.

[33] *Id.* at 1368.

[34] Demaco Corp. v. F. Von Langsdorff Licensing Ltd., 851 F.2d 1387, 1390 (Fed. Cir. 1988) ("The patent statute does not require that a patentable invention be superior to all prior devices.").

[35] *Stiftung*, 945 F.2d at 1180; *see also* Envirotech Corp. v. Al George, Inc., 730 F.2d 753, 762 (Fed. Cir. 1984) ("the fact that an invention has only limited utility and is only operable in certain applications is not grounds for finding lack of utility").

[36] Process Control Corp. v. Hydreclaim Corp., 190 F.3d 1350, 1358 (Fed. Cir. 1999); *Tol-O-Matic*, 945 F.2d at 1553 (referring to the "total incapacity" that could lead to a finding of non-utility). On the other hand, if a claimed invention achieves some of its objectives but not others, it will still be deemed to have utility. *Stiftung*, 945 F.2d at 1180 ("'When a properly claimed invention meets at least one stated objective, utility under § 101 is clearly shown.'"). Note that if a claimed invention is an impossibility, the patent fails on grounds of enablement (see Section 8.6) as well as utility. *Process Control,* 190 F.3d at 1358.

[37] *See* Rasmusson v. Smithkline Beecham Corp., 413 F.3d 1318, 1323 (Fed. Cir. 2005).

occasionally the nature of the invention raises suspicions, as when applicants, defying the most fundamental principles of physics, attempt to patent perpetual motion machines. On such occasions, the applicant may be required to come forward with experimental evidence demonstrating that the invention succeeds.[38] In one case where the claimed device purported to produce more energy than it consumed, the Patent Office arranged for tests to be conducted by the Bureau of Standards. Unfortunately, those tests were unsuccessful.[39]

While the Patent Office has limited means to challenge claims on grounds of inoperability or impossibility, this is not necessarily the case in litigation. A party charged with patent infringement may offer evidence demonstrating that whatever is required by the claim is either physically impossible or useless.[40] On the other hand, if a claim actually has been infringed, a court will be reluctant to find that the invention lacks utility. As one court observed, "People rarely, if ever, appropriate useless inventions."[41]

8.5 DEFINITENESS

The function of patent claims is to identify what is covered by the patent. If patent infringement can be compared to trespassing, the claims serve as the boundary markers that define what is, and what is not, an encroachment on the inventor's exclusive territory.[42] The law therefore requires that the claims have a definite meaning understandable to those skilled in the art.[43] This requirement is embodied in the second paragraph of 35 U.S.C. § 112, which provides that the "specification shall conclude with one or more

---

[38] One example of an invention met with skepticism is discussed in Fregau v. Mossinghoff, 776 F.2d 1034 (Fed. Cir. 1985). The claimed method was supposed to enhance the density and flavor of beverages by passing them through a magnetic field. The Patent Office did not consider the experimental evidence offered by the applicant convincing. Strangely, the Patent Office also found several examples of close, and equally unbelievable, prior art.

[39] *See* Newman v. Quigg, 877 F.2d 1575 (Fed. Cir. 1989). Inventions based on cold fusion are currently treated with great skepticism, but baldness cures have entered the realm of the believable. *See* In re Swartz, 232 F.3d 862 (Fed. Cir. 2000) (cold fusion); In re Cortright, 165 F.3d 1353 (Fed. Cir. 1999) (baldness cures).

[40] *See* Raytheon Co. v. Roper Corp., 724 F.2d 951, 956–57 (Fed. Cir. 1983).

[41] *Raytheon*, 724 F.2d at 959.

[42] *See* S3 Inc. v. Nvidia Corp., 259 F.3d 1364, 1369 (Fed. Cir. 2001) ("The purpose of claims is not to explain the technology or how it works, but to state the legal boundaries of the patent grant.").

[43] *See* Halliburton Energy Servs., Inc. v. M-I LLC, 514 F.3d 1244, 1249 (Fed. Cir. 2008) ("Because claims delineate the patentee's right to exclude, the patent statute requires that the scope of the claims be sufficiently definite to inform the public of the bounds of the protected invention. . . . Otherwise, competitors cannot avoid infringement, defeating the public notice function of patent claims."); Young v. Lumenis, Inc., 492 F.3d 1336, 1346 (Fed. Cir. 2007); All Dental Prodx, LLC v. Advantage Dental Prods., Inc., 309 F.3d 774, 779–80 (Fed. Cir. 2002); Oakley, Inc. v. Sunglass Hut Int'l, 316 F.3d 1331, 1340 (Fed. Cir. 2003).

claims particularly pointing out and distinctly claiming the subject matter which the applicant regards as his invention."

The test for compliance is whether a person experienced in the field of the invention, reading the claims and the patent specification, would understand the scope of the subject matter covered by the claims.[44] If the claims are so vague or unclear that those in the industry cannot reasonably determine what does or does not infringe the patent, the claims may be held unpatentable or invalid. Recently, the Federal Circuit has described the indefiniteness threshold as "somewhat high"[45]–invalidating only claims that are "insolubly ambiguous" and impossible to narrow.[46] A claim is not indefinite merely because it is difficult to interpret.[47]

Because language is inherently imprecise, the law requires only such precision in claim drafting as the subject matter permits.[48] In *Orthokinetics, Inc. v. Safety Travel Chairs, Inc.,*[49] the patent claimed a wheelchair with a part "so dimensioned" that it could be inserted in the space between the seats and door frame of an automobile. The claim did not state what those dimensions should be, nor could it have stated them precisely since they would vary depending on the model of the automobile. The dimensions for any particular automobile could easily be obtained by one skilled in the art. The court held that the claim language was as precise as the subject matter permitted: "The patent law does not require that all possible lengths

---

[44] *See* Microprocessor Enhancement Corp. v. Texas Instruments Inc., 520 F.3d 1367, 1374 (Fed. Cir. 2008); *Young,* 492 F.3d at 1346; IPXL Holdings, L.L.C. v. Amazon.com, Inc., 430 F.3d 1377, 1383–84 (Fed. Cir. 2005); Invitrogen Corp. v. Biocrest Mfg., L.P., 424 F.3d 1374, 1383 (Fed. Cir. 2005). Like enablement, discussed in Section 8.6, definiteness is determined from the perspective of one skilled in the art at the time the patent application was filed. W.L. Gore & Assocs., Inc. v. Garlock, Inc., 721 F.2d 1540, 1557 (Fed. Cir. 1983). A term that can be defined only in terms of a subjective point of view–such as "aesthetically pleasing"–is indefinite. Datamize, LLC v. Plumtree Software, Inc., 417 F.3d 1342, 1350 (Fed. Cir. 2005) ("The scope of claim language cannot depend solely on the unconstrained, subjective opinion of a particular individual purportedly practicing the invention.").

[45] *See* Amgen, Inc. v. Hoechst Marion Roussel, Inc., 314 F.3d 1313, 1342 (Fed. Cir. 2003).

[46] *See Microprocessor Enhancement,* 250 F.3d at 1374; *Halliburton,* 514 F.3d at 1249; *Young,* 492 F.3d at 1346; *Invitrogen,* 424 F.3d at 1383.

[47] *Halliburton,* 514 F.3d at 1249 (claims are not indefinite even if the task of interpreting them is "formidable" and the conclusion "one over which reasonable persons will disagree"); *Invitrogen,* 424 F.3d at 1383; *Datamize,* 417 F.3d at 1374. Moreover, a claim is not indefinite merely because it is difficult to determine whether one's own product infringes. The difficulty may lie in the inadequacy of testing procedures, not imprecision in the claim language. *See Invitrogen,* 424 F.3d at 1384.

[48] Hybritech Inc. v. Monoclonal Antibodies, Inc., 802 F.2d 1367, 1385 (Fed. Cir. 1986); *see also S3,* 259 F.3d at 1367 ("'If the claims when read in light of the specification reasonably apprise those skilled in the art of the scope of the invention, § 112 demands no more.'"). It has been observed that a patent claim is "'one of the most difficult legal instruments to draw with accuracy.'" Slimfold Mfg. Co. v. Kinkead Indus., Inc., 810 F.2d 1113, 1117 (Fed. Cir. 1987).

[49] 806 F.2d 1565 (Fed. Cir. 1986).

corresponding to the spaces in hundreds of different automobiles be listed in the patent, let alone that they be listed in the claims."[50] On the other hand, in *Halliburton Energy Servs., Inc. v. M-I LLC,* the court held indefinite claims describing a "fragile gel." The patent lacked any quantitative measure of fragility, and to say that the gel must be "adequate for the circumstances" did not resolve the ambiguity.[51]

The test for indefiniteness is whether the claim language is understandable when read in light of the specification. One function of the specification is to serve as a dictionary or glossary for any claim terms that might have a specialized meaning.[52] The specification may provide a specific definition for otherwise vague claim language, or it may provide a test for measuring whether a product falls within the intended meaning of the claim.[53] Even if some experimentation is required to determine the boundaries of the claim, the claim will not be held indefinite if the language is as precise as the subject matter permits.[54] The prosecution history also may provide information to clarify the meaning of a disputed term.[55]

In spite of the requirement that claims use definite language, such "words of degree" as "generally," "approximately," and "substantially equal to" are commonly used.[56] While these terms are inherently inexact, they are often tolerated because they are "as precise as the subject matter permits." For example, in *Rosemount, Inc. v. Beckman Instruments, Inc.,*[57] the patent claims described a device having one component "in close proximity" to another. The court found that "close proximity" was a term used and understood in the industry. Had the inventor been forced to specify a precise dimension (e.g., "within 0.5 centimeters"), the claim would likely have been narrower than the true scope of the invention. Moreover, requiring a precise definition of "close proximity" in the patent

---

[50] *Id.* at 1576; *see also Young,* 492 F.3d at 1346 (the term "near" in the context of a procedure for de-clawing a cat was not indefinite, because dependent on the physical characteristics of the cat).

[51] *Halliburton,* 514 F.3d at 1254–56.

[52] *See* Beachcombers, Int'l, Inc. v. Wildwood Creative Prods., Inc., 31 F.3d 1154, 1158 (Fed. Cir. 1994) ("As we have repeatedly said, a patentee can be his own lexicographer provided the patentee's definition, to the extent it differs from the conventional definition, is clearly set forth in the specification.").

[53] *See* Shatterproof Glass Corp. v. Libbey-Owens Ford Co., 758 F.2d 613, 624 (Fed. Cir. 1985); Seattle Box Co. v. Industrial Crating & Packing, Inc., 731 F.2d 818, 826 (Fed. Cir. 1984); W.L. Gore & Assocs., Inc. v. Garlock, Inc., 721 F.2d 1540, 1557–58 (Fed. Cir. 1983).

[54] Exxon Research & Eng'g Co. v. U.S., 265 F.3d 1371, 1379 (Fed. Cir. 2001).

[55] *See All Dental Prodx,* 309 F.3d at 780 ("The prosecution history can . . . be relied upon to clarify claim meaning and hence provide definiteness."); Texas Instruments Inc. v. U.S. Int'l Trade Comm'n, 871 F.2d 1054, 1063 (Fed. Cir. 1989) ("The public is entitled to know the scope of the claims but must look to both the patent specification and the prosecution history, especially where there is doubt concerning the scope of the claims.").

[56] *See* Andrew Corp. v. Gabriel Elec., Inc., 847 F.2d 819, 821 (Fed. Cir. 1988).

[57] 727 F.2d 1540 (Fed. Cir. 1984).

specification would "turn the construction of a patent into a mere semantic quibble that serves no useful purpose."[58]

On the other hand, a court will treat words of degree with suspicion if, in litigation, the patentee argues that the term is broad enough to encompass the accused product but narrow enough to avoid the prior art, with no suggestion as to where the line in between should be drawn.[59] In *Amgen, Inc. v. Chugai Pharmaceuticals Co.*,[60] the patentee claimed a protein having a "specific activity" of "at least about 160,000 IU/AU." A prior art product exhibited a "specific activity" of 128,620 IU/AU. Since nothing in the claims, the specification, the prosecution history, or the prior art provided any hint as to whether, for example, a protein having a "specific activity" of 145,000 IU/AU would come within the scope of the claims, the court held that the term "about" was insufficiently definite in the context of that patent.

A definite claim provides competitors of the patent owner with fair warning of what will or will not infringe the patent. If claim language is vague, competitors must proceed at their peril, and the uncertainty provides the patent owner with what is, in effect, a broader claim. Yet the laudable effects of the definiteness requirement are undermined to some extent by the "doctrine of equivalents."[61] According to that doctrine, even a product that is not literally described by the claim language may infringe, if the differences are "insubstantial." The effect is to add an extra dimension of uncertainty to every patent claim. The tension between the definiteness requirement and the doctrine of equivalents is one of the reasons that the latter doctrine, though long established, is often criticized.[62]

8.6 ENABLEMENT

As discussed in Section 1.1, a patent can be regarded as a bargain between the inventor and the public. In exchange for a monopoly on the invention for a period of years, the inventor must disclose the invention in such clear terms that, when the patent has expired, the public at large can take advantage of the invention. This concept is behind the "enablement" and "best

---

[58] *Id.* at 1547. The Patent Office guidelines also require only a "reasonable degree of particularity and distinctness." MPEP § 2173.02. "Some latitude in the manner of expression and the aptness of terms should be permitted even though the claim language is not as precise as the examiner might desire." *Id. See also Oakley*, 316 F.3d at 1341 ("a patentee need not define his invention with mathematical precision").

[59] *See Datamize*, 417 F.3d at 1347 (claims must "'clearly distinguish what is claimed from what went before in the art and clearly circumscribe what is foreclosed from future enterprise'" (*quoting* United Carbon Co. v. Binney & Smith Co., 317 U.S. 228, 236 (1942)).

[60] 927 F.2d 1200 (Fed. Cir. 1991).

[61] See Section 10.6.

[62] See Section 10.6.3.

mode" requirements.[63] The enablement requirement comes from the following language of 35 U.S.C. § 112 (emphasis added):

> The specification shall contain a written description of the invention, and of the manner and process of making and using it, in such full, clear, concise, and exact terms as to *enable* any person skilled in the art to which it pertains, or with which it is most nearly connected, to make and use the same.

To satisfy the enablement requirement, the patent must describe the invention in such clear and exact terms that persons skilled in the art can make and use the invention without "undue experimentation."[64] Because patents are intended to be read and used by those skilled in the art, the specification need not include information that such persons would already know.[65] A patent on an improved radio antenna need not disclose the entire theory and practice of how to build a radio, beginning with Marconi. Persons skilled in the radio art would know the basics already and would have to be informed only of the inventor's improvement.[66]

A patent can be enabling even though *some* experimentation is necessary, so long as the experimentation is not "undue."[67] The definition of "undue" varies depending on the nature of the invention and expectations in the industry.[68] Even time-consuming experimentation may not be "undue" if the experiments are routine. In the biotechnology industry, for example, isolating cells

---

[63] The enablement requirement also helps to fix the date of invention for purposes of determining priority. See Section 8.9.2. The inclusion of an enabling disclosure in a patent application demonstrates that the applicant had a completed invention no later than the filing date.

[64] Sitrick v. Dreamworks, LLC, 516 F.3d 993, 999 (Fed. Cir. 2008); Koito Mfg. Co. v. Turn-Key-Tech, LLC, 381 F.3d 1142, 1155 (Fed. Cir. 2004); AK Steel Corp. v. Sollac, 344 F.3d 1234, 1244 (Fed. Cir. 2003); Enzo Biochem, Inc. v. Calgene, Inc., 188 F.3d 1362, 1371 (Fed. Cir. 1999).

[65] *Koito*, 381 F.3d at 1156; Chiron Corp. v. Genentech, Inc., 363 F.3d 1247, 1254 (Fed. Cir. 2004); Hybritech Inc. v. Monoclonal Antibodies, Inc., 802 F.2d 1367, 1384 (Fed. Cir. 1986) ("[A] patent need not teach, and preferably omits, what is well known in the art.").

[66] See S3 Inc. v. Nvidia Corp., 259 F.3d 1364, 1371 (Fed. Cir. 2001) ("To hold otherwise would require every patent document to include a technical treatise for the unskilled reader. Although an accommodation to the 'common experience' of lay persons may be feasible, it is an unnecessary burden for inventors and has long been rejected as a requirement of patent disclosures."); Ajinomoto Co. v. Archer-Daniels-Midland Co., 228 F.3d 1338, 1346–47 (Fed. Cir. 2000) (offering similar observations in the context of the best mode requirement).

[67] See *Chiron*, 363 F.3d at 1253; *Enzo*, 188 F.3d at 1371. A patent disclosure is not meant to be a "production specification." *Koito*, 381 F.3d at 1156.

[68] Factors to consider include the amount of experimentation required, the presence or absence of guidance in the patent disclosure, the skill of those practicing in the field, and the extent to which the art is "predictable." See *Enzo*, 188 F.3d at 1371. If the patentee cannot succeed in implementing its own invention, this suggests that the patent disclosure is non-enabling. Ormco Corp. v. Align Tech., Inc., 498 F.3d 1307, 1319 (Fed. Cir. 2007).

that will produce a desired antibody may require testing many cells and discarding all but a few. If the screening is routine and the patent specification tells the experimenter how to proceed, the disclosure is likely to suffice.[69]

Patentees risk violating the enablement requirement when they reserve as a trade secret some piece of information necessary to practice the claimed invention.[70] In one case a patentee claimed a machine tool control system but did not disclose the proprietary software that made the system work.[71] Without better evidence that commercially available software could be substituted, the court found the patent non-enabling. To have constructed the necessary software from scratch would have required 1½ to 2 years of "undue" experimentation. On the other hand, another patent that failed to disclose software passed muster where supplying a substitute would have been a comparatively quick and straightforward task for an experienced programmer.[72]

In the case of inventions that depend on the use of living materials, such as microorganisms or cultured cells, words alone may be insufficient to enable one skilled in the art to make and use the invention. A sample of the biological materials may be necessary to begin. In such cases, inventors can satisfy the enablement requirement by depositing samples of the material in a certified depository where they are available to researchers in the field.[73] In other cases, it may be sufficient to direct researchers to commercial sources of supply or provide them with the directions necessary to produce the materials for themselves.

As far as the enablement requirement is concerned, the specification need disclose only some manner in which the invention can be practiced. It need not disclose every manner of practicing the invention, or even the best manner.[74] Moreover, the inventor need not understand or disclose the principles that make the invention work.[75]

---

[69] *See* In re Wands, 858 F.2d 731 (Fed. Cir. 1988).

[70] See Section 2.3.

[71] White Consolidated Indus. v. Vega Servo-Control, Inc., 713 F.2d 788 (Fed. Cir. 1983).

[72] Northern Telecom, Inc. v. Datapoint Corp., 908 F.2d 931 (Fed. Cir. 1990). The absence of a specific disclosure of software is also a potential best mode violation. See Section 8.7. However, "it is generally sufficient if the functions of the software are disclosed, it usually being the case that creation of the specific source code is within the skill of the art." Robotic Vision Sys., Inc. v. View Eng'g Inc., 112 F.3d 1163, 1166 (Fed. Cir. 1997).

[73] *See* 37 C.F.R. § 1.802; MPEP § 2401 *et seq.*; *Ajinomoto*, 228 F.3d at 1345–46.

[74] Engel Indus., Inc. v. Lockformer Co., 946 F.2d 1528, 1533 (Fed. Cir. 1991). Failure to disclose the best manner known to the inventor may violate the best mode requirement. See Section 8.7.

[75] *See* Process Control Corp. v. Hydreclaim Corp., 190 F.3d 1350, 1359 (Fed. Cir. 1999) ("an otherwise valid patent covering a meritorious invention should not be struck down simply because of the patentee's misconceptions about scientific principles concerning the invention"); In re Cortright, 165 F.3d 1353, 1359 (Fed. Cir. 1999) ("'[I]t is not a requirement of patentability that an inventor correctly set forth, or even know, how or why the invention works.'"); Newman v. Quigg, 877 F.2d 1575, 1581 (Fed. Cir. 1989).

Whether a specification is enabling is measured at the time the patent application was filed.[76] If the claimed invention cannot be practiced without technology developed after that date, the patent is invalid. On the other hand, applicants are not put to the impossible task of describing *additional* means of practicing the claimed invention that have not yet been invented,[77] even though in such cases one could question whether the claim was overbroad.[78]

8.6.1 Scope of Enablement

Enablement questions arise when the patent claims are substantially broader than the specific embodiments disclosed in the specification. Patent claims are often, in a certain sense, generic. A claim might (hypothetically) cover *every* mousetrap that included the combination of (1) a spring, (2) a latch, and (3) a trigger to unhook the latch and release the spring when disturbed by a mouse. The specification might disclose in detail only *one* example of such a trap—with a particular kind of spring, latch, and trigger. If the claim covers other versions of the trap that are not discussed at all, is the specification adequate to enable one skilled in the art to practice the claimed invention?

It is said that the enabling disclosure in the specification must be "commensurate in scope" with the claims.[79] But until recently, at least in the case of "predictable arts," courts seemed to allow patent applicants considerable leeway to claim the invention broadly, even though the specification disclosed very few of the specific alternatives that one might employ.[80] If the specification disclosed a plastic spring for the mousetrap, persons skilled in the art would know how to substitute a steel spring without additional instruction. In "unpredictable arts," such as chemistry and biotechnology, the courts demanded a more extensive disclosure, apparently because one functioning

---

[76] *See* Plant Genetic Sys., N.V. v. DeKalb Genetics Corp., 315 F.3d 1335, 1339 (Fed. Cir. 2003); *Enzo*, 188 F.3d at 1371.

[77] *See* Invitrogen Corp. v. Clontech Labs., Inc., 429 F.3d 1052, 1071 (Fed. Cir. 2005) ("Enablement does not require the inventor to foresee every means of implementing an invention at pains of losing his patent franchise. Were it otherwise, claimed inventions would not include improved modes of practicing those inventions. Such narrow patent rights would rapidly become worthless. . . ."); *Chiron*, 363 F.3d at 1254 ("The law does not expect an applicant to disclose knowledge invented or developed after the filing date. Such disclosure would be impossible.").

[78] See Section 8.6.1.

[79] *See, e.g.,* Chiron Corp. v. Genentech, Inc., 363 F.3d 1247, 1253 (Fed. Cir. 2004); National Recovery Techs., Inc. v. Magnetic Separation Sys., Inc., 166 F.3d 1190, 1195–96 (Fed. Cir. 1999); Amgen, Inc. v. Chugai Pharmaceutical Co., 927 F.2d 1200, 1213 (Fed. Cir. 1991). "Pioneering" inventions that establish an entirely new field of inquiry (see Section 10.6.7), may support broad claims, but they are subject to the same requirement that the claims "bear a reasonable correlation to the scope of enablement." *See* Plant Genetic Sys., N.V. v. DeKalb Genetics Corp., 315 F.3d 1335, 1339–40 (Fed. Cir. 2003).

[80] "If an invention pertains to an art where the results are predictable, e.g., the mechanical as opposed to the chemical arts, a broad claim can be enabled by disclosure of a single embodiment. . . ." Spectra-Physics, Inc. v. Coherent, Inc., 827 F.2d 1524, 1533 (Fed. Cir. 1987).

example leads less reliably to other successful means of practicing the invention. Even a tiny change in the structure of a molecule, for example, may have large and unanticipated effects. One patentee claimed all possible sequences of DNA that would produce the protein EPO, which stimulates the production of red blood cells, or any analog of EPO that would have a similar effect.[81] The specification disclosed the information needed to prepare EPO and just a few of its analogs. The court found that the number of possible DNA sequences within the scope of the claim vastly outstripped the enabling disclosure: "There may be many other genetic sequences that code for EPO-type products. [The patentee] has told us how to make and use only a few of them and is therefore not entitled to claim all of them."[82]

Now the courts are applying a stricter standard even where the invention falls within the mechanical or electronic arts. If the claim encompasses alternative manners of practicing the invention, but the specification teaches only one of those alternatives, the claim may be held invalid for failing to enable the "full scope" of the claim.[83] For example, in *Sitrick v. Dreamworks, LLC*,[84] the patent claimed a system for integrating user-created images into existing movies or video games. Because the specification did not describe how to apply the technology to movies (as opposed to video games), and the teachings of one could not be applied to the other, the patent was invalid.[85] The court observed that enabling the full scope of the claim is a quid quo pro of the patent bargain, and a "patentee who chooses broad claim language must make sure the broad claims are fully enabled."[86] The Federal Circuit seems to have turned to

---

[81] *Amgen*, 927 F.2d at 1212–14.

[82] *Id.*

[83] *Sitrick*, 516 F.3d at 999; *see also* Automotive Techs. Int'l, Inc. v. BMW of North America, Inc., 501 F.3d 1274, 1285 (Fed. Cir. 2007) (because "claims must be enabled to correspond to their scope," a patent on a side-impact crash sensor claiming mechanical and electronic sensors, but enabling only the former, was invalid); Liebel-Flarsheim Co. v. Medrad, Inc., 481 F.3d 1371, 1380 (Fed. Cir. 2007) (claims encompassed injectors with and without pressure jackets, but the patent did not enable the jacketless alternative); AK Steel Corp. v. Sollac, 344 F.3d 1234, 1244 (Fed. Cir. 2003) ("[W]hen a range is claimed, there must be reasonable enablement of the scope of the range."). If the claim encompasses an alternative that the specification positively *discourages* as impractical, it is difficult to argue that the alternative could be implemented with reasonable experimentation. *See AK Steel*, 344 F.3d at 1244.

[84] 316 F.3d 993 (Fed. Cir. 2008).

[85] *Id.* at 1000–01.

[86] *Id.* at 999. That is not to say that the specification must describe explicitly every possible embodiment of the claimed invention; the "'artisan's knowledge of the prior art and routine experimentation can often fill gaps, interpolate between embodiments, and perhaps even extrapolate beyond the disclosed embodiments, depending upon the predictability of the art.'" *AK Steel*, 344 F.3d at 1244; *see also Chiron*, 363 F.3d at 1253. Because persons skilled in the art have few other sources of useful information, "nascent" technologies require a more thorough disclosure. *Chiron*, 363 F.3d at 1254. In *Sitrick*, the alternative embodiment would have differed so much from the disclosed embodiment that it could not have been accomplished through extrapolation.

the enablement requirement, as it earlier turned to the written description requirement,[87] to curb the natural tendency of patentees to claim as broadly as they can. Consequently, patentees are well advised to have some claims, at least, that adhere closely to the disclosed embodiments, particularly where the broader claims include some distinctly implied but incompletely enabled alternatives.

8.7 BEST MODE

The "best mode" requirement, like the enablement requirement, arises from the language of 35 U.S.C. § 112, which provides that a specification "shall set forth the best mode contemplated by the inventor for carrying out his invention." The "best mode" means the best manner of practicing the invention, or the best operative example, known to the inventor. If the inventor of a hypothetical mousetrap envisioned two variants of the claimed invention, one using an inferior plastic spring and the other a superior steel spring, the best mode requirement would demand that the better embodiment be disclosed in the patent, even though both came within the scope of the claim.[88]

Like the enablement requirement, the best mode requirement reflects the bargain model of patent law. If a patentee is to be awarded a monopoly on an invention for a period of years, the public is entitled to disclosure of the best that the patentee has to offer. If there were no best mode requirement, patentees might be tempted to disclose the least effective or most impractical embodiments of their inventions, perhaps reserving the better embodiments as trade secrets. The result would do little to advance the "useful arts."[89]

Where the enablement requirement can be satisfied by the disclosure of *any* operable method of practicing the invention, the best mode requirement

---

[87] *See* Section 8.8.

[88] *See* High Concrete Structures, Inc. v. New Enterprise Stone & Lime Co., 377 F.3d 1379, 1383 (Fed. Cir. 2004) ("The best mode requirement precludes inventors 'from applying for patents while at the same time concealing from the public preferred embodiments of their inventions which they have in fact conceived.'").

[89] "[T]he best mode requirement . . . ensure[s] that a patent applicant plays 'fair and square' with the patent system. It is a requirement that the *quid pro quo* of the patent grant be satisfied. One must not receive the right to exclude others unless at the time of filing he has provided an adequate disclosure of the best mode known to him of carrying out the invention." Amgen, Inc. v. Chugai Pharmaceutical Co., 927 F.2d 1200, 1209–10 (Fed. Cir. 1991). In some cases, a "better mode" may have been devised by someone other than the inventor, after the date of invention but before the filing of the patent application. If the inventor is aware of this "better mode" before the application is filed, it must be disclosed in the specification, even though it does not represent the inventor's own work and he could not claim it in the patent. *See* Graco, Inc. v. Binks Mfg. Co., 60 F.3d 785, 789 (Fed. Cir. 1995).

compels disclosure of the one method believed by the inventor to be the best.[90] The relevant time period is the time at which the patent application was filed, and the relevant perspective is that of the inventor.[91] If the inventor believed the disclosed method superior, the best mode requirement is satisfied even if the inventor was mistaken at the time, or even if better methods were later discovered. The patent does not have to be updated to disclose improvements.[92]

Since satisfaction of the best mode requirement is dependent on the subjective beliefs of the inventor, violation of the requirement may be difficult to prove. Sometimes in litigation the inventor's contemporaneous documents are used to show that a better mode was recognized but not disclosed.[93] One can also consider the means adopted by the patentee for commercializing the invention. For example, in *Northern Telecom, Inc. v. Datapoint Corp.*,[94] the patent described a system for capturing data on standard audio cassettes. Employees of the patent owner testified that cassettes with special characteristics, different from those of ordinary audio cassettes, had been ordered by the patent owner for its own use. This evidence helped to establish a violation of the best mode requirement.[95]

The best mode requirement also has an objective component: was the best mode known to the inventor *disclosed* in the application in such clear terms that persons skilled in the art, reviewing the patent specification, would recognize it as the best mode and have sufficient information to practice it themselves?[96] Even if the specification includes a general reference to the best mode, the reference may be so lacking in detail that, as a practical matter, the best mode is concealed.[97] Alternatively, the best mode may be disclosed together with so many inferior modes that the best mode is inadequately differentiated.[98] The determination of whether the best mode was adequately disclosed must take into account the level of skill in the art and

---

[90] *See* Teleflex, Inc. v. Ficosa North America Corp., 299 F.3d 1313, 1330 (Fed. Cir. 2002) (distinguishing between best mode and enablement requirements).

[91] *See* Bayer A.G. v. Schein Pharmaceuticals, Inc., 301 F.3d 1306, 1314 (Fed. Cir. 2002) ("Unlike enablement, the existence of a best mode is a purely subjective matter depending upon what the inventor actually believed at the time the application was filed.").

[92] *See* Transco Prods. Inc. v. Performance Contracting, Inc., 38 F.3d 551 (Fed. Cir. 1994). Constant changes in patent disclosures, to account for progressive improvements in technology, might cause more administrative difficulties than the benefits would warrant. The addition of new disclosure might also cause difficulty in applying the "new matter" rules. See Section 5.2.

[93] *See, e.g.,* Dana Corp. v. IPC Ltd. Partnership, 860 F.2d 415, 418–20 (Fed. Cir. 1988).

[94] 908 F.2d 931 (Fed. Cir. 1990).

[95] *Id.* at 940.

[96] *See* Go Medical Indus., Pty., Ltd. v. Inmed Corp., 471 F.3d 1264, 1271 (Fed. Cir. 2006); *Bayer*, 301 F.3d at 1320; Eli Lilly & Co. v. Barr Labs., Inc., 222 F.3d 973, 981 (Fed. Cir. 2000).

[97] *See* U.S. Gypsum Co. v. National Gypsum Co., 74 F.3d 1209, 1215 (Fed. Cir. 1996); Spectra-Physics, Inc. v. Coherent, Inc., 827 F.2d 1524, 1536 (Fed. Cir. 1987).

[98] *See* Randomex, Inc. v. Scopus Corp., 849 F.2d 585, 592 (Fed. Cir. 1988) (Mayer, J., dissenting).

the extent to which information would be understood implicitly by those of ordinary skill.[99]

Although a patent specification must reveal the inventor's best mode of practicing the invention, the level of detail that must be included is not unlimited.[100] The focus is on the invention *as claimed*.[101] The specification need not be equivalent to a "product specification" or a blueprint for mass production. It need not, for example, disclose all of the dimensions, tolerances, drawings, and other information that a factory foreman would need to gear up for production.[102] Such detailed information would be impractical to include in every patent, and it would be an unnecessary gift to the patentee's competitors. Still, the line between best mode and product specification can be a difficult one to draw.

In *Christianson v. Colt Indust.*,[103] the court held that patents to various parts of the M-16 rifle were not invalid, even though they failed to disclose the

---

[99] *See* Chemcast Corp. v. Arco Indus. Corp., 913 F.2d 923, 927 (Fed. Cir. 1990). Several cases suggest that "routine details" within reach of those skilled in the art need not be disclosed. *See, e.g.* Liquid Dynamics Corp. v. Vaughan Co., 449 F.3d 1209, 1223 (Fed. Cir. 2006); *Teleflex*, 299 F.3d at 1332. Moreover, the best mode may be adequately described even if "some experimentation is necessary." *Eli Lilly*, 222 F.3d at 984. On the other hand, the best mode requirement cannot be satisfied *solely* by reference to information already known in the art. *Bayer*, 301 F.3d at 1314. The applicant still must *disclose* the best mode. *See* Robotic Vision Sys., Inc. v. View Eng'g, Inc., 112 F.3d 1163, 1165 (Fed. Cir. 1997) ("While a disclosure . . . is to be understood from the standpoint of one skilled in the relevant art, a certain basic disclosure is needed of the best mode.").

[100] *See Bayer*, 301 F.3d at 1314–15 (inventor's "every preference" need not be disclosed).

[101] *See* AllVoice Computing PLC v. Nuance Communications, Inc., 504 F.3d 1236, 1246 (Fed. Cir. 2007); Cardiac Pacemakers, Inc. v. St. Jude Medical, Inc., 381 F.3d 1371, 1379 (Fed. Cir. 2004) (requiring disclosure of unclaimed subject matter would make "'the disclosure . . . boundless, and the pitfalls endless'"); *Teleflex*, 299 F.3d at 1329–30 (best mode analysis "must begin and remain focused on the language of the claim," as opposed, for example, to "unclaimed subject matter relating to production details dictated by customer requirements"). Recent statements by the Federal Circuit suggest that an inventor need not disclose preferred methods of *making or using* the claimed invention, unless the claims show that such methods are a part of "carrying out the invention" or "materially affect[] the properties of the claimed invention." *Bayer*, 301 F.3d at 1315; *see also* Pfizer, Inc. v. Teva Pharmaceuticals USA, Inc., 518 F.3d 1353, 1364 (Fed. Cir. 2008). If the claim described the mechanical aspects of a novel mousetrap, the *enablement* requirement would demand an adequate description of how to make and use the trap without "undue experimentation." See Section 8.6. However, the inventor might not be required to disclose the *best* method of making or using the trap, so long as the claims were about the mechanical aspects of the trap, as opposed to its manufacture or use. The result would be different only if the inferior method of manufacture (or use) resulted in a mechanically inferior mousetrap. If a method of manufacture was disfavored because it was more expensive, but it produced an identical mousetrap, it would have nothing to do with "carrying out the invention" and need not be disclosed. In any event, the analysis in *Bayer* suggests a strong focus on the *claimed* invention, which may assist in resolving some difficult best mode issues.

[102] *Teleflex*, 299 F.3d at 1331 ("[t]he best mode requirement does not extend to 'production details'").

[103] 822 F.2d 1544, 1562–63 (Fed. Cir. 1987).

dimensions and tolerances that would have been necessary for others to manufacture interchangeable parts. Because interchangeability was not required by the claims, the production details were deemed separable from the best mode of the invention, even though, as a practical matter, the absence of those details would prevent others from competing in the market for rifle parts. The patents were still adequate to allow one to manufacture *a* rifle, even if it was not a rifle that the army, which required interchangeability with M-16 parts, would care to purchase.

Similarly, a patent applicant is not always required to disclose the details of components that may be used *with* the claimed invention, but that are not part of the claimed invention itself. To borrow an analogy used by the court in *Randomex, Inc. v. Scopus Corp.*,[104] the inventor of a new engine might have to disclose the kind of fuel that is best for its operation, but the inventor of the engine would not have to disclose the best formula for making that fuel. It would be sufficient to disclose the fuel by brand name, as long as that brand, or its equivalent, was readily available. Engines and fuels are different arts, and a patent claiming only the engine need not disclose how to manufacture the fuel.

One case that put this principle to practice is *DeGeorge v. Bernier*,[105] where the claimed invention was electrical circuitry that would automatically indent paragraphs composed on a word processor. Even though the applicant did not disclose any details of the word processor, the court found no violation of the best mode requirement or the enablement requirement. The applicant did not claim to have invented a word processor, and one could practice the best mode *of the invention* even in conjunction with an inferior word processor.

Whether an inventor is required to disclose such information as the names of companies supplying parts, or the trade names of ingredients used in the inventor's composition, depends on the particular facts of the case.[106] If, for example, only one company sells an ingredient pure enough to produce an effective version of the patented compound, the inventor would probably be required to disclose the name of that company—at least if that information was not already generally known.[107] In other cases, the name of a supplier might be a convenience, but its absence would not prevent others from practicing the inventor's best mode.

Companies that have manufactured a product prior to the filing date of their patent are particularly vulnerable to claims of a best mode violation.

---

[104] 849 F.2d 585, 590 (Fed. Cir. 1988).

[105] 768 F.2d 1318, 1324–25 (Fed. Cir. 1985).

[106] *See Transco*, 38 F.3d at 560.

[107] *See U.S. Gypsum*, 74 F.3d at 1214 (since inventor did not know the composition of or method of manufacturing a critical ingredient, "he was required, at a minimum, to provide supplier/trade name information").

Something can always be found in the patentee's product, or in its manu-facturing methods, that was not disclosed in the patent. Whatever that thing is, it will be singled out by those challenging the validity of the patent, who will argue that the patentee must have considered that thing the "best" choice, or the patentee would have chosen something else.[108] In the end, the court will have to decide whether that choice is sufficiently related to the claimed invention that it should have been disclosed as the best mode, or whether it is a choice that has little to do with the invention itself.

Some cases suggest that an inventor violates the best mode requirement only by *deliberately* concealing information.[109] Other cases, while still speak-ing of "concealment," suggest that concealment can be unintentional.[110] Intentional concealment of the best mode may constitute "inequitable conduct"[111] rendering all claims of the patent, and possibly those of related patents, unenforceable.[112]

A best mode violation occurs only if the best mode contemplated *by the inventor* is inadequately disclosed in the patent specification. Knowledge of better modes will not be imputed to the inventor through legal fictions. For example, if other engineers working for the same corporation knew of an improvement to the basic invention, but the improvement was not communi-cated to the inventor before the filing date of the patent, failure to disclose the improvement in the patent specification would not violate the best mode requirement.[113] This result might encourage a "head in the sand" mentality among corporations, which could isolate researchers just to avoid the disclo-sure of more information than necessary. On the other hand, § 112 literally refers only to the knowledge of the "inventor," not the inventor's colleagues or employer, and it could be difficult to determine whether the inventor had been deliberately shielded from knowledge of improvements to his invention.

---

[108] *See* Wahl Instruments, Inc. v. Acvious, Inc., 950 F.2d 1575, 1581 (Fed. Cir. 1991).

[109] "Invalidation based on a best mode violation requires that the inventor knew of and inten-tionally concealed a better mode than was disclosed." *High Concrete*, 377 F.3d at 1383; *see also Cardiac Pacemakers*, 381 F.3d at 1378; Brooktree Corp. v. Advanced Micro Devices, Inc., 977 F.2d 1555, 1575 (Fed. Cir. 1992). In *High Concrete*, the undisclosed information—that heavy loads should be moved with a crane—was already known to persons skilled in the art. 377 F.3d at 1384. In spite of the "intentionally concealed" language, arguably that was a more significant factor than whether the omission of the information was deliberate. *See* Ajinomoto Co. v. Archer-Daniels-Midland Co., 28 F.3d 1338, 1346–47 (Fed. Cir. 2000) (omitted reference to a publication known in the art was not a best mode violation).

[110] "[O]nly evidence of 'concealment,' whether *accidental* or intentional, is considered." Spectra-Physics, Inc. v. Coherent, Inc., 827 F.2d 1524, 1535 (Fed. Cir. 1987) (emphasis added); *see also U.S. Gypsum*, 74 F.3d at 1215–16.

[111] See Section 9.1.

[112] *See* Consolidated Aluminum Corp. v. Foseco Int'l, Ltd., 910 F.2d 804 (Fed. Cir. 1990) (application's disclosure was of a "fictitious" and "inoperable" mode).

[113] *See* Glaxo Inc. v. Novopharm Ltd., 52 F.3d. 1043, 1050 (Fed. Cir. 1995).

8.8 THE WRITTEN DESCRIPTION REQUIREMENT

Another test of validity is the so-called written description requirement, taken from the following language of 35 U.S.C. § 112, Paragraph 1:

> The specification shall contain a *written description of the invention,* and of the manner and process of making and using it, in such full, clear, concise, and exact terms as to enable any person skilled in the art to which it pertains, or with which it is most nearly connected, to make and use the same.

The written description requirement is one of the more nebulous concepts in patent law, in part because it is so easily confused with the definiteness and enablement requirements, and in part because its function seems largely redundant. It is, after all, the function of the *claims* to describe the invention in precise terms.[114] Why should the *specification* also be required to describe the invention? On the other hand, if the "description" simply means an enabling disclosure, as the remainder of the sentence seems to imply, why not leave that to the enablement requirement?

The Federal Circuit made some attempt to sort out the confusion in *Vas-Cath Inc. v. Mahurkar.*[115] As the court explained, the written description requirement can be characterized in part as an historical accident, traceable to the late eighteenth century, when patents were not required to have claims. In those days, it was the function of the specification to enable the practice of the invention *and* to "describe" it to potential infringers. Today the written description requirement most often comes into play where the claims have changed during prosecution of the patent application.

As discussed in Section 5.1, applicants commonly change or "amend" claims during patent prosecution. The patent examiner may object to the claims as filed for any number of reasons, including the applicant's failure to distinguish the invention from the prior art. The applicant may respond by substituting new language. Such changes are allowed as long as the specification *as filed* supports the modified claims. In most cases, the specification itself remains the same throughout prosecution.

The filing date of the patent application is often critical to establishing the priority of the invention—in other words, whether the applicant is entitled to a patent because he was the first to invent, or whether the applicant is not entitled to a patent because someone else invented first.[116] If the application fully described the claimed invention, then the applicant's date of invention

---

[114] According to the second paragraph of § 112, the specification must conclude with "one or more claims particularly pointing out and distinctly claiming the subject matter which the applicant regards as his invention." See Section 8.5.

[115] 935 F.2d 1555, 1560–64 (Fed. Cir. 1991).

[116] A foreign patent application can be of similar importance if the applicant relies on that application for his "filing date." See Section 12.3.

is, at the very latest, his filing date. But if the applicant amended the claims during prosecution, they might describe a new and different invention than that originally disclosed. Then the application date would have no bearing on the actual date of invention. The written description requirement prevents this result by requiring a match between the invention claimed and the invention "described" in the specification.[117] The test is whether the specification demonstrates, to persons skilled in the art, that the applicant "possessed" the invention set forth in the claims.[118] The level of detail required is said to depend on the scope of the invention and the state of knowledge in the field.[119]

Problems can arise if the specification, as originally filed, disclosed only a single species of a later-claimed genus.[120] For example, in *In re Curtis*,[121] the application claimed dental floss made of PTFE (better known as "Teflon")

---

[117] The description requirement "'guards against the inventor's overreaching by insisting that he recount his invention in such detail that his future claims can be determined to be encompassed within his original creation.'" *Vas-Cath*, 935 F.2d at 1561; *see also* In re Wright, 866 F.2d 422, 424 (Fed. Cir. 1989) ("When the scope of a claim has been changed by amendment in such a way as to justify an assertion that it is directed to a *different invention* than was the original claim, it is proper to inquire whether the newly claimed subject matter was *described* in the patent application when filed as the invention of the applicant. That is the essence of the so-called 'description requirement.'" (emphasis in original)). If the patentee is attempting to rely on the filing date of a "parent" or "grandparent" application (see Section 5.2), and that application does not adequately describe the subsequent claim, the result may be not that the claim is invalid but only that it cannot rely on the earlier filing date. *See* Reiffin v. Microsoft Corp., 214 F.3d 1342, 1346 (Fed. Cir. 2000).

[118] *See* Falkner v. Inglis, 448 F.3d 1357, 1365 (Fed. Cir. 2006); Bilstad v. Wakalopulos, 386 F.3d 1116, 1123 (Fed. Cir. 2004); Purdue Pharma L.P. v. Faulding Inc., 230 F.3d 1320, 1323 (Fed. Cir. 2000) ("Put another way, one skilled in the art, reading the original disclosure, must immediately discern the limitation at issue in the claims."). Note that it is not possession itself that is the issue, but the adequacy of the disclosure to *demonstrate* possession. Hence, the description requirement as a rule cannot be satisfied by other evidence, such as sworn testimony, that the applicant did possess (though he did not adequately describe) the claimed invention. *See* Enzo Biochem, Inc. v. Gen-Probe Inc., 296 F.3d 1316, 1330 (Fed. Cir. 2002). The applicant may "possess" the invention even though there has been no actual reduction to practice. *Falkner*, 448 F.3d at 1366–67. On the other hand, an applicant cannot "possess" technology that did not exist at all. Chiron Corp. v. Genentech, Inc., 363 F.3d 1247, 1255 (Fed. Cir. 2004).

[119] *See* Capon v. Eshhar, 418 F.3d 1343, 1357 (Fed. Cir. 2005). A broad claim is more likely to be supported if results in the field are relatively "predictable." *See id.* at 1359–60; *Bilstad*, 386 F.3d at 1125. If a written description is impossible, as may be the case with biological or chemical discoveries that are not entirely understood, deposit of a physical sample can suffice. *Capon*, 418 F.3d at 1357; *see also Enzo Biochem*, 296 F.3d at 1326.

[120] *See* Regents of the Univ. of California v. Eli Lilly & Co., 119 F.3d 1559, 1567–68 (Fed. Cir. 1997); *Vas-Cath*, 935 F.2d at 1561–62. But sometimes disclosure of a single species *is* sufficient to "describe" an entire genus. *Bilstad*, 386 F.3d at 1124. Similar problems occur if the disclosure is too general. The disclosure of a large genus may lack any "blaze marks" leading persons skilled in the art to (and showing possession of) a particular species later singled out in a claim. *See Purdue Pharma*, 230 F.3d at 1326. "[O]ne cannot disclose a forest in the original application, and then later pick a tree out of the forest and say here is my invention." *Id.*

[121] 354 F.3d 1347 (Fed. Cir. 2004).

improved with a friction-enhancing coating. Because of the non-stick properties for which PTFE is known, it is difficult to find a material that will
adhere to it. The inventor, surprised to find *anything* that would work, discovered and disclosed one possibility: microcrystalline wax. This disclosure
did not show that the inventor was "in possession" of a broad genus including any and all friction-enhancing coatings, particularly when the art was
notoriously unpredictable.[122]

It may appear that the enablement requirement, discussed in Section 8.6,
would prevent an applicant from claiming more than the original application can support. If a modified claim really reflected a new and different
invention, it would seem unlikely that the specification as filed would be adequate to enable one to practice that invention. However, according to the
Federal Circuit and its predecessor court, "'it is possible for a specification to
enable the practice of invention as broadly as it is claimed, and still not
describe that invention.'"[123] An example of this distinction can be found in
Martin v. Mayer,[124] where the invention concerned an electrical cable constructed of various layers, including a conductor, a dielectric, and a "high fre-
quency absorption medium." One of the claims at issue required a "harness"
composed of more than one such cable. The specification as filed disclosed
only a single cable. A person skilled in the art might have been *enabled* by
the description of the solitary cable to construct a "harness" of several cables
(particularly if the later-filed claim suggested it), but the specification
included no written description of the "harness" to demonstrate that the
applicant had conceived of that invention when the application was filed.

A patent satisfies the written description requirement if the specification
"conveys with reasonable clarity to those skilled in the art that, as of the filing
date [of the application], he or she was in possession *of the invention.* The invention is, for purposes of the 'written description' inquiry, *whatever is now
claimed.*"[125] This does not mean that the specification has to describe the later-
claimed invention in the very same terms.[126] In *In re Wright,*[127] for example, the
claim language "not permanently fixed," as applied to a microcapsule powder
used in an imaging process, did not appear in the specification. Yet the specification included enough information, including a warning that the powder
should not be disturbed, to show that the invention as originally contemplated
and disclosed included powder that was "not permanently fixed."

---

[122] *Id.* at 1353.
[123] *Vas-Cath,* 935 F.2d at 1561 (emphasis in original); *see also* Lizardtech, Inc. v. Earth Resource
Mapping, Inc., 433 F.3d 1373, 1374 (Fed. Cir. 2006) ("Our case law has been quite consistent
in holding that the patent law requires a written description of a claimed invention independent of the requirements to enable one skilled in the art to make and use the invention.").
[124] 823 F.2d 500 (Fed. Cir. 1987).
[125] *Vas-Cath,* 935 F.2d at 1563–64 (emphasis in original).
[126] *See* Lampi Corp. v. American Power Prods., Inc., 228 F.3d 1365, 1378 (Fed. Cir. 2000).
[127] 866 F.2d 422, 425 (Fed. Cir. 1989).

The specification must demonstrate that the applicant invented the claimed subject matter, not just that he had a plan for doing so. This problem has been known to arise where the patent claims a particular variety of DNA. "An adequate written description of DNA requires more than a mere statement that it is a part of the invention and reference to a potential method for isolating it; what is required is a description of the DNA itself."[128] In these cases it is difficult to disentangle the written description requirement from the enablement requirement. In *Fiers v. Revel*,[129] for example, the court seemed to fear that the applicants were claiming an invention much broader than what they had so far achieved: "Claiming all DNA's that achieve a result without defining the means that will do so is not in compliance with the description requirement; it is an attempt to preempt the future before it has arrived."[130] Unless the issue arises from a discrepancy between the originally filed specification and a *modified* claim, this concern should be one that can be adequately addressed by the enablement requirement.[131]

The description requirement certainly seems most useful, and most distinct from the other requirements of patentability, when claims have changed during prosecution. Some judges of the Federal Circuit believe that it should be invoked *only* as "a priority policeman."[132] On some occasions, however, the description requirement has been enforced as an absolute requirement of disclosure, even when claims have not been changed so as to make the *timing* of the disclosure the issue.[133] One can still inquire whether the specification demonstrates "possession of the invention" and perhaps, in that way, guard against over-ambitious claiming accompanied by an inadequate quid pro quo of disclosure.[134] Again, the enablement

[128] Fiers v. Revel, 984 F.2d 1164, 1170 (Fed. Cir. 1993). Functional descriptions of genetic material may be adequate. *See Enzo Biochem*, 296 F.3d at 1324.

[129] 984 F.2d 1164 (Fed. Cir. 1993).

[130] *Fiers*, 984 F.2d at 1171.

[131] See Section 8.6.

[132] *See* Enzo Biochem, Inc. v. Gen-Probe Inc., 63 U.S.P.Q.2d 1618, 1624 (Fed. Cir. 2002) (non-precedential opinion; Rader, J., dissenting).

[133] *See Lizardtech*, 433 F.3d at 1375; Moba, B.V. v. Diamond Automation, Inc., 325 F.3d 1306, 1320 (Fed. Cir. 2003). The first case to use the description requirement in this fashion seems to have been *Regents of the Univ. of California v. Eli Lilly & Co.*, 119 F.3d 1559 (Fed. Cir. 1997). In *University of Rochester v. G.D. Searle & Co.*, 358 F.3d 916 (Fed. Cir. 2004), the Federal Circuit, addressing this issue more squarely than before, held that the description requirement applies "whether a question of priority has arisen or not." *Id.* at 924. While earlier cases of this sort had dealt with "genetic materials," the principle "applies to all types of inventions." *Id.* at 925. The Federal Circuit is so divided on this issue that the denial of a rehearing *en banc* in the *University of Rochester* case produced no less than five concurring and dissenting opinions. *See University of Rochester v. G.D. Searle & Co.*, 375 F.3d 1303 (Fed. Cir. 2004).

[134] *See Capon*, 418 F.3d at 1357 ("The written description requirement . . . satisfies the policy premises of the law, whereby the inventor's technical/scientific advance is added to the body of knowledge, as consideration for the grant of patent exclusivity.").

requirement, an easier test to define and perhaps to satisfy, arguably covers that ground already.

8.9 NOVELTY AND OBVIOUSNESS

An invention can be patented only if it is *new*. So an important part of patent prosecution and patent litigation is comparing the claimed invention with prior inventions to determine if the claims are "novel." Prior inventions, as well as patents, patent applications, and publications that disclose prior inventions, are known as "prior art references." The various kinds of prior art references can be found in 35 U.S.C. § 102, a complex provision discussed in detail in the sections that follow. If a claimed invention is identical to one or more prior art references, the claim is "anticipated."[135] If the claimed invention differs from the prior art, but the differences are of the sort that would occur to a person of ordinary skill, the claim is "obvious."[136] Either condition is a sufficient ground for holding a claim unpatentable or invalid.

8.9.1 Categories of Prior Art

One of the most important provisions of the Patent Act is 35 U.S.C. § 102, but because of its length and structure it is also one of the most difficult to grasp. The provision begins "A person shall be entitled to a patent unless . . . ," and the following seven paragraphs (§ 102(a) to § 102 (g)) list various circumstances under which a patent *cannot* be granted, most of them related to a lack of novelty. If a patent issues even though it violates one of these conditions, the patent can be held invalid in the course of infringement litigation.

8.9.1.1   Prior Knowledge, Use, Patents and Publications (§ 102(a))

Section 102(a) reads as follows:

A person shall be entitled to a patent unless—
(a) the invention was known or used by others in this country, or patented or described in a printed publication in this or a foreign country, before the invention thereof by the applicant for patent. . . .

This section identifies four kinds of prior art reference that might invalidate a patent if they occurred before the applicant's date of invention:[137]

- Prior knowledge of the invention by others in *this* country.
- Prior use of the invention by others in *this* country.

---

[135] See Section 8.9.5.
[136] See Section 8.9.6.
[137] The "date of invention" is discussed in Section 8.9.2.

- A prior patent on the invention in *any* country.
- A prior "printed publication" of the invention in *any* country.[138]

Patents, printed publications, prior "use," and prior "knowledge" are four common categories of prior art. One feature they share is that, to some degree, they all place the invention in the possession of the public.[139] If an invention has already been the subject of a patent or printed publication, or if the invention is one that has already been known or used, granting a patent on the invention would not "promote the progress of . . . the useful arts."[140] On the contrary, it would take away an invention that the public had already enjoyed. In § 102, "[s]ociety, speaking through Congress and the courts, has said 'thou shalt not take it away.'"[141]

Although prior use, prior knowledge, prior patents, and prior publications are fairly straightforward concepts, they have been refined through judicial analysis, primarily to clarify the extent to which a reference must be publicly available. For example, although "known or used" could literally refer to secret knowledge or secret use, § 102(a) has been interpreted to require knowledge or use that is accessible to the public.[142] Similarly, the term "patented" means that the invention was *disclosed* in a patent, not merely that it was encompassed within the scope of a broad patent claim.[143] "Patented" can refer to the rights granted by foreign countries, even if they differ somewhat from U.S. patent rights,[144] but the foreign "patent" must be "available to the public."[145]

---

[138] Section 102(a) excludes prior use or knowledge of the invention in a foreign country, perhaps because in an earlier era such knowledge or use would have been difficult to verify. The increasingly global nature of both commerce and scientific research has spurred some commentators to suggest that the national distinctions embodied in § 102(a) are out of date.

[139] *See* Ormco Corp. v. Align Tech., Inc., 463 F.3d 1299, 1305 (Fed. Cir. 2006) ("Art that is not accessible to the public is generally not recognized as prior art."); Carella v. Starlight Archery & Pro Line Co., 804 F.2d 135, 139 (Fed. Cir. 1986). A prior patent at least gives the public *knowledge* of the invention and the expectation of possessing it as soon as the patent has expired.

[140] See Section 1.1.

[141] Kimberly-Clark Corp. v. Johnson & Johnson, 745 F.2d 1437, 1453–54 (Fed. Cir. 1984).

[142] *See* Astra Aktiebolag v. Andrx Pharmaceuticals, Inc., 483 F.3d 1364, 1380 (Fed. Cir. 2007) (secret information is not prior art); Minnesota Mining & Mfg. Co. v. Chemque, Inc., 303 F.3d 1294, 1301 (Fed. Cir. 2002); Woodland Trust v. Flowertree Nursery, Inc., 148 F.3d 1368, 1370 (Fed. Cir. 1998). Public use is also an issue under § 102(b), if it occurs more than one year before the filing date of the patent. In either context, confidentiality obligations may undermine the "public" nature of the use. This issue, which under § 102(b) often arises in the context of the inventor's *own* activities, is discussed in detail in Section 8.10.2.

[143] *See* In re Benno, 768 F.2d 1340, 1346 (Fed. Cir. 1985).

[144] *See* In re Carlson, 983 F.2d 1032 (Fed. Cir. 1992).

[145] *See Carlson,* 983 F.2d at 1037. The standard of "availability" is rather low. *See id.* at 1037–38 (a German Geschmacksmuster can qualify as a publicly available "patent" under § 102, even though one must travel to a courthouse in a remote German city to see the design to which it applies).

"[D]escribed in a printed publication" may be the language of § 102(a) that has received the most intense judicial scrutiny.[146] "Printed" is not to be taken literally. Information distributed through other forms of media—such as photographs, CD-ROMs, and microfilm—can qualify as "printed publications."[147] The two critical characteristics of a "printed publication" are (1) that it is "accessible" to the public and (2) that it includes an "enabling disclosure."

"Accessible" means that "interested members of the public could obtain the information if they wanted to."[148] Most books, journals, and other materials normally thought of as publications are easily accessible to the public, but inventions are sometimes disclosed in classified documents or documents distributed only on a confidential basis (e.g., documents for the internal use of a corporation). Those do not qualify as "publications."[149] On the other hand, distribution of even a small number of copies without restriction can be considered sufficient qualification.[150]

Some of the most difficult cases arise when a document has not been distributed, but has been made available in a library or similar collection. In *In re Hall*,[151] for example, the potentially invalidating reference was a doctoral thesis. The thesis had not been published in the usual sense, but it had been deposited in a university library in Germany, where it was, theoretically, available for review. The court held that "a single catalogued thesis in one university" might

---

[146] The same term also appears in the statutory bar provision of 35 U.S.C. § 102(b). See Section 8.10.

[147] *See* In re Klopfenstein, 380 F.3d 1345, 1348 n.2 (Fed. Cir. 2004) (the meaning of "printed publication" has changed since it was first used; today it means "a perceptible description of the invention, in whatever form it may have been recorded"); In re Hall, 781 F.2d 897, 898 (Fed. Cir. 1986) ("The statutory phrase 'printed publication' has been interpreted to give effect to ongoing advances in the technologies of data storage, retrieval, and dissemination.").

[148] Constant v. Advanced Micro-Devices, Inc., 848 F.2d 1560, 1569 (Fed. Cir. 1988); *see also* SRI Int'l, Inc. v. Internet Security Sys., Inc., 511 F.3d 1186, 1194 (Fed. Cir. 2008) (a publication is "publicly accessible" if it has been "'made available to the extent that persons interested . . . in the subject matter . . . exercising reasonable diligence, can locate it'"). If the publication is "accessible," it is irrelevant whether anyone in particular *actually* reviewed it. *Constant*, 848 F.2d at 1569.

[149] *See* Northern Telecom, Inc. v. Datapoint Corp., 908 F.2d 931, 936–37 (Fed. Cir. 1990); *but cf.* Cooper Cameron Corp. v. Kvaerner Oilfield Prods., Inc., 291 F.3d 1317, 1323–24 (Fed. Cir. 2002) (in spite of a "confidential" label, a report may have been sufficiently available to the public to qualify as prior art). Restricted publications might serve as evidence of a prior invention under § 102(g). See Section 8.9.1.3.

[150] *See* Massachusetts Inst. of Tech. v. A.B. Fortia, 774 F.2d 1104, 1109 (Fed. Cir. 1985) (paper that was discussed at a conference attended by 50 to 100 interested persons, and that was distributed "on request" to at least six persons without restrictions, constituted a "publication"); *but cf.* Preemption Devices, Inc. v. Minnesota Mining & Mfg. Co., 732 F.2d 903, 906 (Fed. Cir. 1984) (six copies of an article sent to a "friend" were not a "publication"). Sometimes the "interested public" to whom the publication must be available is a relatively small group. *See Cooper Cameron*, 291 F.3d at 1324.

[151] 781 F.2d 897 (Fed. Cir. 1986).

"constitute sufficient accessibility to those interested in the art exercising reasonable diligence."[152] On the other hand, in *In re Cronyn*,[153] the court held that
three undergraduate theses did not constitute "printed publications." The court
held that, in this case, the documents "were not accessible to the public because
they had not been either cataloged or indexed in a meaningful way."[154] They
could have been located only by sorting through a collection of index cards
kept in a shoe box in the university's chemistry department. These cases obviously draw fine, and somewhat arbitrary, distinctions. Although the undergraduate theses in *Cronyn* would have been difficult to track down, as a practical
matter the thesis in *Hall* might have been equally elusive.[155]

A *display* of information may also qualify as a "printed publication." In *In
re Klopfenstein*,[156] printed materials were affixed to poster boards and displayed at a professional conference for 2½ days. The materials were seen by
numerous persons skilled in the relevant art, who could have copied the
information at their leisure. Although the materials were neither distributed
nor indexed in a library, the court found that the display qualified as a
"printed publication" because it was accessible to the interested public.[157]

The other important requirement of a "printed publication" is that it
include an "enabling disclosure" of the invention.[158] An enabling disclosure is a
description of the invention that would allow a person skilled in the art to make
and use the invention without undue experimentation.[159] If, for example, a
marketing brochure boasts of the advantages of a process, but it does not

---

[152] *Hall,* 781 F.2d at 900.

[153] 890 F.2d 1158 (Fed. Cir. 1989).

[154] *Cronyn,* 890 F.2d at 1161.

[155] A case illustrating the low standard of accessibility is Bruckelmyer v. Ground Heaters, Inc.,
445 F.3d 1374 (Fed. Cir. 2006). The disputed reference was a Canadian patent application.
Because the relevant illustrations related to canceled claims, they were omitted from the
issued patent. However, a person skilled in the art might have been led by the patent to
investigate the patent's file history, and upon doing so would have discovered the missing
illustrations. The majority found the "roadmap" provided by the issued patent sufficient to
lead a diligent researcher to the original application, although it is difficult to imagine this
actually occurring. *Id.* at 1379.

[156] 380 F.3d 1345 (Fed. Cir. 2004).

[157] Factors relevant to the court's decision included "the length of time the display was exhibited, the expertise of the target audience, the existence (or lack thereof) or reasonable expectations that the material displayed would not be copied, and the simplicity or ease with which
the material displayed could have been copied." *Id.* at 1350.

[158] Elan Pharmaceuticals, Inc. v. Mayo Found., 346 F.3d 1051, 1054 (Fed. Cir. 2003); Amgen,
Inc. v. Hoechst Marion Roussel, Inc., 314 F.3d 1313, 1354 (Fed. Cir. 2003); Constant v.
Advanced Micro-Devices, Inc., 848 F.2d 1560, 1569 (Fed. Cir. 1988). A publication need not
be enabling to serve as evidence of *obviousness,* discussed in Section 8.9.6. *See Amgen,* 314 F.3d
at 1357.

[159] The enabling disclosure requirement also applies to patent applications. See Section 8.6. One
difference is that a prior art reference is enabling if it discloses the invention but does not tell
one how to use it. Patent applications must enable a substantial utility. *See* Rasmusson v.
Smithkline Beecham Corp., 413 F.3d 1318, 1325–26 (Fed. Cir. 2005).

include enough information to allow the process to be duplicated, the brochure lacks an enabling disclosure.[160] In deciding whether a disclosure is "enabling," the knowledge that would be available to those of skill in the art can be taken into account. In other words, the publication does not have to include information that would already be known to persons of ordinary skill.[161]

8.9.1.2   Prior Applications (§ 102(e))[162]

Another category of prior art reference, not discussed in § 102(a), is a patent *application*. The circumstances under which a patent application can constitute prior art are set forth in § 102(e). Section 102(e) has evolved into a complex paragraph freighted with cross-references to other portions of the Patent Act, but the gist of it is the addition of the following to the list of potential prior art references:

> A patent application, filed by another inventor in the United States,[163] before the applicant's date of invention, *if* (eventually) the application issued as a patent or it was published.

If Inventor A had a patent application on file before Inventor B conceived of the same invention, then Inventor A's application would be prior art to Inventor B, even if Inventor A's application neither issued as a patent nor was published as an application until some later date. Note that § 102(e) does not apply to patent applications that are *never* made public.

8.9.1.3   Prior Inventions (§ 102(g))

Section 102(g) establishes a final category of prior art reference:[164]

> A person shall be entitled to a patent unless—
>   (g)(2) before the applicant's invention thereof, the invention was made in this country by another inventor who had not abandoned, suppressed, or concealed it. . . .

Here we are looking for a second inventor—a second inventor who, before the applicant's own date of invention, made the same invention in this country. Two inventors can conceive of the same invention, even if they are working

---

[160] *See* Helefix Ltd. v. Blok-Lok, Ltd., 208 F.3d 1339, 1346–48 (Fed. Cir. 2000).

[161] In re Donohue, 766 F.2d 531, 533 (Fed. Cir. 1985).

[162] There is no apparent logic to the ordering of paragraphs in § 102. They will therefore be discussed in the order that seems easiest to understand, rather than in the order in which they appear in the statute.

[163] Under certain circumstances, an "international application" may qualify. *See* 35 U.S.C. § 102(e)(1).

[164] Other than those that apply only to the statutory bar provisions discussed in Sections 8.10 and 8.11.

independently. The telephone, for example, is said to have been invented independently, and almost simultaneously, by Alexander Graham Bell and Elisha Gray.[165] Other countries award priority to the first inventor to file a patent application, but in the United States the patent goes to the first to *invent*. Section 102(g) denies a patent to an applicant who was not the first to invent.[166]

There is, however, an important exception. The first invention does not count against a later inventor if the first invention was "abandoned, suppressed, or concealed." An invention is "abandoned, suppressed, or concealed if, within a reasonable time after completion, no steps are taken to make the invention publicly known."[167] Abandonment, suppression, or concealment can be inferred if, after a reasonable period of time, the first inventor has not filed a patent application, used the invention in public, embodied the invention in a product for sale, or described the invention in a publication.[168] This exception to the "first to invent" rule rewards those who make inventions available to the public, and penalizes those who hide or abandon inventions.[169]

If the delay in publicizing an invention, or applying for a patent, is more than a few years, abandonment may be presumed.[170] The presumption can be overcome by evidence that efforts to perfect the invention caused the delay.[171] On the other hand, efforts to *commercialize* the invention cannot excuse an applicant's failure to file promptly.[172] In

---

[165] Although a recent book claims that Bell stole essential information from Gray's own patent application, thanks to some chicanery at the Patent Office. *See* SETH SHULMAN, THE TELEPHONE GAMBIT: CHASING ALEXANDER GRAHAM BELL'S SECRET (2008).

[166] Section 102(g)(2) may be invoked in litigation to invalidate an issued patent. *See, e.g.,* Flex-Rest, LLC v. Steelcase, Inc., 455 F.3d 1351, 1358 (Fed. Cir. 2006); Dow Chemical Co. v. Astro-Valcour, Inc., 267 F.3d 1334, 1339 (Fed. Cir. 2001); Apotex USA, Inc. v. Merck & Co., 254 F.3d 1031, 1035 (Fed. Cir. 2001). If the contest for priority occurs in the course of prosecuting a patent application, the result can be an interference proceeding, discussed in Section 5.4. In that event, § 102(g)(1) controls. The rule is much the same, except that work in some foreign countries can suffice to establish priority, whereas § 102(g)(2) is restricted to prior invention in the United States.

[167] *Apotex,* 254 F.3d at 1039; Correge v. Murphy, 705 F.2d 1326, 1330 (Fed. Cir. 1983).

[168] *See Flex-Rest,* 455 F.3d at 1359; *Dow Chemical,* 267 F.3d at 1342.

[169] *See* Checkpoint Sys., Inc. v. U.S. Int'l Trade Comm'n, 54 F.3d 765, 761 (Fed. Cir. 1995).

[170] *See* Lutzker v. Plet, 843 F.2d 1364, 1367 (Fed. Cir. 1988) (discussing cases in which delays of 29 months to 4 years were held sufficient to show abandonment, suppression, or concealment). However, there is no period of time that is unreasonable per se. *See Flex-Rest,* 455 F.3d at 1359; *Dow Chemical,* 267 F.3d at 1342–43. "Rather a determination of abandonment, suppression or concealment has 'consistently been based on equitable principles and public policy as applied to the facts of each case.'" *Checkpoint,* 54 F.3d at 761.

[171] *See Lutzker,* 843 F.2d at 1367.

[172] If the prior inventor never intended to file a patent application but, instead, meant to introduce the invention to the public by a product, courts are far more tolerant of commercial activities as an excuse for delay. *See Flex-Rest,* 455 F.3d at 1360; *Dow Chemical,* 267 F.3d at 1343; *Checkpoint,* 54 F.3d at 762. This means, oddly enough, that the prior inventor who never filed a patent application himself may be better off, since he can more easily invalidate the subsequent patent of someone else.

Lutzker v. Plet,[173] where the invention was a device for making canapés, the first inventor (Lutzker) waited more than four years after completing the invention before disclosing it to the public at a trade show. By the time of the trade show, the second inventor (Plet) had invented the device independently and filed a patent application. Lutzker argued that the delay should be excused because it had been due to efforts to perfect the invention. The Patent Office, affirmed by the court, disagreed. The delay was attributed to the development of a recipe book, packaging, and other things unrelated to the invention itself. Lutzker was therefore found to have abandoned, suppressed, or concealed the invention, and his activities did not prevent the issuance of a patent to Plet.[174]

Two points should be mentioned about the timing of an "abandonment." First, the abandonment can be nullified if the first inventor renews his efforts to patent the invention, or to make it available to the public, before the second inventor "enters the field."[175] The first inventor would be credited with the date of renewed activity as his "date of invention." Thus, if Lutzker had begun work on a patent application before Plet entered the field, his earlier inactivity could have been overlooked. Second, § 102(g) refers to prior inventions that "had" not been abandoned, suppressed, or concealed, implying that an invention abandoned, suppressed, or concealed *after* the entry into the field of the second inventor would still be effective as prior art.[176]

8.9.2 Date of Invention

To evaluate whether a patent, patent application, publication, or other reference is *prior* art under § 102(a) or (e), it is necessary to determine the patentee's (or applicant's) "date of invention." In applying § 102(g), it is necessary to determine the "date of invention" of both the patentee (or applicant) and the alleged prior inventor. References subsequent to the patentee's (or applicant's) date of invention have no relevance under these statutory provisions.[177]

"Invention," as defined in patent law, involves two steps: "conception" and "reduction to practice."[178] "Conception" is the mental act of

---

[173] 843 F.2d 1364 (Fed. Cir. 1988).

[174] The court was influenced by the fact that the recipe book and other items accounting for the delay were not related to the disclosure in Lutzker's patent application. *Lutzker*, 843 F.2d at 1367–68.

[175] *See Lutzker*, 843 F.2d at 1368; Paulik v. Rizkalla, 760 F.2d 1270, 1275–76 (Fed. Cir. 1985).

[176] The language of the statute seems clear. However, the Federal Circuit has not ruled on this issue, and it could be argued that ignoring a later abandonment would hinder the policy of making inventions available to the public.

[177] They may, however, be relevant under the "statutory bar" provisions (see Section 8.10), and they may have a bearing on obviousness as instances of "near-simultaneous invention" (see Section 8.9.6.1).

[178] The Supreme Court regards conception as the more important of the two. *See* Pfaff v. Wells Elecs., Inc., 525 U.S. 55, 60 (1998) ("The primary meaning of the word 'invention' in the Patent Act unquestionably refers to the inventor's conception rather than to a physical embodiment of that idea."). However, as discussed below, reduction to practice still plays an important role in establishing priority.

invention—the moment of insight when the inventor imagines the thing that ultimately will be claimed. As formally defined by the Federal Circuit, conception requires the formation in the inventor's mind of "a definite and permanent idea of the invention, including every feature of the subject matter sought to be patented."[179] If the inventor has done no more than recognize a problem, the conception of the invention is still incomplete.[180] Conception is complete only when the inventor finds the *solution* to a problem, and the solution is worked out in sufficient detail, in the inventor's mind, that persons of ordinary skill in the art could put the inventor's ideas to practice without extensive research or undue experimentation.[181]

"Reduction to practice" means reducing the idea to a physical embodiment and, in most cases, testing it to confirm that it will work.[182] In the case of an apparatus, reduction to practice means that the apparatus was assembled, at least in prototype. In the case of a method, reduction to practice means that the method was actually performed.[183] A patent claim is not reduced to practice until there is a physical embodiment that includes all elements of the claim.[184]

The amount of testing of the physical embodiment necessary to establish reduction to practice varies considerably depending on the nature of the invention. The courts are instructed to employ a "common sense approach."[185] Some devices are so simple, and their effectiveness so obvious, that no testing at all is required.[186] On the other hand, some inventions

---

[179] Sewall v. Walters, 21 F.3d 411, 415 (Fed. Cir. 1994); *see also* Shum v. Intel Corp., 499 F.3d 1272, 1277 (Fed. Cir. 2007) ("'Conception is the formation "in the mind of the inventor of a definite and permanent idea of the complete and operative invention, as it is thereafter to be applied in practice."'"); Stern v. Trustees of Columbia Univ., 434 F.3d 1375, 1378 (Fed. Cir. 2006). A mere research plan coupled with a vague hope of success does not amount to a conception. *See* In re Jolley, 308 F.3d 1317, 1323 (Fed. Cir. 2002); Hitzeman v. Rutter, 243 F.3d 1345, 1356–57 (Fed. Cir. 2001); Burroughs Wellcome Co. v. Barr Labs., Inc., 40 F.3d 1223, 1228 (Fed. Cir. 1994) ("An idea is definite and permanent when the inventor has a specific, settled idea, a particular solution to the problem at hand, not just a general goal or research plan he hopes to pursue."). An inventor who has stumbled across a patentable invention must recognize it, though he need not appreciate that it is, in fact, patentable. *See* Invitrogen Corp. v. Clontech Labs., Inc., 429 F.3d 1052, 1074 (Fed. Cir. 2005); Rosco, Inc. v. Mirror Lite Co., 304 F.3d 1373, 1381 (Fed. Cir. 2002); *Hitzeman*, 243 F.3d at 1358–59.

[180] *See* Morgan v. Hirsch, 728 F.2d 1449 (Fed. Cir. 1994).

[181] *See* Brand v. Miller, 487 F.3d 862, 870 n.4 (Fed. Cir. 2007); *Stern*, 434 F.3d at 1378.

[182] *See* Z4 Techs., Inc. v. Microsoft Corp., 507 F.3d 1340, 1352 (Fed. Cir. 2007); Slip Track Sys., Inc. v. Metal-Lite, Inc., 304 F.3d 1256, 1265 (Fed. Cir. 2002) (reduction to practice "may require testing, depending on the character of the invention and the problem that it solves").

[183] *See* Z4, 507 F.3d at 1352 ("'the inventor must prove that . . . he constructed an embodiment or performed a process that met all of the [claim] limitations'"); *Slip Track*, 304 F.3d at 1265.

[184] *See* Eaton v. Evans, 204 F.3d 1094, 1097 (Fed. Cir. 2000).

[185] Scott v. Finney, 34 F.3d 1058, 1061 (Fed. Cir. 1994).

[186] *See Slip Track*, 304 F.3d at 1265.

require careful evaluation under conditions that duplicate, or simulate, the intended working environment of the invention. The testing required is whatever is reasonably necessary to demonstrate that the invention will work.[187] Even where testing is required, it is not necessary to demonstrate that the invention is so refined that it is ready to market.[188] A prototype that is not yet of commercial quality may be sufficient to show that the principle of the invention is sound.[189] Moreover, "[t]esting need not show utility beyond a possibility of failure, but only utility beyond a probability of failure."[190]

In rare cases, an invention is so unpredictable that it cannot be fully *conceived* until experiments have been performed and the results evaluated. Conception and reduction to practice are, in these cases, simultaneous. This is most likely to occur in the fields of chemistry and biotechnology, where useful combinations sometimes can be discovered only by trial and error.[191] In *Smith v. Bousquet*,[192] for example, the court held that the effectiveness of a chemical as an insecticide, on particular species and under particular conditions, could not be predicted until realistic experiments were carried out. Until then, plans to use the chemical as an insecticide were mere hope or speculation, not an invention.[193]

The "reduction to practice" discussed so far is *actual* reduction to practice. Filing a patent application effects a "*constructive* reduction to practice."[194] "Constructive" is a word often used in the law when an act is treated as though it

---

[187] "[The] common sense approach prescribes more scrupulous testing under circumstances approaching actual use conditions when the problem includes many uncertainties. On the other hand, when the problem to be solved does not present myriad variables, common sense similarly permits little or no testing to show the soundness of the principles of operation of the invention." *Scott*, 34 F.3d at 1063; *see also* Taskett v. Dentlinger, 344 F.3d 1337, 1341 (Fed. Cir. 2003).

[188] "Reduction to practice does not require 'that the invention, when tested, be in a commercially satisfactory stage of development.'" *Scott*, 34 F.3d at 1061; *see also* Loral Fairchild Corp. v. Matsushita Elec. Indus. Co., 266 F.3d 1358, 1362–63 (Fed. Cir. 2001) ("Once the invention has been shown to work for its intended purpose, reduction to practice is complete. . . . Further efforts to commercialize the invention are simply not relevant. . . .").

[189] *See Scott*, 34 F.3d at 1062.

[190] *Id.*

[191] *See* Mycogen Plant Science, Inc. v. Monsanto Co., 243 F.3d 1316, 1330 (Fed. Cir. 2001) ("The doctrine of simultaneous conception and reduction to practice is somewhat rare but certainly not unknown, especially in the unpredictable arts such as chemistry and biology."), *vacated on other grounds*, 535 U.S. 1109 (2002).

[192] 111 F.2d 157 (C.C.P.A. 1940).

[193] More recently, the concept of simultaneous conception and reduction to practice has been applied to inventions involving DNA. *See, e.g., Mycogen*, 243 F.3d at 1330–31; Amgen, Inc. v. Chugai Pharmaceutical Co., 927 F.2d 1200, 1206–07 (Fed. Cir. 1991).

[194] Frazer v. Schlegel, 498 F.3d 1283, 1287 (Fed. Cir. 2007); Hoffman-La Roche, Inc. v. Promega Corp., 323 F.3d 1354, 1377 (Fed. Cir. 2003).

were one thing, when it is actually something else.[195] Although filing a patent application is not a reduction to practice at all, it is treated as though it were for purposes of fixing the date of invention. Consequently, an inventor who never produces a physical embodiment of the invention, or who does so only later, will be considered to have reduced to practice on his filing date.[196]

If "date of invention" were always synonymous with "date of reduction to practice," life would be simpler. In fact, the date of conception must also be taken into account, because of the following complication introduced by § 102(g):

> In determining priority of invention under this subsection, there shall be considered not only the respective dates of conception and reduction to practice of the invention, but also the reasonable diligence of one who was first to conceive and last to reduce to practice, from a time prior to conception by the other.

In other words, when two inventors contend for the title of "first to invent," in the context of either an interference proceeding or a prior art challenge to an issued patent, the inventor who was first to conceive but last to reduce to practice will prevail if, but only if, he was "diligent" in reducing the invention to practice.[197]

The easiest cases to resolve are those in which the first inventor to conceive of the invention is also the first to reduce to practice. Suppose, for example, that Inventor A, who has received a patent, sues an infringer. The infringer argues that the invention of Inventor B is prior art to Inventor A's patent under § 102(g). If Inventor A's date of conception precedes Inventor B's date of conception, *and* Inventor's A's date of reduction to practice precedes Inventor B's date of reduction to practice, Inventor B's work is not prior art. If the situation is reversed (Inventor B's dates of

---

[195] See the discussion of "constructive notice" in Section 11.8.3.2.

[196] Treating the filing of a patent application as equivalent to producing a physical embodiment of the invention is not so far-fetched, since the application should include all of the information necessary to allow one skilled in the art to complete such an embodiment without undue experimentation. If it does not include that information, the patent will be invalid for lack of enablement. See Section 8.6.

[197] *See Pfaff,* 525 U.S. at 61 ("[A]ssuming diligence on the part of the applicant, it is normally the first inventor to conceive, rather than the first to reduce to practice, who establishes the right to patent."); Brand v. Miller, 487 F.3d 862, 869 (Fed. Cir. 2007); Medichem, S.A. v. Rolabo, S.L., 437 F.3d 1157, 1169 (Fed. Cir. 2006). The Federal Circuit has applied the diligence principle in the context of § 102(a). *See* In re Mulder, 716 F.2d 1542, 1545 (Fed. Cir. 1983) (printed publication); Loral Fairchild Corp. v. Matsushita Elec. Indus. Co., 266 F.3d 1358, 1365–66 (Fed. Cir. 2001) (Newman, J., dissenting). However, the recent addition of the phrase "under this subsection" suggests that it is appropriate only in the prior invention context of § 102(g).

conception and reduction to practice precede Inventor A's respective dates), then Inventor B's invention is prior art to Inventor A. In neither case is anyone's diligence an issue. When, however, the first inventor to conceive was last to reduce to practice, diligence comes into play. To return to the example, if Inventor A was the first to conceive of the invention, but before he could reduce the invention to practice Inventor B both conceived and reduced to practice, the patent to Inventor A would be valid only if Inventor A had been diligent from a time *prior* to B's date of conception.[198]

The rules can be more easily visualized with the aid of a time line. In the following examples, C stands for the date of conception and RTP for the date of reduction to practice. Time progresses from left to right. Assume that Inventor A has received a patent. Inventor B developed the same invention independently, and his work is alleged to be prior art under § 102(g). In the first example, B's invention is not prior art because he was last to conceive and last to reduce to practice:

```
A: C - - - - - - - - - RTP
B:           C - - - - - - - - - - - RTP
```

In the second example, B's invention is prior art because he was first to conceive and first to reduce to practice:

```
A:           C - - - - - - - - - - - RTP
B: C - - - - - - - - - RTP
```

In the third example, A was first to conceive, but B was first to reduce to practice. B's invention is not prior art *if* A was diligent, though not as swift as B, in reducing his invention to practice:

```
A: C - - - - - - - - - - - - - - - RTP (diligent?)
B:           C - - - - - RTP
```

In the last example, B was first to conceive, but A was first to reduce to practice. B's invention is prior art *if* B was diligent in reducing his invention to practice:

```
A:           C - - - - - RTP
B: C - - - - - - - - - - - - - - RTP (diligent?)
```

The purpose of this rather confusing set of rules is to reward inventors who are the first to conceive of an idea, and at the same time to encourage

---

[198] *See* Singh v. Brake, 317 F.3d 1334, 1340 (Fed. Cir. 2003); *Jolley*, 308 F.3d at 1326. The time period that begins just before a rival's conception and ends with one's own reduction to practice is frequently called the "critical period" for diligence. *See, e.g.*, Scott v. Koyama, 281 F.3d 1243, 1247 (Fed. Cir. 2002); Bey v. Kollonitsch, 806 F.2d 1024, 1025–26 (Fed. Cir. 1986). Earlier lapses in diligence can be overlooked.

inventors to bring their ideas to a practical end, or a public disclosure, as soon as possible.

"Diligence" in this context means reasonable efforts to reduce the invention to practice or to file a patent application. "Diligent" effort must be relatively continuous. Some excuses for lapses of effort have been recognized—most notably the need to complete some other invention before the first can be reduced to practice.[199] The courts will also consider "the reasonable everyday problems and limitations encountered by an inventor," including illness, poverty, the need for an occasional vacation, or the need to make a living by other means.[200] Time spent on efforts to fund or commercialize the invention, or to develop an unrelated invention, is not considered an adequate excuse for delay.[201]

Although diligence seems the inverse of abandonment or concealment, and the factual considerations are similar, remember that they are distinct issues under § 102(g). Abandonment can negate a prior art reference that was both conceived *and* reduced to practice before the patentee entered the scene. Diligence is an issue only in the rarer circumstance that the first inventor to conceive was the last to reduce to practice.

8.9.3 Burdens of Proof for Conception, Reduction to Practice, and Diligence

If a question of priority turns on the filing date of a patent application or the publication date of a technical journal, the proof is relatively straightforward. The filing date of a patent application is a matter of public record, and the publication date of a journal is usually easy to verify. If, however, priority depends on the dates of conception and reduction to practice, the facts can be much harder to establish. A conception date, in particular, can be a difficult thing to prove because the essential activity occurs entirely in the mind of the inventor.

Whenever a successful invention appears, there are sure to be those who purport to have had the same idea first. By the same token, it is easy for any patentee faced with prior art to claim that his conception occurred even

---

[199] *See, e.g.,* Keizer v. Bradley, 270 F.2d 396 (C.C.P.A. 1959).

[200] *See* Griffith v. Kanamaru, 816 F.2d 624, 626–27 (Fed. Cir. 1987). If the reduction to practice had been a "constructive" reduction to practice, accomplished by filing a patent application, the patent attorney's need to work on other applications can be considered an adequate excuse for delay, if the applications were handled in the order received, or if there was a need to work on related applications as a group. *See Bey,* 806 F.2d at 1028–30.

[201] *See Griffith,* 816 F.2d at 627–28. As in the case of abandonment or concealment, the line between work on the invention and unrelated commercial activity can be difficult to draw. "Precedent illustrates the continuum between, on the one hand, ongoing laboratory experimentation, and on the other hand, pure money-raising activity that is entirely unrelated to practice of the process." *Scott,* 281 F.3d at 1248 (holding that construction of facilities for large-scale practice of the claimed process sufficed to show diligence).

earlier. The courts have therefore established certain rules governing the proof required to establish conception and reduction to practice.

First, the application filing date is presumed to be the applicant's date of invention in the absence of other evidence.[202] During prosecution of a patent application, if the applicant needs to establish an earlier date of invention in order to pre-date a potential prior art reference, this can be accomplished under certain circumstances by means of a sworn affidavit from the inventor establishing prior conception and reduction to practice.[203] This is known as "swearing behind" a reference. In litigation, such claims must be subject to proof. A party challenging a patent must establish prior conception and reduction to practice by "clear and convincing evidence,"[204] and a patentee claiming an invention date prior to the filing date must introduce evidence to support it.[205]

A date of conception cannot be established entirely by the inventor's own testimony, which is likely to be untrustworthy.[206] The date must be *corroborated*, usually by the testimony of a non-inventor who was made aware of the inventor's work soon after the date in question.[207] For this reason, engineers involved in organized research programs often have their laboratory notebooks periodically reviewed, signed and dated by a colleague.[208] A witnessed notebook can be the best evidence of what was conceived and when,[209] and it is a practice strongly recommended to anyone pursuing work that may eventually prove patentable. Dates of reduction to practice and allegations of diligence also must be corroborated by evidence independent of the inventor.[210] Although eyewitness testimony is

---

[202] *See* Ecolochem, Inc. v. Southern California Edison Co., 227 F.3d 1361, 1371 (Fed. Cir. 2000); Bausch & Lomb, Inc. v. Barnes-Hind/Hydrocurve, Inc., 796 F.2d 443, 449 (Fed. Cir. 1986).

[203] *See* 37 C.F.R. § 1.131.

[204] Apotex, USA, Inc. v. Merck& Co., 254 F.3d 1031, 1036 (Fed. Cir. 2001).

[205] The ultimate burden of proof on validity, however, always remains with the party challenging the patent. *See* Innovative Scuba Concepts, Inc. v. Feder Indus., Inc., 26 F.3d 1112, 1115 (Fed. Cir. 1994).

[206] *See* Medichem, S.A. v. Rolabo, S.L., 437 F.3d 1157, 1170 (Fed. Cir. 2006) ("Credibility concerns undergird the corroboration requirement, the purpose of which is to prevent fraud.").

[207] *See* Rosco, Inc. v. Mirror Lite Co., 304 F.3d 1373, 1382 (Fed. Cir. 2002); Sandt Tech., Ltd. v. Resco Metal and Plastics Corp., 264 F.3d 1344, 1350 (Fed. Cir. 2001).

[208] The colleague, however, cannot be a co-inventor. *See Medichem*, 437 F.3d at 1171.

[209] *See Sandt Technology*, 264 F.3d at 1350–51 ("Documentary or physical evidence that is made contemporaneously with the inventive process provides the most reliable proof that the inventor's testimony has been corroborated."). In comparison, "post-invention oral testimony is more suspect, as there is more of a risk that the witness may have a litigation-inspired motive to corroborate the inventor's testimony, and that the testimony may be inaccurate." *Id.* at 1351.

[210] *See Medichem*, 437 F.3d at 1169 (corroboration of reduction to practice); Brown v. Barbacid, 436 F.3d 1376, 1380 (Fed. Cir. 2006) (corroboration of diligence). The Federal Circuit has described the standard for corroborating reduction to practice as "more stringent." Singh v. Brake, 222 F.3d 1362, 1370 (Fed. Cir. 2000). Perhaps that is because reduction to practice requires the inventor to take things farther than does conception. *See id.* ("a notebook page may well show that the inventor *conceived* what he wrote on the page, whereas it may not show that the experiments were *actually performed*, as required for a reduction to practice" (emphasis in original)).

often best, corroboration is subject to a "rule of reason" that allows the inventor's claims to be substantiated by any evidence sufficient to establish credibility.[211] For example, testimony regarding a reduction to practice might be corroborated by dated invoices for the parts that were used to build an embodiment of the invention.[212]

8.9.4 Prior Work by the Same Inventor

The kinds of prior art listed in § 102(a), (e), and (g) are limited, expressly or by implication, to prior inventions, patents, patent applications, printed publications, public knowledge, or public use attributable to persons *other than the inventor*.[213] This limitation can be difficult to apply in cases where a patent names two or more joint inventors.[214] For example, is a publication by A alone prior art to the joint invention of A and B? In these cases, courts resort to the concept of the "inventive entity," which is simply a way of referring to a specific group of inventors. A reference can be considered prior art to a patent or patent application if it is attributable to a different inventive entity. This is true whether the prior inventive entity is composed of entirely different individuals, or whether some individuals are common to both inventive entities. Thus, a publication by A, describing his work alone, could invalidate the subsequent patent of A

---

[211] *See Medichem,* 437 F.3d at 1170–71 ("'[I]t is not necessary to produce an actual over-the-shoulder observer. Rather, sufficient circumstantial evidence of an independent nature can satisfy the corroboration requirement.'"); *Sandt Technology,* 264 F.3d at 1350 ("rule of reason" test, examining "all pertinent evidence"); Cooper v. Goldfarb, 154 F.3d 1321, 1330 (Fed. Cir. 1998). In *Woodland Trust v. Flowertree Nursery, Inc.,* 148 F.3d 1368, 1371 (Fed. Cir. 1998), the court listed a number of factors relevant to whether the testimony of a corroborating witness satisfies the rule of reason. These include the interest of the corroborating witness in the subject matter of the suit and the amount of time that has elapsed since the events in question.

[212] *See* Lacotte v. Thomas, 758 F.2d 611, 613 (Fed. Cir. 1985).

[213] In re Katz, 687 F.2d 450, 454 (C.C.P.A. 1982); *see also* Invitrogen Corp. v. Biocrest Mfg., L.P., 424 F.3d 1374, 1381 (Fed. Cir. 2005); Rapoport v. Dement, 254 F.3d 1053, 1056 (Fed. Cir. 2001) (report cannot be cited as prior art against its author). Section 102(a) refers to an invention "patented or described in a printed publication . . . before the invention thereof by the applicant." While there is no explicit exception for the applicant's own work, clearly the applicant himself cannot patent or describe an invention in a printed publication before he has at least conceived it. It might be possible for the applicant to produce a patent or publication in comparison with which his later invention is *obvious* (see Section 8.9.6), but the courts have generally ruled out the use of an inventor's own work as the basis for an obviousness challenge. *See Katz,* 687 F.2d at 454. The *statutory bar* provisions (see Sections 8.10 and 8.11) create an important exception. A statutory bar, based on either anticipation or obviousness, can be triggered by the inventor's own activities, if they occur more than one year before an application is filed. *See Invitrogen,* 424 F.3d at 1381. A prior patent by the same inventor can raise issues of double patenting. See Section 8.12.

[214] See Section 6.1.

and B together.[215] A publication describing the work of A and B together could invalidate a subsequent patent to A alone. But a publication describing the work of A and B together would not be prior art to the subsequent patent of A and B.[216] Note that the question is not who *wrote* the publication, but rather whose *invention* the publication describes. A publication by A and B describing the work of A alone would not be § 102(a) prior art to A's subsequent patent.[217]

Section 103(c) provides another twist. Even if a prior invention is attributable to a different inventive entity, if the invention is *only* a potential reference under § 102(e), (f), or (g), and if the prior invention and the subsequent application are owned by the *same person* (or both are subject to an obligation to assign to the same person), the prior invention cannot render the subsequent patent invalid for obviousness.[218] This provision applies most often where several people are working on a project for the same corporation,[219] and it prevents the work of one person from invalidating the work of a colleague, recognizing that both are generally working under the same direction and toward the same goal.

8.9.5 Anticipation

Establishing that a patent, patent application, publication, or other potential reference falls within one of the categories of prior art is only a first step. Next one must ask whether or not the claimed invention is novel when compared with the reference. If the claim includes subject matter identical to that disclosed or embodied in a prior art reference, the claim is "anticipated" and invalid for lack of novelty.

Testing for anticipation is much like testing for infringement.[220] First, one "construes" the claim to determine exactly what it means.[221] The same claim construction must be used for all issues of infringement and validity. After construing the claim, one compares the claim to the reference.[222] The claim serves as a checklist, and if every element of the

---

[215] This is one occasion on which A and B might reconsider whether B was properly named as a joint inventor. If B's contribution did not rise to the level of invention, and if B was named as an inventor only accidentally, it would be possible to correct the patent to name only A as the inventor, thereby removing the prior publication as a potential prior art reference. See Section 6.1.

[216] Unless, again, it could suffice for a statutory bar under § 102(b). See Section 8.10.

[217] *See Katz,* 687 F.2d at 455.

[218] See Section 8.9.6.

[219] The law generally treats a corporation as a "person." People are "natural persons."

[220] See Chapter 10.

[221] See Chapter 7.

[222] *See* Teleflex, Inc. v. Ficosa North America Corp., 299 F.3d 1313, 1335 (Fed. Cir. 2000) (describing the "two-step procedure").

claim finds an exact match in the reference, the claim is anticipated.[223] Anticipation requires that all claim elements appear in a *single* reference.[224] This is because combining the teachings of one reference with the teachings of another reference might be sufficiently inventive to warrant a patent.[225] The question in such a case is whether the combination was "non-obvious," a separate issue discussed in the next section.

If the prior art reference is a patent or printed publication, it anticipates only if it discloses or "teaches" every element of the claimed invention, when read by a person skilled in the art.[226] A particular claim element can be mentioned *explicitly* in the reference,[227] or it can be *inherent*.[228] Suppose, for example, that a claim to a mousetrap required a "flexible" spring, and a

---

[223] *See* Hakim v. Cannon Avent Gp., PLC, 479 F.3d 1313, 1319 (Fed. Cir. 2007); Impax Labs., Inc. v. Aventis Pharmaceuticals Inc., 468 F.3d 1366, 1381 (Fed. Cir. 2006); Amgen Inc. v. Hoechst Marion Roussel, Inc., 457 F.3d 1293, 1304 (Fed. Cir. 2006). The tests of anticipation and literal infringement (see Section 10.5) are so similar, it is sometimes said that whatever would literally infringe a claim if it came later in time, anticipates if it came before. *See* Upsher-Smith Labs., Inc. v. Pamlab, L.L.C., 412 F.3d 1319, 1322 (Fed. Cir. 2005) (referring to the "century-old axiom"). However, since anticipation can be based on references that would not infringe (for example, the description of an invention in a publication), the "infringement test" of anticipation may be more confusing than helpful.

[224] *Hakim*, 479 F.3d at 1219; *Impax*, 468 F.3d at 1381.

[225] *See* Clearstream Wastewater Sys., Inc. v. Hydro-Action, Inc., 206 F.3d 1440, 1445 (Fed. Cir. 2000) (combination claims "can consist of new combinations of old elements"; individual elements of those combinations "may, and often do, read on the prior art").

[226] Like a patent disclosure, an anticipating reference must be "enabling." *See Impax*, 468 F.3d at 1381; *Amgen*, 457 F.3d at 1306; Elan Pharmaceuticals, Inc. v. Mayo Foundation for Medical Education and Research, 346 F.3d 1051, 1054 (Fed. Cir. 2003) ("The disclosure in an assertedly anticipating reference must be adequate to enable possession of the desired subject matter. It is insufficient to name or describe the desired subject matter, if it cannot be produced without undue experimentation."). On the other hand, a reference can be enabling, and anticipating, even if what it describes has not actually been attempted. *See Elan*, 346 F.3d at 1055. For anticipation, a reference may be enabling even if it does not describe how the invention can be usefully applied. *See Impax*, 468 F.3d at 1381–82.

[227] The reference does not have to describe a claim element in precisely the same words used in the patent claim. *See* In re Bond, 910 F.2d 831, 832 (Fed. Cir. 1990) (anticipation is not an "ipsissimis verbis" test).

[228] *See* Abbott Labs. v. Baxter Pharmaceutical Prods., Inc., 471 F.3d 1363, 1368 (Fed. Cir. 2006); Eli Lilly & Co. v. Barr Labs., Inc. 251 F.3d 955, 970 (Fed. Cir. 2001) ("A reference is anticipatory if it discloses every limitation of the claimed invention either explicitly or inherently. . . . A reference includes an inherent characteristic if that characteristic is the 'natural result' flowing from the reference's explicitly explicated limitations.");Telemac Cellular Corp. v. Topp Telecom, Inc., 247 F.3d 1316, 1327 (Fed. Cir. 2001) ("'Under the principles of inherency, if the prior art necessarily functions in accordance with, or includes, the claimed limitation, it anticipates.'"). Although anticipation requires that every claim element be found in a single reference, other references can be used to prove the fact of inherency. *Teleflex*, 299 F.3d at 1335; Continental Can Co. v. Monsanto Co., 948 F.2d 1264, 1268–69 (Fed. Cir. 1991).

prior publication disclosed a mousetrap with a steel spring of certain dimensions. Even if the publication did not refer to the flexibility of the spring, the spring described might be inherently flexible because of its materials and design. In this situation, the "flexible" spring element of the claim would be met by the reference, even though it was not explicit.[229]

Although anticipation requires that all of the elements of a claim be found in one reference, it may be proper to look to other references as an aid to *understanding* the anticipatory reference.[230] It is not proper to look to other references to fill in claim elements missing in the primary reference.[231] This relatively clear distinction was blurred somewhat by the decision in *In re Graves*.[232] There the Federal Circuit held that a reference lacking a claim element could still be held to anticipate, if the missing element was "within the knowledge of a skilled artisan."[233] This sounds suspiciously close to an obviousness test, rather than the classic test of anticipation, and it is not clear how far in this direction the Federal Circuit is willing to go.[234]

---

[229] The Federal Circuit has issued conflicting statements on whether an inherent characteristic must have been *recognized* in order to count for anticipation. Some opinions state that the inherent characteristic must be "necessarily present" and "so recognized by persons of ordinary skill." Finnegan Corp. v. International Trade Comm'n, 180 F.3d 1354, 1365 (Fed. Cir. 1999); *see also* Crown Operations Int'l, Ltd. v. Solutia Inc., 289 F.3d 1367, 1377 (Fed. Cir. 2002). On other occasions, the court has observed that "[i]nherency is not necessarily coterminous with the knowledge of those of ordinary skill in the art," and "[a]rtisans of ordinary skill may not recognize the inherent characteristics of functioning of the prior art." In re Cruciferous Sprout Litigation, 301 F.3d 1343, 1349 (Fed. Cir. 2002). The more recent decisions disavow the requirement of recognition. *See, e.g., Abbott*, 471 F.3d at 1367–68; Prima Tek II, L.L.C. v. Polypap, S.A.R.L., 412 F.3d 1284, 1289 (Fed. Cir. 2005); Toro Co. v. Deere & Co., 355 F.3d 1313, 1320–21 (Fed. Cir. 2004). Recognition may be superfluous if beneficial characteristics were present in the prior art, and the advantages were enjoyed whether anyone knew it or not. If certain vegetable sprouts always included cancer-preventing chemicals, the people who ate them reaped the benefits, even if unknowingly. *See Cruciferous Sprout*, 301 F.3d at 1350 (the inherent characteristics "have existed as long as the sprouts themselves. . . . It matters not that those of ordinary skill heretofore may not have recognized these inherent characteristics of the sprouts"). In some instances, however, failure to recognize an inherent characteristic may negate the benefits. For example, if a diet described in a publication could cure cancer but no one realized it, the diet would not be prescribed to those who could profit from it. The Federal Circuit has not explained things in quite this fashion, but it seems a plausible way to resolve the conflict.

[230] *See Teleflex*, 299 F.3d at 1335; Bristol-Meyers Squibb Co. v. Ben Venue Labs., Inc., 246 F.3d 1368, 1379 (Fed. Cir. 2001). When used in that limited fashion, the additional references need not be *prior* art. *See Bristol-Meyers*, 246 F.3d at 1379.

[231] *Teleflex*, 299 F.3d at 1335.

[232] 69 F.3d 1147 (Fed. Cir. 1995).

[233] *Id.* at 1152.

[234] *See Teleflex*, 299 F.3d at 1334–35 (rejecting an argument based on *Graves* and reiterating that additional prior art references cannot fill gaps in the allegedly anticipating reference).

If a patent claims a broad genus, a reference that includes a single species of the genus will anticipate the claim.[235] For example, a claim that specified a fuel composed of (among other things) "10 to 50 percent methane" would be anticipated by a prior fuel that met all of the other claim elements and that was composed of 25 percent methane. The claim is anticipated because it would otherwise prevent the practice of at least one fuel combination already in use. The converse, however, is not true. If a claim called for a fuel composed of exactly 25 percent methane, and a prior publication discussed such a fuel with a methane concentration of anywhere from 10 to 50 percent, the claim requiring exactly 25 percent would not be anticipated.[236] It might or might not be invalid for obviousness.

8.9.6 Obviousness (§ 103)

Obviousness is a concept drawn from the following language of 35 U.S.C. § 103(a):

> A patent may not be obtained though the invention is not identically disclosed or described as set forth in section 102 of this title, if the differences between the subject matter sought to be patented and the prior art are such that the subject matter as a whole would have been obvious at the time the invention was made to a person having ordinary skill in the art to which said subject matter pertains.

Like anticipation, obviousness is a ground for rejecting a patent claim in the course of prosecution or invalidating a patent claim in the course of infringement litigation. Obviousness, however, does not require that the claimed invention be identical to the prior art. Instead, obviousness focuses on the differences between the claim and the prior art, and asks whether those differences are really inventive, or whether they are differences that might have occurred to anyone of ordinary skill.[237] Like § 102, § 103 prevents a patent claim from taking from the public what, in a sense, it already possesses.

---

[235] *See Eli Lilly,* 251 F.3d at 971 ("Our case law firmly establishes that a later genus claim limitation is anticipated by, and therefore not patentably distinct from, an earlier species claim."); Atlas Powder Co. v. Ireco, Inc., 190 F.3d 1342, 1346 (Fed. Cir. 1999) ("[I]f granting patent protection on the disputed claim would allow the patentee to exclude the public from practicing the prior art, then that claim is anticipated, regardless of whether it also covers subject matter not in the prior art.").

[236] *See* Atofina v. Great Lakes Chemical Corp., 441 F.3d 991, 999 (Fed. Cir. 2006); *Upsher-Smith,* 412 F.3d at 1323. Disclosure of a sufficiently limited genus *might* anticipate a species of the genus, even if the prior art did not name that species specifically. *See Bristol-Meyers,* 246 F.3d at 1380. The detailed description of a small genus might be equivalent to an explicit description of each of its members. *See Atofina,* 441 F.3d at 999; *but cf. Impax,* 468 F.3d at 1381 (disclosure in reference of "hundreds of compounds" did not allow a person skilled in the art to separately envision each member of the class).

[237] Although obviousness looks to the differences between the claimed invention and the prior art, the invention still must be viewed "as a whole." *See* 35 U.S.C. § 103; Princeton Biochemicals, Inc. v. Beckman Coulter, Inc., 411 F.3d 1332, 1337 (Fed. Cir. 2005); Para-Ordnance Mfg., Inc. v. SGS Imports Int'l, Inc., 73 F.3d 1085, 1087 (Fed. Cir. 1995).

Obviousness must be judged from the perspective of the "person of ordinary skill in the art" at the time the invention was made.[238] The "person of ordinary skill in the art" is a mythical everyman whose viewpoint is often called upon in patent law, not only in context of obviousness but also, for example, in deciding whether a patent specification enables the practice of the claimed invention.[239] The person of ordinary skill is not an inventor or innovator, but a person of ordinary competence who does the expected thing.[240] The level of expertise and education required of the person of ordinary skill varies depending on the art. In a very sophisticated art, a person of ordinary skill might have a Ph.D. and years of hands-on experience. In a less sophisticated art, the person of ordinary skill might be a shade tree mechanic. A court must decide what level of skill represents "ordinary skill" in the art at the time the invention was made.[241]

Non-obviousness should not be confused with complexity. Sometimes the simplest inventions are the most innovative.[242] Nor must the invention embrace a "flash of genius"—the kind of sudden inspiration that led Archimedes to shout

---

[238] *See* 35 U.S.C. § 103; Arkie Lures, Inc. v. Gene Larew Tackle, Inc., 119 F.3d 953, 956 (Fed. Cir. 1997) (obviousness must be approached "not from the viewpoint of the inventor, but from the viewpoint of a person of ordinary skill in the field of the invention"); Custom Accessories, Inc. v. Jeffrey-Allan Indus., Inc., 807 F.2d 955, 962 (Fed. Cir. 1986) ("obvious" mean obvious to a person of ordinary skill—"not to the judge, or to a layman, or to those skilled in remote arts, or to geniuses in the art").

[239] See Section 8.6.

[240] Life Techs., Inc. v. Clontech Labs., Inc., 224 F.3d 1320, 1325 (Fed. Cir. 2000); Standard Oil Co. v. American Cyanamid Co., 774 F.2d 448, 454 (Fed. Cir. 1985) ("A person of ordinary skill in the art is . . . presumed to be one who thinks along the lines of conventional wisdom in the art and is not one who undertakes to innovate, whether by patient, and often expensive, systematic research or by extraordinary insights, it makes no difference which.").

[241] *See* KSR Int'l Co. v. Teleflex Inc., 127 S. Ct. 1727, 1734 (2007); Abbott Labs. v. Andrx Pharmaceuticals, Inc., 452 F.3d 1331, 1336 (Fed. Cir. 2006); Ruiz v. A.B. Chance Co., 234 F.3d 654, 666 (Fed. Cir. 2000). Factors that may be considered include "'(1) the educational level of the inventor; (2) [the] type of problems encountered in the art; (3) prior art solutions to those problems; (4) [the] rapidity with which innovations are made; (5) [the] sophistication of the technology; and (6) [the] educational level of active workers in the field.'" Daiichi Sankyo Co. v. Apotex, Inc., 501 F.3d 1254, 1256 (Fed. Cir. 2007). An invention may be obvious to a person of "ordinary skill" even if it would not be obvious to a layperson. On the other hand, an invention that would be obvious to an inventor can still be patentable. Inventors and patentees are often assumed to be persons of extraordinary skill. *See Life Technologies,* 224 F.3d at 1325; Kloster Speedsteel AB v. Crucible Inc., 793 F.2d 1565, 1574 (Fed. Cir. 1986). However, the "person of ordinary skill" is someone who *makes* things, not someone who only *uses* the technology supplied by others. *See* Dystar Textilfarben GmbH v. C.H. Patrick Co., 464 F.3d 1356, 1362–63 (Fed. Cir. 2006) (person skilled in the art of dyeing would be someone familiar with chemistry, not the high school–educated equipment operator who merely "flips the switches").

[242] *See* Gentry Gallery, Inc. v. Berkline Corp., 134 F.3d 1473, 1478 (Fed. Cir. 1998) ("simplicity alone is not determinative of obviousness"); In re Oetiker, 977 F.2d 1443, 1447 (Fed. Cir. 1992) ("Simplicity is not inimical to patentability."); Demaco Corp. v. F. Von Langsdorff Licensing Ltd., 851 F.2d 1387, 1390-91 (Fed. Cir. 1988).

"Eureka!" An invention that is the product of patient experimentation, or that is discovered entirely by accident, is just as patentable as one that arises from pure mental effort.[243] The only requirement is that the invention would not have occurred to a person of ordinary skill. This principle accounts for the first sentence of § 103(c), which provides, rather cryptically, that "[p]atentability shall not be negatived by the manner in which the invention was made."[244]

While anticipation requires that all the elements of the claimed invention be found in a single prior art reference, obviousness can be based on the *combination* of more than one reference. For example, if some elements of the claimed invention were found in one technical journal, and the remaining elements were found in another journal, the combination might have been obvious to a person of ordinary skill in the art. Courts sometimes imagine this hypothetical person standing in a workshop, surrounded by all of the relevant patents, publications, and other prior art references.[245] The question then becomes, would such a person, confronting the problem solved by the invention and aware of all of these references, have found it obvious to make the claimed combination?

The references that may be considered include any of the kinds of prior art set forth in § 102, as long as they are "analogous art." A reference qualifies as analogous art if (1) it comes from the "the field of the inventor's endeavor," or (2) it is "reasonably pertinent to the problem with which the inventor was concerned."[246] The latter includes material from other fields

---

[243] *See* Graham v. John Deere Co., 383 U.S. 1, 15 (1966); *Life Techs.*, 224 F.3d at 1325 ("the path that leads an inventor to the invention is . . . irrelevant to patentability"); In re Dow Chemical Co., 837 F.2d 469, 472 (Fed. Cir. 1988) ("[m]ost technological advance is the fruit of methodical, persistent investigation").

[244] An invention may have been obvious from a technological point of view, but not from a *business* point of view. Because patents are meant to encourage the technological arts, even an advancement ingenious from a marketing perspective is unpatentable if it is obvious from a technological perspective. *See* Orthopedic Equipment Co. v. U.S., 702 F.2d 1005, 1013 (Fed. Cir. 1983) ("[T]he fact that the two disclosed apparatus would not be combined by businessmen for economic reasons is not the same as saying that it could not be done because skilled persons in the art felt that there was some technological incompatibility that prevented their combination. Only the latter fact is telling on the issue of nonobviousness.").

[245] *See Para-Ordnance*, 73 F.3d at 1088. However, the visual image of the art "tableau" was criticized by the judge who first created it, perhaps because it suggests the use of hindsight in selecting the references to "hang in the workshop." *See* Standard Oil Co. v. American Cyanamid Co., 774 F.2d 448, 454 n.3 (Fed. Cir. 1985) (referring to the "unfortunate popularity" of the tableau imagery).

[246] In re Kahn, 441 F.3d 977, 987 (Fed. Cir. 2006); *see also Princeton Biochemicals*, 411 F.3d at 1339. The pertinent art should be defined in terms of the *problem* faced by the inventor, not the *solution* embodied in the patented invention. The latter would introduce inappropriate hindsight. *See* Monarch Knitting Machinery Corp. v. Sulzer Morat GmbH, 139 F.3d 877, 881 (Fed. Cir. 1998). Sometimes it is difficult to define the "field of the inventor's endeavor." In *Bigio*, the court affirmed findings by the PTO that toothbrushes and hairbrushes are in the same field of endeavor. Their construction is similar and a small hairbrush (perhaps for a moustache) would be much like a toothbrush. *Id.* at 1325–27. Judge Newman, dissenting, wrote that "[a] brush for hair has no more relation to a brush for teeth than does hair resemble teeth." *Id.* at 1327.

that, as a source of ideas, "logically would have commended itself to an inventor's attention."[247] For example, in *In re Paulsen*,[248] the claimed invention concerned a case for a portable computer, hinged in such a way that it could be closed tight for carrying or latched in an upright position for viewing the display screen. The court found it appropriate to consider references concerning hinges and latches, even if they were not in the portable computer field:

> The problems encountered by the inventors . . . were problems that were not unique to portable computers. They concerned how to connect and secure the computer's display housing to the computer while meeting certain size constraints and functional requirements. . . . We agree with the Board that given the nature of the problems confronted by the inventors, one of ordinary skill in the art "would have consulted the mechanical arts for housings, hinges, latches, springs, etc."[249]

In *In re Oetiker*,[250] on the other hand, the court found insufficient evidence that a person working on hose clamps would have been motivated to consider fasteners used in clothing.[251]

Sometimes a prior reference "teaches away" from the claimed invention. To "teach away" means to suggest that the claimed combination should be avoided as undesirable or ineffective.[252] This is one factor to consider in deciding whether certain references render a claimed invention obvious. Nevertheless, sufficient disclosure can render an invention obvious and unpatentable, even if the reference suggests that the invention is an inferior approach.[253]

It is no easy task to adopt the perspective of a different person (a person of ordinary skill in the art) at a different time (the time the invention was

---

[247] In re Icon Health & Fitness, Inc., 496 F.3d 1374, 1379–80 (Fed. Cir. 2007); *see also Princeton Biochemicals*, 411 F.3d at 1339; Wang Labs., Inc. v. Toshiba Corp., 993 F.2d 858, 864 (Fed. Cir. 1993).

[248] 30 F.3d 1475 (Fed. Cir. 1994).

[249] *Id.* at 1481–82. Similarly, in *Icon Health* the court found that an inventor designing a folding treadmill might have considered earlier work on folding beds. Even though beds and treadmills are in different fields of endeavor, the invention had more to do with the problem of folding than with treadmills per se. *Icon Health*, 496 F.3d at 1380.

[250] 977 F.2d 1443 (Fed. Cir. 1992).

[251] *Id.* at 1447.

[252] *See Icon Health*, 496 F.3d at 1381 ("'A reference may be said to teach away when a person of ordinary skill, upon reading the reference, would be discouraged from following the path set out in the reference, or would be led in a direction divergent from the path that was taken by the applicant.'"); *Kahn,* 441 F.3d at 990; In re Gurley, 27 F.3d 551, 553 (Fed. Cir. 1994). "Teaching away" is not relevant to anticipation. Celeritas Techs., Ltd. v. Rockwell Int'l Corp., 150 F.3d 1354, 1361 (Fed. Cir. 1998) ("A reference is no less anticipatory if, after disclosing the invention, the reference then disparages it.").

[253] *See Gurley,* 27 F.3d at 553 ("A known and obvious composition does not become patentable simply because it has been described as somewhat inferior to some other product for the same use.").

made). One can easily fall prey to hindsight. Once you have seen the invention and how it solves a problem, it may seem like the obvious thing to do[254]–particularly if, as is often the case, the *ingredients* of the solution were already available. Concerned that worthy inventions might, in retrospect, be held obvious simply because their component parts already existed,[255] the Federal Circuit held that a combination can be found obvious only if there was some "teaching, suggestion or motivation" to support it.[256] In other words, one cannot prove the obviousness of combination A plus B simply by showing that A already existed and so did B. One has to show that persons of ordinary skill would have been led, in some fashion, to combine A with B to solve the problem at hand.[257] In a similar vein, the Federal Circuit emphasized that the standard of obviousness is not whether something would have been "obvious to try."[258] Instead, one has to show that the invention was obvious to *do*, and that a person of ordinary skill would have proceeded with a reasonable expectation of success.[259]

These rules, when strictly applied, made obviousness difficult to establish–too difficult, in the end, for the Supreme Court to approve. In one of the more important patent cases of recent years, *KSR Int'l Co. v. Teleflex Inc.*,[260] the court considered the obviousness of a height-adjustable accelerator pedal equipped with an electronic sensor. Height-adjustable pedals already existed, as did electronic sensors for pedals that were not adjustable, but no one had combined them as the patentee did. Finding no "teaching, suggestion or motivation" to support the combination, the Federal Circuit

---

[254] "Good ideas may well appear 'obvious' after they have been disclosed, despite having been previously unrecognized." *Arkie Lures*, 119 F.3d at 956.

[255] *See Crown*, 289 F.3d at 1376 ("'Determination of obviousness cannot be based on the hindsight combination of components selectively culled from the prior art to fit the parameters of the patented invention.'"); *Life Techs.*, 224 F.3d at 1326 ("It is axiomatic that a claimed invention is not obvious solely because it is composed of elements that are all individually found in the prior art."); In re Gorman, 933 F.2d 982, 987 (Fed. Cir. 1991).

[256] Pfizer, Inc. v. Apotex, Inc., 480 F.3d 1348, 1362 (Fed. Cir. 2007); *Kahn*, 441 F.3d at 986; In re Fulton, 391 F.3d 1195, 1200 (Fed. Cir. 2004).

[257] *See Crown*, 289 F.3d at 1376 ("There must be a teaching or suggestion within the prior art, within the nature of the problem to be solved, or within the general knowledge of a person of ordinary skill in the field of the invention, to look to particular sources, to select particular elements, and to combine them as combined by the inventor.").

[258] *Pfizer*, 480 F.3d at 1365 (it is a "truism" that "obvious to try" is not the correct standard of obviousness); Novo Nordisk A/S v. Becton Dickinson & Co., 304 F.3d 1216, 1220 (Fed. Cir. 2002).

[259] *See* Pharmastem Therapeutics, Inc. v. Viacell, Inc., 491 F.3d 1342, 1360 (Fed. Cir. 2007); *Pfizer,* 480 F.3d at 1364; In re O'Farrell, 853 F.2d 894, 903–04 (Fed. Cir. 1988). An "obvious to try" situation might occur if a publication included "a general disclosure [to] pique the scientist's curiosity, such that further investigation might be done as a result of the disclosure, but the disclosure itself [did] not contain a sufficient teaching of how to obtain the desired result." In re Eli Lilly & Co., 902 F.2d 943, 945 (Fed. Cir. 1990).

[260] 127 S. Ct. 1727 (2007).

reversed the district court's judgment that the invention was obvious. On appeal, the Supreme Court found that the "teaching, suggestion or motivation" test had been applied too woodenly in this case.[261] There may have been no explicit teaching encouraging persons skilled in the art to combine a height-adjustable pedal with an electronic sensor, yet the course of the industry made the combination inevitable, even with ordinary levels of ingenuity. Electronic sensors were becoming standard, so eventually persons skilled in the art would add them to adjustable pedals—just as the patentee had done.[262]

Although it recognized the need to avoid hindsight, the Supreme Court endorsed "common sense" as a better guide to obviousness than any rigid formula.[263] Even the "obvious to try" approach can be useful. If there were only a few options to try, and one could have tried them with a fair expectation of success, then the solution might be considered obvious.[264] The court also observed that combinations are more likely to be obvious if they consist of known components performing their usual functions—e.g., a known perfume added to a known sunblock, each behaving as one would expect.[265] On the other hand, a combination might be non-obvious if it creates some unexpected "synergy"—perhaps a perfume combined with a sunblock producing an unexpected mosquito repellent. In *KSR*, the sensor and pedal in combination produced nothing more than the sum of the parts. Common sense showed, in the end, that the improvement did not rise to the level of a patentable invention.

Although obviousness determinations are highly fact-specific,[266] two additional examples will give the reader some flavor for how the decisions are made. In *In re Gorman*,[267] the claimed invention was a novelty lollipop in the

[261] *Id.* at 1741 ("The obviousness analysis cannot be confined by a formalistic conception of the words teaching, suggestion, and motivation, or by overemphasis on the importance of published articles and the explicit content of issued patents.").

[262] *See id.* at 1744–45. In some fields, "market demand, rather than scientific literature, will drive design trends." *Id.* at 1741.

[263] *Id.* at 1742–43; *see also* Leapfrog Enterprises, Inc. v. Fisher-Price, Inc., 485 F.3d 1157, 1161 (Fed. Cir. 2007).

[264] "When there is a design need or a market pressure to solve a problem and there are a finite number of identified, predictable solutions, a person of ordinary skill has good reason to pursue the known options within his or her technical grasp. If this leads to the anticipated success, it is likely the product not of innovation but of ordinary skill and common sense. In that instance the fact that a combination was obvious to try might show that it was obvious under § 103." *Id.* at 1742; *see also* Takeda Chemical Indus., Ltd. v. Alphapharm Pty., Ltd., 492 F.3d 1350, 1359 (Fed. Cir. 2007).

[265] *Id.* at 1739 ("The combination of familiar elements according to known methods is likely to be obvious when it does no more than yield predictable results."); *see also Leapfrog,* 485 F.3d at 1161.

[266] *See Pfizer,* 480 F.3d at 1366. Once the facts are determined, the *ultimate* decision on obviousness is a "question of law." See Section 11.4.

[267] 933 F.2d 892, 897 (Fed. Cir. 1991).

shape of a thumb. The elements of the claimed invention included a thumb-shaped candy core; a protective covering, also thumb-shaped, which served first as a mold for the candy core and then as a "toy and novelty item for placement upon the thumb of the user"; a lollipop stick; a plug of chewing gum or similar edible material to seal the bottom of the candy; and a plastic or cardboard disk at the base of the "thumb."

The prior art located by the Patent Office included 13 references. Some showed candy or ice cream formed in a rubbery mold, which served double-duty as a wrapper for the product. One ice cream product on a stick included a similar cardboard base. Other references (believe it or not) disclosed thumb-shaped candies and confections. Edible plugs also had been disclosed for sealing liquid inside of candy and ice cream products. Although Gorman's claim was very detailed, and none of the references included all of the things that Gorman claimed, the Patent Office found that the combination still would have been obvious to any person of ordinary skill. The Federal Circuit affirmed: "The various elements Gorman combined . . . are all shown in the cited references in various subcombinations, used in the same way, for the same purpose as in the claimed invention."[268]

In *Moleculon Research Corp. v. CBS, Inc.*,[269] on the other hand, the Federal Circuit upheld the determination of the trial court that the claimed invention was not obvious. There the invention was a cube puzzle of the kind popularized by Rubik's Cube. In fact, Rubik's Cube was the product accused of infringement. The claims described a puzzle in the shape of a subdivided cube, the pieces of which could be scrambled and restored by rotating the facets of the cube. CBS, which owned the rights to Rubik's Cube, argued that the claims were obvious in light of a prior patent, to one Gustafson, disclosing a spherical puzzle with a subdivided, rotating shell. A person skilled in the art might have *considered* converting Gustafson's sphere puzzle into a cube with rotating faces, but nothing in the art suggested that such a change would have been desirable. On the contrary, the evidence showed that Gustafson, while considering other shapes, had dismissed a cube as inadequate.[270] Moreover, one expert described the cube as a "quantum leap" from the sphere.[271] On the basis of this evidence, the lower court properly concluded that even someone aware of Gustafson's sphere would not have found it obvious to make the cube.

Even these two examples are enough to prove the Federal Circuit's observation that "[t]he obviousness standard, while easy to expound, is sometimes difficult to apply."[272] It is not hard to imagine *Gorman* or *Moleculon* reaching an opposite conclusion.

[268] *Gorman*, 933 F.2d at 987.
[269] 793 F.2d 1261 (Fed. Cir. 1986).
[270] *Id.* at 1268.
[271] *Id.*
[272] Uniroyal, Inc. v. Rudkin-Wiley Corp., 837 F.2d 1044, 1050 (Fed. Cir. 1988).

8.9.6.1   *Secondary Considerations*

Because the obviousness determination is such a difficult and subjective one, courts have increasingly emphasized the importance of "secondary considerations"—factors thought to provide objective evidence of non-obviousness. In *Graham v. John Deere Co.*,[273] the Supreme Court suggested that these "secondary considerations," including "commercial success, long felt but unsolved needs, failure of others, etc.,"[274] might be illuminating. Under subsequent Federal Circuit precedent, secondary considerations have become a mandatory aspect of the obviousness analysis.[275]

Secondary considerations include the following:

- Commercial success
- Long-felt need
- Failure of others
- Industry recognition
- Expressions of skepticism or disbelief
- Unexpected results
- Copying
- Near-simultaneous invention

The secondary consideration most frequently encountered is "commercial success." Commercial success means evidence that a product covered by a patent claim has earned substantial profits in the marketplace. In theory, an invention that has been successful in the marketplace could not have been an obvious one. Otherwise, someone else would have stepped ahead of the inventor in order to reap the available rewards.[276]

There are at least three possible objections to this theory. First, the theory works only if the success of the invention had been foreseeable. Second,

---

[273] 383 U.S. 1 (1966).

[274] *Id.* at 17–18. The factors specifically mentioned in *Graham* may be given greater weight than others subsumed in the "etc." *See* Ecolochem, Inc. v. Southern California Edison Co., 227 F.3d 1361, 1380 (Fed. Cir. 2000).

[275] *See* Ruiz v. A.B. Chance Co., 234 F.3d 654, 667 (Fed. Cir. 2000) ("Our precedents clearly hold that secondary considerations, when present, must be considered in determining obviousness."); Hybritech, Inc. v. Monoclonal Antibodies, Inc., 802 F.2d 1367, 1380 (Fed. Cir. 1986) (secondary considerations are more than "icing on the cake"); Stratoflex, Inc. v. Aeroquip Corp., 713 F.2d 1530, 1539 (Fed. Cir. 1983).

[276] *See* Syntex (USA) LLC v. Apotex, Inc., 407 F.3d 1371, 1383 (Fed. Cir. 2005) ("commercial success permits the inference that others have tried and failed"); Dickey-John Corp. v. Int'l Tapetronics Corp., 710 F.2d 329, 346–47 (7th Cir. 1983) ("If individuals believe there is 'a fortune waiting in the wings' for the person who solves the problem, we infer that with such an incentive, many artisans were actually attempting to find the solution. The longer they failed to do so, the stronger the inference that it took extraordinary skill to solve the problem.").

someone has to be first to invent, even if the invention is an obvious one and the rewards are substantial. Finally, commercial success can be due to any number of factors other than the claimed invention, including marketing know-how, advertising, manufacturing techniques, quality control, price, or features of the product other than those covered by the claim. In order to meet this last objection, a "nexus" must exist between the success and the claimed invention.[277] Nexus means a logical, cause-and-effect relationship between the success of the product and the claimed invention. Such a connection might be shown in a number of ways, including consumer surveys, comparisons to similar products, or testimony concerning the relative advantages of the claimed invention.[278]

Commercial success is useful as a secondary consideration to patentees or applicants who have marketed a product covered by the claim. Commercial success can also be premised on a product marketed by someone else—even an infringer—as long as there is a nexus between the success of the product and the invention claimed.[279] Success in licensing[280] may also be offered as evidence of commercial success.[281]

The other secondary considerations are relatively straightforward. If there had been a "long-felt need" for an invention, or if others had tried and failed to solve the problem addressed by the invention, it is reasonable to infer that the invention was not an obvious one. Otherwise the problem would have been solved before, and the need already satisfied.[282] Reactions to the invention by persons skilled in the art can also be important. If experts in the field praised the invention or, even better, if they expressed skepticism or disbelief that anyone had solved the problems overcome by the invention, this

---

[277] *See* Ormco Corp. v. Align Tech., Inc., 463 F.3d 1299, 1311–12 (Fed. Cir. 2006); Iron Grip Barbell Co. v. USA Sports, Inc., 392 F.3d 1317, 1324 (Fed. Cir. 2004); Demaco Corp. v. F. Von Langsdorff Licensing Ltd., 851 F.2d 1387, 1392 (Fed. Cir. 1988).

[278] *See Demaco*, 851 F.2d at 1392–93. "[I]f the marketed product embodies the claimed features, and is coextensive with them, then a nexus is presumed and the burden shifts to the party asserting obviousness to present evidence to rebut the presumed nexus." Brown & Williamson Tobacco Corp. v. Philip Morris Inc., 229 F.3d 1120, 1130 (Fed. Cir. 2000). One way to rebut the presumption might be to show that other products embodying the patented invention were commercial failures; hence, the successful product must owe its success to something other than the invention. *See id.*

[279] *See Brown & Williamson*, 229 F.3d at 1130.

[280] See Section 6.3.

[281] *See* In re GPAC Inc., 57 F.3d 1573, 1580 (Fed. Cir. 1995). Here the nexus requirement is essential because the reason for a license may be nothing more than avoidance of litigation. *See Iron Grip*, 392 F.3d at 1324.

[282] *See* Advanced Display Sys., Inc. v. Kent State Univ., 212 F.3d 1272, 1285 (Fed. Cir. 2000) (failure of others); Gambro Lundia AB v. Baxter Healthcare Corp., 110 F.3d 1573, 1579–80 (Fed. Cir. 1997); In re Dow Chemical Co., 837 F.2d 469, 472 (Fed. Cir. 1988) ("Recognition of need, and difficulties encountered by those skilled in the field, are classical indicia of unobviousness."). On the other hand, "mere passage of time without the claimed invention" does not prove non-obviousness. In re Kahn, 441 F.3d 977, 990 (Fed. Cir. 2006).

also serves as evidence of non-obviousness.[283] "Unexpected results" can be useful in showing that an invention was not an obvious one, particularly where the results are unexpectedly good.[284] Finally, since imitation is the sincerest form of flattery, copying of the invention can be taken as objective evidence that the invention was not obvious.[285]

All of the secondary considerations discussed so far are potential evidence of *non-obviousness.*[286] "Near-simultaneous invention" is one secondary consideration that is positive evidence of *obviousness.* If an invention is made independently by another inventor, at nearly the same time as the applicant or patentee, this is evidence that the invention was not the result of uncommon effort or insight. Rather, the art may simply have progressed to the point where the claimed invention was the obvious next step.[287] Note that an independent near-simultaneous invention can serve as objective evidence of obviousness, even if that invention occurred shortly after the invention by the patentee or applicant, thereby disqualifying it as potential prior art under § 102.

8.9.7 Derivation (§ 102(f))

One rule of patentability that almost goes without saying is that an applicant cannot claim someone else's invention. This rule is embodied in 35 U.S.C. § 102(f), which states that a patent cannot be obtained if the applicant "did not himself invent the subject matter sought to be patented." If the purported inventor took the idea from someone else, the claim is unpatentable or, if already issued, invalid. A defense based on § 102(f) is

---

[283] *See* Ortho-McNeil Pharmaceutical, Inc. v. Mylan Labs., Inc., 520 F.3d 1358, 1365 (Fed. Cir. 2008) (expert skepticism); *Ecolochem,* 227 F.3d at 1380 (acclamation); Monarch Knitting Machinery Corp. v. Sulzer Morat GmbH, 139 F.3d 877, 885 (Fed. Cir. 1998) ("general skepticism" as evidence of non-obviousness); Gillette Co. v. S.C. Johnson & Son, Inc., 919 F.2d 720, 726 (Fed. Cir. 1990) (skepticism toward "new-fangled approach"). "Teaching away" (see Section 8.9.6) can be one form of expressing skepticism. *See Monarch Knitting,* 139 F.3d at 885 ("[i]n effect, 'teaching away' is a more pointed and probative form of skepticism").

[284] *See Ortho-McNeil,* 520 F.3d at 1365; Kao Corp. v. Unilever U.S., Inc., 441 F.3d 963, 970 (Fed. Cir. 2006); Richardson-Vicks Inc. v. Upjohn Co., 122 F.3d 1476, 1483 (Fed. Cir. 1997). Unexpected results should match the scope of the claim. Unexpected results for only a subset of a claimed range do not support the non-obviousness of the entire claimed invention. *See* In re Harris, 409 F.3d 1339, 1344 (Fed. Cir. 2005); In re Peterson, 315 F.3d 1325, 1330–31 (Fed. Cir. 2003).

[285] *Ortho-McNeil,* 520 F.3d at 1365; *Advanced Display,* 212 F.3d at 1285–86; Diversitech Corp. v. Century Steps, Inc., 850 F.2d 675, 679 (Fed. Cir. 1988). *But cf. Ecolochem,* 227 F.3d at 1380 (Copying "is only equivocal evidence of non-obviousness in the absence of more compelling objective indicia"; copying could have occurred only because of "'a general lack of concern for patent property.'").

[286] The absence of commercial success, long-felt need, and the other indicia of non-obviousness has generally been held a "neutral factor," rather than positive evidence of obviousness. *See* Gentry Gallery, Inc. v. Berkline Corp., 134 F.3d 1473, 1478 (Fed. Cir. 1998).

[287] *See Ecolochem,* 227 F.3d at 1379; In re Merk & Co., 800 F.2d 1091, 1098 (Fed. Cir. 1986).

usually referred to as a "derivation" defense, because the claim is said to be "derived" from someone else's invention.[288]

A derivation defense requires proof, by clear and convincing evidence, (1) that the invention was fully conceived by another person before it had been conceived by the purported inventor, and (2) that the conception was communicated to the purported inventor.[289] The information communicated must have been an "enabling disclosure" of the invention,[290] not merely information that could have made the invention obvious.[291]

8.10 SECTION 102(b) STATUTORY BARS

The previous discussion of § 102 concerned the effect of events occurring before the applicant's *date of invention*. The portions of § 102 that deal with these events (paragraphs (a), (e) and (g)) ensure that on the date of the applicant's invention, the invention was new. Paragraph (b) of § 102 serves a different purpose. Section 102(b) ensures that the applicant did not delay too long in filing a patent application, after the occurrence of certain key events.

Section 102(b) provides as follows:

A person shall be entitled to a patent unless—
(b) the invention was patented or described in a printed publication in this or a foreign country or in public use or on sale in this country, more than one year prior to the date of the application for patent in the United States. . . .

Section 102(b) is similar to 102(a) in that both refer to prior patents, printed publications, and public use. However, § 102(b) differs fundamentally from § 102(a) in three respects. First, § 102(b) adds the "on sale" language. Second, a § 102(b) issue often arises from the actions of the applicant, whereas a § 102(a) issue can arise only from the acts of a third party. Finally, the important date for § 102(b) is not the date of the invention, but a date exactly *one year before the patent application was filed*.[292] This date is known as the application's "critical date."

---

[288] *See* Eaton Corp. v. Rockwell Int'l Corp., 323 F.3d 1332, 1344 (Fed. Cir. 2003); Price v. Symsek, 988 F.2d 1187, 1190 (Fed. Cir. 1993).

[289] International Rectifier Corp. v. Ixys Corp., 361 F.3d 1363, 1376 (Fed. Cir. 2004); *Eaton*, 323 F.3d at 1344; Gambro Lundia AB v. Baxter Healthcare Corp., 110 F.3d 1573, 1576 (Fed. Cir. 1997). The claim of prior conception must be corroborated (see Section 8.9.3). Lacks Indus., Inc. v. McKechnie Vehicle Components USA, Inc., 322 F.3d 1335, 1349 (Fed. Cir. 2003).

[290] *Eaton*, 323 F.3d at 1344. Enabling disclosures are discussed in Section 8.6.

[291] *Gambro*, 110 F.3d at 1577–78. *Gambro* suggests that one could never base a finding of obviousness on the kind of disclosure contemplated in § 102(f). However, the Federal Circuit later decided that a § 102(f) disclosure, combined with other references, *can* lead to a finding of obviousness. Oddzon Prods., Inc. v. Just Toys, Inc., 122 F.3d 1396, 1403–04 (Fed. Cir. 1997).

[292] When prosecution results in a chain of related applications, a later application may be entitled to the effective filing date of a preceding application for purposes of § 102(b). See Section 5.2.

Imagine the following scenario. On January 1, 2000, an inventor conceives of a better mousetrap and reduces the invention to practice by constructing a prototype in his workshop. January 1, 2000 is the "date of the invention," and that date is corroborated by a witnessed laboratory notebook. The inventor submits a complete description of the mousetrap to the *Inventor's Newsletter*, which publishes the description on February 1, 2000. On February 2, 2001, the inventor files a patent application. The "critical date" of the application, under § 102(b), is February 2, 2000. The publication in the *Inventor's Newsletter* on February 1, 2000 is not prior art under § 102(a) because it did not occur before the applicant's date of invention. However, the publication did occur before the "critical date." Consequently, if the publication included a complete and enabling description of the invention, the patent application would be rejected under § 102(b).

In essence, § 102(b) provides a one-year grace period after the first patent, publication, public use, or offer to sell that relates to the claimed invention.[293] An inventor has that long to file a patent application, or the right to a patent is lost. Any problems that might arise from the inventor's own activities can be avoided simply by ensuring that a patent application is on file within one year of the date of invention. This practice should be adopted by all inventors, though frequently it is not.

The rationale for § 102(b) is threefold. First, and most generally, it encourages diligence by penalizing inventors who are lazy, or inclined to suppress their inventions, or who for some other reason delay in filing a patent application.[294] Second, it prevents the public from being misled where the availability of the invention to the public, without evidence that the inventor intends to obtain a patent, might create the impression that the invention is up for grabs.[295] Finally, it prevents what could be an unwarranted extension of the inventor's monopoly powers beyond the 20 years contemplated by the patent system.[296] If there were no § 102(b), an inventor might delay seeking patent protection indefinitely, and the mere threat that he would do so eventually could prevent potential competitors from daring to compete. On the other hand, an inventor does need a certain amount of time to perfect

---

[293] *See* Gemmy Indus. Corp. v. Chrisha Creations Ltd., 452 F.3d 1353, 1358 (Fed. Cir. 2006); Woodland Trust v. Flowertree Nursery, Inc., 148 F.3d 1368, 1370 (Fed. Cir. 1998).

[294] *See* Special Devices, Inc. v. OEA, Inc., 270 F.3d 1353, 1357 (Fed. Cir. 2001); La Bounty Mfg., Inc. v. U.S. Int'l Trade Comm'n, 958 F.2d 1066, 1071 (Fed. Cir. 1992) ("The general purpose behind [the] section 102(b) bars is to require inventors to assert with due diligence their right to a patent through the prompt filing of a patent application.").

[295] *See* Continental Plastic Containers v. Owens Brockway Plastic Prods., Inc., 141 F.3d 1073, 1079 (Fed. Cir. 1998) ("[t]he primary policy underlying the 'public use' case is that of detrimental public reliance"); Baxter Int'l, Inc. v. Cobe Labs., Inc., 88 F.3d 1054, 1058 (Fed. Cir. 1996).

[296] *See* Atlanta Attachment Co. v. Leggett & Platt, Inc., 516 F.3d 1361, 1365 (Fed. Cir. 2008) ("The overriding concern of the on-sale bar is an inventor's attempt to commercialize his invention beyond the statutory term."); *Continental Plastic*, 141 F.3d at 1079.

the invention, judge whether it is worth pursuing, and prepare a patent application.[297] Section 102(b) establishes one year as the period that most effectively balances the needs of the inventor against the needs of the public.

The prohibitions of § 102(b) are commonly known as "statutory bars." A statutory bar can prevent the issuance of a claim in a patent application, or it can be used to challenge the validity of an issued patent in subsequent infringement litigation. A reference that qualifies under § 102(b) can also be used as the basis for a finding of obviousness.[298] In some cases, a reference can qualify as prior art under either § 102(a) or § 102(b). If so, § 102(b) can provide the simpler analysis since it relies on the easily determined "critical date" of the patent application, rather than the often difficult to determine "date of invention."

8.10.1 "On-Sale Bar"

The most frequently encountered statutory bar is probably the "on-sale bar" created when the inventor, or a third party,[299] takes steps to commercialize the claimed invention more than one year before the filing date of the patent application.[300] A single sale, or a single offer to sell, is sufficient to invoke the statutory bar.[301]

Disputes frequently arise over whether certain activity did or did not constitute a sale or definite offer to sell. For example, an inventor may contend that a commercial relationship with a potential customer was not related to a bona fide sale of patented product, but rather to joint development effort.

---

[297] *See Baxter Int'l,* 88 F.3d at 1058 (policies behind § 102(b) include "'allowing the inventor a reasonable amount of time following sales activity to determine the potential economic value of a patent'").

[298] *See* Dippin' Dots, Inc. v. Mosey, 476 F.3d 1337, 1344 (Fed. Cir. 2007); Elmer v. ICC Fabricating, Inc., 67 F.3d 1571, 1574 (Fed. Cir. 1995).

[299] *See* Special Devices, Inc. v. OEA, Inc., 270 F.3d 1353, 1355 (Fed. Cir. 2001) ("By phrasing the statutory bar in the passive voice, Congress indicated that it does not matter who places the invention 'on sale'; it only matters that someone—inventor, supplier or other third party—placed it on sale.").

[300] *See* Atlanta Attachment Co. v. Leggett & Platt, Inc., 516 F.3d 1361, 1365 (Fed. Cir. 2008) ("Our patent laws deny a patent to an inventor who applies for a patent more than one year after making an attempt to profit from his invention by putting it on sale."); Honeywell Int'l Inc. v. Universal Avionics Sys. Corp., 488 F.3d 982, 998 (Fed. Cir. 2007).

[301] Electromotive Div. of General Motors Corp. v. Transportation Sys. Div. of General Electric Co., 417 F.3d 1203, 1209 (Fed. Cir. 2005). An offer to sell must be so definite and final that, applying traditional principles of contract law, acceptance of that offer would form a binding contract. *See* MEMC Elec. Materials, Inc. v. Mitsubishi Materials Silicon Corp., 420 F.3d 1369, 1376 (Fed. Cir. 2005) (emails with technical data did not include price terms); Lacks Indus., Inc. v. McKechnie Vehicle Components USA, Inc., 322 F.3d 1335, 1347–48 (Fed. Cir. 2003); Group One, Ltd. v. Hallmark Cards, Inc., 254 F.3d 1041, 1046 (Fed. Cir. 2001). The *offer* itself is sufficient even if no sale was completed. Cargill, Inc. v. Canbra Foods, Ltd., 476 F.3d 1359, 1370 (Fed. Cir. 2007); Scaltech, Inc. v. Retec/Tetra, L.L.C., 269 F.3d 1321, 1328 (Fed. Cir. 2001).

In *Continental Can Co. v. Monsanto Co.*,[302] a plastics company entered into an agreement with the Coca-Cola Company to develop a plastic bottle. Under the agreement, the companies would work together to produce a suitable bottle, with the plastics company making the bottles and Coca-Cola testing them. If a satisfactory bottle were developed, Coca-Cola would purchase the bottles from the plastics company, under terms that were partially negotiated. The plastics company produced bottles in a variety of shapes, including one that allegedly embodied the patent claim in question, but the project was abandoned when tests proved unsuccessful.[303] Although the trial court found that the relationship had placed the patented bottle "on sale" before the critical date, the Federal Circuit disagreed and reversed:

> Although Admiral Plastic's hope was surely commercial sales, and the record shows that prices and quantities were discussed, this does not of itself place the subject matter "on sale" in the sense of § 102(b). The . . . bottle was a part of a terminated development project that never bore commercial fruit and was cloaked in confidentiality. While the line is not always bright between development and being on sale . . . in this case the line was not crossed.[304]

A transaction does not constitute a bar under § 102(b) if it is part of an "experimental use"—that is, if the primary object of the "sale" was not to profit from the invention, but to test it in the field.[305] Although a court will consider a variety of factors in deciding if a sale was for purposes of commerce or of experiment,[306] at a minimum the seller must inform the

---

[302] 948 F.2d 1264 (Fed. Cir. 1991).

[303] *See id.* at 1269.

[304] *Id.* at 1270. A sale or offer to sell must be to a separate entity. A transaction between related corporations completed purely for accounting purposes would not constitute a genuine "sale," at least if the "selling" entity "so controls the purchaser that the invention remains out of the public's hands." *See* Ferag AG v. Quipp, Inc., 45 F.3d 1562, 1567 (Fed. Cir. 1995). On the other hand, sales *to the patentee* by an independent supplier, not for purposes of experiment or development but in preparation for release to the general public, can invalidate a patent. *See Special Devices,* 270 F.3d at 1355–57. Licensing someone to practice the invention (see Section 6.3) is not a sale that triggers § 102(b). Elan Corp. v. Andrx Pharmaceuticals, Inc. 366 F.3d 1336, 1341 (Fed. Cir. 2004); In re Kollar, 286 F.3d 1326, 1330–34 (Fed. Cir. 2002).

[305] *See* Pfaff v. Wells Elecs., Inc., 525 U.S. 55, 64 (1998) ("[A]n inventor who seeks to perfect his discovery may conduct extensive testing without losing his right to obtain a patent for his invention—even if such testing occurs in the public eye. The law has long recognized the distinction between inventions put to experimental use and products sold commercially."); *Electromotive,* 417 F.3d at 1210; EZ Dock, Inc. v. Schafer Sys., Inc., 276 F.3d 1347, 1352–53 (Fed. Cir. 2002) (sale may have been primarily to test dock in rougher waters). To qualify as experimental, the transaction must have been primarily for purposes of experimentation, rather than profit. *Electromotive,* 417 F.3d at 1210; Allen Eng'g Corp. v. Bartell Indus., Inc., 299 F.3d 1336, 1352–53 (Fed. Cir. 2002). Sales may have been experimental even though they did not result in any changes to the claimed invention. Honeywell Int'l Inc. v. Universal Avionics Sys. Corp., 488 F.3d 982, 997 (Fed. Cir. 2007).

[306] *See Electromotive,* 417 F.3d at 1213 (listing 13 nonexclusive factors).

purchaser that the goods are experimental, and the seller must retain sufficient control over the goods to conduct the required monitoring or tests.[307] A court will also consider whether payment was made, whether the seller kept the kind of records that would suggest experimentation, and whether the seller required the purchaser to keep the activities confidential.[308] Keeping track of customer responses and complaints after sale of a new product is not sufficient to show that the sales were primarily experimental.[309] Moreover, the experiments have to relate to the *claimed invention*. If the experiments relate to some other aspect of a product, or if they are nothing more than marketing tests to gauge consumer demand, the sale is not within the experimental use exception.[310]

One issue that long divided opinion is the extent to which the invention must be complete before it can be offered for sale in a manner triggering § 102(b).[311] The Supreme Court eventually decreed, in *Pfaff v. Wells Electronics, Inc.*,[312] that the invention must be "ready for patenting" before the critical date in order for a sale or offer to sell to be invalidating.[313] Once the invention is "ready for patenting," there is no excuse to delay (more than one year) filing a patent application. One way to demonstrate that the invention was ready for patenting is an actual reduction to practice.[314] An inventor who has reduced the invention to practice—building the claimed apparatus or performing the claimed method—should be ready to prepare the kind of enabling disclosure required in a patent application.[315] Alternatively, one can

---

[307] *See id.* at 1213–14; Paragon Podiatry Lab., Inc. v. KLM Labs., Inc. 984 F.2d 1182, 1186–87 (Fed. Cir. 1993); La Bounty Mfg., Inc. v. U.S. Int'l Trade Comm'n, 958 F.2d 1066, 1071–72 (Fed. Cir. 1992).

[308] *See* Eli Lilly & Co. v. Zenith Goldline Pharmaceuticals, Inc., 471 F.3d 1369, 1381 (Fed. Cir. 2006); *Allen Eng'g*, 299 F.3d at 1353–55; U.S. Environmental Prods. Inc. v. Westall, 911 F.2d 713, 717 (Fed. Cir. 1990). An inventor's subjective intent to experiment is not relevant. *See Electromotive*, 417 F.3d at 1212.

[309] *See Paragon*, 984 F.2d at 1187–88.

[310] *See* Dippin' Dots, Inc. v. Mosey, 476 F.3d 1337, 1344 (Fed. Cir. 2007); Smithkline Beecham Corp. v. Apotex Corp., 365 F.3d 1306, 1317 (Fed. Cir. 2004); In re Smith, 714 F.2d 1127, 1135–36 (Fed. Cir. 1983). Testing features that are not mentioned in the claim but that are *inherent* to the invention—such as durability—may suffice. *See Electromotive*, 417 F.3d at 1211–12.

[311] *See, e.g.,* UMC Elecs. Co. v. United States, 816 F.2d 647 (Fed. Cir. 1987) (where the majority held that an invention need not be reduced to practice to be offered for sale, and Judge Smith penned a sharp dissent).

[312] 525 U.S. 55 (1998).

[313] *Id.* at 67. The court speaks of the invention being "ready for patenting" *before the critical date*, rather than before the date of the offer to sell. *Id.* This suggests that the event triggering the commencement of the one-year grace period could be the event that makes the invention "ready for patenting" (such as a reduction to practice), if that event occurs subsequent to the offer.

[314] *Id.*; *Atlanta Attachment*, 516 F.3d at 1366–67; *Honeywell*, 488 F.3d at 997. An invention cannot, under any circumstances, be offered for sale before the date on which it was *conceived*. Sparton Corp. v. United States, 399 F.3d 1321, 1324 (Fed. Cir. 2005).

[315] See Section 8.6.

demonstrate that an invention was ready for patenting through "drawings or other descriptions of the invention that were sufficiently specific to enable a person skilled in the art to practice the invention."[316] If these "descriptions" were available to the inventor, they could have been incorporated in a patent application. Consequently, an offer to sell an invention that has yet to be built can bar or invalidate a subsequent patent. In *Pfaff*, for example, the inventor had such confidence in his ability to proceed directly from an engineering drawing to a finished product that he offered to sell the product in large quantities before any had been made.[317] The drawing showed that the invention was ready for patenting, so the offer, before the critical date, invalidated the patent.

8.10.2 Public Use Bar

Public use of the claimed invention before the application's critical date can also operate as a bar under § 102(b). A use of the invention by any person, other than the inventor, who is under no obligation of secrecy may constitute a "public use" of the invention.[318] It is "public use" even if not communicated to a wider public, as was likely true in the celebrated case of a corset steel used by the lady friend of the man who invented it.[319] On the other hand, because § 102(b) refers to "public" use, a use that is observed only by persons under an obligation of secrecy does not invoke the statutory bar.[320] The public use bar is subject to the same experimental use exception

---

[316] *Pfaff*, 525 U.S. at 67. An invention may be fully conceived but not yet ready for patenting if the development necessary for putting the invention to practice is incomplete. *See* Space Sys./Loral, Inc. v. Lockheed Martin Corp., 271 F.3d 1076, 1080–81 (Fed. Cir. 2001). On the other hand, the invention can be ready for patenting even if the inventor does not yet have perfect confidence that it will work. *See* Robotic Vision Sys., Inc. v. View Eng'g, Inc., 249 F.3d 1307, 1312 (Fed. Cir. 2001) ("It will be a rare case indeed in which an inventor has no uncertainty concerning the workability of his invention before he has reduced it to practice."). Whether an invention was "ready for patenting" or "not quite ready for patenting" is certain to be a matter of frequent dispute.

[317] *See Pfaff*, 525 U.S. at 58. As the inventor testified at his deposition: "Q. It was in a drawing. Is that correct? A. Strictly in a drawing. Went from the drawing to the hard tooling. That's the way I do my business. Q. Boom-boom? A. You got it. Q. You are satisfied, obviously, when you come up with some drawings that it is going to go–'it works'? A. I know what I am doing, yes, most of the time." *Id.* at 58 n.3.

[318] American Seating Co. v. USSC Gp., Inc., 514 F.3d 1262, 1267 (Fed. Cir. 2008); Adenta GmbH v. OrthoArm, Inc., 501 F.3d 1364, 1371 (Fed. Cir. 2007); Motionless Keyboard Co. v. Microsoft Corp., 486 F.3d 1376, 1384 (Fed. Cir. 2007). The public use bar is said to "discourage 'the removal of inventions from the public domain which the public justifiably comes to believe are freely available.'" *American Seating*, 514 F.3d at 1267.

[319] Egbert v. Lippman, 104 U.S. 333 (1881); *see also Motionless Keyboard*, 486 F.3d at 1384.

[320] *See Motionless Keyboard*, 486 F.3d at 1385 (keyboard tester had signed a nondisclosure agreement); Eli Lilly & Co. v. Zenith Goldline Pharmaceuticals, Inc., 471 F.3d 1369, 1381 (Fed. Cir. 2006) (restricted access to information on drug tests).

as the on-sale bar.[321] Some inventions must be tested in a more or less public environment, and if it is clear that the use is experimental it will not invalidate a claim.[322]

When the inventor demonstrates his invention to a few friends or associates, the determination of whether such use was "public" can be difficult. In *Moleculon Research Corp. v. CBS, Inc.*,[323] the inventor displayed a model of his cube puzzle to a few university colleagues. The "personal relationships and surrounding circumstances" were sufficient for the court to find that the inventor had retained control over the invention and the distribution of information concerning it, even though there was no express agreement of confidentiality.[324] In contrast, a jury in *Beachcombers v. Wildwood Creative Products, Inc.*[325] found that a demonstration of an improved kaleidoscope to 20 to 30 party guests was a public use, and the Federal Circuit affirmed. The purpose of the demonstration was "getting feedback on the device," and the host made no efforts toward secrecy.[326]

Although it does not fit neatly in the categories of "public use" or "on-sale," a commercial use of the invention by the applicant before the critical date, even if that use does not make the invention itself a matter of public knowledge, is considered sufficient to invoke the statutory bar.[327] Suppose, for example, that the applicant invented a more efficient method of manufacturing copper wire. If the finished product resembled any other copper wire, no one outside of the factory might know anything of the improved process. Nevertheless, if the applicant used that process, and profited from it, prior to

---

[321] *See* Honeywell Int'l Inc. v. Universal Avionics Sys. Corp., 488 F.3d 982, 998 (Fed. Cir. 2007); *Eli Lilly*, 471 F.3d at 1381. The "ready for patenting" test of *Pfaff* applies here as well. Invitrogen Corp. v. Biocrest Mfg., LP, 424 F.3d 1374, 1379 (Fed. Cir. 2005).

[322] *See* Pfaff v. Wells Electronics, Inc., 525 U.S. 55, 64 (1998); Netscape Communications Corp. v. Konrad, 295 F.3d 1315, 1320 (Fed. Cir. 2002); Allied Colloids Inc. v. American Cyanamid Co., 64 F.2d 1570, 1574 (Fed. Cir. 1995).

[323] 793 F.2d 1261 (Fed. Cir. 1986).

[324] *Id.* at 1266; *see also American Seating*, 514 F.3d at 1268 (limited group who saw the invention "shared a general understanding of confidentiality"); *Invitrogen*, 424 F.3d at 1381 (confidentiality obligations need not be express); Bernhardt, L.L.C. v. Collezione Europa USA, Inc., 386 F.3d 1371, 1381 (Fed. Cir. 2004).

[325] 31 F.3d 1154 (Fed. Cir. 1994).

[326] *Id.* at 1160.

[327] *See American Seating*, 514 F.3d at 1267 (bar applies if invention is publicly accessible *or* "commercially exploited"); *Invitrogen*, 424 F.3d at 1382 ("secrecy of use alone is not sufficient to show that existing knowledge has not been withdrawn from public use: commercial exploitation is also forbidden"); Special Devices, Inc. v. OEA, Inc., 270 F.3d 1353, 1357 (Fed. Cir. 2001); Woodland Trust v. Flowertree Nursery, Inc., 148 F.3d 1368, 1370–71 (Fed. Cir. 1998). Sometimes the bar is characterized as an on-sale bar, sometimes as a public use bar. *See Special Devices*, 270 F.3d at 1357 (characterizing *Woodland Trust* as referring to the on-sale bar); *Woodland Trust*, 148 F.3d at 1998 (citing cases referring to "public use"). In the paradoxical words of *Kinzenbaw v. Deere & Co.*, 741 F.2d 383, 390 (Fed. Cir. 1984), "[a] commercial use is a public use even if it is kept secret."

the critical date of the patent application, the Federal Circuit has held that such use forfeits the right to obtain a patent.[328] Here there is a difference between the activities of the patent applicant and unrelated third parties. If a third party made commercial use of the method before the applicant's critical date, but such use did not disclose the invention to the public, § 102(b) does not apply.[329] Perhaps the distinction exists because an inventor's own secret but commercial use, or a third party's non-secret commercial use, can put the inventor on notice of the need to file promptly.[330] A secret third-party use, on the other hand, could catch the inventor off guard.

8.11 OTHER STATUTORY BARS (§ 102(c), (d))

A similar type of "statutory bar" is created by 35 U.S.C. § 102(d), which provides as follows:

A person shall be entitled to a patent unless—
(d) the invention was first patented or caused to be patented, or was the subject of an inventor's certificate, by the applicant or his legal representatives or assigns in a foreign country prior to the date of the application for patent in this country on an application for patent or inventor's certificate filed more than twelve months before the filing of the application in the United States. . . .

Simply put, an inventor who applies for a patent in a foreign country, waits more than twelve months before filing in the United States, and receives the foreign patent before filing in the United States, will be denied a United States patent.[331] As in the case of § 102(b), § 102(d) promotes diligence in filing and prevents the extension of the patent monopoly.[332] Anyone who applies for a patent in a foreign country and plans to obtain a United States patent is well advised to file in the United States no more than 12 months later, thereby avoiding the risk that the foreign patent will be granted sooner than expected.

Finally, one other rarely used form of "statutory bar" arises from § 102(c), which provides that an inventor is not entitled to a patent if "he

---

[328] *See* D.L. Auld Co. v. Chroma Graphics Corp., 714 F.2d 1144, 1147–48 (Fed. Cir. 1983) (secret commercial use by "applicant for patent or his assignee" triggers § 102(b)). Sale of a product that *embodies* the patented invention, without, somehow, disclosing it, triggers § 102(b) regardless of who sold it. In re Epstein, 32 F.3d 1559, 1568 (Fed. Cir. 1994); J.A. LaPorte, Inc. v. Norfolk Dredging Co., 787 F.2d 1577, 1583 (Fed. Cir. 1986). Perhaps that is because the sale of the claimed invention itself does not straddle the "public use" and "on-sale" bars as problematically as the sale of a product made by a secret *process*.

[329] *Woodland Trust*, 148 F.3d at 1371 ("when an asserted prior use is not that of the applicant, § 102(b) is not a bar when that prior use or knowledge is not available to the public").

[330] *See Special Devices*, 270 F.3d at 1355.

[331] *See* Bayer AG v. Schein Pharmaceuticals, Inc., 301 F.3d 1306, 1312 (Fed. Cir. 2002).

[332] *See* In re Kathawala, 9 F.3d 942, 947 (Fed. Cir. 1993).

has abandoned the invention."[333] "Abandoning the invention" means abandoning the right to *patent* the invention. Mere delay in filing a patent application does not show that the invention was "abandoned,"[334] although it can have important consequences in a priority contest under § 102(g),[335] and it can allow the imposition of an on-sale or similar bar under § 102(b). However, if an inventor were to announce to the public that he would not patent his invention, such an announcement might constitute an abandonment.[336]

8.12 DOUBLE PATENTING

An inventor is entitled to one patent on one invention.[337] If more than one patent could be obtained on the same invention, an inventor could extend the period of exclusivity beyond what the law intends.[338] For example, an inventor could apply for one patent in 2005 and a second on the same invention in 2015, thereby obtaining the equivalent of a 30-year patent. To prevent this result, a claim can be held unpatentable or invalid if it duplicates the subject matter of a claim in an earlier patent to the same inventor. This is known as "double patenting." Double patenting can also be found where the claims are attributable to different "inventive entities"[339] but are owned by a common assignee.[340]

Double patenting comes in two forms. The first is "same invention" double patenting, which means that the later claim is substantially identical in scope to the earlier claim.[341] The prohibition against "same invention" double patenting is said to have a statutory basis in 35 U.S.C. § 101, which states that "[w]hoever invents or discovers any new and useful process . . . may obtain *a* patent therefor."[342] The more common form of double patenting is "obviousness-type double patenting," which means that the later claim, though not identical, is only an obvious variation of the earlier claim.[343] The reasoning behind this prohibition is that once a patent has expired, the public should be

---

[333] *See* Oddzon Prods., Inc. v. Just Toys, Inc., 122 F.2d 1396, 1402 (Fed. Cir. 1997).

[334] *See* Paulik v. Rizkalla, 760 F.2d 1270, 1272 (Fed. Cir. 1985) ("'the mere lapse of time' will not prevent the inventor from receiving a patent").

[335] See Section 8.9.1.3.

[336] An *application* can be "abandoned" and then refiled, without abandoning the invention in terms of § 102(c). The abandonment could, however, sacrifice the early filing date of the application for purposes of § 102(b).

[337] Perricone v. Medicis Pharmaceutical Corp., 432 F.3d 1368, 1373 (Fed. Cir. 2005); Geneva Pharmaceuticals, Inc. v. Glaxosmithkline PLC, 349 F.3d 1373, 1377 (Fed. Cir. 2003).

[338] *See* AstraZeneca AB v. KV Pharmaceutical Co., 494 F.3d 1011, 1016 (Fed. Cir. 2007); *Perricone*, 432 F.3d at 1372; In re Goodman, 11 F.3d 1046, 1053 (Fed. Cir. 1993).

[339] See Section 8.9.4.

[340] *See AstraZeneca*, 494 F.3d at 1016; In re Longi, 759 F.2d 887, 893 (Fed. Cir. 1985).

[341] *See* In re Lonardo, 119 F.3d 960, 965 (Fed. Cir. 1997); *Goodman*, 11 F.3d at 1052; *Longi*, 759 F.2d at 892.

[342] *See Perricone*, 432 F.3d at 1372–73.

[343] *See AstraZeneca*, 494 F.3d at 1016; *Perricone*, 432 F.3d at 1373; Eli Lilly & Co. v. Barr Labs., Inc., 251 F.3d 955, 967–68 (Fed. Cir. 2001).

at liberty to use not only the precise invention claimed, but also variations that would be obvious to one of ordinary skill.[344]

Issues of obviousness-type double patenting often arise where an inventor seeks to patent both a broad genus and a narrow species of that genus. For example, an inventor might conceive of both a generic design for a new mouse-trap and a specific variation of that design using a particularly sensitive trigger. If the inventor obtained a patent on the broad invention first and then sought a patent on the variation or improvement, the question would be whether the variation was obvious in light of the more general design. If not, the inventor would be entitled to both patents.[345] On the other hand, if the inventor obtained the narrower patent first and the broader patent second, the second patent would almost certainly be held "obvious" in light of the first.[346] This result conforms with the rule derived in the context of § 102 that a claim to a genus is anticipated if a single species of that genus is found in the prior art.[347]

On rare occasions the inventor actually filed the application for the broader patent *first,* and it issued second only because of delays in prosecution over which the inventor had no control. Under these circumstances, the second patent has been denied only if each claimed invention would be obvious in light of the other—a so-called two-way test of obviousness.[348] While this can result in an extension of the patent monopoly beyond the contemplated period, where it was not the patentee's fault the extension is not "unjustified."[349] Note that the term of patents applied for after June 7, 1995 runs from their filing date rather than their issue date, as was previously the case, so this particular concern will eventually be eliminated.

---

[344] *See Geneva Pharmaceuticals,* 349 F.3d at 1378; *Lonardo,* 119 F.3d at 965; *Longi,* 759 F.2d at 892–93.

[345] It is true that the combination of both patents, issued at different times, might prevent anyone from making the specific mousetrap for a period of more than 20 years. This is not improper. If one product embodies several distinct patentable inventions, each such invention can result in a patent. When a particular patent expires, that invention is available to the public *as long as* it is practiced in a way that does not violate some other patent. *See* In re Kaplan, 789 F.2d 1574, 1577–78 (Fed. Cir. 1986).

[346] *See Perricone,* 432 F.3d at 1374 (double patenting where second patent claimed a treatment for skin damage, and the earlier patent claimed the same treatment for sunburn—a species of skin damage).

[347] See Section 8.9.5. Although this is classified as an instance of "obviousness-type" double patenting, *see Goodman,* 11 F.3d at 1052–53, one can conceive of cases in which the full scope of a genus is not obvious merely from the disclosure of a species of the genus. Perhaps this would be better classified as "anticipation-type" double patenting. *See Eli Lilly,* 251 F.3d at 968 (claim in second patent is not "patentably distinct . . . if the later claim is obvious over, or anticipated by, the earlier claim").

[348] A "two-way" approach for obviousness-type double patenting is also adopted whenever when one of the patents at issue is a utility patent and the other is a design patent. *See* In re Dembiczak, 175 F.3d 994, 1002 (Fed. Cir. 1999).

[349] In re Braat, 937 F.2d 589, 595 (Fed. Cir. 1991). The "two-way" test is not appropriate if the applicant is at least partially responsible for the delay in issuing the first-filed application. *See Eli Lilly,* 251 F.3d at 968 n.7. Nor is it appropriate if the applicant could have filed all of the claims in one application. *See* In re Berg, 140 F.3d 1428, 1434 (Fed. Cir. 1998).

Obviousness-type double patenting can be cured, in a sense, by filing a "terminal disclaimer" with the Patent Office.[350] A terminal disclaimer is a binding statement that (1) a later patent will expire at the same time as a prior patent, and (2) the later patent will be enforceable only as long as it and the prior patent are commonly owned.[351] The voluntary curtailment of the term of the second patent removes any concern that the existence of two similar patents will improperly extend the duration of the patent monopoly. The requirement of common ownership eliminates the additional risk that the two similar patents might be assigned to different parties, each of whom could press duplicative and harassing claims against a potential infringer.[352]

The terminal disclaimer mechanism provides inventors with some incentive to further develop their patented ideas, even in ways that might be considered obvious, and to disclose those developments to the public through additional patents.[353] This procedure applies only to obviousness-type double patenting; "same invention" double patenting cannot be remedied by a terminal disclaimer. A terminal disclaimer is also no protection against grounds of invalidity other than double patenting.[354]

Sometimes related patents will issue as the result of a "restriction requirement."[355] A restriction requirement results when the patent examiner, during prosecution, finds that an application claims two or more distinct inventions. The applicant must elect which invention to pursue in the pending application, and if the applicant wishes to pursue one of the other inventions, the applicant must file a "divisional" application. That application and the original application may each result in a patent. Because, in this case, the existence of two separate patents is attributable to the Patent Office's determination that each application represents a distinct invention, the patents are immune from a challenge of double patenting.[356] A different result would be unfair to the applicant. But if the claims of the separate applications evolve during the course of prosecution, as they sometimes do, the applicant must maintain "consonance"—that is, the claims cannot be changed in such a way that what was formerly patentably distinct is no longer so. If "consonance" is lost, so is the immunity from double patenting.[357]

---

[350] *See* 35 U.S.C. § 253; *Perricone*, 432 F.3d at 1375; *Goodman*, 11 F.3d at 1052; *Longi*, 759 F.2d at 894.

[351] *See* 37 C.F.R. § 1.321(c); In re Van Ornum, 696 F.2d 937, 944–48 (C.C.P.A. 1982).

[352] *See Van Ornum*, 686 F.2d at 944–45.

[353] *See* Quad Environmental Technologies Corp. v. Union Sanitary Dist., 946 F.2d 870, 873 (Fed. Cir. 1991).

[354] *See id.* at 874.

[355] See Section 5.3.

[356] *See* 35 U.S.C. § 121; *Geneva Pharmaceuticals*, 349 F.3d at 1378; Applied Materials, Inc. v. Advanced Semiconductor Materials America, Inc., 98 F.3d 1563, 1568 (Fed. Cir. 1996); Gerber Garment Technology, Inc. v. Lectra Sys., Inc., 916 F.2d 683, 687 (Fed. Cir. 1990).

[357] *See Geneva Pharmaceuticals*, 349 F.3d at 1381; *Gerber*, 916 F.2d at 688.

CHAPTER 9

Enforceability Defenses

Certain defenses to a claim of patent infringement produce, if successful, a holding that the patent is "unenforceable" rather than invalid. The most important of these are the inequitable conduct and misuse defenses.[1] If a patent is unenforceable, it cannot be the basis of an infringement claim.

9.1 INEQUITABLE CONDUCT

In court proceedings, the adversarial system keeps litigants honest. If a party shades the truth or withholds important evidence from the court, the other party will expose the error, if it can. As discussed in Section 5.1, patent prosecution is *ex parte*, meaning that persons who might oppose the issuance of a patent have no opportunity to participate. So when applicants misrepresent the facts, there is no one to contradict them. The Patent Office must rely heavily on information provided by applicants. An applicant's sales activities, for example, might be enough to raise a statutory bar under § 102(b),[2] but the patent examiner generally knows about those activities only what the applicant chooses to tell. Nevertheless, every issued patent enjoys a presumption of validity.

---

[1] Transferring ownership of a patent subject to a terminal disclaimer, contrary to the requirement that patents linked by a terminal disclaimer remain commonly owned, might also create an unenforceability defense. See Section 8.12.

[2] See Section 8.10.1.

Because applicants could take unfair advantage of this situation, they are charged with a duty of candor more demanding than what is normally expected of parties in an adversarial proceeding.[3] Applicants must disclose to the patent examiner any information that is "material" to the issuance of the patent.[4] Applicants do not have to *search* for such information. They do not, for example, have to search the prior art for potentially invalidating references.[5] But an applicant aware of such a reference must inform the patent examiner. This duty extends to the applicant, to the applicant's attorneys, and to anyone else who has substantial involvement in the application process.[6] Failure to meet the required duty of candor is known as "inequitable conduct."

Inequitable conduct may be raised as a defense in patent infringement litigation, and, if it is proven, the patent will be held unenforceable.[7] Although technically the patent may not be *invalid*, the effect is much the same, with one important exception. If a single claim of a patent is invalid, the remaining claims of the patent survive if they do not suffer the same defect.[8] In contrast, if an applicant obtained a single patent claim through inequitable conduct, the *entire patent* is unenforceable.[9] This result often

---

[3] *See* Honeywell Int'l Inc. v. Universal Avionics Sys. Corp., 488 F.3d 982, 999 (Fed. Cir. 2007) ("Applicants for patents have a duty to prosecute patent applications in the Patent Office with candor, good faith, and honesty.").

[4] 37 C.F.R. § 1.56.

[5] *See* Frazier v. Roessel Cine Photo Tech., Inc., 417 F.3d 1230, 1238 (Fed. Cir. 2005); Brasseler, U.S.A. I, L.P. v. Stryker Sales Corp., 267 F.3d 1370, 1382 (Fed. Cir. 2001); FMC Corp. v. Hennessy Indus., Inc., 836 F.2d 521, 526 n.6 (Fed. Cir. 1987). The "possibility that material information may exist" is not enough to trigger a duty to inquire; there must be some clue "suggest[ing] the existence of specific information the materiality of which may be ascertained with reasonable inquiry." *Brasseler*, 267 F.3d at 1382. On the other hand, an applicant cannot cultivate ignorance if there are sufficient warnings of invalidating prior art. *See* Bruno Independent Living Aids, Inc. v. Acorn Mobility Servs., Ltd., 394 F.3d 1348, 1352 (Fed. Cir. 2005) ("'an applicant who knew of the art or information cannot intentionally avoid learning of its materiality . . . it may be found that the applicant "should have known" of that materiality'"); Hewlett-Packard Co. v. Bausch & Lomb Inc., 882 F.2d 1556, 1562 (Fed. Cir. 1989) (wrongful intent may be inferred from evidence of "studied ignorance"). Usually an attorney can rely on information provided by the applicant, unless there is reason to doubt its accuracy or completeness. *See Brasseler*, 267 F.3d at 1382–83 ("[t]here is no need for an attorney to pursue a fishing expedition").

[6] 37 C.F.R. § 1.56(c); Evident Corp. v. Church & Dwight Co., 399 F.3d 1310, 1315-16 (Fed. Cir. 2005); *Brasseler*, 267 F.3d at 1383 n.6. Note that "inventors represented by counsel are presumed to know the law." *Id.* at 1385.

[7] Liquid Dynamics Corp. v. Vaughan Co., Inc., 449 F.3d 1209, 1226 (Fed. Cir. 2006).

[8] 35 U.S.C. § 288.

[9] Impax Labs., Inc. v. Aventis Pharmaceuticals Inc., 468 F.3d 1366, 1375 (Fed. Cir. 2006); Pharmacia Corp. v. Par Pharmaceuticals, Inc., 417 F.3d 1369, 1374–75 (Fed. Cir. 2005); Baxter Int'l, Inc. v. McGaw, Inc., 149 F.3d 1321, 1332 (Fed. Cir. 1998) ("It is . . . settled law that inequitable conduct with respect to one claim renders the entire patent unenforceable."). Unenforceability can even extend to another patent if the patents are sufficiently related. This is sometimes called "infectious unenforceability." *See Baxter*, 149 F.3d at 1327.

makes inequitable conduct a more attractive defense than, for example, anticipation, even though both defenses could rely on the same prior art reference.

An inequitable conduct defense can be based on a misrepresentation made to the Patent Office, or a withholding of information.[10] In either case, two elements must be proven: *materiality* and *intent*.[11] Both standards have been subject to conflicting definitions over the years, suggesting that the courts have had difficulty in defining the conduct that should be considered inequitable.

"Materiality" means that the information withheld or misrepresented was of sufficient importance to warrant the penalties associated with inequitable conduct. One test of materiality is whether there is a *substantial likelihood* that a *reasonable patent examiner* would have considered the information *important* in deciding whether the application should issue as a patent.[12] Information can be material as defined by this test even if, ultimately, the examiner would have decided that the patent should issue.[13] This test has often been adopted by the Federal Circuit as the threshold test of materiality. If the withheld or misrepresented information does not meet this threshold, the inequitable conduct defense necessarily fails.

The source of the "reasonable examiner" standard was the Patent Office's own Rule 56, which changed in 1992 to adopt a new definition of materiality. According to the new definition, information is material if, by itself or in combination with other information, it is inconsistent with a position taken by the applicant, or it is sufficient to establish a *prima facie* case of unpatentability.[14] The latter means that the information initially compels a conclusion of unpatentability (under a preponderance-of-the-evidence burden of proof), before any evidence in favor of patentability is

---

[10] *See Honeywell,* 488 F.3d at 999; Cargill, Inc. v. Canbra Foods, Ltd., 476 F.3d 1359, 1363 (Fed. Cir. 2007); Flex-Rest, LLC v. Steelcase, Inc., 455 F.3d 1351, 1362 (Fed. Cir. 2006).

[11] *Honeywell,* 488 F.3d at 999; *Brasseler,* 267 F.3d at 1379-80; PerSeptive Biosystems, Inc. v. Pharmacia Biotech, Inc., 225 F.3d 1315, 1318–19 (Fed. Cir. 2000). The party challenging the patent must prove both materiality and intent by "clear and convincing" evidence. Dippin' Dots, Inc. v. Mosey, 476 F.3d 1337, 1345 (Fed. Cir. 2007); *Flex-Rest,* 455 F.3d at 1363.

[12] *Honeywell,* 488 F.3d at 1000; *Cargill,* 476 F.3d at 1364. In a close case, it is best to assume that the information is material. *See Flex-Rest,* 455 F.3d at 1363 ("When materiality of information is close . . . a patent applicant should err on the side of disclosure."). "[A]ffirmative misrepresentations by the patentee, in contrast to misleading omissions, are more likely to be regarded as material." Hoffman-La Roche, Inc. v. Promega Corp., 323 F.3d 1354, 1367 (Fed. Cir. 2003).

[13] *See Cargill,* 476 F.3d at 1366; Digital Control, Inc. v. Charles Machine Works, 437 F.3d 1309, 1318 (Fed. Cir. 2006); Li Second Family Ltd. Partnership v. Toshiba Corp., 231 F.3d 1373, 1380–81 (Fed. Cir. 2000).

[14] 37 C.F.R. § 1.56(b).

considered.[15] In the Federal Circuit's view, the new standard supplements rather than replaces its own "reasonable examiner" standard. An omission or misstatement may be material under *either* standard—warranting further inquiry into the applicant's intent.[16]

Information cannot be material, under any standard, if it is cumulative of other information available to the examiner.[17] For example, if the information is a withheld prior art reference, it is not material if the examiner considered prior art that was just as pertinent, or more pertinent, than the reference in question.[18] Similarly, if the applicant withheld information but the examiner discovered it independently, the applicant's action does not qualify as inequitable conduct.[19]

The intent threshold of inequitable conduct is as important as the materiality threshold. If the applicant withheld or misrepresented information because of an innocent mistake, the applicant did not commit inequitable conduct, no matter how material the information may have been.[20] At one time, some courts considered *gross negligence* to be sufficient intent to warrant a finding of inequitable conduct.[21] However, in *Kingsdown Medical Consultants v. Hollister Inc.*,[22] the Federal Circuit, resolving conflicting precedent, held that inequitable conduct can occur only if the applicant or attorney deliberately attempted to deceive the Patent Office. Hence, a lapse that is the result of carelessness, even gross carelessness, does not amount to inequitable conduct.[23]

Intent to deceive can be proven by indirect evidence. It is rare that inequitable conduct will be proven by an applicant's admission or a "smoking gun" document referring to a planned deception. Rather, the proof is likely to be found in circumstances where the information was so important,

---

[15] *Id.*

[16] *Digital Control,* 437 F.3d at 1316; *see also Cargill,* 476 F.3d at 1364; *Impax,* 468 F.3d at 1374.

[17] *Honeywell,* 488 F.3d at 1000; Tap Pharmaceuticals Prods., Inc. v. Owl Pharmaceuticals, L.L.C., 419 F.3d 1346, 1351 (Fed. Cir. 2005).

[18] *See* LNP Eng'g Plastics, Inc. v. Miller Waste Mills, Inc., 275 F.3d 1347, 1360 (Fed. Cir. 2001); GFI, Inc. v. Franklin Corp., 265 F.3d 1268, 1274 (Fed. Cir. 2001).

[19] Molins PLC v. Textron, Inc., 48 F.3d 1172, 1185 (Fed. Cir. 1995); Scripps Clinic Research Foundation v. Genentech, Inc., 927 F.2d 1565, 1582 (Fed. Cir. 1991).

[20] *See Cargill,* 476 F.3d at 1364 ("'the involved conduct, viewed in light of all the evidence, including evidence indicative of good faith, must indicate sufficient culpability to require a finding of intent to deceive'"); *Impax,* 468 F.3d at 1375; *Liquid Dynamics,* 449 F.3d at 1227 ("Intent is a subjective inquiry into whether the inventor knew the information was material and chose not to disclose it."). Although "subjective good faith can support a defense to inequitable conduct . . . there is no such thing as a good faith intent to deceive." *Cargill,* 476 F.3d at 1367–68.

[21] *See, e.g.,* Driscoll v. Cebalo, 731 F.2d 878, 885 (Fed. Cir. 1984).

[22] 863 F.2d 867 (Fed. Cir. 1988) (resolution of conflicting precedent decided *en banc*).

[23] *Id.; see also Brasseler,* 267 F.3d at 1382 ("a finding of deceptive intent may not be based solely on gross negligence").

and the situation so devoid of any possibility of an excuse, that one must conclude that the deception was deliberate.[24]

If the information withheld or misrepresented meets the threshold test of materiality, and if there is also proof of intent to deceive, the ultimate decision of whether there was inequitable conduct is left to the discretion of the judge,[25] who must balance the materiality of the information against the seriousness of the intent.[26] The more important the information, the less the required showing of intent before the patent will be held unenforceable.[27]

Charges of inequitable conduct have become so routine in patent litigation that the Federal Circuit has referred to them as "an absolute plague."[28] It is difficult to say whether this reflects a low standard of ethics among applicants and patent attorneys, or just the readiness of accused infringers to raise every conceivable defense.

9.2 MISUSE

The patent system strikes a delicate balance between, on the one hand, the desire to encourage innovation by rewarding inventors with exclusive rights to their inventions and, on the other hand, the desire to promote healthy competition in the marketplace. While the essence of the patent system is the grant of a monopoly, it is still a monopoly of limited scope and duration. If a patent owner attempts to leverage the advantage of a patent into something beyond its intended boundaries, the patent owner may be held to have

---

[24] *See Cargill*, 476 F.3d at 1366 (intent may be inferred where the applicant knew, or should have known, that the information was material); *Impax*, 468 F.3d at 1375 ("intent to deceive is generally inferred from the facts and circumstances surrounding the applicant's overall conduct"); *Dippin' Dots*, 476 F.3d at 1345 ("'[S]moking gun' evidence is not required in order to establish an intent to deceive. . . ."); *Hoffman-La Roche*, 323 F.3d at 1371 ("a finding of intent does not require a confession from the stand by the inventor or the prosecuting attorney"). If the circumstantial evidence is sufficient to infer the necessary intent, "a mere denial of intent to mislead (which would defeat every effort to establish inequitable conduct) will not suffice [to rebut that evidence]." *GFI*, 265 F.3d at 1275. Sometimes the absence of a credible explanation for nondisclosure is enough to infer bad intent. *See Bruno*, 394 F.3d at 1354 ("Normally . . . an innocent party will be motivated to try to present convincing reasons for its actions or inaction.").

[25] *See* Kemin Foods, L.C. v. Pigmentos Vegetales Del Centro S.A. de C.V., 464 F.3d 1340, 1346 (Fed. Cir. 2006); *Hoffman-La Roche*, 323 F.3d at 1372; *PerSeptive Biosystems*, 225 F.3d at 1318 ("The defense of inequitable conduct is entirely equitable in nature, and thus not an issue for a jury to decide.").

[26] *See Honeywell*, 488 F.3d at 999; *Cargill*, 476 F.3d at 1364; AGFA Corp. v. Creo Prods. Inc., 451 F.3d 1366, 1377 (Fed. Cir. 2006).

[27] *See Cargill*, 476 F.3d at 1364 ("'[t]he more material the omission or the misrepresentation, the lower the level of intent required to establish inequitable conduct, and vice versa'"); *Impax*, 468 F.3d at 1375; Purdue Pharma L.P. v. Endo Pharmaceuticals Inc., 438 F.3d 1123, 1128–29 (Fed. Cir. 2006).

[28] Burlington Indus., Inc. v. Dayco Corp., 849 F.2d 1418, 1422 (Fed. Cir. 1988).

committed "misuse."[29] Like the inequitable conduct defense, the misuse defense leads, if successful, to a holding that the patent is unenforceable.

An early example of overreaching by a patent owner can be found in *Morton Salt Co. v. G.S. Suppiger.*[30] Suppiger obtained a patent on a machine used in the canning industry for adding salt tablets to the contents of the cans. Only the machine was patented; the salt tablets were not. Nevertheless, when Suppiger leased its machines to canneries, it licensed the canneries to use the machines only if they agreed to buy all of their salt tablets from a Suppiger subsidiary. The Supreme Court viewed this extension of the patent grant as improper and held that a patent owner guilty of such practices could not look to a court for relief.[31] Today such conduct might be characterized as misuse.

Although there is no exhaustive list of the kinds of behavior that constitute misuse, the following may raise questions:

- A patent license, such as that discussed in *Morton Salt,* which compels the licensee to purchase separate, unpatented goods from the patent owner. This is called a "tying" arrangement.[32]
- A patent license that forbids the licensee from dealing with the patent owner's competitors. This is sometimes called "tying out," in contrast to the "tying in" found in *Morton Salt.*
- A patent license granted on the condition that *other* patents are also licensed, even though the other patents may be undesired or even invalid.[33]

---

[29] *See* Monsanto Co. v. Scruggs, 459 F.3d 1328, 1339 (Fed. Cir. 2006) ("In order for competitive behavior to amount to patent misuse, one must 'impermissibly broaden[] the scope of the patent grant with anticompetitive effect.'"); Monsanto Co. v. McFarling, 363 F.3d 1336, 1341 (Fed. Cir. 2004); C.R. Bard, Inc. v. M3 Sys., Inc., 157 F.3d 1340, 1372 (Fed. Cir. 1998) ("Patent misuse relates primarily to a patentee's actions that affect competition in unpatented goods or that otherwise extend the economic effect beyond the scope of the patent grant."); Windsurfing Int'l, Inc. v. AMF, Inc., 782 F.2d 995, 1001 (Fed. Cir. 1986) (a misuse defense "requires that the alleged infringer show that the patentee has impermissibly broadened 'the physical or temporal scope' of the patent grant with anticompetitive effect"). "In cases in which the restriction is reasonably within the patent grant, the patent misuse defense can never succeed." *Monsanto,* 363 F.3d at 1341.

[30] 314 U.S. 488 (1941).

[31] *Id.* at 492–94.

[32] *See Monsanto,* 363 F.3d at 1341; Virginia Panel Corp. v. Mac Panel Co., 133 F.3d 860, 869 (Fed. Cir. 1997) (referring to tying of "staple good[s]" as an example of "*per se* patent misuse"). It is not misuse to demand that licensees purchase from the patent owner goods which, if purchased from someone else, could supply the basis of a claim of contributory infringement— for example, goods useful only in practicing the patented invention. *See* 35 U.S.C. § 271(d). Contributory infringement is discussed in Section 10.4.

[33] It is common for patent owners to license a group of related patents as a package—an arrangement that may be convenient for the licensee as well as for the patent owner. *See* U.S. Philips Corp. v. Int'l Trade Comm'n, 424 F.3d 1179, 1192–93 (Fed. Cir. 2005). The *U.S. Philips* case casts some doubt on whether package licensing can ever be anticompetitive, even if the licensee has no alternative. The negotiated price for the package will reflect the value of the technology that the licensee *does* need, and the "extra" licenses do not compel the licensee to use those technologies instead of others. *See* 424 F.3d at 1190–91.

- Extending the collection of royalty payments past the expiration of the patent term.[34]
- Charging royalties on products that do not use the patented invention.[35]

The misuse defense covers some of the same territory as the federal antitrust laws,[36] at least where the challenged activity takes the form of a threat to competition. Conduct may rise to the level of misuse without violating the antitrust laws,[37] but similar considerations of "market power," anticompetitive effects, and business justifications appear in either context,[38] particularly after changes to 35 U.S.C. § 271. The latter now states that it is misuse to condition a patent license on the sale of a separate, unpatented product only if the patent owner has "market power" in the relevant market.[39] The same limitation applies to patent licenses offered only as a group.[40]

"Market power" is a concept developed in the setting of antitrust law, and perhaps only an economist could provide a thorough definition. In general terms, market power means the ability to alter the conditions of trade, and in particular to raise prices, beyond what could be accomplished in a competitive market. Whether a company has market power depends on the availability of acceptable substitutes for whatever goods or services that company controls. Thus, if *Morton Salt* had applied the current version of § 271, the court might have considered whether Suppiger's patented salt depositing machines were so superior that it could compel canneries to obtain a patent license, even at the cost of having to purchase unpatented salt tablets from Suppiger's subsidiary. If the canneries could easily have chosen another machine without such restrictions, Suppiger would not have had the "power" to restrain competition.

Even where a misuse defense is dependent on a demonstration of anticompetitive effects, it is not necessary that the party raising the defense have

---

[34] *See* Brulotte v. Thys Co., 379 U.S. 29, 33 (1964); *Virginia Panel*, 133 F.3d at 869.

[35] *See U.S. Philips*, 424 F.3d at 1184.

[36] The federal antitrust laws (e.g., the Sherman Antitrust Act, 15 U.S.C. §§ 1–7) are designed to protect competition in the marketplace. Because a patent is a *legal* form of monopoly, efforts to enforce a patent within its legitimate scope do not violate the antitrust laws. *See* In re Independent Service Organizations Antitrust Litigation, 203 F.3d 1322, 1326 (Fed. Cir. 2000) (generally a patent owner who brings suit to enforce right to exclude is exempt from antitrust laws). Antitrust concerns should arise only if the patent was obtained by fraud, or was known to be invalid, or if the suit for infringement was a "mere sham." *See id.*; Atari Games Corp. v. Nintendo of America, Inc., 897 F.2d 1572, 1576 (Fed. Cir. 1990).

[37] *U.S. Philips*, 424 F.3d at 1185–86; *Monsanto*, 459 F.3d at 1339.

[38] *See Virginia Panel*, 133 F.3d at 869 (discussing "rule of reason" applied to some practices alleged to be misuse); *Windsurfing*, 782 F.2d at 1002 (unless conduct has been deemed *per se* anticompetitive, there must be a showing that it "tends to restrain competition unlawfully in an appropriately defined market").

[39] 35 U.S.C. § 271(d). A patent does not confer market power automatically, nor can a court presume that a patent confers such power. Illinois Tool Works Inc. v. Independent Ink, Inc., 547 U.S. 28, 45–46 (2006).

[40] 35 U.S.C. § 271(d).

suffered those anticompetitive effects personally. Protection of the public from abusive practices, and denial of relief to those undeserving of the court's protection, are sufficient reasons to hold a patent unenforceable, no matter what effect the challenged conduct has had on the litigants in a particular case.[41]

Some conduct that might seem anticompetitive is not considered misuse. For example, it is not misuse to grant only a limited number of licenses to a patent, to grant no licenses to a patent, or to completely suppress an invention by neither practicing it nor licensing it.[42] Generally, it is up to the patentee to decide whether the invention will be exploited during the term of the patent. On the other hand, recent decisions give courts some leeway to deny an injunction even after a successful suit for infringement. One factor courts may consider is the impact on the public if the patentee does not permit the invention to be made available for its use.[43]

Unlike invalidity, or unenforceability resulting from inequitable conduct, unenforceability resulting from misuse is reversible. The patent can be enforced again as soon as the objectionable conduct has ceased and any lingering effects have "dissipated."[44]

---

[41] *Morton Salt,* 314 U.S. at 493–94.

[42] *See* 35 U.S.C. § 271(d) (stating that "refus[al] to license or use any rights to the patent" is not an act of misuse); *Independent Service Organizations,* 203 F.3d at 1326; Cygnus Therapeutics Sys. v. Alza Corp., 92 F.3d 1153, 1160 (Fed. Cir. 1996) ("a patentee may, if it wishes, do nothing with the subject matter of the patent"); King Instruments Corp. v. Perego, 65 F.3d 941, 950 (Fed. Cir. 1995) ("The market may well dictate that the best use of a patent is to exclude infringing products, rather than to market the invention.").

[43] *See* eBay Inc. v. MercExchange, L.L.C., 547 U.S. 388, 391 (2006).

[44] *Morton Salt,* 314 U.S. at 493; *see also* Senza-Gel Corp. v. Seiffhart, 803 F.2d 661, 668 n.10 (Fed. Cir. 1986).

CHAPTER 10

Infringement

The owner of a patent has the exclusive right to make, use, sell, offer to sell, or import into the United States the invention described by the claims.[1] Anyone else who engages in those activities, without the permission of the patent owner, is an "infringer." An infringer can be sued for money damages[2] and can be compelled by a court to cease the infringing activities.

10.1 PATENT TERM

Generally speaking, the exclusive rights conferred by a patent begin on the date the patent issues and expire 20 years after the *filing date* of the application (or any earlier application cited for purposes of priority).[3] Consequently, the term of the patent will vary depending on how long it takes for the application to make its way through the Patent Office. A patent issued in 2005 on an application filed in 2000 would last only 15 years, expiring in 2020.[4]

---

[1] *See* 35 U.S.C. § 271(a).
[2] See Section 11.8.
[3] 35 U.S.C. § 154(2).
[4] The 20-year term applies to utility patents. Design patents, discussed in Section 12.1, have a term of 14 years from the date of issue. 35 U.S.C. § 173.

The term of a patent used to be 17 years from the date of *issue.*[5] Consequently, long delays in prosecution,[6] sometimes due to maneuvering by the applicant, occasionally resulted in patents issuing on inventions that had already been in public use for decades.[7] In 1990, for example, computer chip manufacturers learned that a patent had been issued to one Gilbert Hyatt claiming the basic concept of the microprocessor—already the subject of a long-established and lucrative industry. This patent appeared at such a late date because it took 21 years and the prosecution of a long chain of related applications before the patent issued. Since the application process was conducted in secret, none of the chip manufacturers knew of the patent until, from their perspective, it was too late to do anything about it. The current practice of measuring the effective term of a patent from its filing date reduces the incentive for applicants to delay prosecution and surprise an industry with a so-called submarine patent.

Under the current rules, if the examination is unduly delayed and the PTO bears the blame, the term of the patent may be extended accordingly.[8] The term may also be extended if a successful appeal,[9] an interference proceeding,[10] or certain kinds of regulatory delay,[11] such as FDA review of the patented product, prevent the patentee from enjoying the full term of its commercial monopoly.

In the event a patent application is published before its date of issue,[12] the patentee enjoys "provisional rights," meaning the right to demand a reasonable royalty from anyone who practiced the patented invention in the interval.[13] These rights apply only against parties with actual notice of the patent application,[14] and they can be collected only after the patent has issued. Such rights are one incentive for applicants to publish their applications, even when the law does not require it.[15] Except for these

---

[5] Due to the change from a 17-year to a 20-year term, patents applied for prior to June 8, 1995 are entitled to the greater of the 20-year term provided by the current statute, or the term of 17 years from issue provided by the former statute. 35 U.S.C. § 154(c).

[6] The record holder in this respect might be U.S. Patent No. 6,130,946, disclosing a cryptography machine resembling the German Enigma device. The patent issued on October 10, 2000, based on an application filed on October 23, 1936.

[7] Calculated delay may allow an accused infringer to raise the defense of "prosecution laches." See Section 11.8.3.3.

[8] *See* 35 U.S.C. § 154(b).

[9] *See* 35 U.S.C. § 154(b)(1)(C).

[10] *See* 35 U.S.C. § 154(b)(1)(C). Interference proceedings are discussed in Section 5.4.

[11] *See* 35 U.S.C. §§ 155, 156.

[12] See Section 5.1.

[13] 35 U.S.C. § 154(d). The invention claimed in the issued patent must be "substantially identical" to the invention claimed in the published application. *Id.*

[14] 35 U.S.C. § 154(d)(1)(B).

[15] See Section 5.1.

provisional rights, an applicant with a "patent pending" has no exclusive rights until the patent issues. On the other hand, with few exceptions,[16] the patentee can demand that infringing activity cease when the patent issues, even if it had already begun. Warnings of a "patent pending" advise potential infringers that they should not begin what they may not be permitted to continue. On the other hand, one should remember that many pending applications result in relatively narrow patent claims, or are denied altogether.

10.2 GEOGRAPHIC LIMITATIONS

United States patent law does not apply to activities that take place entirely in another country.[17] The sale or use of a patented product in Japan, for example, is not an infringement of a United States patent, although it could be an infringement of a corresponding Japanese patent. The law also provides an explicit exception for inventions built into vehicles, such as aircraft, that may enter the United States temporarily. If a United States patent covered a design for landing gear, and a Japanese airliner with the claimed landing gear flew into the United States to deliver passengers, the use of the landing gear in the United States would not infringe the patent.[18]

In two respects, United States patent law does take notice of activities occurring in another country. First, supplying the *components* of a patented invention from the United States to a foreign country, where they will be assembled into the claimed combination, can be an infringement of a United

---

[16] One exception involves a claim to a "method of doing or conducting business." See 35 U.S.C. § 173(a)(3). An accused infringer who can demonstrate that, acting in good faith, it (1) reduced to practice the claimed method at least one year before the filing date of the patent, and (2) used the method commercially before the filing date of the patent, may continue to use the method without the patentee's consent. See 35 U.S.C. § 273(b). This recently created defense to infringement protects parties who already invested in a method of doing business, but whose use of that method was not sufficiently public to trigger a statutory bar. See Section 8.10. It remains to be seen how broadly the term "method of doing or conducting business" will be interpreted. The other instance of "intervening rights" arises in the context of reissued patents. See Section 5.5.

[17] See Microsoft Corp. v. AT&T Corp., 127 S. Ct. 1746, 1750 (2007) ("It is the general rule under United States patent law that no infringement occurs when a patented product is made and sold in another country."); Rotec Indus., Inc. v. Mitsubishi Corp., 215 F.3d 1246, 1251 (Fed. Cir. 2000) ("'[t]he right conferred by a patent under our law is confined to the Unites States and its territories, and infringement of this right cannot be predicated of acts wholly done in a foreign country'").

[18] See 35 U.S.C. § 272; National Steel Car, Ltd. v. Canadian Pacific Railway, Ltd., 357 F.3d 1319, 1326 (Fed. Cir. 2004). The exception applies to countries offering reciprocal privileges.

States patent.[19] The legal analysis mirrors that of "contributory infringement" or "inducement" of infringement in the United States, topics discussed in Section 10.4. Second, it can be an infringement of a United States patent to import, use, sell, or offer to sell in the United States a product made in a foreign country by a *process* patented in the United States.[20] This prevents the evasion of United States patents by moving production overseas.[21]

The latter provision does not apply if the product is "materially changed by subsequent processes" or if the product "becomes a trivial and nonessential component of another product."[22] So, for example, if the patent claimed a process for refining aluminum, it would probably not be an infringement to import an automobile having an aluminum ashtray, even if the material from which the ashtray was made could be traced back to the patented process. At some point, the imported product becomes too far removed from the claimed process for the importation of that product to be regarded as an infringement.

10.3 STATE OF MIND

Generally speaking, the intentions of the infringer are irrelevant to infringement. A patent can be infringed even by someone who is unaware

---

[19] *See* 35 U.S.C. § 271(f). The components must be supplied with the intent that they be combined in an infringing manner. *See* Liquid Dynamics Corp. v. Vaughan Co., 449 F.3d 1209, 1222 (Fed. Cir. 2006). The *intention* is what counts. Proof that they were actually combined is unnecessary. Waymark Corp. v. Porta Sys. Corp., 245 F.3d 1364, 1367–68 (Fed. Cir. 2001). In that respect, § 271(f) differs from contributory infringement or inducement. *See id.* In *Microsoft Corp. v. AT&T Corp.*, 127 S. Ct. 1746 (2007), the Supreme Court held that sending software code to a foreign country does not qualify as supplying a "component" of a patented combination. A component is a tangible thing. Software is more like a construction blueprint–something not covered by § 271(f). *Id.* at 1755 ("A blueprint may contain precise instructions for the construction and combination of the components of a patented device, but it is not itself a combinable component of that device."); *see also* Pellegrini v. Analog Devices, Inc., 375 F.3d 1113, 1118 (Fed. Cir. 2004). On the other hand, some Federal Circuit decisions hold that § 271(f) may be applied to a component of a patented *process*, which might include an article uniquely adapted to be used in that process. *See* Union Carbide Chemicals & Plastics Tech. Corp. v. Shell Oil Co., 425 F.3d 1366, 1378–80 (Fed. Cir. 2005) (catalyst used in patented process); *but cf.* NTP, Inc. v. Research in Motion, Ltd., 418 F.3d 1282, 1322 (Fed. Cir. 2005) (U.S. sales of BlackBerry devices did not violate § 102(f), even if used abroad in a patented process).

[20] 35 U.S.C. § 271(g); Kinik Co. v. Int'l Trade Comm'n, 362 F.3d 1359, 1361–62 (Fed. Cir. 2004); Biotec Biologische Naturverpackungen GmbH v. Biocorp, Inc., 249 F.3d 1341, 1351–52 (Fed. Cir. 2001). The patent must be in force when the steps of the process are performed abroad. Monsanto Co. v. Syngenta Seeds, Inc., 503 F.3d 1352, 1360 (Fed. Cir. 2007). Section 271(g) applies only to physical products made abroad; it does not apply to intangible products like information. *NTP*, 418 F.3d at 1323; Bayer AG v. Housey Pharmaceuticals, Inc. 340 F.3d 1367, 1377 (Fed. Cir. 2003).

[21] *See* Eli Lilly & Co. v. American Cyanamid Co., 82 F.3d 1568, 1571–72 (Fed. Cir. 1996).

[22] 35 U.S.C. § 271(g); *see also Biotec*, 249 F.3d at 1352; *Eli Lilly*, 82 F.3d at 1572; Bio-Technology General Corp. v. Genentech, Inc., 80 F.3d 1553, 1560 (Fed. Cir. 1996).

that the patent exists.[23] On the other hand, infringement that *is* intentional, referred to as "willful infringement," can result in an award of increased damages, up to three times the amount of damages that could be recovered from an innocent infringer, together with attorneys' fees. These increased awards, intended as a penalty or deterrent, are discussed in Section 11.8.2.

Indirect infringement, discussed in Section 10.4, is an exception to the general rule. "Inducement" of infringement and "contributory infringement," both forms of indirect infringement, do require an awareness of the patent and knowledge of the infringing acts.

10.4 DIRECT AND INDIRECT INFRINGEMENT

One who, without authority, makes, uses, sells, offers to sell, or imports into the United States a product covered by a patent is a "direct infringer." One who is not a direct infringer may be held equally liable for encouraging or contributing to infringement by someone else. This is sometimes referred to as "indirect" or "dependent" infringement.[24]

Indirect infringement comes in two forms—"inducement" of infringement and "contributory infringement." The concept of inducement is the simpler one. Anyone who "actively induces" the infringement of a patent by another may be held liable as an infringer.[25] Consider the case of *Moleculon Research Corp. v. CBS, Inc.*[26] CBS sold the popular toy known as Rubik's Cube, a product that Moleculon believed to infringe its patent on a rotating-cube puzzle. Some of the claims, rather than describing the puzzle as a physical object, instead claimed a method of solving the puzzle by rotating the facets of the cube. These method claims could be directly infringed only by someone

---

[23] Hilton Davis Chemical Co. v. Warner-Jenkinson Co., 62 F.3d 1512, 1519 (Fed. Cir. 1995) (*en banc*) ("Intent is not an element of infringement. . . . A patent may exclude others from practicing the claimed invention, regardless of whether the infringers even know of the patent."), *rev'd on other grounds*, Warner-Jenkinson Co. v. Hilton-Davis Chemical Co., 520 U.S. 17 (1997); *see also* Florida Prepaid Postsecondary Education Expense Board v. College Savings Bank, 527 U.S. 627, 645 (1999) ("Actions predicated on direct patent infringement . . . do not require any showing of intent to infringe."); Jurgens v. CBK, Ltd., 80 F.3d 1566, 1570 n.2 (Fed. Cir. 1996) (infringement is "a strict liability offense").

[24] *See* RF Delaware, Inc. v. Pacific Keystone Techs., Inc., 326 F.3d 1255, 1268 (Fed. Cir. 2003) ("dependent infringement"); Moba, B.V. v. Diamond Automation, Inc., 325 F.3d 1306, 1318 (Fed. Cir. 2003) ("indirect infringement"). In any case of indirect infringement, there must be evidence of a related *direct* infringement by someone else. *See* Acco Brands, Inc. v. ABA Locks Mfrs. Co., 501 F.3d 1307, 1312–13 (Fed. Cir. 2007); Glenayre Elecs., Inc. v. Jackson, 443 F.3d 851, 858 (Fed. Cir. 2006); Aquatex Indus., Inc. v. Techniche Solutions, 419 F.3d 1374, 1380 (Fed. Cir. 2005). However, that direct infringement can be shown by circumstantial evidence. *See* Golden Blount, Inc. v. Robert H. Peterson Co., 438 F.3d 1354, 1362 (Fed. Cir. 2006).

[25] 35 U.S.C. § 271(b).

[26] 793 F.2d 1261 (Fed. Cir. 1986).

performing the steps of the method—that is, by someone using the puzzle. It would have been impractical, however, to file suit against every consumer who purchased Rubik's Cube. Even though CBS did not directly infringe those method claims, the court found that it could be held liable for inducing infringement by purchasers, largely because it sold puzzles and instruction sheets that would lead purchasers to practice the method.[27]

Although a direct infringer can be completely unaware of the existence of the patent, one who induces infringement must know of the patent and must intend to cause the infringing acts.[28] Where such intent is found, it is even possible to hold officers or directors of a corporation liable for an infringement by their corporation, if they "actively assisted" in that infringement.[29] This is one instance in which the corporate form will not shield officers or directors from personal liability for the acts of their corporation. Such liability still is comparatively rare since it is seldom possible to prove the necessary intent.[30]

A "contributory infringer" is one who imports, sells or offers to sell a *component* of a patented combination, or a material or apparatus to be used in a patented process, if all of the following conditions are met:[31]

- The item is a "*material part* of the patented invention."
- The item is imported, sold, or offered for sale with *knowledge* that the item was "*especially made or especially adapted*" for use in an infringing manner.[32]
- The item is *not* a "staple article or commodity of commerce suitable for substantial noninfringing use."

---

[27] *Id.* at 1272.

[28] *See ACCO*, 501 F.3d at 1312; DSU Medical Corp. v. JMS Co., 471 F.3d 1293, 1304 (Fed. Cir. 2006) (resolution of conflicting precedent *en banc*); *Moba*, 325 F.3d at 1318 ("Although § 271(b) does not use the word 'knowingly,' this court has uniformly imposed a knowledge requirement."). Some courts impose a "knew *or should have known*" standard of knowledge. *See DSU*, 471 F.3d at 1304; Ferguson Beauregard/Logic Controls v. Mega Sys., LLC, 350 F.3d 1327, 1342 (Fed. Cir. 2003); Manville Sales Corp. v. Paramount Sys., Inc., 917 F.2d 544, 553 (Fed. Cir. 1990). This may be another way of saying that the necessary intent can be proven by circumstantial evidence. *See* nCube Corp. v. SeaChange Int'l, Inc., 436 F.3d 1317, 1324 (Fed. Cir. 2006). Although it is difficult to distinguish between intending to cause infringing acts and intending to cause infringement, the Federal Circuit seems to require consciousness of the legal implications. *See DSU*, 471 F.3d at 1305–06; *Ferguson*, 350 F.3d at 1342.

[29] *See Manville*, 917 F.2d at 553; Orthokinetics, Inc. v. Safety Travel Chairs, Inc., 806 F.2d 1565, 1578–79 (Fed. Cir. 1986).

[30] *See* Al-Site Corp. v. VSI Int'l, Inc., 174 F.3d 1308, 1331 (Fed. Cir. 1999).

[31] 35 U.S.C. § 271(c); Husky Injection Molding Sys. Ltd. v. R & D Tool Eng'g Co., 291 F.3d 780, 784 (Fed. Cir. 2002).

[32] Although it is not apparent on the face of the statute, contributory infringement requires both knowledge that the component is adapted to a particular use and knowledge of the patent that proscribes that use. Hewlett-Packard Co. v. Bausch & Lomb Inc., 909 F.2d 1464, 1469 (Fed. Cir. 1990). Someone who is not aware of a patent cannot be a contributory infringer, at least until notified that the patent exists. However, in contrast to inducement, contributory infringement does not require intent to cause the infringing acts. *See id.*

Many patented combinations include individual elements that themselves are common and unpatentable. The Oviatt mousetrap design (see Appendix A) includes an ordinary Ping-Pong ball. The Oviatt patent cannot prevent anyone from making, using, importing, selling or offering to sell Ping-Pong balls, which have obvious uses unrelated to the mousetrap invention. The inventor's legitimate monopoly extends only to the claimed combination. Suppose, however, that someone sold the remaining components of the Oviatt mousetrap, without the Ping-Pong ball. Since all of the claims of the Oviatt patent require a ball, selling the remaining pieces would not directly infringe the patent.[33] However, it is likely that anyone who purchased the incomplete trap would eventually supply the missing ball, thereby forming an infringing combination. If the patent owner were forced to sue only those who formed that combination–consumers who purchased an incomplete trap and supplied their own Ping-Pong ball–enforcement of the Oviatt patent would be impractical.

Patent law treats as contributory infringement the importation, sale, or offer to sell a component of a claimed combination if the component is "especially made" for use in the patented combination (like the tubed structure depicted in the Oviatt patent) and not a "staple article or commodity of commerce suitable for substantial noninfringing use" (like a Ping-Pong ball). Originally, the law made no distinction between contributory infringement and inducement, and it is still useful to consider contributory infringement in the inducement context. The sale of a Ping-Pong ball could not, by itself, be legitimately regarded as an inducement to infringe the Oviatt patent, since the Ping-Pong ball could be used for something else. The sale of the single-purpose apparatus could, however, be viewed as an inducement to infringe, since the apparatus has no other plausible use.

The concept of a "staple article of commerce" most obviously applies to basic materials sold in large quantities and useful in numerous applications. Ordinary nuts and bolts and common chemicals would be considered "staples," and their sale would not trigger contributory infringement.[34] But in this context "staple" also applies to goods having even one "substantial" noninfringing use.[35] If it did not, in practical effect the patentee's monopoly would extend to unpatented uses and combinations. If Oviatt could prevent the unlicensed sale of Ping-Pong balls, he would have an effective monopoly not only on his own invention, but also on the game of Ping-Pong.

Issues of contributory infringement often arise in the context of replacing worn or broken parts in a patented device. One who obtains a patented

---

[33] See Section 10.5.

[34] There might be a legitimate claim of inducement, however, if the sale were accompanied by instructions telling the purchaser how to use the goods in an infringing manner. *See* Dynacore Holdings Corp. v. U.S. Philips Corp., 363 F.3d 1263, 1277 n.6 (Fed. Cir. 2004).

[35] *See id.* at 1275; Preemption Devices, Inc. v. Minnesota Mining & Mfg. Co., 803 F.2d 1170, 1174 (Fed. Cir. 1986).

device from a legitimate source is permitted to repair that device, or replace a broken or exhausted part, without further obligation to the patent owner.[36] On the other hand, one cannot "reconstruct" the patented device to such an extent that one is, in effect, building a new and unlicensed device.[37] If the substitution of a part effects a reconstruction rather than a repair of the patented device, that reconstruction can constitute an infringement, and whoever supplied the part may be found liable as a contributory infringer.[38]

The line between "repair" and "reconstruction" is a difficult one to draw,[39] but courts generally have taken a broad view of what may be repaired or replaced.[40] If it is simply a matter of replacing a spent and easily replaceable component, the replacement will probably not be considered an infringement, as long as the component is not the subject of a patent in its own right.[41] For example, the Federal Circuit held that supplying replacement liners for a biohazard disposal system was not an infringement of the related patent because

[36] *See* Fuji Photo Film Co. v. Int'l Trade Comm'n, 474 F.3d 1281, 1296 (Fed. Cir. 2007) ("the replacement of a spent part [is] a fundamental example of a permissible repair"); *Husky,* 291 F.3d at 785–86; Surfco Hawaii v. Fin Control Sys., Ltd., 264 F.3d 1062, 1065 (Fed. Cir. 2001). This is true whether or not the replaced part is one "essential" to the combination, and whether or not the replaced part is the thing that distinguished the invention from the prior art. *See Fuji,* 474 F.3d at 1297; *Husky,* 291 F.3d at 786–87; Porter v. Farmers Supply Service, Inc., 790 F.2d 882, 885–86 (Fed. Cir. 1986). Parts can also be exchanged to *modify* the patented combination for reasons other than extending its useful life. *See Husky,* 291 F.3d at 786, 788 (modifications that are "kin to repair," involving a substitution for an easily replaceable part, are permitted); *Surfco,* 264 F.3d at 1065–66 (owner may replace fins on a surfboard, even though fins are not worn out, in order to make the surfboard safer).

[37] *See* Aro Mfg. Co. v. Convertible Top Replacement Co., 365 U.S. 336, 346 (1961).

[38] *See* FMC Corp. v. Up-Right, Inc., 21 F.3d 1073, 1076 (Fed. Cir. 1994).

[39] *See Husky,* 291 F.3d at 784–85 (the courts "have struggled for years to appropriately distinguish between repair of a patented machine and reconstruction"). One court, in a passage cited with approval by the Federal Circuit, declined to adopt any bright-line test to distinguish between repair and reconstruction, placing its reliance instead on "'the exercise of sound common sense and an intelligent judgment.'" *FMC,* 21 F.3d at 1079 (quoting Goodyear Shoe Machinery Co. v. Jackson, 112 F. 146, 150 (1st Cir. 1901)); *see also* Bottom Line Management, Inc. v. Pan Man, Inc., 228 F.3d 1352, 1355 (Fed. Cir. 2000) (no "bright line test"). The Federal Circuit has suggested a "concept of proportionality inherent in the distinction between repair and reconstruction." *Husky,* 291 F.3d at 786–87; *see also Fuji,* 474 F.3d at 1296 (no contention that refurbishment was "disproportionate to the overall value of the parts that were not replaced"). Such "proportionality" would lead one to distinguish between replacing the spark plugs on a vehicle (a permissible repair) and replacing the rest of the vehicle at a single stroke, retaining *only* the spark plugs (an impermissible reconstruction). Of course, few cases will be so easy to categorize.

[40] Sage Prods., Inc. v. Devon Indus., Inc., 45 F.3d 1575, 1578 (Fed. Cir. 1995).

[41] Although the distinction between replacement and repair is difficult to draw, the Federal Circuit has recently implied that the substitution of a new part for one that is "readily replaceable" is conduct within a "safe harbor." *See Husky,* 291 F.3d at 787. Consequently, the difficult cases involve parts that are *not* easily replaced. *See, e.g., Fuji,* 474 F.3d at 1296 (reloading film in a "single use" camera was not impermissible reconstruction, even though the back of the camera had to be broken and replaced); *Bottom Line,* 228 F.3d at 1356 (refurbishing cooking surfaces with worn Teflon coatings was not impermissible reconstruction, even though it meant breaking welds).

the liners, only a component of the patented combination, were meant to be replaced after a single use.[42] In fact, though it defies logic, one may be allowed to replace an entire device over a period of time, by the successive replacement of worn out or spent parts, as long as in no single instance are the replacements so extensive that they amount to "reconstruction."[43] On the other hand, if the entire product is spent, as a patented torpedo would be following its explosion,[44] construction of a new item from what remains would not be permitted. Also, the courts have sometimes balked at the replacement of a component clearly not meant to be, nor customarily considered to be, replaceable.[45]

10.5 LITERAL INFRINGEMENT

Determining if a patent is infringed is a two-step process.[46] First, one must examine the language of the claims at issue and determine what the claims mean. This step, referred to as "claim construction" or "claim interpretation," proceeds according to the rules discussed in Chapter 7. Although it is a principle difficult to apply in practice, claims are supposed to be construed without any reference to the thing that has been accused of infringing.[47]

---

[42] *Sage Prods.*, 45 F.3d 1575 (Fed. Cir. 1995).

[43] *See Husky*, 291 F.3d at 786; *FMC*, 21 F.3d at 1077.

[44] *See Husky*, 291 F.3d at 785.

[45] In Sandvik Aktiebolag v. E.J. Co., 121 F.3d 669 (Fed. Cir. 1997), the Federal Circuit held that replacement of a carbide drill tip constituted reconstruction of the patented drill, rather than repair, even though the tip was only a component of the claimed combination. A number of factors influenced the court, including the elaborate procedures necessary to replace the tip, the long useful life of the tip compared with other components of the drill, the lack of any substantial industry in replacement tips, and the lack of any evidence that the patentee intended for the drill tip to be replaced. *Id.* at 673.

[46] Elbex Video, Ltd. v. Sensormatic Elecs. Corp., 508 F.3d 1366, 1370 (Fed. Cir. 2007); Stumbo v. Eastman Outdoors, Inc., 508 F.3d 1358, 1361 (Fed. Cir. 2007); Wilson Sporting Goods Co. v Hillerich & Bradsby Co., 442 F.3d 1322, 1326 (Fed. Cir. 2006).

[47] SRI Int'l v. Matsushita Elec. Corp., 775 F.2d 1107, 1118 (Fed. Cir. 1985) (*en banc*) ("[C]laims are not construed 'to cover' or 'not to cover' the accused device. That procedure would make infringement a matter of judicial whim. It is only *after* the claims have been *construed without reference to the accused device* that the claims, as so construed, are applied to the accused device to determine infringement." (emphasis in original)). *But see* Serio-US Indus., Inc. v. Plastic Recovery Techs. Corp., 459 F.3d 1311, 1319 (Fed. Cir. 2006) ("a trial court may consult the accused device for context that informs the claim construction process"); *Wilson Sporting Goods,* 442 F.3d at 1326–27 ("[W]hile a trial court should certainly not prejudge the ultimate infringement analysis by construing claims with an aim to include or exclude an accused product or process, knowledge of that product or process provides meaningful context for the first step of the infringement analysis, claim construction."); Vivid Techs., Inc. v. American Science & Eng'g, Inc., 200 F.3d 795, 803 (Fed. Cir. 1999) ("although the claims are construed objectively and without reference to the accused device, only those terms need be construed that are in controversy, and only to the extent necessary to resolve the controversy"); Scripps Clinic & Research Found. v. Genentech, Inc., 927 F.2d 1565, 1580 (Fed. Cir. 1991) ("Of course the particular accused product (or process) is kept in mind, for it is efficient to focus on the construction of only the disputed elements or limitations of the claims.").

Once the claims have been properly construed, they must be compared with the accused product or method to see if the claims are infringed. A patent is said to be "literally infringed" if the claims literally or "exactly" describe the thing accused of infringement.[48]

A claim cannot be literally infringed if any claim element is missing entirely from the accused product.[49] This is so even if the missing element seems an insignificant part of the invention as a whole. If a mousetrap claim refers to a hook for hanging the trap on a wall when the trap is not in use, a trap that has no hook does not literally infringe. This principle is often called the "all elements" rule. It can be helpful to think of a patent claim as a kind of checklist of features, every one of which must be found in the accused product in order for the claim to be infringed.

On the other hand, infringement is not avoided by adding things that are not described in the claim.[50] Suppose, for example, that a first inventor claimed a mousetrap comprising the combination of a spring, a latch, a mouse-trapping jaw, and a trigger that releases the latch and closes the jaw. A later inventor improves the combination by adding an audible alarm that sounds when the trap has sprung. The improved trap would still literally infringe, as long as it had the spring, latch, jaw and trigger claimed.[51]

---

[48] DeMarini Sports, Inc. v. Worth, Inc., 239 F.3d 1314, 1331 (Fed. Cir. 2001); General Am. Transp. Corp. v. Cryro-Trans, Inc., 93 F.3d 766, 770 (Fed. Cir. 1996); Southwall Techs., Inc. v. Cardinal IG Co., 54 F.3d 1570, 1575 (Fed. Cir. 1995).

[49] See BMC Resources, Inc. v. Paymentech, L.P., 498 F.3d 1373, 1378 (Fed. Cir. 2007); Gemstar-TV Guide Int'l, Inc. v. Int'l Trade Comm'n, 383 F.3d 1352, 1360 (Fed. Cir. 2004); Techsearch, L.L.C. v. Intel Corp., 286 F.3d 1360, 1371 (Fed. Cir. 2002) ("To establish literal infringement, all of the elements of the claim, as correctly construed, must be present in the accused system.").

[50] See Free Motion Fitness, Inc. v. Cybex Int'l, Inc., 423 F.3d 1343, 1353 (Fed. Cir. 2005) ("Basic patent law holds that a party may not avoid infringement of a patent claim using an open transitional phrase, such as comprising, by adding additional elements."); Suntiger, Inc. v. Scientific Research Funding Gp., 189 F.3d 1327, 1336 (Fed. Cir. 1999); Northern Telecom, Inc. v. Datapoint Corp., 908 F.2d 931, 945 (Fed. Cir. 1990) ("Nor is infringement avoided if a claimed feature performs not only as shown in the patent, but also performs an additional function."). The same principle applies to method claims. See Smith & Nephew, Inc. v. Ethicon, Inc., 276 F.3d 1304, 1311 (Fed. Cir. 2001) ("Infringement arises when all of the steps of a claimed method are performed, whether or not the infringer also performs additional steps."). There is an exception if the claim is limited by its terms to the recited elements *and no others*. See *Suntiger*, 189 F.3d at 1336 ("If a claim is specific as to the number of elements and the addition of an element eliminates an inherent feature of the claim, then that additional element will prevent a finding of literal infringement."). When a claim preamble ends with the words "consisting of" (rather than the more common "comprising"), the claim is limited to only the elements recited. See Section 7.6.

[51] See Innogenetics, N.V. v. Abbott Labs., 512 F.3d 1363, 1371–72 (Fed. Cir. 2008) ("Abbott argues that a patent can never be literally infringed by embodiments that did not exist at the time of the filing. Our case law allows for after-arising technology to be captured within the literal scope of valid claims that are drafted broadly enough."); JVW Enters., Inc. v. Interact Accessories, Inc., 424 F.3d 1324, 1333 (Fed. Cir. 2005) (additional features and improvements do not avoid infringement).

Some accused infringers mistakenly believe that if they have obtained a patent covering their own product, they are immune from charges of infringing another patent. This is simply not the case. A patent conveys only the right to *exclude others*; it does not convey a right to produce or sell the invention claimed.[52] Even if the inventor of the trap-with-alarm had obtained a patent on the improvement (which is perfectly proper as long as the improvement is "non-obvious"), the product would still infringe.[53] However, the new patent would prevent the first inventor from adding an alarm to his invention, without a license from the second inventor.

The concept of literal infringement is relatively straightforward–a patent is literally infringed if the accused product is exactly what the claims describe. But this is not the end of the infringement inquiry. Even if the accused product is *not* exactly what the claims describe, it can still be found infringing under the "doctrine of equivalents." Alternatively, if an accused product *is* exactly what the claims describe, it can still theoretically be found non-infringing under the "reverse doctrine of equivalents." These doctrines are discussed in the sections that follow.

10.6 THE DOCTRINE OF EQUIVALENTS

The "doctrine of equivalents" is one of the most important doctrines in patent law, and one of the most perplexing. It is not based on the patent statutes passed by Congress, but is entirely a product of judicial reasoning. Some critics view the doctrine as inconsistent with other fundamental principles of patent law. However, the doctrine has a long history, and, having survived recent criticisms, it is clearly here to stay.

10.6.1 Winans v. Denmead

Winans v. Denmead,[54] an ancient but important case in the evolution of the doctrine of equivalents, provides a useful introduction. Winans obtained a patent on a coal-carrying railroad car shaped like the base (or "frustum") of a cone, with the smaller end extending below the level of the axles. The circular cross section and tapered dimensions of the car equalized the pressures

---

[52] Bio-Technology General Corp. v. Genentech, Inc., 80 F.3d 1553, 1559 (Fed. Cir. 1996) ("'[T]he existence of one's own patent does not constitute a defense to infringement of someone else's patent. It is elementary that a patent grants only the right to *exclude others* and confers to right on its holder to make, use, or sell.'" (emphasis in original)); Atlas Powder Co. v. E.I. Du Pont de Nemours & Co., 750 F.2d 1569, 1580 (Fed. Cir. 1984).

[53] *See Atlas Powder*, 750 F.2d at 1580 ("if Atlas patents A+B+C and Du Pont then patents the improvement A+B+C+D, Du Pont is liable to Atlas for any manufacture, use, or sale of A+B+C+D because the latter directly infringes claims to A+B+C"). A second patent can bear on whether an improvement is "equivalent" to the original, if there is no literal infringement. See Section 10.6.

[54] 56 U.S. 330 (1853).

on the load-bearing surfaces, with the result that a lighter car could carry a relatively larger burden without damage. Winans' patent claim specifically referred to a car "in the form of a frustum of a cone." The car accused of infringing Winans' patent was similarly tapered, but it had an octagonal rather than a circular cross section. Rather than the "frustum of a cone," the shape of the car was closer to an octagonal pyramid. The accused car did not fall within the literal language of the claim, but it provided similar (though reduced) benefits in equalizing the pressures exerted by the load.

Even though the accused car was outside of the literal language of the claim, the court found that it employed the principle of Winans' invention. The differences were merely differences of "form," and the court held these differences insufficient to avoid infringement.

> The exclusive right to the thing patented is not secured, if the public are at liberty to make substantial copies of it, varying its form or proportions. And, therefore, the patentee, having described his invention, and shown its principles, and claimed it in that form which most perfectly embodies it, is, in contemplation of law, deemed to claim every form in which his invention may be copied, unless he manifests an intention to disclaim some of those forms.[55]

A dissenting justice rejected this "substance over form" approach to infringement and emphasized the importance of definite claims in informing the public of the limits of the patentee's monopoly. A patentee, he felt, should be held to the limitations made explicit in the claims. He also warned that nothing could be "more mischievous, more productive of oppressive and costly litigation, or exorbitant and unjust pretensions and vexatious demands" than relaxation of the requirement that patentees be bound by definite claims.[56]

10.6.2 Graver Tank

The modern history of the doctrine of equivalents begins in 1950 with *Graver Tank & Mfg. Co. v. Linde Air Prods. Co.*[57] The patent at issue claimed a material to be used in an electric welding process, including as a principal ingredient an "alkaline earth metal" such as magnesium. The accused product used manganese instead of magnesium, and while the names of the ingredients are nearly the same, manganese is *not* an "alkaline earth metal" as specifically required by the patent claims. Nevertheless, invoking the doctrine of equivalents as expressed in *Winans v. Denmead,* the court found the patent infringed. The following paragraph summed up the majority's support for the doctrine:

> [T]o permit imitation of a patented invention which does not copy every literal detail would be to convert the protection of the patent

---

[55] *Id.* at 343.
[56] *Id.* at 347 (Campbell, J., dissenting).
[57] 339 U.S. 605 (1950).

grant into a hollow and useless thing. Such a limitation would leave room for—indeed encourage—the unscrupulous copyist to make unimportant and insubstantial changes and substitutions in the patent which, though adding nothing, would be enough to take the copied matter outside the claim, and hence outside the reach of law. . . . Outright and forthright duplication is a dull and very rare type of infringement. To prohibit no other would place the inventor at the mercy of verbalism and would subordinate substance to form.[58]

The court declined to establish any definite test of whether something outside of the literal scope of a patent claim is still "equivalent." "Equivalence," said the court, "is not the prisoner of a formula."[59] Rather, the judgment must be made in the context of the particular invention, the functions performed by the claimed and the substituted element, and the knowledge available to those skilled in the art. In addition, "[a]n important factor is whether persons reasonably skilled in the art would have known of the interchangeability of an ingredient not contained in the patent with one that was."[60] The court also referred to an earlier case inquiring whether the accused product performs "'substantially the same function in substantially the same way to obtain the same result,'"[61] reasoning that "'if two devices do the same work in substantially the same way, and accomplish substantially the same result, they are the same, even though they differ in name, form or shape.'"[62]

Applying these principles to the case before it, the court found the patent infringed, even though the accused welding material did not include the "alkaline earth metal" apparently required by the claim. The manganese served the same purpose as an "alkaline earth metal," and persons skilled in the art knew the two ingredients to be interchangeable. The substitution was nothing more than a slight and obvious variation of the invention literally described.[63]

10.6.3 Challenges to the Doctrine

The doctrine of equivalents is intended to free the infringement inquiry from excessive literalism and to elevate substance over form.[64] From that perspective, the doctrine seems an enlightened policy. On the other hand,

---

[58] *Id.* at 607.

[59] *Id.* at 609.

[60] *Id.*

[61] *Id.* at 608 (quoting *Sanitary Refrigerator Co. v. Winters*, 280 U.S. 30, 42 (1929)).

[62] *Id.* at 608 (quoting *Union Paper-Bag Machine Co. v. Murphy*, 97 U.S. 120, 125 (1877)).

[63] *Id.* at 612.

[64] "Unfortunately, the nature of language makes it impossible to capture the essence of a thing in a patent application. . . . If patents were always interpreted by their literal terms, their value would be greatly diminished. Unimportant and insubstantial substitutes for certain elements could defeat the patent, and its value to inventors could be destroyed by simple acts of copying." Festo Corp. v. Shoketsu Kinzoku Kogyo Kabushiki Co., 535 U.S. 722, 731 (2002).

the doctrine is at odds with the requirement of claims "particularly pointing out and distinctly claiming the subject matter which the applicant regards as his invention."[65] Ideally, claims notify the public of what can or cannot be done without risk of infringing the patent.[66] But when the doctrine of equivalents applies, claims can be positively misleading, by seeming to include restrictions that, in the end, a court will disregard. Attempting to honor the "competitor's need for precise wording as an aid in avoiding infringement" while avoiding "the risk of injustice that may result from a blindered focus on words alone,"[67] *Graver Tank* committed courts to a narrow and difficult path.

Recognizing the tension between the doctrine of equivalents and fair notice to potential infringers, the Federal Circuit has warned that

> [a]pplication of the doctrine of equivalents is the exception . . . not the rule, for if the public comes to believe (or fear) that the language of patent claims can never be relied on, and that the doctrine of equivalents is simply the second prong of every infringement charge, regularly available to extend protection beyond the scope of the claims, then claims will cease to serve their intended purpose. Competitors will never know whether their actions infringe a granted patent.[68]

Yet in practice, allegations of infringement under the doctrine of equivalents have become the rule, not the exception. Wherever there is any doubt as to literal infringement, patent owners routinely invoke the doctrine of equivalents as a fallback position. Indeed, attorneys representing patent owners would be remiss if they failed to take advantage of the opportunities the doctrine provides. The principle that "the protected invention is what the claims say it is"[69] appears increasingly "utopian."[70]

Eventually, critics began to suggest ways in which application of the doctrine of equivalents might be limited. For example, because *Graver Tank* had alluded to the "pirating" of an invention, or a "fraud on the patent" by an "unscrupulous copyist," some critics suggested that the doctrine of equivalents ought to be applied only in such egregious circum-

---

[65] 35 U.S.C. § 112.

[66] *See* Slimfold Mfg. Co., Inc. v. Kinkead Indus., Inc., 932 F.2d 1453, 1457 (Fed. Cir. 1991) ("Inherent in our claim-based patent system is also the principle that the protected invention is what the claims say it is, and thus that infringement can be avoided by avoiding the language of the claims.").

[67] Laitram Corp. v. Cambridge Wire Cloth Co., 863 F.2d 855, 856–57 (Fed. Cir. 1988).

[68] London v. Carson Pirie Scott & Co., 946 F.2d 1534, 1538 (Fed. Cir. 1991).

[69] *Slimfold*, 932 F.2d at 1457.

[70] Paper Converting Machine Co. v. Magna-Graphics Corp., 745 F.2d 11, 19 (Fed. Cir. 1984).

stances.[71] Had this approach been adopted, it would have significantly changed the prevailing practice of applying the doctrine even against "innocent infringers."

In *Warner-Jenkinson Co. v. Hilton Davis Chemical Co.*,[72] the Supreme Court entered the debate for the first time since *Graver Tank*. Although the court "share[d] the concern . . . that the doctrine of equivalents . . . has taken on a life of its own, unbounded by the patent claims,"[73] it declined the invitation to abolish the doctrine of equivalents or limit it to "unscrupulous copyists."[74] Instead, it reaffirmed the principles of *Graver Tank* and the generalized application of the doctrine, with some refinements discussed below. Unless Congress enacts new legislation, which seems very unlikely, the doctrine of equivalents will be with us for the foreseeable future.[75]

10.6.4 Tests of Equivalence

One of the most intractable problems raised by the doctrine of equivalents is how a court, or in many cases a jury, can decide what is "equivalent" and what is not. Fulfilling the prophecy of the dissenting justice in *Winans v.*

---

[71] *See, e.g.,* International Visual Corp. v. Crown Metal Mfg. Co., 991 F.2d 768, 773–75 (Fed. Cir. 1993) (Lourie, J., concurring). Note, however, that one person's "piracy" is another person's "designing around" a patent claim. The latter, which refers to the deliberate avoidance of a patent claim, is encouraged as a means of furthering the "useful arts" promoted by patent law. *See* State Indus., Inc. v. A.O. Smith Corp., 791 F.2d 1226, 1235–36 (Fed. Cir. 1985) ("One of the benefits of a patent system is its so-called 'negative incentive' to 'design around' a competitor's products, even when they are patented, thus bringing a steady flow of innovations to the marketplace."). As the Supreme Court remarked in rejecting an "equitable" distinction, "one wonders how ever to distinguish between the intentional copyist making minor changes to lower the risk of legal action, and the incremental innovator designing around the claims, yet seeking to capture as much as is permissible of the patented advance." Warner-Jenkinson Co. v. Hilton Davis Chemical Co., 520 U.S. 17, 36 (1997).

[72] 520 U.S. 17 (1997).

[73] *Id.* at 28–29.

[74] *Id.* at 34–36.

[75] In 2002, the Supreme Court reaffirmed the doctrine of equivalents, while taking note of the usual arguments against it. As the court explained:

> It is true that the doctrine of equivalents renders the scope of patents less certain. It may be difficult to determine what is, or is not, an equivalent to a particular element of an invention. If competitors cannot be certain about a patent's extent, they may be deterred from engaging in legitimate manufactures outside its limits, or they may invest by mistake in competing products that the patent secures. In addition the uncertainty may lead to wasteful litigation between competitors, suits that a rule of literalism might avoid. These concerns with the doctrine of equivalents, however, are not new. Each time the Court has considered the doctrine, it has acknowledged this uncertainty as the price of ensuring the appropriate incentive for innovation, and it has affirmed the doctrine over dissents that urged a more certain rule.

Festo, 535 U.S. at 732.

Denmead, the issue of equivalence has been as "productive of oppressive and costly litigation" as any other, primarily because the results are unpredictable.[76] In virtually any case, the patentee can produce evidence of similarities between the accused product and the invention described in the claims, seemingly leading to a conclusion of equivalence. At the same time, the defendant can produce evidence of dissimilarities, seemingly leading to a conclusion of non-equivalence. How is a judge or jury to decide? What Justice Story observed as long ago as 1818 remains true today:

> In all my experience I can scarcely recollect a single instance, in which the general question, whether the principles of two machines were the same or different, has not produced from different witnesses, equally credible and equally intelligent, opposite answers.[77]

Although the *Graver Tank* court declined to reduce equivalence to a formula, its reference to equivalence based on performing "substantially the same function in substantially the same way to obtain the same result" was adopted in many subsequent Federal Circuit decisions as the touchstone of infringement.[78] Indeed, this function-way-result test of equivalence (also referred to as the "three-prong" test or "triple identity" test of equivalence) took on a significance that the *Graver Tank* court may not have intended or foreseen. The Federal Circuit went so far as to require that a patentee produce independent evidence on *each* part of the three-prong test—in other words, evidence that the substituted ingredient or apparatus (1) performs substantially the same function, in (2) substantially the same way, to (3) achieve substantially the same result as that which is literally claimed.[79] Without such close adherence to the three-prong test, the court feared that juries would be "put to sea without guiding charts."[80] Still, the debate commonly boils down to the second prong of the test—whether the accused product and the claimed invention function in "substantially the same way"[81]—and the answer to that question is rarely straightforward.

---

[76] *See* Paper Converting Machine Co. v. Magna-Graphics Corp., 745 F.2d 11, 19 (Fed. Cir. 1984) ("In view of [the doctrine of equivalents], a copier rarely knows whether his product 'infringes' a patent or not until a district court passes on the issue.").

[77] Barrett v. Hall, 2 F. Cas. 914, 923 (C.C.D. Mass. 1818).

[78] *See, e.g.,* Malta v. Schulmerich Carillons, Inc., 952 F.2d 1320, 1327 (Fed. Cir. 1991); Lear Siegler, Inc. v. Sealy Mattress Co., 873 F.2d 1422, 1425 (Fed. Cir. 1989).

[79] *See Malta,* 952 F.2d at 1327; *Lear Siegler,* 873 F.2d at 1425.

[80] *Lear Siegler,* 873 F.2d at 1426–27. A patentee invoking the three-part test should offer "particularized testimony and linking argument" showing, specifically, how the accused product performs substantially the same function as the claimed invention, in substantially the same way, to achieve substantially the same result. "Generalized testimony as to . . . overall similarity" will not suffice. Paice LLC v. Toyota Motor Co., 504 F.3d 1293, 1304–05 (Fed. Cir. 2007).

[81] *See* Slimfold Mfg. Co., Inc. v. Kinkead Indus., Inc., 932 F.2d 1453, 1457 (Fed. Cir. 1991).

Another important consideration is whether the item found in the accused product is known to be interchangeable with the item literally claimed.[82] This is not a definitive test of equivalence.[83] Things may be interchangeable in the broadest sense if they produce similar results but still operate in substantially different ways. A word processor may be interchangeable with a ballpoint pen for the purpose of preparing a grocery list, but the two may not be equivalent in an infringement analysis.[84] On the other hand, a physical incompatibility that would complicate the substitution of one thing for another (e.g., putting instant film in a 35 mm camera) does not, necessarily, prevent those things from being equivalent in a more conceptual sense.[85]

In recent years, the trend has been to downplay the function-way-result test as the conclusive test of equivalency.[86] Instead, the three-prong test has been described as just one approach to the fundamental inquiry, which is whether the differences between the claimed and the accused product are "insubstantial."[87]

---

[82] *See* Graver Tank & Mfg. Co. v. Linde Air Prods. Co., 339 U.S. 605, 609 (1950); Vulcan Eng'g Co. v. Fata Aluminium, Inc., 278 F.3d 1366, 1374 (Fed. Cir. 2002) ("Known interchangeability is an important factor in determining equivalence.").

[83] *See* Warner-Jenkinson Co. v. Hilton Davis Chemical Co., 520 U.S. 28, 37 (1997) (known interchangeability "is not relevant for its own sake, but rather for what it tells the fact-finder about the similarities or differences between those elements"); Abraxis Bioscience, Inc. v. Mayne Pharma (USA) Inc., 467 F.3d 1370, 1382 (Fed. Cir. 2006) (absence of known interchangeability is not determinative: "known interchangeability is only one factor to consider in a doctrine of equivalents analysis"); Key Mfg. Gp., Inc. v. Microdot, Inc., 925 F.2d 1444, 1449 (Fed. Cir. 1991) ("an interchangeable device is not necessarily an equivalent device"); Perkin-Elmer Corp. v. Westinghouse Elec. Corp., 822 F.2d 1528, 1535 (Fed. Cir. 1987) (interchangeable devices "still must perform substantially the same function in substantially the same way to obtain the same result").

[84] *See Perkin-Elmer*, 822 F.2d at 1535 (devices were "interchangeable" only in "entirely different and unrelated environments" and were not interchangeable for performing certain functions).

[85] *See* Interactive Pictures Corp. v. Infinite Pictures, Inc., 274 F.3d 1371, 1383 (Fed. Cir. 2001) ("Rather than focusing on physical or electronic compatibility, the known interchangeability test looks to the knowledge of a skilled artisan to see whether that artisan would contemplate the interchange as a design choice."); *but cf.* Frank's Casing Crew & Rental Tools, Inc. v. Weatherford Int'l, Inc., 389 F.3d 1370, 1378 (Fed. Cir. 2004) (mechanical incompatibility "underscored" a finding of substantial differences).

[86] *See Warner-Jenkinson*, 520 U.S. at 39–40 ("[W]hile the triple identity test may be suitable for analyzing mechanical devices, it often provides a poor framework for analyzing other products or processes."); Toro Co. v. White Consolidated Indus., Inc., 266 F.3d 1367, 1370 (Fed. Cir. 2001) (the function-way-result test "offers additional guidance" in "appropriate cases").

[87] *See* Stumbo v. Eastman Outdoors, Inc., 508 F.3d 1358, 1364 (function-way-result test is "one way" to show that the differences are insubstantial); Aquatex Indus., Inc. v. Techniche Solutions, 479 F.3d 1320, 1326 (Fed. Cir. 2007); Upjohn Co. v. Mova Pharmaceutical Corp., 225 F.3d 1306, 1309 (Fed. Cir. 2000) (three-prong test is "[t]he usual test of the substantiality of the differences"). As one court explained the test, an equivalent is "an insubstantial change which, from the perspective of one of ordinary skill in the art, adds nothing of significance to the claimed invention." Valmont Indus., Inc. v. Reinke Mfg. Co., 983 F.2d 1039, 1043 (Fed. Cir. 1993).

Yet to ask whether a difference is "substantial" or "insubstantial" seems more a rephrasing of the equivalence question than a clarification.[88] For its part, the Supreme Court in *Warner-Jenkinson* declined to endorse any particular "linguistic framework" for deciding the ultimate question of equivalence.[89] In short, the question of equivalence is likely to remain a perennial source of confusion and difficulty.

10.6.5 Improvements

Equivalency calls on the perspective of the person of ordinary skill in the art *at the time of the alleged infringement*.[90] Consequently, variations that the patentee had not even imagined, much less enabled, can be held infringing under the doctrine of equivalents. For example, if a transistor were substituted for a vacuum tube referenced in a patent claim, that claim might still be infringed under the doctrine of equivalents even if, when the patent application was filed, transistors had not been invented yet. If the rule were otherwise, technological advancements would allow competitors to take the substance of an invention but still avoid infringement. This does not mean, however, that technological advancements are irrelevant in judging equivalency. A transistor might be such a marked advancement over a vacuum tube that, in the context of a particular invention, the differences between the two would be thought substantial even at the time of infringement.

One factor that bears on whether an improvement is still an equivalent is whether the improvement is itself the subject of a patent. If we limit equivalence to "insubstantial variations," a change worthy of its own patent seems beyond reach. However, while it is a factor to be considered and given "due weight,"[91]

---

[88] *See Warner-Jenkinson*, 520 U.S. at 40 ("the insubstantial differences test offers little additional guidance as to what might render a given difference 'insubstantial'"). However, "[i]n some cases, the change in the accused device is so facially 'unimportant and insubstantial' that little additional guidance is needed." *Toro*, 266 F.3d at 1370.

[89] *Warner-Jenkinson*, 520 U.S. at 40.

[90] Warner-Jenkinson Co. v. Hilton Davis Chemical Co., 520 U.S. 28, 37 (1997) ("[T]he proper time for evaluating equivalency—and thus knowledge of interchangeability between elements—is at the time of infringement, not at the time the patent was issued."); Lighting World, Inc. v. Birchwood Lighting, Inc., 382 F.3d 1354, 1357 (Fed. Cir. 2004).

[91] National Presto Indus., Inc. v. West Bend Co., 76 F.3d 1185, 1192 (Fed. Cir. 1996); *see also* Zygo Corp. v. Wyko Corp., 79 F.3d 1563, 1570 (Fed. Cir. 1996) ("The nonobviousness of the accused device, evidenced by the grant of a United States patent, is relevant to the issue of whether the change therein is substantial.").

it cannot be said categorically that a patented improvement is never equivalent.[92]

Texas Instruments, Inc. v. U.S. Int'l Trade Comm'n[93] illustrates the difficulty of applying the equivalency concept in fields subject to rapid technological change.[94] Texas Instruments obtained the first patent ever issued on a pocket calculator. The court acknowledged it as a "pioneering invention"[95] and noted that the prototype had become part of the permanent collection at the Smithsonian's Museum of History and Technology. In essence, the claims of the patent called for the basic combination of a keyboard, a processing circuit, a memory, and a display, but because the claims were drafted in "means-plus-function" format,[96] the claims literally incorporated only the particular keyboard, processing circuit, memory, and display described in the patent specification, and their "equivalents."

About 17 years after filing its patent application, and 10 years after the patent issued, Texas Instruments brought an action to prevent the importation of pocket calculators by foreign manufacturers. During those years, the field had advanced in significant ways. MOS transistors had replaced bipolar transistors, liquid crystal displays had replaced thermal printer displays, and so forth. The Federal Circuit found that each substitution, by itself, might be considered the substitution of an equivalent, but when considered *as a whole*, all of the technological changes were sufficient to take the accused devices beyond the protection of the doctrine of equivalents.[97] The decision was a controversial one, even among the judges of the Federal Circuit.

Years later, and in spite of the result in *Texas Instruments*, the Federal Circuit announced in *Chiuminatta Concrete Concepts, Inc. v. Cardinal Indus., Inc.*[98] that

[92] Fiskars, Inc. v. Hunt Mfg. Co., 221 F.3d 1318, 1324 (Fed. Cir. 2000) ("it is well established that separate patentability does not avoid equivalency as a matter of law"); *National Presto*, 76 F.3d at 1192; Atlas Powder Co. v. E.I. Du Pont de Nemours & Co., 750 F.2d 1569, 1580 (Fed. Cir. 1984). In *Festo Corp. v. Shoketsu Kinzoku Kogyo Kabushiki Co.*, 493 F.3d 1368, 1379 (Fed. Cir. 2007), the court observed that "[w]e have not directly decided whether a device—novel and separately patentable because of the incorporation of an equivalent feature—may be captured by the doctrine of equivalents." However, "there is a strong argument that an equivalent cannot be both non-obvious and insubstantial." *Id.* at 1380. Just as an improvement is sometimes still an equivalent, an inferior variation may also be equivalent. *See* Whapeton Canvas Co. v. Frontier, Inc., 870 F.2d 1546, 1548 n.2 (Fed. Cir. 1989) ("inferior infringement is still infringement"). The question, as before, is whether or not the differences are "insubstantial."

[93] 805 F.2d 1558 (Fed. Cir. 1986). Also see the opinion on denial of rehearing *en banc*, 846 F.2d 1369 (Fed. Cir. 1988).

[94] The opinion deals with equivalence under 35 U.S.C. § 112, ¶ 6, discussed in Section 10.7, and under the doctrine of equivalents. At the time, the court treated the analysis as essentially the same. *See Texas Instruments*, 805 F.2d at 1571. More recently, the court has suggested a difference—confining § 112, ¶ 6 equivalence to structures that existed in the art when the patent was filed, and equivalence under the doctrine of equivalents to later-developed structures. See Section 10.7.

[95] See Section 10.6.7.

[96] See Section 7.7.4.

[97] *Texas Instruments*, 805 F.2d at 1570–72.

[98] 145 F.3d 1303 (Fed. Cir. 1998).

the unpredictability of technological developments is the primary reason, perhaps the *only* reason, to invoke the doctrine of equivalents. "The doctrine of equivalents is necessary," the court observed, "because one cannot predict the future."[99] If the applicant knew about the unclaimed equivalent (because it is "technology that predates the invention itself"), and *could* have claimed it in the patent, the court knew of "no policy-based reason why a patentee should get two bites at the apple."[100] In other words, unless the failure to claim the full scope of the invention explicitly can be excused by historical necessity, the court may refuse to apply the doctrine of equivalents.

Chiuminatta's emphasis on later-developed technology may be overdone.[101] The Supreme Court has justified the doctrine of equivalents, at least in part, by reference to the inherent imprecision of language[102]—a problem that goes beyond that of advancing technologies. *Graver Tank* itself dealt with an equivalent known at the time the patent application was filed. Later cases have interpreted *Chiuminatta's* "two bites at the apple" reasoning as applying only to means-plus-function claims, where equivalence of structure is already an issue for literal infringement.[103] Except in those cases, "the mere fact that the asserted equivalent structure was pre-existing technology does not foreclose a finding of infringement under the doctrine of equivalents."[104] The rhetoric of *Chiuminatta* is, however, representative of recent efforts by the Federal Circuit to confine the doctrine of equivalents to situations where the uncertainty it creates is easiest to justify.[105]

10.6.6 Impact of the "All Elements" Rule on Equivalence

One of the most important refinements of the principles announced in *Graver Tank* involves the "all elements" rule, which states that every element of the claimed invention must be found in an infringing product.[106] In *Pennwalt Corp. v. Durand-Wayland, Inc.*,[107] the Federal Circuit, in the form of

---

[99] *Id.* at 1310.

[100] *Id.* at 1311.

[101] The paragraphs discussing the "after-developed technology" rationale for the doctrine of equivalents are uncharacteristically free of citations to precedent. *See id.* at 1310–13.

[102] "[T]the nature of language makes it impossible to capture the essence of a thing in a patent application." Festo Corp. v. Shoketsu Kinzoku Kogyo Kabushiki Co., 535 U.S. 722, 731 (2002).

[103] See Section 10.7.

[104] Kraft Foods, Inc. v. International Trading Co., 203 F.3d 1362, 1373 (Fed. Cir. 2000).

[105] A more specific application of the *Chiuminatta* reasoning is the Federal Circuit's refusal to recognize equivalents that were actually *disclosed* in the application, without being explicitly claimed. See Section 10.6.9.

[106] *See* Cook Biotech Inc. v. Acell, Inc., 460 F.3d 1365, 1379 (Fed. Cir. 2006); Freedman Seating Co. v. American Seating Co., 420 F.3d 1350, 1358 (Fed. Cir. 2005); Forest Labs., Inc. v. Abbott Labs., 239 F.3d 1305, 1310 (Fed. Cir. 2001).

[107] 833 F.2d 931 (Fed. Cir. 1987) (*en banc*).

an expanded *en banc* panel, considered whether the doctrine of equivalents could be applied if the claimed invention and the accused product were similar *as a whole*, even though individual claim elements were entirely absent in the accused product.

The invention in *Pennwalt* was a machine used to sort fruit by color and weight. One of the claimed components of the machine was a "position indicating means," which kept track of the physical location of a piece of fruit as it passed through the sorter. The accused product—also a sorting device—produced comparable results. However, it did so without any means for keeping track of the physical location of a piece of fruit. Although a number of judges dissented, the majority held that an accused product cannot infringe a claim under the doctrine of equivalents unless every claim element, or its equivalent, can be found in the accused product. Overall similarity is insufficient if any claim element is entirely missing.[108] In *Warner-Jenkinson Co. v. Hilton Davis Chemical Co.*,[109] the Supreme Court reaffirmed the rule established in *Pennwalt*, stating that a strict, element-by-element application of the doctrine would ensure fair notice to potential infringers.[110]

As a corollary to the "all elements" rule, courts resist any argument, even one couched in terms of equivalence, that seems to ignore completely a very clear claim limitation. As the Supreme Court stated, "[i]t is important to ensure that the application of the doctrine, even as to an individual element, is not allowed such broad play as to effectively eliminate that element in its

---

[108] *Pennwalt*, 833 F.2d at 935, 939; *see also* E-Pass Technologies, Inc. v. 3Com Corp., 473 F.3d 1213, 1221 (Fed. Cir. 2007) ("Under the 'all elements' rule, 'the doctrine of equivalents must be applied to individual elements of the claim, not to the invention as a whole.'"); Depuy Spine, Inc. v. Medtronic Sofamor Danek, Inc., 469 F.3d 1005, 1017 (Fed. Cir. 2006); *Freedman*, 420 F.3d at 1358 ("an accused product or process is not infringing unless it contains each limitation of the claim, either literally or by an equivalent"). On the other hand, there need not be a "one-to-one correspondence" between the claim and the accused product. A single component of an accused product can perform the functions of several components described in the claim, and the single component can be considered the equivalent of *each* claimed component. Dolly, Inc. v. Spalding & Evenflo Co., 16 F.3d 394, 398 (Fed. Cir. 1994); Sun Studs, Inc. v. ATA Equipment Leasing, Inc., 872 F.2d 978, 989 (Fed. Cir. 1989) ("elements or steps may be combined without *ipso facto* loss of equivalency"). This principle allows somewhat greater flexibility in applying the doctrine of equivalents than the "all elements" rule might suggest.

[109] 520 U.S. 17 (1997)

[110] *Id.* at 29–30 ("Each element in a patent claim is deemed material to defining the scope of the patented invention, and thus the doctrine of equivalents must be applied to individual elements of the claim, not to the invention as a whole."). Interestingly, the Supreme Court did not mention *Pennwalt*, and discussed the "all elements" approach as though it were a newly discovered compromise solution to the problems posed by the doctrine of equivalents.

entirety."[111] When a claim limitation specifically excludes an alternative, a court may refuse to find them equivalent.[112] For example, in *Moore U.S.A., Inc. v. Standard Register Co.*,[113] the patent claims described a "business type mailer form" having adhesive strips extending "the majority of the lengths" of the margins.[114] The accused product had adhesive strips covering only a minority of the margins, but the plaintiff argued that the product was still equivalent. The court rejected that argument, in part because "it would defy logic to conclude that a minority—the very antithesis of a majority—could be insubstantially different from a claim limitation requiring a majority."[115] Of course, whether something is an opposite or "antithesis" as opposed to an insignificant difference is sometimes a matter of perspective. "Majority" seems the opposite of "minority," but, as a dissenting judge in *Moore* pointed out, just under 50 percent might differ insubstantially from just over 50 percent.[116]

10.6.7 Impact of the Prior Art on Equivalence

The prior art imposes another limitation on the doctrine of equivalents.[117] The doctrine of equivalents cannot expand the scope of a claim so far that it

---

[111] *Warner-Jenkinson*, 520 U.S. at 29; *see also Depuy*, 469 F.3d at 1017; Planet Bingo, LLC v. Gametech Int'l, Inc., 472 F.3d 1338, 1344 (Fed. Cir. 2006); Primos, Inc. v. Hunter's Specialties, Inc., 451 F.3d 841, 850 (Fed. Cir. 2006) ("The 'all limitations rule' restricts the doctrine of equivalents by preventing its application when doing so would vitiate a claim limitation."); Lear Siegler, Inc. v. Sealy Mattress Co., 873 F.2d 1422, 1425 (Fed. Cir. 1989) ("'a court may not, under the guise of applying the doctrine of equivalents, erase a plethora of meaningful structural and functional limitations of the claims[s] on which the public is entitled to rely in avoiding infringement.'"). There is "no set formula" for deciding if a broad reading of equivalence would actually "vitiate" the relevant claim limitation. "Rather, courts must consider the totality of the circumstances of each case and determine whether the alleged equivalent can be fairly characterized as an insubstantial change . . . without rendering the pertinent limitation meaningless." *Freedman*, 420 F.3d at 1359. It does not "vitiate" a claim element each time a court or jury finds an equivalent for a claim element not literally met. That approach would "'swallow the doctrine of equivalents entirely.'" *See* Abbott Labs. v. Andrx Pharmaceuticals, Inc., 473 F.3d 1196, 1212 (Fed. Cir. 2007); *Depuy*, 469 F.3d at 1018 (the doctrine of equivalents "'*necessarily* deals with subject matter that is "beyond," "ignored" by, and not included in the literal scope of the claim'" (emphasis in original)).

[112] *See Cook Biotech*, 460 F.3d at 1379 ("'the concept of equivalency cannot embrace a structure that is specifically excluded from the scope of the claims'"); Scimed Life Sys., Inc. v. Advanced Cardiovascular Sys., Inc., 242 F.3d 1337, 1345 (Fed. Cir. 2001) ("Having specifically identified, criticized, and disclaimed the dual lumen configuration, the patentee cannot now invoke the doctrine of equivalents to 'embrace a structure that was specifically excluded from the claims.'"); Athletic Alternatives, Inc. v. Prince Mfg., Inc., 73 F.3d 1573, 1582 (Fed. Cir. 1996). A detailed claim may be read to exclude alternatives implicitly. *See* Bicon, Inc. v. Straumann Co., 441 F.3d 945, 955 (Fed. Cir. 2006).

[113] 229 F.3d 1091 (Fed. Cir. 2000).

[114] *Id.* at 1095.

[115] *Id.* at 1106; *see also* Asyst Techs., Inc. v. Emtrak, Inc., 402 F.3d 1188, 1195 (Fed. Cir. 2005) ("the term 'mounted' can fairly be said to specifically exclude objects that are 'unmounted'").

[116] *See Moore*, 229 F.3d at 1119 (Newman, J., concurring in part and dissenting in part).

[117] Section 8.9 discusses "prior art."

encompasses the prior art.[118] One method of analyzing the problem (though it is not an exclusive method) is to imagine a "hypothetical claim" that would be *literally* infringed by the product at issue.[119] If the patentee could not have obtained such a claim—because it would have been anticipated by the prior art or rendered obvious[120]—then the accused product does not infringe. The purpose of this limitation is to ensure that patentees do not achieve indirectly, through the doctrine of equivalents, a monopoly that could not have been obtained directly by prosecution of a broader claim.[121]

The restrictions imposed by the prior art create, in effect, a "safe harbor" insofar as the doctrine of equivalents is concerned, if the accused product in all relevant respects is identical to an invention in the prior art. No hypothetical claim could encompass such a product yet avoid invalidity. The restriction applies only to the claim as a whole, so there is no immunity from infringement by equivalence unless all of the relevant features of the accused product are found in the prior art, either in one reference or in several that, together, made the combination obvious. Because patents are often granted to novel combinations of known elements, one cannot escape infringement, either literal or under the doctrine of equivalents, merely by identifying isolated features of the accused product in the prior art.[122]

The prior art also influences the doctrine of equivalents in a subtler fashion, through the concept of the "pioneer patent." Whereas most patents are granted to incremental improvements of inventions that have gone before, a pioneer patent is one that breaks with the past so distinctly that it creates an entirely new field. Patents such as Bell's on the telephone, or the Texas Instruments calculator patent, have staked claims to "pioneering" status. Some cases have held that a pioneer patent, as a very basic advancement in technology, should be given a correspondingly broad scope of equivalence. A patent on a narrow improvement, on the other hand, should be held more

---

[118] Tate Access Floors, Inc. v. Interface Architectural Resources, Inc., 279 F.3d 1357, 1367 (Fed. Cir. 2002); Interactive Pictures Corp. v. Infinite Pictures, Inc., 274 F.3d 1371, 1380 (Fed. Cir. 2001) ("It is well settled law that a patentee cannot assert a range of equivalents that encompasses the prior art.").

[119] Abbott Labs. v. Dey, L.P., 287 F.3d 1097, 1105 (Fed. Cir. 2002); *Interactive Pictures*, 274 F.3d at 1380; Wilson Sporting Goods Co. v. David Geoffrey & Assoc., 904 F.2d 677, 684 (Fed. Cir. 1990).

[120] See Sections 8.9.5 and 8.9.6.

[121] *See Tate Access Floors*, 279 F.3d at 1367 ("the doctrine of equivalents is an equitable doctrine and it would not be equitable to allow a patentee to claim a scope of equivalents encompassing material that had been previously disclosed by someone else, or that would have been obvious in light of others' earlier disclosures"); *Wilson Sporting Goods*, 904 F.2d at 684 ("The doctrine of equivalents exists to prevent fraud on a patent . . . *not* to give a patentee something which he could not lawfully have obtained from the PTO had he tried.").

[122] *See Abbott Labs.*, 287 F.3d at 1106; Corning Glass Works v. Sumitomo Elec. U.S.A., Inc., 868 F.2d 1251, 1261 (Fed. Cir. 1989).

strictly to the language of the claims.[123] Of course, whether or not a patent deserves to be called "pioneering" will often be a subject for debate.[124]

For the most part, the Federal Circuit has declined to divide patents into "pioneering" and "non-pioneering" categories. Instead, it has treated pioneering patents as just one end of a spectrum that embraces various degrees of inventiveness.[125] Moreover, it has emphasized that pioneer patents are not subject to different legal standards than other patents, as a reward for merit or otherwise.[126] A pioneering patent merely enjoys a potentially broader scope of equivalence because it is not hemmed in by large numbers of similar inventions in the prior art, as is generally true of an incremental improvement in an already crowded field.[127]

10.6.8 Prosecution History Estoppel

One of the most important limitations on the doctrine of equivalents is "prosecution history estoppel." The prosecution history is the written record of an applicant's dealings with the Patent Office, including any actions taken by the examiner and any statements, arguments, or modifications of the claims made by the applicant.[128] "Estoppel" means that a claim is barred because the claimant's prior actions are inconsistent with that claim. Simply put, prosecution history estoppel prevents a patent owner

---

[123] *See* Sun Studs, Inc. v. ATA Equipment Leasing, Inc., 872 F.2d 978, 987 (Fed. Cir. 1989) ("The concept of the 'pioneer' arises from an ancient jurisprudence, reflecting judicial appreciation that a broad breakthrough invention merits a broader scope of equivalents than does a narrow improvement in a crowded technology.").

[124] "That an improvement enjoys commercial success and has some industry impact, as many do, cannot compel a finding that an improvement falls within the pioneer category." Perkin-Elmer Corp. v. Westinghouse Elec. Corp., 822 F.2d 1528, 1532 (Fed. Cir. 1987). Even the pioneering status of Texas Instruments' calculator patent was challenged. *See* Texas Instruments, Inc. v. U.S. Int'l Trade Comm'n, 846 F.2d 1369, 1370 (Fed. Cir. 1988).

[125] *See* Sun Studs, 872 F.2d at 987 ("[T]he 'pioneer' is not a separate class of invention, carrying a unique body of law. The wide range of technological advance between pioneering breakthrough and modest improvement accommodates gradations in scope of equivalency."); *Texas Instruments*, 846 F.2d at 1370 ("[t]here is not a discontinuous transition from 'mere improvement' to 'pioneer'").

[126] *See* Augustine Medical, Inc. v. Gaymar Indus., Inc., 181 F.3d 1291, 1301 (Fed. Cir. 1999) ("no objective legal test separates pioneers from non-pioneers").

[127] *See* Abbott Labs., 287 F.3d at 1105 ("A pioneer patent by definition will have little applicable prior art to limit it, whereas an improvement patent's scope is confined by the existing knowledge on which the improvement is based."); *Augustine Medical*, 181 F.3d at 1301 ("Without extensive prior art to confine and cabin their claims, pioneers acquire broader claims than non-pioneers who must craft narrow claims to evade the strictures of a crowded art field."); *Texas Instruments*, 846 F.2d at 1370 (the "liberal" scope of equivalency afforded to pioneer patents "flows directly from the relative sparseness of prior art in nascent fields of technology").

[128] See Section 5.1.

from contradicting the prosecution history, by claiming as an equivalent subject matter *given up* during prosecution in order to obtain the patent.[129]

Brenner v. United States[130] illustrates the principle. The patented invention in *Brenner* concerned a system for coding and sorting mail. The claims described a means for applying a "codable" material, such as a magnetic strip, to an article of mail. The material would carry the information needed for the sorting. Initially, the claims referred to a "coded" rather than "codable" material, implying that the information was encoded beforehand. However, the applicant changed the claim language to "codable," telling the examiner that the new language more accurately described the invention "'since when the material is placed on the mail it is not yet coded.'"[131] When compelled to distinguish certain prior art, the applicant stressed this distinction and also emphasized that the material could be erased after encoding.

The system accused of infringing used an ink jet printer to spray bar codes directly on the mail to be sorted. The only article applied to the mail was the ink itself, and the ink was not literally "codable." By the time the ink hit the paper, it was fixed in a predetermined pattern, and it could not be altered or erased afterward. The trial court, affirmed by the Federal Circuit, found that the accused system could not be held equivalent to the system claimed because the applicant, during prosecution, had clearly limited the invention to "codable" material.[132]

Prosecution history estoppel checks the inclination of some patent owners to treat claims as a "nose of wax," to be twisted in one direction to avoid invalidity and in another to ensure infringement. An applicant who represents the invention as one thing in prosecution must be prepared to live with that interpretation in litigation. There can be no "second bite at the abandoned apple."[133] The doctrine also provides better notice to a

---

[129] *See* Festo Corp. v. Shoketsu Kinzoku Kogyo Kabushiki Co., 535 U.S. 722, 741 (2002); Regents of the Univ. of California v. Dakocytomation California, Inc., 517 F.3d 1364, 1376 (Fed. Cir. 2008); Cross Medical Prods., Inc. v Medtronic Sofamor Danek, Inc., 480 F.3d 1335, 1341 (Fed. Cir. 2007). While the clearest cases of estoppel arise when the applicant narrows a claim by amendment, *see Cross Medical*, 480 F.3d at 1341 ("a narrowing amendment classically invokes the doctrine"), estoppel can also result when the applicant argues in favor of a narrow claim interpretation. *See* Pods, Inc. v. Porta Stor, Inc., 484 F.3d 1359, 1368 (Fed. Cir. 2007); Conoco, Inc. v. Energy & Environmental Int'l, L.C., 460 F.3d 1349, 1363 (Fed. Cir. 2006). As the Supreme Court has observed, "the doctrine of equivalents is premised on language's inability to capture the essence of innovation"—a premise "undercut" when the applicant specifically abandoned material now urged to be equivalent. *Festo*, 535 U.S. at 734. Applicant arguments may create an estoppel even if they were unnecessary to secure the issuance of the patent. *See Pods*, 484 F.3d at 1368. However, estoppel does require that the prosecution history demonstrate a "clear and unmistakable surrender of subject matter." *Id.* at 1367; *Conoco*, 460 F.3d at 1364.

[130] 773 F.2d 306 (Fed. Cir. 1985).

[131] *Id.* at 307.

[132] *Id.* at 308.

[133] Lemelson v. General Mills, Inc., 968 F.2d 1202, 1208 (Fed. Cir. 1992).

patentee's competitors of the scope of the patented invention, at least in those cases where the competitors have an opportunity to review the prosecution history.[134] Most important, the doctrine of prosecution history estoppel prevents applicants from circumventing the process of patent examination. If the scope of equivalence were not limited by the prosecution history, an applicant could narrow the claims as much as necessary to satisfy the examiner, while resorting to the doctrine of equivalents to preserve what amounts to a broader claim. Prosecution history estoppel helps to ensure that a patent claim is no broader in scope than the examiner understood it to be.[135]

In *Festo Corp. v. Shoketsu Kinzoku Kogyo Kabushiki Co.*,[136] the Federal Circuit, to the surprise of many patent attorneys, announced that if a claim element had been narrowed during prosecution, for reasons related to patentability, the doctrine of equivalents could not be applied to that element *at all* in any subsequent litigation.[137] Suppose, for example, that a claim to a mousetrap originally called for "at least one spring," but the examiner found the claim to be anticipated by a prior trap with a single spring. The applicant might amend the claim to call for "two springs," perhaps pointing out how the two springs of the preferred embodiment produced non-obvious advantages compared to the one-spring prior art. The patentee could not argue afterward that a trap with *three* springs infringed by equivalency, even though the difference between two and three springs might be insignificant. By specifically referring to "two springs," the applicant disclaimed anything else. The majority of the court viewed this as the only "workable" approach, fostering predictability and respect for the notice function of claims.[138] However, the decision contradicted earlier cases promoting a more flexible brand of estoppel, and it confounded the expectations of many patent attorneys who had routinely amended claims without being aware of the drastic effect.[139]

---

[134] *See id.* at 1208 ("Other players in the marketplace are entitled to rely on the record made in the Patent Office in determining the meaning and scope of the patent."). For the same reason, a patentee may be barred from claiming as an equivalent an alternative distinguished and criticized in the patent specification. *See* L.B. Plastics, Inc. v. Amerimax Home Prods., Inc., 499 F.3d 1303, 1309 (Fed. Cir. 2007); Astrazeneca AB v. Mutual Pharmaceutical Co., 384 F.3d 1333, 1342 (Fed. Cir. 2004) (clear disavowal in specification bars claim of equivalence).

[135] *See* Genentech, Inc. v. Wellcome Found. Ltd., 29 F.3d 1555, 1564 (Fed. Cir. 1994) ("An applicant should not be able deliberately to narrow the scope of examination to avoid during prosecution scrutiny by the PTO of subject matter . . . and then, obtain in court, either literally or under the doctrine of equivalents, a scope of protection which encompasses that subject matter.").

[136] 234 F.3d 558 (Fed. Cir. 2000) (*en banc*).

[137] *Id.* at 574.

[138] *Id.* at 575–77.

[139] *See Festo*, 234 F.3d at 638 (Newman, J., concurring in part and dissenting in part).

The Supreme Court accepted the appeal and reversed.[140] The court reaffirmed the principle of prosecution history estoppel[141] and held that the scope of equivalence could be limited by any claim amendment made in order to secure a patent (and not merely to avoid prior art).[142] On the other hand, the court rejected the notion that a claim amendment leads automatically to a complete bar on equivalents:

> By amending the application, the inventor is deemed to concede that the patent does not extend as far as the original claim. It does not follow, however, that the amended claim becomes so perfect in its description that no one could devise an equivalent. After amendment, as before, language remains an imperfect fit for invention. The narrowing amendment may demonstrate what the claim is not; but it may still fail to capture precisely what the claim is. There is no reason why a narrowing amendment should be deemed to relinquish equivalents unforeseeable at the time of the amendment and beyond a fair interpretation of what was surrendered. Nor is there any call to foreclose claims of equivalence for aspects of the invention that have only a peripheral relation to the reason the amendment was submitted.

Consequently, one must consider whether the thing now claimed as an equivalent is precisely what the patentee relinquished. In changing "at least one spring" to "two springs," did the patent applicant surrender the three-spring mousetrap?

The more subtle approach breeds uncertainty, but this is alleviated, to some degree, by the Supreme Court's assignment of the burden of proof. First, one must presume that a narrowing claim amendment offered during prosecution was occasioned by a "substantial reason related to patentability."[143] The burden is on the patent owner to rebut that presumption by showing that the amendment had another explanation "sufficient to overcome prosecution history estoppel."[144] It might have been, for example, a "truly cosmetic"[145] or clarifying amendment, having no impact on the scope of the claim. Second, if the amendment was related to patentability, the patentee also "bear[s] the burden of showing that the amendment [did] not surrender the particular equivalent in question."[146] If the patentee cannot meet

---

[140] 535 U.S. 722 (2002).

[141] *Id.* at 733–34.

[142] *Id.* at 736–37.

[143] Warner-Jenkinson, Inc. v. Hilton Davis Chemical Co., 520 U.S. 17, 33 (1997).

[144] *Warner-Jenkinson,* 520 U.S. at 33. Alternative reasons for claim amendment should be demonstrated by evidence in the prosecution history, not by an after-the-fact declaration of the patentee's intentions. *See* Pioneer Magnetics, Inc. v. Micro Linear Corp., 330 F.3d 1352, 1356 (Fed. Cir. 2003) (rejecting patent attorney's contention that a narrowing amendment had been made "through sheer inadvertence").

[145] *Festo,* 535 U.S. at 736–37.

[146] *Id.* at 740.

that burden, a court will presume that the patentee gave up, irretrievably, all of the subject matter excluded from the claim due to the amendment—like the three-spring mousetrap encompassed, in our hypothetical, by the original claim language.[147]

After remand of *Festo* from the Supreme Court, the Federal Circuit explained that the presumption of surrender can be rebutted in three ways. First, the patentee can show that "the rationale underlying the amendment [bore] no more than a tangential relation to the equivalent in question."[148] If the amendment in our example had depended on a fundamental distinction between a single spring and multiple springs (perhaps it had been questioned whether any single spring could generate the force required), the patentee might argue that the one-spring-versus-two-spring rationale had been, at best, tangential to the issue of equivalence between two springs and three. Second, the patentee can demonstrate that the alleged equivalent was unforeseeable at the time of the amendment.[149] If a three spring mousetrap had been inconceivable, perhaps because of some technical barrier in the art

---

[147] If the applicant adds a narrowing limitation to one claim, and that same term was already present in another claim, the estoppel may limit the range of equivalents available to *both* claims, a phenomenon dubbed "infectious estoppel" by one litigant. *See* Glaxo Wellcome Inc. v. Impax Labs. Inc., 356 F.3d 1348, 1356 (Fed. Cir. 2004) ("[S]ubject matter surrendered via claim amendments during prosecution is also relinquished for other claims containing the same limitation. . . . This court follows this rule to ensure consistent interpretation of the same claim terms in the same patent.").

[148] Festo Corp. v. Shoketzu Kinzoku Kogyo Kabushiki Co., 344 F.3d 1359, 1365 (Fed. Cir. 2003) (*en banc*) (quoting *Festo*, 535 U.S. at 740); *see also Regents of the Univ. of California*, 517 F.3d at 1378 (claim narrowed for reasons tangential to the issue at hand); Primos, Inc. v. Hunter's Specialties, Inc., 451 F.3d 841, 849 (Fed. Cir. 2006) (same). The Federal Circuit has warned that the "tangential relation criterion for overcoming the *Festo* presumption is very narrow." *Cross Medical*, 480 F.3d at 1342.

[149] "This criterion presents an objective inquiry, asking whether the alleged equivalent would have been unforeseeable to one of ordinary skill in the art at the time of the amendment." *Festo*, 344 F.3d at 1369. Patentees who argue, for purposes of infringement, that the alleged equivalent was a known substitute (see Section 10.6.4) may have a particularly difficult time arguing that unforeseeability rebuts the presumption of estoppel. *See* Ranbaxy Pharmaceuticals Inc. v. Apotex, Inc. 350 F.3d 1235, 1241 (Fed. Cir. 2003). In a recent opinion still related to the *Festo* dispute, the Federal Circuit held that a known technology is not "unforeseeable" merely because a person skilled in the art would not have expected it to be an equivalent capable of performing substantially the same function, in substantially the same way, to achieve substantially the same result. Festo Corp. v. Shoketsu Kinzoku Kogyo Kabushiki Co., 493 F.3d 1368, 1382 (Fed. Cir. 2007) ("An equivalent is foreseeable if one skilled in the art would have known that the alternative existed . . . even if the suitability of the alternative for the particular purposes defined by the amended claim scope were unknown."). In other words, if transistors were known of at the time of the amendment, the estoppel effect of narrowing a vacuum tube claim to exclude transistors could not be undone on grounds of unforeseeability, even if no one knew they could perform like a vacuum tube. Judge Newman penned a strong dissent, arguing that unknown capabilities produce unforeseeable equivalents. *See id.* at 1385.

that no one expected to overcome, the applicant could not have anticipated the limiting effect of the amendment, nor might an objective observer, equally skilled in the art, have expected such an effect. Generally, if the alleged equivalent embodies technology unknown in the art at the time of the claim amendment—for example, a variant with transistors unforeseeable when vacuum tubes were the state of the art—the equivalent will be considered unforeseeable. Old technology, particularly if found in prior art in the field of the invention, is likely to be considered foreseeable.[150] Finally, the patentee may rebut the presumption by showing "some other reason" it could not have been expected to express the claim amendment in such a way as to still include what is now argued to be equivalent.[151] This catch-all category is necessarily vague, but it might include arguments based on a "shortcoming of language."[152] Whether the patentee has met its burden of proof will be determined by the judge as a matter of law, not by the jury.[153]

If *Festo* is not the watershed it might have been had the original Federal Circuit decision been allowed to stand, it does at least promise a more predictable analysis for prosecution history estoppel. The focus on foreseeability recognizes both the difficulties of patent applicants, who hope to reap the rewards of their efforts for years to come, and the interests of potential infringers, who deserve fair warning of prohibited conduct.

10.6.9 Disclosure of Unclaimed Embodiments

Even when an alleged "equivalent" is beyond the literal scope of the claims, sometimes it is discussed in the specification. In some ways this seems to bolster the patentee's argument in favor of infringement. At least it shows that the patentee was aware of the equivalent, and it suggests the possibility of substituting that equivalent for the matter literally claimed. But the effect of the disclosure can be quite the opposite, as illustrated in the case of *Maxwell v. J. Baker, Inc.*[154]

Maxwell was a store employee who invented a system for tying together pairs of shoes for display. Previous systems had relied on plastic filaments strung through the eyelets of the shoes, but this only worked for shoes that *had* eyelets. This led some retailers to punch holes in the shoes, just to provide a way of tying them together. Maxwell's idea was to anchor plastic tabs inside the shoes and use holes or loops in the tabs as the attachment point

---

[150] *Festo*, 344 F.3d at 1369. Expert testimony may be useful in determining what would have been foreseeable at the time of the claim amendment. *See id.*

[151] *Id.* at 1370.

[152] Amgen Inc. v. Hoechst Marion Roussel, Inc. 457 F.3d 1293, 1313–16 (Fed. Cir. 2006); *Festo*, 344 F.3d at 1370. The Federal Circuit cautions that this third category of excuse is, like the tangential relation argument, "a narrow one." *Amgen*, 457 F.3d at 1313.

[153] *Festo*, 344 F.3d at 1369.

[154] 86 F.3d 1098 (Fed. Cir. 1996).

for the filament. The figures in Maxwell's patent specification showed the tabs anchored between the inner and outer soles of the shoes, and the claims explicitly referred to this construction, but the specification also observed that the tabs could be stitched into the lining of the shoes. The court held that shoes having tabs sewn into the lining did not infringe Maxwell's patent under the doctrine of equivalents, precisely because that option had been disclosed, *but not claimed,* in Maxwell's patent. Such unclaimed disclosures are "dedicated to the public" and cannot be recaptured through the doctrine of equivalents.[155]

The court's position tends to penalize applicants for making their disclosures more thorough and informative. If Maxwell had kept silent about the unclaimed alternative, it might well have been found infringing. On the other hand, from the perspective of a competitor trying to determine what would infringe, it may be reasonable to conclude that things discussed in the patent, but specifically excluded from the claims, were not meant to be covered by the patent. In addition, the Supreme Court has stressed the inability of language to capture the essence of an invention as the rationale for the doctrine of equivalents.[156] A patentee who described an alleged equivalent in the specification can hardly claim that he "lacked the words to describe the subject matter in question."[157] Finally, the "dedication to the public" of unclaimed embodiments forces applicants to subject to the rigors of PTO examination claims as broad as the monopoly they ultimately attempt to enforce.

For a time, it was uncertain whether the principle of *Maxwell* would find broad application,[158] but in 2002 the Federal Circuit's *en banc* opinion in *Johnson & Johnston Assoc., Inc. v. R.E. Serv. Co.*[159] reaffirmed the rule that "when a patent drafter discloses but declines to claim subject matter . . . this action dedicates that unclaimed subject matter to the public."[160] In this case, the patentee, whose claims called for an "aluminum sheet," could not argue that

---

[155] *Id.* at 1106–07; *see also* Unique Concepts, Inc. v. Brown, 939 F.2d 1558, 1562–63 (Fed. Cir. 1991).

[156] *See* Festo Corp. v. Shoketsu Kinzoku Kogyo Kabushiki Co., 535 U.S. 722, 734–38 (2002).

[157] *Festo,* 535 U.S. at 734 (applying the same reasoning where claims were narrowed to exclude the alleged equivalent).

[158] *See* YBM Magnex, Inc. v. Int'l Trade Comm'n, 145 F.3d 1317 (Fed. Cir. 1998) (holding that *Maxwell* creates no "blanket rule" regarding disclosed but unclaimed embodiments, but offering little to clarify the limits of the *Maxwell* principle).

[159] 285 F.3d 1046 (Fed. Cir. 2002).

[160] *Johnson & Johnston,* 285 F.3d at 105; *see also* PSC Computer Prods. Inc. v. Foxconn Int'l Inc., 355 F.3d 1353, 1357–60 (Fed. Cir. 2004). Although in the landmark Supreme Court case of *Graver Tank* the equivalent alternative of manganese was disclosed in the specification, the Federal Circuit distinguished that case as one in which the applicant at least *tried* to obtain the broader claim, though it failed when the PTO rejected it. That reasoning presents some difficulties, but at least the *Graver Tank* situation is less likely an instance of a patentee attempting to "game the system." *See Johnson & Johnston,* 285 F.3d at 1060 (Dyk, J., concurring).

a steel sheet was equivalent when the patent specifically disclosed, without claiming, the steel alternative.[161] The court cited the usual concerns regarding the primacy of claims and the desirability of fair notice to the public.[162] Like its unsuccessful attempt in *Festo*,[163] the "disclosure-dedication rule" can be seen as another effort by the Federal Circuit to rein in the doctrine of equivalents and restore some certainty to the patent system.

10.7 EQUIVALENCE IN THE CONTEXT OF MEANS-PLUS-FUNCTION CLAIMS

Patent law would be less confusing if equivalence were an issue arising solely in connection with the doctrine of equivalents. However, equivalence is also an issue affecting *literal* infringement if the claim is a means-plus-function claim, drafted in accordance with Paragraph 6 of 35 U.S.C. § 112.[164] Section 7.7.4 discusses means-plus-function claims. To summarize, literal infringement where a claim element recites a "means" for performing a specified function requires (1) that the accused product perform that function and (2) that it use a structure identical or "equivalent" to the corresponding structure disclosed in the patent specification.[165]

Suppose that a mousetrap claim includes "a means for snapping the trap shut," and the specification discloses a steel spring to perform that function. The first step in addressing infringement is to see if the accused mousetrap has *any* means for "snapping the trap shut." If no component of the accused mousetrap performs that function, the claim is not literally infringed.[166] If the

---

[161] *Id.* at 1055.

[162] *Id.* at 1052. In order to be "dedicated to the public," the unclaimed alternative must be described in the patent with sufficient specificity that it can be identified by a person of ordinary skill in the art as a variation disclosed but not claimed. *PSC*, 355 F.3d at 1360; *see also* Pfizer, Inc. v. Teva Pharmaceuticals, USA, Inc., 429 F.3d 1364, 1379 (Fed. Cir. 2005) (the dedicated subject matter must have been "identified by the patentee as an alternative to a claim limitation"). Whether the patentee subjectively intended to disclaim is not a factor. Toro Co. v. White Consolidated Indus., Inc., 383 F.3d 1326, 1333 (Fed. Cir. 2004).

[163] See Section 10.6.8.

[164] "An element in a claim for a combination may be expressed as a means or step for performing a specified function without the recital of structure, material, or acts in support thereof, and such claim shall be construed to cover the corresponding structure, material or acts described in the specification and equivalents thereof."

[165] Frank's Casing Crew & Rental Tools, Inc. v. Weatherford Int'l, Inc., 389 F.3d 1370, 1378 (Fed. Cir. 2004); Momos Corp. v. Brainlab USA, Inc., 357 F.3d 1364, 1369 (Fed. Cir. 2004); Overhead Door Corp. v. Chamberlain Gp., Inc., 194 F.3d 1261, 1273 (Fed. Cir. 1999).

[166] One might inquire, however, whether it performs an equivalent function sufficient to apply the doctrine of equivalents. *See* Interactive Pictures Corp. v. Infinite Pictures, Inc., 274 F.3d 1371, 1382 (Fed. Cir. 2001) ("[I]nfringement under the doctrine of equivalents may be premised on the accused and the patented component having *substantially* the same function, whereas structure corresponding to the disclosed limitation in a means-plus-function clause must perform the *identical* function." (emphasis in original)).

accused mousetrap does have some means for "snapping the trap shut," we then ask whether the structure performing that function is identical or equivalent to the steel spring. If the accused mousetrap uses a rubber band, we have to decide whether a rubber band and a steel spring are equivalent in the context of the invention.

Paradoxically, this is one case in which literal infringement does not involve taking the language of the claims literally. Literally, a claim requiring a "means for snapping the trap shut" would be satisfied by *any* means performing that function. The compromise embodied in § 112, ¶ 6 is that patentees are allowed to express a claim element as a "means" (which otherwise might be considered indefinite), but literal infringement is restricted to equivalents of the corresponding structure shown in the specification.[167]

Equivalency for purposes of § 112, ¶ 6 should not to be confused with equivalency for purposes of the doctrine of equivalents. The contexts are different, since the latter is a specialized subset of the *literal* infringement inquiry.[168] The basis for comparison is also different. Section 112, ¶ 6 requires comparison of the accused product with the structures disclosed in the *specification,* while the doctrine of equivalents requires comparison of the accused product with the *claims.*

The tests of equivalence are generally similar. Both "invoke[] the familiar concept of an insubstantial change which adds nothing of significance."[169] It is less clear whether the traditional function-way-result test of the doctrine of equivalents can also be applied to equivalence under § 112, ¶ 6. In the *Texas Instruments* case, the court stated that in either instance "the test is the same three-part test of history: does the asserted equivalent perform substantially the same function in substantially the same way to accomplish substantially the same result?"[170] Later, the court held that "[a] determination of section 112 equivalence does not involve the . . . tripartite

---

[167] *See* Warner-Jenkinson Co. v. Hilton Davis Chemical Co., 520 U.S. 17, 28 (1997) (equivalence under §112, ¶ 6 is "an application of the doctrine of equivalents in a restrictive role, narrowing the application of broad literal claim elements"); Al-Site Corp. v. VSI Int'l, Inc., 174 F.3d 1308, 1320 (Fed. Cir. 1999); Johnston v. IVAC Corp., 885 F.2d 1574, 1580 (Fed. Cir. 1989) (§ 112, ¶ 6 "operates to *cut back* on the types of *means* which could literally satisfy the claim language" (emphasis in original)).

[168] *See* Valmont Indus., Inc. v. Reinke Mfg. Co., 983 F.2d 1039, 1043 (Fed. Cir. 1993) ("The doctrine of equivalents has a different purpose and application than section 112.").

[169] *Valmont,* 983 F.2d at 1043; *see also* Chiuminatta Concrete Concepts, Inc. v. Cardinal Indus., Inc., 145 F.3d 1303, 1310 (Fed. Cir. 1998) (both forms of equivalency "protect the substance of a patentee's right to exclude by preventing mere colorable differences or slight improvements from escaping infringement," and they do so "by applying similar analyses of insubstantiality of the differences").

[170] Texas Instruments, Inc. v. United States Int'l Trade Comm'n, 805 F.2d 1558, 1571 (Fed. Cir. 1986).

test of the doctrine of equivalents."[171] Perhaps the most that can really be said is that equivalence under § 112, ¶ 6, like the equivalence discussed in *Graver Tank*, is "not the prisoner of a formula," but depends on the circumstances of each case.[172]

In *Chiuminatta Concrete Concepts, Inc. v. Cardinal Indus., Inc.*,[173] the Federal Circuit distinguished the rationales for the doctrine of equivalents and equivalency under § 112, ¶ 6. The reason for the doctrine of equivalents, the court said, is that unforeseen technological advances may allow minor variations in what the applicant has literally described.[174] It would not be fair to an applicant whose claims required a "vacuum tube" to allow the substitution of its modern equivalent, the solid-state transistor.[175] In cases of newly developed technology, the court seemed willing to permit a broader range of equivalents than would be permitted under § 112, ¶ 6.[176] If, on the other hand, the alleged equivalent is "technology that predates the invention itself" rather than a newly developed variation, a finding of non-equivalence under § 112, ¶ 6 should preclude a finding of equivalence under the doctrine of equivalents.[177]

The *Chiuminatta* opinion is not a model of clarity, and it seems to overstate the differences in rationale between the doctrine of equivalents and § 112, ¶ 6. Arguably, each is a remedy for the inherent inability of language to capture the essence of an invention, whether that inability is due to evolving technologies

---

[171] *Valmont*, 983 F.2d at 1043. The function-way-result test may be inappropriate to the literal infringement analysis under § 112, ¶ 6 because the function must be *identical*, not merely "substantially the same." *See* IMS Tech., Inc. v. Haas Automation, Inc., 206 F.3d 1422, 1435 (Fed. Cir. 2000) ("[A] reduced version of the well-known tripartite test for the doctrine of equivalents has been applied in the § 112, ¶ 6 context to determine if the differences are insubstantial, i.e., after determining that the accused device performs the identical function, as required by statute, whether it performs the function in substantially the same way to achieve substantially the same result.").

[172] *See IMS Tech.*, 206 F.3d at 1436 ("the context of the invention should be considered when performing a § 112, ¶ 6 equivalence analysis just as it is in a doctrine of equivalents determination"); Intel Corp. v. U.S. Int'l Trade Comm'n, 946 F.2d 821, 842–43 (Fed. Cir. 1991) ("[A]ids for determining a structural equivalent to the structure disclosed in the patent specification are the same as those used in interpreting any other type of claim language, namely, the specification, the prosecution history, other claims in the patent, and expert testimony.").

[173] 145 F.3d 1303 (Fed. Cir. 1998).

[174] See Section 10.6.5.

[175] *See Chiuminatta*, 145 F.3d at 1310.

[176] *See id.* at 1310 ("Even if [a later-developed] element is found not to be a § 112, ¶ 6, equivalent because it is not equivalent to the structure disclosed in the patent, this analysis should not foreclose it from being an equivalent under the doctrine of equivalents.").

[177] *Id.* at 1311; *see also Frank's Casing*, 389 F.3d at 1379 (the difference between § 112, ¶ 6 and the doctrine of equivalents is "a question of timing"; after-arising technology should be analyzed under the doctrine of equivalents, but existing technology under § 112, ¶ 6 (into which the doctrine of equivalents analysis "collapses")).

or to lack of foresight and suitable vocabulary.[178] Later interpretations of *Chiuminatta* suggest that an important difference is between equivalence of *structure*, where the issues of equivalence may merge, and equivalence of *function*, where only the doctrine of equivalents is relevant.[179] This line of cases, however, has produced one important distinction, which may explain how the results could differ when the tests of equivalence seem to be identical. Under the doctrine of equivalents, equivalence is judged as of the date of the alleged infringement.[180] Equivalence under § 112, ¶ 6 is judged as of the date the patent issued, since the literal meaning of a claim should be fixed at that time.[181] Accordingly, an alternative that a person skilled in the art might not have considered equivalent when the patent issued—perhaps because he had never heard of it—might be considered equivalent at a later date.

10.8 THE REVERSE DOCTRINE OF EQUIVALENTS

The doctrine of equivalents has a judicially devised counterpart known as the "reverse doctrine of equivalents." The source of the "reverse doctrine" is the following language in *Graver Tank*:[182]

> The wholesome realism of [the doctrine of equivalents] is not always applied in favor of a patentee but is sometimes used against him. Thus, where a device is so far changed in principle from a patented article that it performs the same or a similar function in a substantially different way, but nevertheless falls within the literal words of the claim, the doctrine of equivalents may be used to restrict the claim and defeat the patentee's action for infringement.

Thus, a product literally described by a claim can be held non-infringing if it is "so far changed in principle" that it functions in a "substantially different way" compared with what the patentee actually invented.

---

[178] *See* Kraft Foods, Inc. v. International Trading Co., 203 F.3d 1362, 1372–73 (Fed. Cir. 2000) (except in the case of means-plus-function claims, where equivalent structures known at the time of the patent already literally infringe, infringement under the doctrine of equivalents is *not* limited to later-developed technologies).

[179] *See Interactive Pictures*, 274 F.3d at 1381–82; WMS Gaming, Inc. v. International Game Technology, 184 F.3d 1339, 1353 (Fed. Cir. 1999). The later cases, however, still preserve the possibility of newly developed structure that is equivalent only under the doctrine of equivalents. *Interactive Pictures,* 274 F.3d at 1381; *Al-Site,* 174 F.3d at 1320 n.2 (because of the problem of unforeseeable technological change, "the doctrine of equivalents appropriately allows marginally broader coverage than § 112, ¶ 6").

[180] *Warner-Jenkinson*, 520 U.S. at 37.

[181] *Al-Site*, 174 F.3d at 1320.

[182] Graver Tank & Mfg. Co. v. Linde Air Prods. Co., 339 U.S. 605, 608–09 (1950); *see also* Scripps Clinic & Research Found. v. Genentech, Inc., 927 F.2d 1565, 1581 ("the purpose of the 'reverse' doctrine is to prevent unwarranted extension of the claims beyond a fair scope of the patentee's invention"); SRI Int'l v. Matsushita Elec. Corp., 775 F.2d 1107, 1123 (Fed. Cir. 1985) (*en banc*).

The language in *Graver Tank* suggests that the doctrine of equivalents is a two-way street, but in practice the "reverse doctrine" has proven to be far less potent than its counterpart. Cases won on the reverse doctrine of equivalents are exceedingly rare.[183] In 2002 the Federal Circuit observed that it had never, in its 20-year history, affirmed a finding of non-infringement based on the reverse doctrine.[184] Before the legislative adoption of means-plus-function claims and their explicit limitations, the judicially created reverse doctrine of equivalents may have served to restrict the scope of overly broad claims. Today, the court found, the strictures of § 112—including the definiteness, description, and enablement requirements—left the reverse doctrine an "anachronistic exception . . . long mentioned but rarely applied."[185] Absent a problem of enablement or description, it would be difficult to persuade a court that an accused product literally described by a patent claim was still so "changed in principle" as to avoid infringement.

10.9 EXPERIMENTAL USE EXCEPTION TO INFRINGEMENT

A rarely invoked defense to a charge of infringement is that the challenged activity was done for purposes of experimentation rather than profit. This defense finds some support in a number of older cases in which a patented device was constructed not to sell it, but to test its advantages. For example, in *Akro Agate Co. v. Master Marble Co.*,[186] the court held that the use of a patented machine to make glass marbles was not an infringement because the marbles had been made only as an experiment, the results were unsatisfactory, and the marbles themselves were not sold. In *Kaz Mfg. Co. v. Chesebrough-Ponds, Inc.*,[187] the defendant constructed a patented vaporizer solely for the purpose of a television commercial in which it compared the design unfavorably with its own (using the slogan "steam is dangerous"). The court did not view this as an infringement either.

The Federal Circuit has viewed the experimental use exception as an extremely narrow one, applicable only when the experiments were conducted "solely for amusement, to satisfy idle curiosity, or for strictly philosophical inquiry."[188] In other words, a kitchen experimenter amusing himself on a rainy afternoon might practice a patent without infringing, but experiments conducted

---

[183] *See, e.g.,* Precision Metal Fabricators Inc. v. Jetstream Sys. Co., 6 U.S.P.Q.2d 1704 (N.D. Cal. 1988); Lesona Corp. v. United States, 530 F.2d 896, 905–06 (Ct. Cl. 1976).

[184] Tate Access Floors, Inc. v. Interface Architectural Resources, Inc., 279 F.3d 1357, 1368 (Fed. Cir. 2002).

[185] *Tate Access Floors,* 279 F.3d at 1368.

[186] 318 F. Supp. 305, 315, 333 (N.D. W. Va. 1937).

[187] 317 F.2d 679 (2d Cir. 1963).

[188] Madey v. Duke Univ., 307 F.3d 1351, 1362 (Fed. Cir. 2002); Embrex, Inc. v. Service Eng'g Corp., 216 F.3d 1343, 1349 (Fed. Cir. 2000).

for commercial purposes are likely to violate a patent, if they involve making or using the claimed invention.[189] Any use "in keeping with the legitimate business of the alleged infringer" fails to qualify for the limited exception,[190] including research undertaken by a university solely for purposes of education and discovery.[191]

In 35 U.S.C. § 271(e), Congress established a narrow experimental use exception to cover the testing of patented pharmaceuticals.[192] When a patent on a particular drug expires, rival manufacturers are, of course, permitted to market their own versions of the drug. But before this can happen, the new drug must undergo extensive government-required tests of safety and effectiveness. If manufacturing and using the drug for purposes of such tests were held to be an infringement, the tests could not *begin* until after the patent had expired. Consequently, there would be a considerable delay between the expiration of the patent and the opportunity to market a competitive drug. The patent owner would have, in effect, a patent of longer duration than the patent laws intend. Section 271(e) prevents this by allowing these tests to occur prior to the expiration of the patent, without fear of liability.

---

[189] *See* Douglas v. United States, 181 U.S.P.Q. 170, 176–77 (Ct. Cl. 1974). In the former instance, the infringement is seemingly excused on the legal principle of "de minimis non curat lex," or "the law does not concern itself with trifles." *But see Embrex*, 216 F.3d at 1352–53 (Rader, J., concurring) (arguing that patent law does not permit *de minimis* infringement; "the statute leaves no leeway to excuse infringement because the infringer only infringed a little").

[190] *Madey*, 307 F.3 at 1362.

[191] Id. at 1362 ("[M]ajor research universities . . . often sanction and fund research projects with arguably no commercial application whatsoever. However, these projects unmistakably further the institution's legitimate business objectives, including educating and enlightening students and faculty participating in these projects. These projects also serve . . . to increase the status of the institution and lure lucrative research grants, students and faculty.").

[192] *See* Merck KGaA v. Integra Life Sciences I, Ltd., 545 U.S. 193, 202 (2005) (the statute "provides a wide berth for the use of patented drugs in activities related to the federal regulatory process"). Although the statute is not clear on this point, it has been held to cover both drugs and *medical devices* that must undergo government-required tests. Eli Lilly & Co. v. Medtronic, Inc., 496 U.S. 661 (1990).

CHAPTER 11

Patent Litigation

A patent owner whose rights have been infringed can file a lawsuit in a Federal District Court.[1] If the suit is successful, the court can compel the infringer to stop the infringing activity and pay the patent owner for infringement that has already occurred. Litigation, or the threat of litigation, is what gives a patent its "teeth."

The suit may be brought by the original recipient of the patent, or its successor if rights to the patent have been transferred by assignment.[2] Either may be referred to as the "patentee." If the owner of the patent transfers "all substantial rights," the new owner may sue in its name alone.[3] A licensee who possesses an exclusive license,[4] but not "all substantial rights," may sue for infringement but must join the patent owner in the suit, to guard against the possibility of multiple judgments against the same infringer.[5] A licensee who does *not* have an exclusive license lacks the kind of injury necessary for "standing" to sue.[6] A non-exclusive licensee cannot expect to be the only party making, using, or selling the patented invention. On the other hand,

---

[1] The patent owner cannot sue in a state court because the federal courts have "exclusive jurisdiction." *See* 28 U.S.C. § 1338(a). If the defendant imports infringing goods, the patent owner may initiate proceedings in the International Trade Commission in lieu of, or in addition to, a suit in a district court. See Section 11.9. Suits against the United States government must be brought in the Court of Claims. *See* 28 U.S.C. § 1498.

[2] *See* 35 U.S.C. §§ 281 (patentee's right to sue for infringement), 100(d) ("patentee" includes successors in interest); Morrow v. Microsoft Corp., 499 F.3d 1332, 1339 (Fed. Cir. 2007).

[3] *Morrow*, 499 F.3d at 1340.

[4] See Section 6.3.

[5] *Morrow*, 499 F.3d at 1340.

[6] Id.

the licensee may be disadvantaged in competition if it is paying for the right to practice the patented invention and the infringer is not, so the licensee may wish to persuade the patent owner to bring suit—something the owner should be willing to consider in order to preserve the value of a license.

A typical lawsuit involves three issues:

- Is the patent valid and enforceable?
- Are the claims infringed?
- If the claims are infringed, what relief should be awarded?

The patentee can prevail only if the patent is valid *and* infringed. On occasion, the defendant[7] will concede that the patent is valid and will challenge only the charge of infringement, or it will concede infringement and argue invalidity, but it is more common for the defendant to make war on both fronts. Patent litigation may also involve related claims (e.g., breach of contract, unfair competition, or antitrust claims) if they arise from the same factual situation.

Infringement litigation is often a complicated, time-consuming, and costly process. Patent cases typically involve both subtle issues of law and complex questions of technology. In order to try such a case, both parties have to acquire a thorough understanding of, at a minimum, the patent and its file history, the accused products, and any prior art that might be used to challenge the validity of the patent. As a result, just the "discovery" phase of the litigation, in which both parties gather the evidence needed to try the case, often takes more than a year. It is not unusual for an infringement suit to last several years from the day it is filed until the final disposition of the case, and worse examples can be found.[8]

Patent cases are difficult for courts and juries, both because the law is unfamiliar and because an understanding of complex technology may be critical. Imagine how difficult it would be for an average juror to determine whether one complex procedure in genetic engineering is "equivalent" to another. Simply mastering the vocabulary can be a daunting task. These difficulties contribute to a certain level of unpredictability in the outcome of patent litigation.

11.1 JURISDICTION AND VENUE

The geographical location where a suit for patent infringement must be filed (for example, in the Northern District of California or in the Eastern District of New York) depends on the rules of "in personam jurisdiction" and "venue." A

---

[7] It is convenient to use the term "defendant" interchangeably with "accused infringer," but in a declaratory judgment action (see Section 11.2) the accused infringer may technically be the plaintiff.

[8] For example, in March 1999 the Supreme Court denied the last appeal in *United States v. Hughes Aircraft Co.*, a case filed in 1973. *See* 525 U.S. 1177 (1999).

federal court has in personam jurisdiction (or jurisdiction over the person) only if the individual or corporate defendant has had certain "minimum contacts" with the district in which that court resides.[9] If an accused infringer has had no contact whatsoever with, for example, the state of Florida, then suit cannot be filed there. The minimum contacts doctrine has constitutional origins in the due process clause. The rules are subtle and depend in part on the jurisdictional rules of the state where the court is located.[10] If the accused infringer has an office in the district, or regularly transacts business in the district, or conducts infringing activity in the district, the minimum contacts test will likely be satisfied.[11] It may even be sufficient that the infringer intended the accused products to enter the district via the "stream of commerce."[12]

If a court has jurisdiction over the defendant, the next question is that of venue. The rules of venue create further restrictions on where suit can be filed. In a patent case, venue is appropriate in the following districts:

- Where the defendant "resides," *or*
- Where the defendant has committed acts of infringement *and* has a regular and established place of business.[13]

In 1988 the federal venue statutes were altered so that corporate defendants are now held to "reside" in any district where the corporation is subject

---

[9] *See* International Shoe Co. v. State of Washington, 326 U.S. 310, 316 (1945) (defendant must have "certain minimum contacts with [the forum] such that the maintenance of the suit does not offend 'traditional notions of fair play and substantial justice'"). The defendant's contacts with the forum must be such that "he should reasonably anticipate being haled into court there." *See* World-Wide Volkswagen Corp. v. Woodson, 444 U.S. 286, 297 (1980); LSI Indus. Inc. v. Hubbell Lighting, Inc., 232 F.3d 1369, 1375 (Fed. Cir. 2000). The emphasis is on deliberate or "purposeful" contacts rather than those that may occur by accident. *See* Beverly Hills Fan Co. v. Royal Sovereign Corp., 21 F.3d 1558, 1565 (Fed. Cir. 1994).

[10] *See* Trintec Indus., Inc. v. Pedre Promotional Prods., Inc., 395 F.3d 1275, 1279–80 (Fed. Cir. 2005) (discussing the state "long-arm statute").

[11] If the accused infringer's contacts with the forum are "continuous and systematic," the court may have "general jurisdiction" concerning *any* matter involving the accused infringer. *See id.* at 1279; Deprenyl Animal Health, Inc. v. University of Toronto Innovations Found., 297 F.3d 1343, 1350 (Fed. Cir. 2002). If the contacts are more sporadic but relate specifically to the subject matter of the suit, the court may exercise "specific jurisdiction," so long as that is consistent with "fair play and substantial justice." *See Trintec,* 395 F.3d at 1279; *Deprenyl,* 297 F.3d at 1350–51. A thorny issue is whether a corporate internet website accessible in the region is sufficient to establish jurisdiction. The answer may depend on whether the site is a passive one, available only for reading, or an interactive one that permits business transactions. *See Trintec,* 395 F.3d at 1281.

[12] *See* Viam Corp. v. Iowa Export-Import Trading Co., 84 F.3d 424, 427–28 (Fed. Cir. 1996); *Beverly Hills Fan,* 21 F.3d at 1565 ("The allegations are that defendants purposefully shipped the accused fan into Virginia through an established distribution channel. The cause of action for patent infringement is alleged to arise out of those activities. No more is usually required to establish specific jurisdiction.").

[13] 28 U.S.C. § 1400(b).

to in personam jurisdiction—in other words, wherever it has established "minimum contacts."[14] Most patent cases are filed against corporations rather than against individuals or partnerships, so the minimum contacts standard is generally the test of whether a suit can or cannot be filed in a particular judicial district.

Because a corporate defendant typically has "minimum contacts" with several states—possibly all 50—patent owners may have a number of choices in deciding where to file suit. The choice is likely to be governed by factors such as geographical convenience, the experience of the court in dealing with patent litigation, whether the court's docket permits a speedy trial, and any perceived "home field" advantages. Within the limits set by the rules of jurisdiction and venue, the location of the lawsuit is generally within the control of the plaintiff. If, however, the defendant can show that another district would be more suitable (for the "convenience of parties and witnesses" and "in the interest of justice"[15]), the court in which the suit was filed has the power to transfer the case to another district, if it is a district in which the suit could have been filed in the first instance.

11.2 DECLARATORY JUDGMENT

Patent cases generally arise when a patent owner files suit against a party it accuses of infringement. However, it is also possible for the accused infringer to launch a preemptive strike by filing suit against a patentee. A suit of this kind is called an action for "declaratory judgment" because it asks the court to declare that the party filing suit is *not* liable to the patent owner, either because the patent is invalid or is not infringed, or for some other reason.[16] The potential infringer in such a case is nominally the plaintiff, and the patent owner is the defendant.[17]

If it were not for declaratory judgment actions, parties accused of infringement would have to wait until the patent owner chose to litigate before the dispute could be resolved. In the meantime, the accused infringer would have to give in to the patent owner's demands, or proceed as before with the risk that investments would be lost, and accumulated damages assessed, when the patent owner finally did sue.[18] A suit for declaratory judgment

---

[14] *See* 28 U.S.C. § 1391(c); *Trintec,* 395 F.3d at 1280 ("Venue in a patent action against a corporate defendant exists wherever there is personal jurisdiction."); VE Holding Corp. v. Johnson Gas Appliance Co., 917 F.2d 1574 (Fed. Cir. 1990).

[15] 28 U.S.C § 1404(a).

[16] *See* 22 U.S.C. § 2201 (Declaratory Judgment Act).

[17] Even if the patent owner initiates the lawsuit, the accused infringer may choose to file a *counterclaim* for declaratory judgment.

[18] *See* Cardinal Chemical Co. v. Morton Int'l, Inc., 508 U.S. 83, 95 (1993) (discussing the Declaratory Judgment Act as a cure for the "scarecrow patent").

allows the potential infringer to bring matters to a head. It also gives the accused infringer more control over the forum in which the case will be heard.

Federal courts generally follow a "first to file" rule in deciding where a case will be tried.[19] Suppose that a patent owner in California accused a company in Illinois of infringement. For the sake of convenience, and possibly in the hope of sympathy from a local jury, the patent owner would likely prefer that any litigation take place in California, while the accused infringer, for the same reasons, would prefer Illinois. If the accused infringer sues for declaratory judgment in Illinois before the patent owner sues in California, the first-to-file rule generally means that the case will be heard in Illinois. The first-to-file rule is not absolute, however. An exception can be made if the interests of justice or expediency so require.[20]

A federal court can try a case only if there is a genuine dispute—a "case or controversy," in constitutional terms.[21] A potential infringer cannot file an action for declaratory judgment simply because there is a hypothetical possibility that a patent owner will allege infringement;[22] the threat must be definite and concrete. The Federal Circuit long applied strict standards of immediacy, including a reasonable apprehension of imminent litigation by the patentee.[23] In 2007 the Supreme Court criticized that test,[24] saying that the dispute must be "real and substantial," and one that admits of concrete relief rather than an advisory opinion.[25] The patent owner's pattern of suing similar businesses, together with public statements that it will pursue an aggressive litigation strategy, may be sufficient grounds for a potential defendant to file for declaratory judgment.[26] Or a licensee may file suit to have a patent declared invalid, without first breaching the license agreement to create the circumstances under which it could be sued for infringement.[27]

---

[19] *See* Electronics for Imaging, Inc. v. Coyle, 394 F.3d 1341, 1347 (Fed. Cir. 2005); Genentech, Inc. v. Eli Lilly & Co., 998 F.2d 931, 937 (Fed. Cir. 1993).

[20] *See Electronics for Imaging,* 394 F.3d at 1347–48; Serco Services Co. v. Kelley Co., 51 F.3d 1037, 1039 (Fed. Cir. 1995); *Genentech,* 998 F.2d at 937.

[21] *See* Micron Tech., Inc. v. Mosaid Techs., Inc., 518 F.3d 897, 901 (Fed. Cir. 2008); Sandt Tech,, Ltd. v. Resco Metal & Plastics Corp., 264 F.3d 1344, 1356 n.4 (Fed. Cir. 2001).

[22] *See* Vanguard Research, Inc. v. Peat, Inc., 304 F.3d 1249, 1254–55 (Fed. Cir. 2002) ("To invoke the court's declaratory judgment jurisdiction, a plaintiff must show 'more than the nervous state of mind of a possible infringer,' but does not have to show that the patentee is 'poised on the courthouse steps.'").

[23] *See* Phillips Plastics Corp. v. Kato Hatsujou K.K., 57 F.3d 1051, 1052–54 (Fed. Cir. 1995) (ongoing license negotiations did not create a reasonable apprehension of litigation).

[24] MedImmune, Inc. v. Genentech, Inc., 127 S. Ct. 764, 774 n.11 (2007).

[25] *Id.* at 771; *see also Micron,* 518 F.3d at 901.

[26] *See Micron,* 518 F.3d at 901.

[27] *MedImmune,* 127 S. Ct. at 777.

11.3 BURDEN OF PROOF

The patent owner has the burden of proving infringement by a "preponderance of the evidence."[28] In other words, based on the evidence presented, it must be more likely than not that the patent is infringed. If the evidence on each side is equally persuasive, the claim must fail.

If the accused infringer raises a defense of invalidity or unenforceability, the defendant bears the burden of proof with respect to that defense.[29] Moreover, the burden is one of "clear and convincing" evidence, a higher standard of proof than a mere preponderance of the evidence.[30] The evidence not only must favor the accused infringer's version of the facts; it must be sufficient to produce an "abiding conviction" that the facts are "highly probable."[31] The reason for this higher standard of proof is the "presumption of validity," discussed in Section 8.2.

11.4 THE ROLE OF JUDGE AND JURY

Litigants in a patent case are entitled to trial by jury.[32] This right can be waived, by consent of both parties, in favor of a bench trial, in which the judge decides all issues.[33] Even if the trial does involve a jury, the judge will still decide certain questions. Generally speaking, a judge decides "questions of law," whereas the jury decides "questions of fact."[34] In reality, most questions have a factual aspect and a legal aspect. For example, to decide if an accused product is "equivalent" to a claimed invention, one has to address questions of fact (how does the accused product differ from the

---

[28] Warner-Lambert Co. v. Teva Pharmaceuticals USA, Inc., 418 F.3d 1326, 1342 (Fed. Cir. 2005); Centricut, LLC v. ESAB Gp., Inc., 390 F.3d 1361, 1367 (Fed. Cir. 2004); Advanced Cardiovascular Sys., Inc. v. Scimed Life Sys., Inc., 261 F.3d 1329, 1336 (Fed. Cir. 2001).

[29] 35 U.S.C. § 282; PowerOasis, Inc. v. T-Mobile USA, Inc., 522 F.3d 1299, 1303 (Fed. Cir. 2008); Adenta GmbH v. OrthoArm, Inc., 501 F.3d 1364, 1371 (Fed. Cir. 2007); Pfizer, Inc. v. Apotex, Inc., 480 F.3d 1348, 1359 (Fed. Cir. 2007).

[30] Zenith Electronics Corp. v. PDI Communications Sys., Inc., 522 F.3d 1348, 1363 (Fed. Cir. 2008); Sitrick v. Dreamworks, LLC, 516 F.3d 993, 999 (Fed. Cir. 2008); *Pfizer*, 480 F.3d at 1359.

[31] *Pfizer*, 480 F.3d at 1359 n.5; Am-Pro Protective Agency, Inc. v. United States, 281 F.3d 1234, 1239–40 (Fed. Cir. 2002) (also referring to the standard as one of "well-nigh irrefragable" proof).

[32] *See* Markman v. Westview Instruments, Inc., 517 U.S. 370, 377 (1996) ("there is no dispute that infringement cases today must be tried to a jury, as their predecessors were more than two centuries ago").

[33] *See* Rule 38 of the Federal Rules of Civil Procedure.

[34] *See* Jurgens v. McKasy, 927 F.2d 1552, 1557 (Fed. Cir. 1991) ("In a jury trial, there are two decisionmakers, the judge and the jury. In general, the judge decides issues of law and issues committed to his discretion, and the jury decides issues of fact that are material to the case and in genuine dispute.").

claimed invention?) and questions of law (how much can the accused product differ from the claimed invention before the law no longer considers them "equivalent"?).

Because there is no practical way to separate every nuance of fact and law, certain issues have, somewhat arbitrarily, been deemed questions of law for the judge, and others questions of fact for the jury.[35] Anticipation is a question of fact,[36] but obviousness is a question of law.[37] Compliance with the enablement and definiteness requirements are questions of law.[38] Compliance with the written description and utility requirements are questions of fact.[39] Claim interpretation is a question of law,[40] while infringement is a question of fact.[41] Some questions of law, such as obviousness, depend in part on underlying issues of fact that can be submitted to the jury.[42]

The judge also rules on "equitable" claims and defenses. In the eighteenth century, there were two varieties of court—courts of law and courts of equity—and they differed in the kinds of claims that could be heard and the remedies that could be granted. Only courts of law provided a right to a jury trial. In the United States, courts of law and equity were merged long ago, so the distinction would be little more than a historical curiosity if not for the language of the Seventh Amendment of the Constitution. In lieu of setting forth the right to a jury trial in explicit terms, the Seventh Amendment provides that "the right of trial by jury shall be *preserved*" as it was under English common law. To this day courts are required to examine claims from a historical perspective and try to determine whether, applying eighteenth-century standards, the claim is "legal" or "equitable." If the latter, there is no right to a jury.[43]

For purposes of patent litigation, it is enough to know that a claim seeking *money damages* is a legal claim with a right to a jury trial, but a claim to an

---

[35] Frequent disagreements among the Federal Circuit judges as to whether something is a question of law or a question of fact illustrates how arbitrary the distinctions can be. *See, e.g.,* Markman v. Westview Instruments, Inc., 52 F.3d 967 (Fed. Cir. 1995) (*en banc* panel split on whether claim interpretation is an issue of law decided by the judge alone); Lough v. Brunswick Corp., 103 F.3d 1517 (Fed. Cir. 1997) (panel split on whether "experimental use" in the context of § 102(b) is a question of fact or law).

[36] Finisar Corp. v. DirecTV Group, Inc., 523 F.3d 1323, 1334 (Fed. Cir. 2008).

[37] Agrizap, Inc. v. Woodstream Corp., 520 F.3d 1337, 1343 (Fed. Cir. 2008).

[38] Ormco Corp. v. Align Tech., Inc., 498 F.3d 1307, 1318 (Fed. Cir. 2007) (enablement); IPXL Holdings, L.L.C. v. Amazon.com, Inc., 430 F.3d 1377, 1380 (Fed. Cir. 2005) (definiteness).

[39] Falkner v. Inglis, 448 F.3d 1357, 1363 (Fed. Cir. 2006) (written description); In re Swartz, 232 F.3d 862, 863 (Fed. Cir. 2000) (utility).

[40] *Markman,* 517 U.S. at 372.

[41] *Finisar,* 523 F.3d at 1332.

[42] *See* Mycogen Plant Science, Inc. v. Monsanto Co., 243 F.3d 1316, 1331 (Fed. Cir. 2001) (questions of law with underlying issues of fact can be submitted to the jury, accompanied by appropriate instructions on the law).

[43] *See* Tegal Corp. v. Tokyo Electron America, Inc., 257 F.3d 1331, 1339 (Fed. Cir. 2001).

injunction is an equitable claim. In the rare instance that a patentee chooses to forgo damages and sue only for an injunction, neither party has a right to a jury trial.[44] Certain defenses are also equitable in nature and are reserved for the judge to decide. These include inequitable conduct[45] (discussed in Section 9.1), laches, and estoppel[46] (discussed in Sections 11.8.3.3 and 11.8.3.4). The Federal Circuit has held that infringement under the doctrine of equivalents (discussed in Section 10.6), often referred to as the "*equitable* doctrine of equivalents," is in fact a matter for decision by a jury.[47]

In spite of the latter development, there may be a trend toward assigning more decision-making responsibility to judges and less to juries. At least certain disapproving Federal Circuit judges perceive such a trend.[48] This shift, if there is one, may reflect a feeling that juries are overmatched by the complex and difficult issues often presented in patent cases.

11.5 BIFURCATION

Patent cases are often tried in phases rather than all at once. A trial divided into two phases is "bifurcated," but division into three or more phases is also possible. The purpose of holding trial in stages is to focus the issues, avoid confusion, and save unnecessary effort.

One common practice is to hold separate trials on liability and damages. If the court does not find the accused infringer liable, there is no need to proceed with the damages phase. Another option is to hold a preliminary bench trial on those issues that do not require fact finding by the jury. For example, if a patent has been challenged on grounds of inequitable conduct (an "equitable" defense reserved to the judge), that part of the case can be tried before the jury has been selected.

When the Supreme Court held in *Markman v. Westview Instruments*[49] that claim interpretation is a matter within the province of the judge rather than the jury, questions arose as to how and when judges should decide questions of claim interpretation, and how judges should communicate their findings to the jury. Many courts have responded by scheduling a "*Markman* hearing" before the jury trial. During the hearing, the court may receive evidence and argument from all parties regarding their proposed claim interpretations.

---

[44] *See id.* at 1341.

[45] Kingsdown Medical Consultants, Ltd. v. Hollister, Inc., 863 F.2d 867, 876 (Fed. Cir. 1988) ("the ultimate question of whether inequitable conduct occurred is equitable in nature").

[46] A.C. Aukerman Co. v. R.L. Chaides Construction Co., 960 F.2d 1020, 1028 (Fed. Cir. 1992).

[47] Miken Composites, L.L.C. v. Wilson Sporting Goods Co., 515 F.3d 1331, 1336 (Fed. Cir. 2008).

[48] See Judge Newman's dissent in *Lough v. Brunswick Corp.*, 103 F.3d 1517, 1519 (Fed. Cir. 1997) ("In converting the factual question of experimental purpose into a matter of law, our court has cut another notch in the removal of patent issues from the trier of fact.").

[49] 517 U.S. 370, 372 (1996).

The judge's findings are then incorporated into the jury instructions so that the jury can determine whether or not the claims have been infringed.[50]

11.6 PRELIMINARY INJUNCTIONS

Patent litigation often begins with a motion for a preliminary injunction.[51] A preliminary injunction is a court order preventing the accused infringer from making, using, selling, offering to sell, or importing the accused product until the case has been decided. In effect, it forces the accused infringer to put its activities on hold. On occasion, the Federal Circuit has characterized a preliminary injunction as "a drastic and extraordinary remedy that is not to be routinely granted."[52]

The judge decides whether to grant the motion for a preliminary injunction by weighing the following factors:[53]

- The likelihood that the patent owner will ultimately prevail in the litigation—in other words, the likelihood that the patent will be held valid, enforceable, and infringed. This requires the judge to make a preliminary assessment of the evidence, including any defenses that may be raised by the accused infringer.
- Whether the patent owner would suffer "irreparable harm" if the injunction were denied. Irreparable harm is harm that cannot be cured by the eventual payment of money damages. If the only harm to the patentee is a temporary loss of royalty income pending trial, this loss is one that probably can be made up, with interest, when damages are received. However, the harm might be irreparable if the accused infringer would not have the funds to pay damages after trial, or if sales of infringing articles would create some form of intangible harm. For example, if the patent owner itself sold an article within the scope of the patent, the infringer's sales of an inferior product pending trial might injure the patent owner's reputation and market share in ways that would be difficult to translate into a payment of money. Note that if the patent owner fails to seek a preliminary injunction at the first opportunity, it may be difficult to convince the court that there is a threat of immediate harm.[54]

---

[50] *See* Sulzer Textile A.G. v. Picanol, N.V., 358 F.3d 1356, 1366 (Fed. Cir. 2004) ("[I]t is the duty of trial courts . . . to inform jurors both of the court's claim construction rulings on all disputed claim terms and of the jury's obligation to adopt and apply the court's determined meanings of disputed claim terms to the jury's deliberation of the facts.").

[51] *See* 35 U.S.C. § 283.

[52] National Steel Car, Ltd. v. Canadian Pacific Railway, Ltd., 357 F.3d 1319, 1324 (Fed. Cir. 2004).

[53] *See* Erico Int'l Corp. v. Vutec Corp., 516 F.3d 1350, 1353–54 (Fed. Cir. 2008); Abbott Labs. v. Andrx Pharmaceuticals, Inc., 473 F.3d 1196, 1200–01 (Fed. Cir. 2007); PHG Technologies, LLC v. St. John Cos., Inc., 469 F.3d 1361, 1365 (Fed. Cir. 2006).

[54] *See, e.g.,* High Tech Medical Instrumentation, Inc. v. New Image Indus., Inc., 49 F.3d 1551, 1557 (Fed. Cir. 1995) ("Absent a good explanation, not offered or found here, 17 months is a substantial period of delay that militates against the issuance of a preliminary injunction by demonstrating that there is no apparent urgency to the request for injunctive relief.").

- The balance of hardships if the motion is granted or denied. In other words, would the harm to the patent owner if the injunction were denied outweigh the harm to the accused infringer if the injunction were granted? The harm to the accused infringer is often more tangible and immediate. If the accused product accounts for a substantial portion of the accused infringer's business, the loss of that business pending trial could result in diminished profits, employee layoffs, or even bankruptcy. A court is unlikely to grant an injunction with such severe consequences unless it is very clear that the patent owner will prevail on the merits.
- The public interest. A court may hesitate to grant an injunction that would deny the public an important product–for example, a drug or medical device–even temporarily.[55] On the other hand, the enforcement of valid patents ultimately benefits the public by encouraging innovation.

A court must weigh each of these factors and determine whether a preliminary injunction is appropriate. The stronger the patent owner's case, the lesser the showing of irreparable harm necessary to justify an injunction.[56]

11.7 SUMMARY JUDGMENT

Sometimes the merits of a case are so clear that it is unnecessary to conduct a full-blown jury trial. The mechanism for cutting short such a case is known as "summary judgment." The judge grants summary judgment when there is no "genuine issue of material fact" for decision by a jury.[57] In other words, the evidence is so one-sided that the outcome of the case cannot reasonably be disputed, and a competent jury could reach only one decision.[58] Either party to a patent infringement suit may bring a motion for summary judgment, supported by evidence in its favor (usually in the form of documents and sworn testimony), or pointing out the absence of evidence supporting claims on which the other party bears the burden of proof.[59] The

---

[55] *See* Hybritech Inc. v. Abbott Labs., 849 F.2d 1466, 1458 (Fed. Cir. 1988).

[56] *See* New England Braiding Co. v. A.W. Chesterton Co., 970 F.2d 878, 883 n.5 (Fed. Cir. 1992).

[57] Rule 56(c) of the Federal Rules of Civil Procedure states that summary judgment "shall be rendered forthwith if the pleadings, depositions, answers to interrogatories, and admissions on file, together with the affidavits, if any, show that there is no genuine issue as to any material fact and that the moving party is entitled to a judgment as a matter of law." A dispute as to an "immaterial fact"–one that need not be decided to render judgment–does not preclude summary judgment. "A disputed fact is material to the outcome of the suit if a finding of that fact is necessary and relevant to the proceeding." Madey v. Duke Univ., 307 F.3d 1351, 1358 (Fed. Cir. 2002).

[58] *See Madey*, 307 F.3d at 1358 ("Issues of fact are genuine only 'if the evidence is such that a reasonable jury could return a verdict for the nonmoving party.'").

[59] *See* Exigent Tech., Inc. v. Atrana Solutions, Inc., 442 F.3d 1301, 1308–09 (Fed. Cir. 2006); Golan v. Pingel Enter., Inc., 310 F.3d 1360, 1367–68 (Fed. Cir. 2002); Celotex Corp. v. Catrett, 477 U.S. 317, 325 (1986). The party opposing the motion "must show more than a mere metaphysical doubt regarding the material facts" and must produce more than "a mere scintilla of evidence." *Golan*, 310 F.3d at 1368.

opposing party naturally submits its own evidence in an attempt to convince the judge that there is, at least, a "genuine issue of material fact" to be decided.

An entire matter may be decided by summary judgment, or the judge may determine that individual questions raise no genuine issue of fact, even if they do not resolve the entire case.[60] For example, a court might grant summary judgment (or "summary adjudication"), finding that a particular invention predates the patentee's invention, while leaving to the jury the genuinely disputed question of whether the prior invention anticipates the claims at issue. Occasionally courts grant summary judgment that a patent is infringed,[61] but usually the accused infringer can at least raise a "genuine issue of fact" regarding alleged differences between the accused product and the claimed invention. More frequently, a court holds a patent *not* infringed on summary judgment,[62] often because of prosecution history estoppel.[63] Sometimes courts grant summary judgment that patents are invalid or unenforceable.[64] Since liability can be found only if a patent is valid, enforceable, *and* infringed, a negative judgment on one of these issues can dispose of the entire case.

11.8 REMEDIES

When a court determines that a patent is both valid and infringed, it must decide what remedies to grant the patentee. Permanent injunctions against further infringement were once granted to victorious patent owners almost automatically.[65] But in *eBay Inc. v. MercExchange, L.L.C.*,[66] the Supreme Court held that courts should not enter injunctions routinely, simply because infringement has been proven. Instead, the plaintiff must

---

[60] See Rule 56(d) of the Federal Rules of Civil Procedure.

[61] *See, e.g.*, Monsanto Co. v. Scruggs, 459 F.3d 1328, 1332 (Fed. Cir. 2006); Amgen Inc. v. Hoechst Marion Roussel, Inc., 314 F.3d 1313, 1351 (Fed. Cir. 2003); McGinley v. Franklin Sports, Inc., 262 F.3d 1339, 1348–49 (Fed. Cir. 2001).

[62] *See, e.g.*, PSN Illinois, LLC v. Ivoclar Vivadent, Inc., 525 F.3d 1159 (Fed. Cir. 2008); Schwarz Pharma, Inc. v. Paddock Labs., Inc., 504 F.3d 1371, 1378 (Fed. Cir. 2007); Planet Bingo, LLC v. Gametech Int'l, Inc., 472 F.3d 1338, 1345 (Fed. Cir. 2006).

[63] See Section 10.6.8.

[64] *See, e.g.*, Automotive Techs. Int'l, Inc. v. BMW of North America, Inc., 501 F.3d 1274, 1276 (Fed. Cir. 2007) (enablement); Ferring B.V. v. Barr Labs., Inc., 437 F.3d 1181, 1183 (Fed. Cir. 2006) (inequitable conduct); Electromotive Div. of General Motors Corp. v. Transportation Sys. Div. of General Electric Co., 417 F.3d 1203, 1205–06 (Fed. Cir. 2005) (on-sale bar); Mazzari v. Rogan, 323 F.3d 1000, 1002 (Fed. Cir. 2003) (obviousness and anticipation).

[65] *See* Richardson v. Suzuki Motor Co., 868 F.2d 1226, 1246–47 (Fed. Cir. 1989) ("Infringement having been established, it is contrary to the laws of property, of which the patent law partakes, to deny the patentee's right to exclude others from use of his property. . . . It is the general rule that an injunction will issue when infringement has been adjudged, absent a sound reason for denying it.").

[66] 547 U.S. 388 (2006).

demonstrate the following conditions traditionally required in other types of lawsuit: (1) that it has suffered irreparable injury, (2) that monetary damages cannot compensate for the injury, (3) that the balance of hardships warrants injunctive relief, and (4) that the public interest would not be disserved by a permanent injunction.[67] If these conditions do not prevail, a court may decide to impose what amounts to a compulsory license; the infringer may continue, but owes the patentee an ongoing royalty payment in an amount fixed by the court.[68] This new approach may benefit the public, perhaps ensuring the supply of products needed by consumers or preventing economic disruptions such as unemployment. On the other hand, patent owners have lost a significant bargaining chip because it is no longer certain that infringing activity must cease following a successful lawsuit.

11.8.1 Damages

The other remedy available to a patentee is an award of money damages to compensate for past infringement. While injunctions are a matter within the discretion of the judge, the calculation of damages is a question of fact for the jury.[69] A patentee can elect to pursue damages in either of two forms. One is *lost profits* attributable to the infringement.[70] This form of recovery is appropriate if the infringer competed with the patentee in the marketplace, and it can be shown that sales made by the infringer were sales lost to the patentee.[71] The standard of proof is one of "reasonable probability."[72]

---

[67] *Id.* at 391.

[68] *See* Paice LLC v. Toyota Motor Corp., 504 F.3d 1293, 1313–14 (Fed. Cir. 2007).

[69] Utah Medical Prods., Inc. v. Graphic Controls Corp., 350 F.3d 1376, 1381 (Fed. Cir. 2003); Micro Chemical, Inc. v. Lextron, Inc., 317 F.3d 1387, 1394 (Fed. Cir. 2003). "A court is not at liberty to supplant its own judgment on the damages amount for the jury's findings." Oiness v. Walgreen Co., 88 F.3d 1025, 1030 (Fed. Cir. 1996). The award can be rejected by the court only if "the amount is grossly excessive or monstrous, clearly not supported by the evidence or based only on speculation or guesswork." Monsanto Co. v. McFarling, 488 F.3d 973, 981 (Fed. Cir. 2007). This assumes that the case was tried by a jury. If the parties waived their right to a jury trial, the judge would determine all issues of fact, including the amount of damages.

[70] The infringer cannot be compelled to turn over *its* profits in lieu of calculating the *patentee's* lost profits, except where the infringed patent is a design patent. *See* 35 U.S.C. § 289.

[71] *See* American Seating Co. v. USSC Gp., Inc., 514 F.3d 1262, 1268 (Fed. Cir. 2008); Stryker Corp. v. Intermedics Orthopedics, Inc., 96 F.3d 1409, 1417 (Fed. Cir. 1996). Lost profits are most easily proven in a two-supplier market, but they can also be based on suppositions relating to market share. *See* King Instruments Corp. v. Perego, 65 F.3d 941, 953 (Fed. Cir. 1995). In the two-supplier situation (the two suppliers being the patentee and the infringer), proof of lost profits typically focuses on the following factors: (1) the demand for the patented product; (2) the absence of acceptable substitutes; (3) the capacity of the patentee to exploit the demand had there been no infringement (for example, did the patentee have the manufacturing capacity to make the sales that the infringer made?); and (4) the amount of profit the patentee would have made if the patentee, rather than the infringer, had made the sales. *See* *Stryker*, 96 F.3d at 1418.

[72] *See* Wechsler v. Macke Int'l Trade, Inc., 486 F.3d 1286, 1297 (Fed. Cir. 2007).

The calculation of lost profits is often complicated by disputes over collateral sales that the patentee might have lost together with sales of the patented item. Suppose, for example, that the patent covered a component of a larger item—perhaps an improved lens for a flashlight. The patentee would demand the profits that could have been made from the sale of *flashlights* if the infringer had not misappropriated the lens design. The infringer, on the other hand, might attempt to apportion the profits in some way so that only profits from the *lens* could be recovered. The patentee might argue further that lost flashlight sales led to lost sales of accessories and spare parts—for example, spare bulbs, batteries, and so forth. The infringer would likely attempt to exclude these from the calculation.

These disputes are resolved by the "entire market value" rule, which "allows calculation of damages based on the value of an entire apparatus containing several features, when the patent-related feature in the 'basis for customer demand.'"[73] The patented and unpatented features must constitute "components of a single assembly or parts of a complete machine," or together they must operate as "a single functional unit."[74] Recovery cannot be had for functionally unrelated items sold together with the patented invention as a matter of convenience, or to satisfy customer demand for a package deal.[75] Returning to the example, the entire flashlight would likely be held the appropriate base for calculating lost profits because the patented lens, together with the unpatented bulb and housing, form a "single functional unit." On the other hand, if the flashlights were sold as part of a tool kit, the other tools would likely be excluded from the calculation of lost profits because their use and function are unrelated to the patented lens.[76]

Another issue is whether a patentee can recover profits lost on sales of an *unpatented* item that competes with sales of an *infringing* item. Suppose, for example, that the inventor of the improved flashlight lens decided, for whatever reason, to market only flashlights that are *not* covered by the patent. Meanwhile, the infringer marketed flashlights that *are* covered by the patent.

[73] Imonex Servs., Inc. v. W.H. Munzprufer Dietmar Trenner GmbH, 408 F.3d 1374, 1380 (Fed. Cir. 2005).

[74] *American Seating*, 514 F.3d at 1268; Rite-Hite Corp. v. Kelley Co., 56 F.3d 1538, 1550 (Fed. Cir. 1995) (*en banc*).

[75] *See American Seating*, 514 F.3d at 1268; *Rite-Hite*, 56 F.3d at 1550.

[76] The flashlight batteries might be a close call. They are a necessary part of a functioning flashlight but are often sold separately. The infringer might argue that when batteries are sold with a flashlight, it is done only as a matter of "convenience and business advantage." *Rite-Hite*, 56 F.3d at 1550. Alternatively, a distinction might be drawn between the original batteries, which are sold as a part of the flashlight, and replacement batteries, which the patentee could not have expected to sell. *See* Kaufman Co. v. Lantech, Inc., 926 F.2d 1136, 1144 (Fed. Cir. 1991) (whether "accessories" should be included in the calculation of lost profits depends on whether there is a reasonable probability that the patentee would have made the sale if not for the infringement).

Can the patentee recover the profits that it would have made on unpatented flashlights if not for the sales of the infringing ones? According to the Federal Circuit, those profits can be recovered, as long as it can be shown that the sales of the unpatented flashlights would have been made if not for the infringement.[77]

In many cases lost profits are difficult to calculate, or the patentee did not lose any profits through competition because the patentee did not sell a product of its own. In these situations, the patentee may choose to pursue a *reasonable royalty* as the measure of damages. This is, by statute, the minimum that a patentee can be awarded.[78] A reasonable royalty is the amount that the infringer would have paid the patentee if, instead of infringing the patent, it had negotiated a license. This is generally assessed as a percentage of the sales price of the infringing goods, multiplied by total sales.

The best guide to calculating a reasonable royalty is evidence of an established royalty.[79] If the patentee has already licensed the patent to others at a standard royalty of 3 percent, then 3 percent appears to be an amount that the market will bear, and that is adequate to satisfy the patentee. If there is no established royalty, then a reasonable royalty must be determined through a difficult mental exercise. One must imagine what would have occurred if, at the time the infringement began, the patentee and the infringer sat down together and negotiated the terms of a patent license. The amount that the patentee would have been willing to accept, and that the infringer would have been willing to pay, is the amount of a reasonable royalty.[80]

The courts have identified a number of factors that should be considered in the context of this "hypothetical negotiation." These are commonly known as "*Georgia-Pacific* factors"—a reference to one of the first opinions to set them down.[81] The *Georgia-Pacific* factors include the following:[82]

[77] *Rite-Hite*, 56 F.3d at 1548–49.

[78] 35 U.S.C. § 284 ("Upon finding for the claimant the court shall award the claimant damages adequate to compensate for the infringement, but in no event less than a reasonable royalty for the use made of the invention by the infringer, together with interest and costs as fixed by the court.").

[79] Monsanto Co. v. McFarling, 488 F.3d 973, 978–79 (Fed. Cir. 2007) ("An established royalty is usually the best measure of a 'reasonable' royalty for a given use of an invention because it removes the need to guess at the terms to which parties would hypothetically agree."); Nickson Indus., Inc. v. Rol Mfg. Co., 847 F.2d 795, 798 (Fed. Cir. 1988).

[80] *See* Mitutoyo Corp. v. Central Purchasing, LLC, 499 F.3d 1284, 1292 (Fed. Cir. 2007); Applied Medical Resources Corp. v. U.S. Surgical Corp., 435 F.3d 1356, 1361 (Fed. Cir. 2006); *Rite-Hite*, 56 F.3d at 1554.

[81] Georgia-Pacific Corp. v. United States Plywood Corp., 318 F. Supp. 1116 (S.D.N.Y. 1970); *see also* Parental Guide of Texas, Inc. v. Thomson, Inc., 446 F.3d 1265, 1270 (Fed. Cir. 2006); *Micro-Chemical*, 317 F.3d at 1393; Interactive Pictures Corp. v. Infinite Pictures, Inc., 274 F.3d 1371, 1385–86 (Fed. Cir. 2001).

[82] *See Georgia-Pacific*, 318 F. Supp. at 1120.

- Any evidence of an established royalty rate;
- Rates paid by the infringer for rights to similar patents;
- Whether the patentee had a policy of refusing licenses;
- Whether the patentee and the infringer were competitors;
- Whether sales of the patented item would generate (for the infringer or the patentee) additional sales of non-patented items, including such things as accessories and spare parts;[83]
- The time remaining before the patent's expiration;
- The established success and profitability of items within the scope of the patent;
- The advantages of the patented invention over available substitutes;
- The portion of both selling price and profits that could be attributed to the patented invention rather than to other product components or features.

The hypothetical negotiation exercise is difficult and imprecise, in part because it requires the jury, or the judge in a bench trial, to imagine the state of affairs as they existed when the infringement began, putting aside knowledge of subsequent events.[84] It also requires that the patentee and the infringer be pictured as a willing licensor and a willing licensee, respectively, when the reality may have been very different.[85]

Even if the hypothetical negotiation could be imagined perfectly, basing a damages figure on the result would seem to make infringement a "no-lose" proposition.[86] The potential infringer who would otherwise pay for a license might decide to take its chances, knowing that, at worst, it would be forced to pay after litigation no more than would have been required for a license. In reality, things are not so easy for the would-be infringer. First, courts recognize that the hypothetical negotiation is only a mental exercise. In the end, an infringer may be compelled to pay more than an actual licensee would have paid.[87] More important, if the infringement was "willful," damages can be increased as a punishment.

---

[83] These additional sales are known as "convoyed sales" or "derivative sales."

[84] *See* Unisplay, S.A. v. American Elec. Sign Co., 69 F.3d 512, 518 (Fed. Cir. 1995); Hanson v. Alpine Ski Area, Inc., 718 F.2d 1075, 1079 (Fed. Cir. 1983) ("'The key element in setting a reasonable royalty . . . is the necessity for return to the date when the infringement began.'"). In seeming contradiction to this rule, some cases have approved the use of later information to suggest what a reasonable royalty might have been. *See* Fromson v. Western Litho Plate & Supply Co., 853 F.2d 1568, 1575 (Fed. Cir. 1988) (the law "permits and often requires a court to look to events and facts that occurred thereafter and that could not have been known to or predicted by the hypothesized negotiators").

[85] *See Rite Hite*, 56 F.3d at 1554 n.13 (imagining the patentee as a willing licensor is "inaccurate, and even absurd").

[86] *See Fromson*, 853 F.2d at 1574–75.

[87] *See King Instruments*, 65 F.3d at 951 n.6; *Fromson*, 853 F.2d at 1575 n.11 ("Courts have on occasion recognized the need to distinguish between royalties payable by infringers and non-infringers.").

11.8.2 Willful Infringement

Although unintentional infringement is still infringement, the law recognizes a difference in culpability between the innocent infringer and the deliberate infringer. A court can as much as triple the damages assessed against a "willful" infringer.[88] Willfulness is a question of fact,[89] and the standard of proof is one of clear and convincing evidence.[90] Whether or not to increase the damages, and by how much, is a decision left to the discretion of the trial judge.[91]

To behave willfully means to behave recklessly—to ignore a high likelihood that one's actions infringe a valid patent. The patentee must demonstrate that the risk would have been apparent to an objectively reasonable observer, and that the danger was known, "or so obvious that it should have been known," to the infringer.[92] Willfulness depends on the totality of the circumstances,[93] but an important consideration is whether the infringer sought out and relied on competent advice of counsel. Although the advice must have been mistaken (because willfulness is an issue only after the defendant has been found to infringe), the fact that it was solicited tends to show that the infringer acted reasonably and in good faith. The Federal Circuit has retreated from earlier suggestions that one must always, or almost always, seek legal advice, even when such precautions seem unnecessary.[94] Nevertheless, an accused infringer is wise to seek such advice. If it is competent advice, a patentee will find it difficult to prove that the infringer who relied upon it acted recklessly.[95]

---

[88] *See* 35 U.S.C. § 284 ("the court may increase the damages up to three times the amount found or assessed"). Although the statute does not specify the circumstances under which damages may be increased, the courts have held that "an award of enhanced damages requires a showing of willful infringement." In re Seagate Tech., LLC, 497 F.3d 1360, 1368 (Fed. Cir. 2007) (*en banc*).

[89] Biotec Biologische Naturverpackungen GmbH v. Biocorp, Inc., 249 F.3d 1341, 1356 (Fed. Cir. 2001) (willful infringement "is quintessentially a question of fact, for it depends on findings of culpable intent and deliberate or negligent wrongdoing").

[90] *Seagate*, 497 F.3d at 1371.

[91] *See* Electro Scientific Indus., Inc. v. General Scanning Inc., 247 F.3d 1341, 1353 (Fed. Cir. 2001) ("A finding of willfulness does not mandate enhanced damages."); Graco, Inc. v. Binks Mfg. Co., 60 F.3d 785, 792 (Fed. Cir. 1995).

[92] *Seagate*, 497 F.3d at 1371. Prior to its *en banc* decision in *Seagate*, the Federal Circuit applied a standard of willfulness closer to negligence than to recklessness. In other words, a *careless* defendant might willfully infringe. The new standard appears to require a *knowing* disregard of serious risk, though the "should have been known" language introduces some ambiguity.

[93] Liquid Dynamics Corp. v. Vaughan Co., Inc., 449 F.3d 1209, 1225 (Fed. Cir. 2006); Knorr-Bremse Systeme Fuer Nutzfahrzeuge GmbH v. Dana Corp., 383 F.3d 1337, 1342 (Fed. Cir. 2004) (*en banc*).

[94] *See Seagate*, 497 F.3d at 1371 ("Because we abandon the affirmative duty of due care, we also reemphasize that there is no affirmative obligation to obtain opinion of counsel.").

[95] There may be some legal advice so lacking in substance or preparation that one could not reasonably rely upon it. *See* Comark Communications, Inc. v. Harris Corp., 156 F.3d 1182, 1191 (Fed. Cir. 1998). Competent advice is advice from a qualified attorney, based on a thorough investigation, with support for its conclusions spelled out in reasonable detail.

Although communications between attorney and client are privileged, the client waives that privilege, exposing to discovery matters it would rather keep confidential, if it relies on those communications in court. Until recently, defendants who might rely on advice of counsel to rebut claims of willfulness were put to a difficult choice. If the accused infringer chose to stand on its right to attorney-client privilege, courts would infer that legal advice received by the infringer, if it received any advice at all, was unfavorable.[96] If it wished to avoid that inference, the infringer *had* to waive the privilege. In *Knorr-Bremse*, the Federal Circuit *en banc* removed the adverse inference, giving accused infringers a more realistic choice.[97] Moreover, in the subsequent *Seagate* decision, also *en banc*, the Federal Circuit limited the scope of the privilege waiver. The waiver allows the patentee to examine attorney-client communications between the infringer and the counsel who rendered the advice, to make sure that the advice was what the infringer claims it to have been. But in most cases the patentee cannot inquire into communications between the infringer and its *trial* counsel, who are often different attorneys than those offering pre-litigation advice.[98]

A court may consider as evidence of willfulness whether the infringer deliberately set out to copy the patentee's invention.[99] On the other hand, an attempt to "design around" the claims of the patent (making changes deemed necessary to avoid the scope of the claims) may be viewed as evidence of good faith.[100] The conduct of the infringer during litigation and the closeness of the questions decided against it may also be weighed in the balance.[101]

Another potential remedy against a willful infringer is an award of reasonable attorneys' fees. The general rule in the United States is that each litigant must bear its own legal costs, regardless of the outcome of the case, but 35 U.S.C. § 285 provides for an award of attorneys' fees in an "exceptional case." Willful infringement may create such an exceptional

---

[96] *See* Electro Medical Sys., S.A. v. Cooper Life Sciences, Inc., 34 F.3d 1048, 1056 (Fed. Cir. 1994); L.A. Gear, Inc. v. Thom McAn Shoe Co., 988 F.2d 1117, 1126 (Fed. Cir. 1993).

[97] *Knorr-Bremse*, 383 F.3d at 1344 ("[I]nference that withheld opinions are adverse to the client's actions can distort the attorney-client relationship, in derogation of the foundations of that relationship. We conclude that a special rule affecting attorney-client relationships in patent cases is not warranted.").

[98] *Seagate*, 497 F.3d at 1374.

[99] *See Liquid Dynamics*, 449 F.3d at 1225; Crystal Semiconductor Corp. v. Tritech Microelectronics Int'l, Inc., 246 F.3d 1336, 1352 (Fed. Cir. 2001).

[100] *See* Westvaco Corp. v. International Paper Co., 991 F.2d 735, 745 (Fed. Cir. 1993); Rolls-Royce Ltd. v. GTE Valeron Corp., 800 F.2d 1101, 1109–10 (Fed. Cir. 1986). Yet often it is difficult to distinguish between "designing around" a patent claim and introducing an "insubstantial variation" that subjects the potential infringer to liability under the doctrine of equivalents. See Section 10.6.3.

[101] *Liquid Dynamics*, 449 F.3d at 1225.

case,[102] though it is still a matter for the judge's discretion.[103] On occasion courts award attorneys' fees to the accused infringer, generally when the patentee committed inequitable conduct or the claim of infringement was frivolous.[104] It is by no means proper to award attorneys' fees to the prevailing party as a matter of routine.[105]

11.8.3 Limitations

Recovery of damages for patent infringement can be limited under certain circumstances. Some of the most important limiting factors are the statute of limitations, failure to properly mark products or give notice of infringement, laches, and equitable estoppel.

11.8.3.1 Statute of Limitations

Under 35 U.S.C. § 286, no damages may be recovered for infringement that occurred more than 6 years prior to the filing of a claim. This statute of limitations is equivalent to those found in many other areas of the law, and the purpose is the usual one of encouraging the prompt disposition of potential claims. Section 286 does not prevent the filing of a suit, unless the only relief that could be granted is damages for infringement more than 6 years ago. If, for example, the defendant had infringed continuously for the past 10 years, the patentee could still sue to recover damages for the most recent 6 years of infringement and could obtain an injunction against future infringement.[106]

---

[102] *See* Serio-US Indus. v. Plastic Recovery Techs. Corp., 459 F.3d 1311, 1321 (Fed. Cir. 2006) ("[e]xceptional cases usually feature some material, inappropriate conduct related to the matter in litigation, such as willful infringement"); Tate Access Floors, Inc. v. Maxcess Techs., Inc., 222 F.3d 958, 972 (Fed. Cir. 2000). Even if the infringement was not willful, "vexatious conduct" by the infringer in the course of the litigation may justify an award of attorneys' fees. *See* Beckman Instruments, Inc. v. LKB Produkter AB, 892 F.2d 1547, 1551–52 (Fed. Cir. 1989).

[103] Odetics, Inc. v. Storage Tech. Corp., 185 F.3d 1259, 1274 (Fed. Cir. 1999). Where the jury has found willful infringement, a judge's *unexplained* failure to treat the case as "exceptional" may be an abuse of discretion. *See Tate Access Floors*, 222 F.3d at 972.

[104] *See* Monsanto Co. v. Bayer Bioscience N.V., 514 F.3d 1229, 1242 (Fed. Cir. 2008) (inequitable conduct); Haynes Int'l, Inc. v. Jessop Steel Co., 8 F.3d 1573, 1579 (Fed. Cir. 1993) (a "frivolous" lawsuit justifying an award of attorneys' fees is one that "the patentee knew or, on reasonable investigation, should have known, was baseless"); Stevenson v. Sears Roebuck & Co., 713 F.2d 705, 713 (Fed. Cir. 1983) ("There must be some finding of unfairness, bad faith, or inequitable conduct on the part of the unsuccessful patentee."). A patentee's failure to investigate thoroughly before bringing an unsuccessful claim of infringement may render the case "exceptional." *See* Superior Fireplace Co. v. Majestic Prods. Co., 270 F.3d 1358, 1378 (Fed. Cir. 2001) ("From the record on appeal, it is unclear if Superior inspected the allegedly infringing products, prepared claim charts, construed the claims at issue, or even read those claims.").

[105] *See* Revlon, Inc. v. Carson Prods. Co., 803 F.2d 676, 679 (Fed. Cir. 1986).

[106] *See* Teva Pharmaceuticals USA, Inc. v. Novartis Pharmaceuticals Corp., 482 F.3d 1330, 1341 (Fed. Cir. 2007).

11.8.3.2 Notice and Marking

Many manufactured articles bear markings referring to a specific patent or patents. These are the result of 35 U.S.C. § 287, which states that such markings provide "notice to the public" that the article is patented. They may not provide *actual notice* to a particular individual who has never seen the article, but the law considers them "constructive notice" to anyone.[107] Where it is not practical to mark a patent number on the article itself, the number can be displayed on packaging.[108] If a patent owner or licensee makes, sells, offers to sell, or imports into the United States articles covered by the patent but not marked in this fashion, no damages for infringement can be recovered until (1) marking begins or (2) the infringer receives from the patent owner actual notice of the infringement.[109] This limitation of damages provides an incentive to patent owners to mark their goods and provide at least that much notice to the public.[110]

The marking of goods must be "substantially consistent and continuous."[111] If the patentee sells a large shipment of unmarked goods, this resets the damages clock, so to speak. The obligation to mark applies to goods made or sold by the patent owner *or* licensee (express or implied).[112] Patent owners therefore have to make sure that licensees are properly marking their goods, or the patent owner's ability to recover damages for infringement will be impaired.[113] Section 287 does not apply to patents with just method claims, for the simple reason that a method cannot be marked.[114] If neither the patent owner nor the patent owner's licensees have sold any products covered by the patent, no marking or other notice is required to begin the accumulation of damages for infringement.

If products have not been properly marked, the patentee can provide *actual notice* to the infringer.[115] The notice can come in the form of a warning

[107] *See* Syngenta Seeds, Inc. v. Delta Cotton Coop., Inc., 457 F.3d 1269, 1276 (Fed. Cir. 2006); Sentry Protection Prods., Inc. v. Eagle Mfg. Co., 400 F.3d 910, 918 (Fed. Cir. 2005).

[108] 35 U.S.C. § 287(a).

[109] *See id.*; SRI Int'l, Inc. v. Advanced Tech. Labs., Inc., 127 F.3d 1462, 1469 (Fed. Cir. 1997); Maxwell v. J. Baker, Inc., 86 F.3d 1098, 1111 (Fed. Cir. 1996).

[110] *See* Nike, Inc. v. Wal-Mart Stores, Inc., 138 F.3d 1437, 1443 (Fed. Cir. 1998).

[111] *Maxwell*, 86 F.3d at 1111; American Medical Sys., Inc. v Medical Eng'g Corp., 6 F.3d 1523, 1537 (Fed. Cir. 1993).

[112] *Maxwell*, 86 F.3d at 1111; Amstead Indus. Inc. v. Buckeye Steel Castings Co., 24 F.3d 178, 185 (Fed. Cir. 1994).

[113] This obligation is subject to a "rule of reason," and "substantial compliance" may be held sufficient. *See Maxwell*, 86 F.3d at 1111–12 (patentee's reasonable efforts were sufficient, even though a "numerically large number" of goods–although still a small percentage of the total–were not properly marked).

[114] *American Medical*, 6 F.3d at 1538. If a patent includes both method and apparatus claims, and the method is related to an apparatus that can be marked, such marking will likely be required, at least if both method and apparatus claims are infringed. *See id.* at 1538–39.

[115] *See* U.S. Philips Corp. v. Iwasaki Elec. Co., 505 F.3d 1371, 1375 (Fed. Cir. 2007).

letter from the patentee or without ceremony in the form of a suit for infringement.[116] Once such notice has been provided, damages with respect to that infringer can begin to accrue. The notice must come from the patent owner; it is not sufficient that the accused infringer discovered the infringement on its own or through a third party.[117] Moreover, the notice must identify the patent, and it must specifically charge the recipient with infringement of that patent.[118] In *Amstead Indus. Inc. v. Buckeye Steel Castings Co.*,[119] the infringer (Buckeye) received a form letter from the patent owner mentioning the patent and warning it not to infringe. The same letter had been sent to other companies throughout the industry. The court found that this was not actual notice of infringement to Buckeye because it did not specifically charge Buckeye with infringement, nor did it identify any infringing device.[120]

11.8.3.3 Laches

The equitable principle of "laches" may also bar recovery of damages accrued before suit was filed. As explained by the Federal Circuit in *A.C. Aukerman Co. v. R. L. Chaides Construction Co.*,[121] laches may bar the recovery of pre-filing damages if (1) the patentee unreasonably and inexcusably delayed in filing suit and (2) the accused infringer was materially harmed by the delay.[122] If the patentee delayed filing suit for more than six years,

---

[116] *See American Medical*, 6 F.3d at 1537.

[117] *U.S. Philips*, 505 F.3d at 1375; Lans v. Digital Equipment Corp., 252 F.3d 1320, 1327 (Fed. Cir. 2001).

[118] *See U.S. Philips*, 505 F.3d at 1375 (actual notice "requires the affirmative communication of a specific charge of infringement by a specific accused product or device"). It is immaterial whether the patent owner "threatens suit, demands cessation of infringement, or offers a license under the patent." *SRI*, 127 F.3d at 1470. The important thing is that "the recipient is notified, with sufficient specificity, that the patent holder believes that the recipient of the notice may be an infringer." *Id.*

[119] 24 F.3d 178, 185–87 (Fed. Cir. 1994).

[120] *Id.* at 187. Somewhat clouding the picture, the Federal Circuit has stated that the notice of infringement must be specific, but not necessarily an "unqualified charge of infringement." Gart v. Logitech, Inc., 254 F.3d 1334, 1344 (Fed. Cir. 2001). Specific reference to the patent and the potentially infringing product, together with advice that the recipient seek an opinion of counsel to determine "whether a non-exclusive license under the patent is needed," is sufficient to warn the recipient that it is believed to be infringing. *Id.*

[121] 960 F.2d 1020 (Fed. Cir. 1992) (*en banc*).

[122] *Aukerman*, 960 F.2d at 1032; *see also* Symantec Corp. v. Computer Assocs. Int'l, Inc., 522 F.3d 1279, 1294 (Fed. Cir. 2008); Intirtool, Ltd. v. Texar Corp., 369 F.3d 1289, 1297 (Fed. Cir. 2004); State Contracting & Eng'g Corp. v. Condotte America, Inc., 346 F.3d 1057, 1065 (Fed. Cir. 2003). Enforcement of the laches defense is still left to the judge's discretion and sense of fairness. *See* Gasser Chair Co. v. Infanti Chair Mfg. Corp., 60 F.3d 770, 773 (Fed. Cir. 1995). If the infringer itself has behaved unfairly (perhaps by deliberately copying the patentee's invention), the court may decline to exercise its equitable powers. *See id.*

measured from the time it first knew or should have known of the alleged infringement, [123] laches is presumed, though that presumption can be overcome with the introduction of contrary evidence.[124]

The harm to the accused infringer can be either "economic" or "evidentiary."[125] Economic harm means the loss of investments or the incurring of additional damages that could have been avoided if suit had been filed earlier. For example, during the period of delay the accused infringer might have made unrecoverable investments in a factory to manufacture the accused product. A patentee cannot delay unreasonably while such investments are made, nor can it "lie silently in wait watching damages escalate."[126] Evidentiary prejudice refers to the loss of evidence that the accused infringer might have used in its defense had the case been brought sooner. Such prejudice can arise where, for example, important documents have been lost, memories have faded, or witnesses have died.[127]

Laches is an equitable defense that depends on the exercise of the judge's discretion, in view of all the circumstances.[128] Those circumstances include the length of the delay and any excuses or justifications offered by the patentee. Excuses for delay that may be acceptable include the demands of other litigation, negotiations with the accused infringer, and disputes over ownership of the patent.[129] Fairness may sometimes require that the patentee notify the accused infringer of the reason for its delay.[130]

---

[123] *See* Wanlass v. General Elec. Co., 148 F.3d 1334, 1337 (Fed. Cir. 1998) ("The period of delay begins at the time the patentee had actual or constructive knowledge of the defendant's potentially infringing activities."). Because laches can arise based on what the patentee *should* have known, patentees are, in effect, required to "police their rights" by keeping themselves reasonably informed of potentially infringing activity. *Id.* at 1338. A patentee cannot remain "negligently or willfully oblivious," where the potentially infringing activity is so "pervasive, open, and notorious" that a reasonable patentee would investigate. *Id.*

[124] *Symantec*, 522 F.3d at 1294; *Aukerman*, 960 F.2d at 1028, 1037-39; *Wanlass*, 148 F.3d at 1337 ("A delay of more than six years raises a presumption that it is unreasonable, inexcusable, and prejudicial.").

[125] *State Contracting*, 346 F.3d at 1066; *Aukerman*, 960 F.2d at 1033.

[126] *Id.* at 1033. The court must find that the potential infringer would have acted differently if the infringer had made its claim more promptly. In other words, the losses must have been *caused* by the delay. *See State Contracting*, 346 F.3d at 1066; *Gasser*, 60 F.3d at 775.

[127] *Aukerman*, 960 F.2d at 1033.

[128] *Id.* at 1032.

[129] *Id.* at 1033. Poverty or inability to find an attorney willing to work for a contingent fee has not been recognized as a valid excuse for delay. *See* Hall v. Aqua Queen Mfg., Inc., 93 F.3d 1548, 1554 (Fed. Cir. 1996).

[130] *See Aukerman*, 960 F.2d at 1033; Vaupel Textilmaschinen KG v. Meccanica Euro Italia S.P.A., 944 F.2d 870, 877 (Fed. Cir. 1991) (for the "other litigation" excuse to apply, the patentee must inform the accused infringer of the other litigation and of its intention to enforce the patent when the other litigation concludes).

The effect of a successful laches defense is to bar recovery of damages incurred *before* the lawsuit was filed.[131] The patentee can still recover damages for subsequent infringement, as well as an injunction against future infringement.

Recently the Federal Circuit endorsed the concept of "prosecution laches," which bars enforcement of a patent issuing after unreasonable and unexplained delays in prosecution, even though the applicant complied with the relevant PTO regulations.[132] The defense prevents an applicant from unreasonably delaying the issuance of a patent, simply to put itself in a more advantageous position with respect to others who, not knowing of the pending application, may be investing in infringing technology. In this instance, a successful laches defense appears to render the claims generally unenforceable.[133] A severe remedy, prosecution laches "should be applied only in egregious cases of misuse of the statutory patent system."[134]

11.8.3.4   Equitable Estoppel

"Equitable estoppel" is an equitable defense similar to laches, but it depends on a somewhat different set of circumstances. In order for this defense to apply, the patentee must somehow have *communicated* to the potential infringer the idea that the patentee would not press a claim.[135] This communication can be in the form of words, conduct, or even silence if, under the circumstances, one would expect the patentee to voice any objections to the potential infringer's activities.[136] In addition, the potential

---

[131] Odetics, Inc. v. Storage Tech. Corp., 185 F.3d 1259, 1272–73 (Fed. Cir. 1999); *Aukerman*, 960 F.2d at 1041.

[132] *See* Symbol Techs., Inc. v. Lemelson Medical, Educ. & Research Found., LP, 277 F.3d 1361, 1363–65 (Fed. Cir. 2002).

[133] *See id.* at 1364.

[134] Symbol Techs., Inc. v. Lemelson Medical, Educ. & Research Found., LP, 422 F.3d 1378, 1385 (Fed. Cir. 2005). An example of such egregious misuse is "refiling an application solely containing previously-allowed claims for the business purpose of delaying their issuance," particularly when it is done repeatedly. *Id.* The tactics employed by the patentee in *Symbol Techs.* resulted in gaps of 18 to 39 years between filing and issue. *Id.* at 1386.

[135] Vanderlande Indus. Nederland BV v. Int'l Trade Comm'n, 366 F.3d. 1311, 1324 (Fed. Cir. 2004); A.C. Aukerman Co. v. R.L. Chaides Construction Co., 960 F.2d 1020, 1042 (Fed. Cir. 1992) (*en banc*).

[136] *Id.* at 1041–42. If the "communication" is in the form of inaction, then there must have been some contact or relationship with the patentee that would allow the inaction to be reasonably interpreted as a sign of abandonment. *Id.* at 1042. For example, the patentee might have threatened immediate enforcement of its patents and then failed to follow through, which could reasonably be interpreted as a change of heart. *See* Meyers v. Asics Corp., 974 F.2d 1304, 1309 (Fed. Cir. 1993). Ironically, the patentee who insists most emphatically that it will enforce its patent rights is the patentee most likely to be found to have abandoned those rights by its subsequent inaction.

infringer must have *relied* on the communication and suffered material harm as a result of that reliance.[137] Equitable estoppel is most easily applied where, for example, the patentee told the potential infringer that it would not interfere, the potential infringer relied on that communication and invested in a new factory, and the patentee then reversed itself and filed suit.[138] The more difficult cases are those where the patentee did nothing and the potential infringer interpreted that inaction as tacit permission.

As in applying the laches defense, the court must weigh all of the circumstances and determine what fairness dictates.[139] If the defense of equitable estoppel applies, it bars *any* relief to the patentee.[140] In this respect, the consequences are more severe than those of the traditional laches defense, which prevents only the recovery of past damages.

11.9 THE INTERNATIONAL TRADE COMMISSION

If allegedly infringing products are being *imported* into the United States, a patent owner can request an investigation by the International Trade Commission (ITC). In many ways, an ITC investigation is similar to a suit for patent infringement in a district court, but there are important differences.

First, the matter will be handled by an administrative law judge (ALJ) rather than a conventional judge or jury. The decision of the ALJ is reviewed by the ITC commissioners and, if an exclusion of infringing goods is ordered, by the president of the United States.[141] Second, the patent owner must demonstrate that importation of infringing articles threatens a "domestic industry" in those articles—in other words, there must be significant business activity in the United States, either under way or imminent, that will be injured by the illicit competition of infringing goods.[142] Third, the ITC can award no money damages for past infringement; it can only order that the importation of infringing goods be stopped.[143] Finally, although an ITC investigation involves much of the same effort as does a suit in a district court, the schedule is generally more compressed. An ITC investigation, from start to finish, is generally completed in a little more than a year.

---

[137] *See Vanderlande*, 366 F.3d. at 1324; *Aukerman*, 960 F.2d at 1042–43. The accused infringer "must have knowledge of the patentee and its patent and must reasonably infer that the patentee acquiesced to the allegedly infringing activity for some time." Winbond Elecs. Corp. v. International Trade Comm'n, 262 F.3d 1363, 1374 (Fed. Cir. 2001).

[138] Unlike the laches defense, equitable estoppel does not require any element of delay. *Aukerman*, 960 F.2d at 1041–42.

[139] *Id.* at 1043.

[140] *Id.* at 1041.

[141] *See* 19 U.S.C. § 1337(c), (j).

[142] *See* 19 U.S.C. § 1337(a)(2)-(3).

[143] *See* 19 U.S.C. § 1337(d).

11.10 JUDGMENTS OF INVALIDITY

When a court has held a patent invalid, and all avenues of appeal have been exhausted, the patent cannot in the future be asserted against any potential infringer.[144] In a sense, a patent owner has only one chance to defend the validity of the patent. On the other hand, an unsuccessful attempt by one accused infringer to challenge the validity of a patent generally does not preclude another accused infringer from raising similar arguments.

---

[144] Assuming that the patent owner had a "full and fair opportunity" to defend the patent. *See* Blonder-Tongue Labs., Inc. v. Univ. of Illinois Found., 402 U.S. 313, 328 (1971).

CHAPTER 12

Special Topics

This chapter covers a number of specialized topics outside the mainstream of patent law but still worthy of discussion. These include design patents, plant patents, foreign patents, and the complex problem of extending patent protection to computer software. The concluding section discusses the prospect of patent reform legislation.

12.1 DESIGN PATENTS

Throughout this book, the term "patent" generally refers to a *utility patent.* A utility patent is a patent on a device, method, or composition of matter having a practical use.[1] Most of the inventions one commonly thinks of—from mousetraps, to pharmaceuticals, to communications satellites—are things properly within the domain of a utility patent. However, the Patent Office also issues *design patents.* A design patent is a curious hybrid similar in some respects to an ordinary utility patent but applied to the kinds of artistic (or, at any rate, decorative) expression that also fall in the domain of copyright or trademark protection.[2] Whereas utility patents exist to promote the "useful arts," design patents exist to promote the "decorative arts."[3]

---

[1] "Utility" is defined rather broadly, however, and can be applied to inventions such as toys that have minimal practical value. See Section 8.4.

[2] See Sections 2.1 and 2.2.

[3] Avia Group Int'l, Inc. v. L.A. Gear California, Inc., 853 F.2d 1557, 1563 (Fed. Cir. 1988).

The PTO issues design patents to new, original, and ornamental designs, as they are embodied in manufactured objects.[4] The design can be a surface ornament, such as a pattern on a cream pitcher, or it can derive from the shape and configuration of the object itself. A sleek new shape for a telephone, for example, could be the subject of a design patent. Copies of three design patents can be found in Appendix B. They depict a candle holder, a faucet, and an automobile tire, respectively.

A design patent cannot be awarded to an entirely abstract design, not associated with any particular utilitarian object. One could not, for example, obtain a design patent on a painting of sunflowers.[5] One could, however, obtain a design patent on a vase that bears the same painting as a decoration. Although a design patent must claim an article of manufacture, the design cannot be dictated by functional considerations.[6] If the shape of a new tennis racket were dictated by a scheme to enlarge the "sweet spot," that shape should not be the subject of a design patent. Instead, the shape should be protected by a utility patent, assuming that it meets the criteria of patentability. One factor to consider in judging whether a design is functional or ornamental is whether the same functions could be accomplished by designs of significantly different appearance.[7]

Although neither the Patent Office nor the courts are well suited to judge artistic merit, a design must be "ornamental" before it can be granted a design patent. The design need not be a fine example of artistic expression, but it must, in some way, appeal to the "aesthetic sense." On occasion, design patents have been denied because the depicted article failed to meet this criterion.[8] On the other hand, design patents have been

---

[4] 35 U.S.C. § 171.

[5] *See* MPEP § 1504.01A.

[6] *See* PHG Techs., LLC v. St. John Co., 469 F.3d 1361, 1366 (Fed. Cir. 2006) ("If the patented design is primarily functional rather than ornamental, the patent is invalid."); Door-Master Corp. v. Yorktowne, Inc., 256 F.3d 1308, 1312 (Fed. Cir. 2001) ("only 'the non-functional aspects of an ornamental design as shown in a patent' are proper bases for design patent protection"); L.A. Gear, Inc. v. Thom McAn Shoe Co., 988 F.2d 1117, 1123 (Fed. Cir. 1993).

[7] *See PHG*, 469 F.3d at 1366–37; Rosco, Inc. v. Mirror Lite Co., 304 F.3d 1373, 1378 (Fed. Cir. 2002) ("[I]f other designs could produce the same or similar functional capabilities, the design of the article in question is likely ornamental, not functional."); *L.A. Gear*, 988 F.2d at 1123. Even if every element of the design has a function, the overall configuration may be a matter of patentable aesthetic expression. *See L.A. Gear*, 988 F.2d at 1123; *Avia*, 853 F.2d at 1563.

[8] *See, e.g.,* Blisscraft of Hollywood v. United Plastics Co., 294 F.2d 694, 696 (2d Cir. 1961) (finding a pitcher design insufficiently ornamental: "Plaintiff's pitcher has no particularly aesthetic appeal in line, form, color, or otherwise. . . . The reaction which the pitcher inspires is simply that of the usual, useful and not unattractive piece of kitchenware."). In more recent cases, designs are unlikely to be criticized for failing to look attractive. Instead, the debate is likely to center on whether aesthetic aspirations (however successful) or functional necessity dictated the design. *See* Seiko Epson Corp. v. Nu-Kote Int'l, Inc., 190 F.3d 1360, 1368 (Fed. Cir. 1999) ("Nor need the design be aesthetically pleasing. . . . The design may contribute distinctiveness or consumer recognition to the [product], but an absence of artistic merit does not mean that the design is purely functional.").

granted to objects that would not ordinarily be thought of as having an ornamental aspect—for example, a hip prosthesis.[9] Apparently, a physician selecting a hip prosthesis might be moved to select the one that appeals to the eye.

Because design patents protect visually appealing designs, they may be denied to objects hidden from view.[10] A vacuum cleaner bag, for example, was denied a design patent on that ground.[11] Nevertheless, a design may be sufficiently ornamental if its appearance is "a matter of concern" during some significant portion of its life cycle.[12] A hip prosthesis, for example, is not visible in use, but it is visible when displayed at a trade show or in advertising.

Whereas utility patents include many pages describing the invention in words, design patents describe the invention only through drawings.[13] This is appropriate since the purpose of the patent is to protect a visual design. A utility patent can have many claims. A design patent has only one,[14] typically in the form "the ornamental design for the [object] as shown."[15] The bracketed portion would name the kind of object depicted—for example, a candle holder, faucet, or automobile tire.

A patented design need not have utility, but it must be new and nonobvious.[16] Obviousness is difficult to judge in aesthetic matters,[17] and the prior art available for the Patent Office to consult—primarily earlier design patents and utility patents—may barely scratch the surface. Nevertheless, a design patent, like a utility patent, carries a presumption of validity.

The term of a design patent is 14 years from the date of issue.[18] An object can infringe a design patent if it presents substantially the same appearance

---

[9] *See* In re Webb, 916 F.2d 1553 (Fed. Cir. 1990).

[10] *See Door-Master*, 256 F.3d at 1312 ("generally concealed features are not proper bases for design patent protection because their appearance cannot be a 'matter of concern'"); *Webb*, 916 F.2d at 1557.

[11] *See* Ex parte Fesco, 147 U.S.P.Q. 74 (Pat. Off. Bd. App. 1965).

[12] *See* Contessa Food Prods., Inc. v. Conagra, Inc., 282 F.3d 1370, 1379 (Fed. Cir. 2002); Keystone Retaining Wall Sys., Inc. v. Westrock, Inc., 997 F.2d 1444, 1451 (Fed. Cir. 1993); *Webb*, 916 F.2d at 1557–58.

[13] *See* Amini Innovation Corp. v. Anthony California, Inc., 439 F.3d 1365, 1371 (Fed. Cir. 2006) ("It is the drawings of the patent . . . that define the patented design."); Hupp v. Siroflex of America, Inc., 122 F.3d 1456, 1464 (Fed. Cir. 1997) ("A design patent contains no written description; the drawings are the claims to the patented subject matter.").

[14] *See* 37 C.F.R. § 1.153.

[15] *See* MPEP § 1503.03.

[16] 35 U.S.C. §§ 171, 103; *L.A. Gear*, 988 F.2d at 1124; *Avia*, 853 F.2d at 1563.

[17] As in the case of a utility patent, factors to consider include the scope and content of the prior art, the differences between the prior art and the claimed subject matter, the level of ordinary skill in the art, and secondary considerations such as commercial success or copying. *Avia*, 853 F.2d at 1564. See Section 8.9.6. In the case of a design patent, obviousness must be judged from the perspective of a designer of ordinary capabilities. Litton Sys., Inc. v. Whirlpool Corp., 728 F.2d 1423, 1443 (Fed. Cir. 1984).

[18] 35 U.S.C. § 173.

to an ordinary observer.[19] Differences will not avoid infringement if the patented design and the accused product are sufficiently similar overall.[20] It is not an infringement to copy only the functional aspects of a patented design.[21]

In addition to the ordinary observer test of infringement, the Federal Circuit required that the accused product incorporate the patented design's "point of novelty"—the element or elements that distinguished the patented design from the prior art—in order to infringe. Recently, in the *en banc* decision *Egyptian Goddess, Inc. v. Swisa, Inc.,*[22] the court abandoned that requirement. However, the court held that the hypothetical observer must compare the patented design and the accused product with knowledge of the prior art and attention to the distinguishing elements of the patented design. If the patented design and the accused product resemble each other primarily because of elements also found in the prior art, then the accused product does not infringe.

The patentee can recover the "entire profit" of an infringer who has sold an article covered by a design patent.[23]

12.2 PLANT PATENTS

A new plant variety can be the subject of a utility patent,[24] but only if the variety is non-obvious,[25] and only if the patent disclosure satisfies the usual requirements, such as the enablement and written description requirements.[26] These are often problematic in the case of a plant variety. If the difference between a newly discovered rose and a known variety is a subtle difference in color and perfume, it is difficult to describe these differences in

---

[19] "'[I]f, in the eye of an ordinary observer, giving such attention as a purchaser usually gives, two designs are substantially the same, if the resemblance is such as to deceive such an observer, inducing him to purchase one supposing it to be the other, the first one patented is infringed by the other.'" *Amini,* 439 F.3d at 1371; *see also* Lawman Armor Corp. v. Winner Int'l, LLC, 437 F.3d 1383, 1384 (Fed. Cir. 2006); *Contessa,* 282 F.3d at 1377. If the item is specialized, the court may adopt the perspective of an ordinary purchaser of that item. *See* Goodyear Tire & Rubber Co. v. Hercules Tire & Rubber Co., 162 F.3d 1113, 1117 (Fed. Cir. 1998). Note the similarity to the test of trademark infringement, discussed at Section 2.2. The proper comparison, however, is between the accused product and the design depicted in the patent, not between the accused product and the patentee's own commercial embodiment, which may include features not depicted in the patent. *See* Sun Hill Indus., Inc. v. Easter Unlimited, Inc., 48 F.3d 1193, 1196 (Fed. Cir. 1995).

[20] *See Contessa,* 282 F.3d at 1376–78.

[21] *See* Lee v. Dayton-Hudson Corp., 838 F.2d 1186, 1189 (Fed. Cir. 1988).

[22] 2008 U.S. App. LEXIS 20104 (Fed. Cir. 2008) (*en banc*).

[23] 35 U.S.C. § 289.

[24] J.E.M. AG Supply, Inc. v. Pioneer Hi-Bred Int'l, Inc., 534 U.S. 124, 127 (2001).

[25] See Section 8.9.6.

[26] See Sections 8.6.8 and 8.8.

words and equally difficult to decide if the differences are non-obvious. Congress addressed these difficulties by providing a special form of patent for plant varieties, thereby putting agriculture on a more even footing with industry when it comes to encouraging, and rewarding, innovation.

A plant patent can be obtained by one who "invents or discovers and asexually reproduces any distinct and new variety of plant, including cultivated spores, mutants, hybrids, and newly found seedlings, other than a tuber propagated plant or a plant found in an uncultivated state."[27] Asexual reproduction refers to reproduction by grafting, budding, and similar procedures that reproduce a genetically identical plant from a portion of the first plant or its progeny.[28] The "invention" is complete only when the new variety has been discovered, its distinguishing characteristics have been identified, and it has been asexually reproduced. If the asexually reproduced plant has the distinctive characteristics of its parent, this demonstrates that the characteristics likely represent a genetic rather than an environmental variation.

A patent cannot be granted for the discovery of a new plant in the wild—that is, in an "uncultivated state." However, patents can be granted for varieties that arise from unplanned sports or mutations of cultivated crops. *Imazio Nursery, Inc. v. Dania Greenhouses,*[29] for example, discusses a patented variety of heather discovered as a seedling in a cultivated field. This variety, dubbed "Erica Sunset," blooms during the Christmas season, much earlier than the ordinary heather from which it arose.

Plant patents have only one claim, which typically refers to the plant variety "shown and described" in the specification, usually with a brief recital of the characteristics that distinguish the new variety.[30] In contrast to a utility patent, a description found in a plant patent need only be "as complete as is reasonably possible."[31] Because of their function in identifying the patented variety, illustrations are an important part of a plant patent, and they must be "artistically and competently executed."[32]

---

[27] 35 U.S.C. § 161. According to the Manual of Patent Examining Procedure, tubers (such as potatoes) are excluded because "this group alone, among asexually reproduced plants, is propagated by the same part of the plant that is sold as food." MPEP § 1601. The term "plant" is used in its popular sense rather than a strict scientific sense, so species such as bacteria are also excluded. *Id.*

[28] See MPEP § 1601. The Plant Variety Protection Act, 7 U.S.C. § 2321 *et seq.*, provides similar legal protection for sexually reproduced plant varieties (e.g., plants grown from seed), but not as a part of the patent system. The Plant Variety Protection Act is administered by the Department of Agriculture.

[29] 69 F.3d 1560 (Fed. Cir. 1995).

[30] *See* 35 U.S.C. § 162 ("The claim in the specification shall be in formal terms to the plant shown and described.").

[31] 35 U.S.C. § 162.

[32] MPEP § 1606. Either drawings or color photographs are acceptable. *Id.* Examples of plant patents have been omitted from the appendices due to the difficulty of reproducing the illustrations.

A plant variety is patentable if it is "distinct and new"[33]—a threshold of novelty less demanding than "non-obviousness." The patent confers the right to exclude others from asexually reproducing the claimed plant or from using or selling such a plant.[34] It is not an infringement of a plant patent to grow the claimed plant from seed.[35] It is also not an infringement to develop independently a variety that is indistinguishable from the patented variety. An infringement occurs only if the accused variety is an *offspring* of the original, which means that an element of proving infringement is evidence that the accused infringer had access to the original plant or its asexually reproduced progeny.[36] This is in contrast to the usual rule (applied to utility patents) that independent development is not a defense to infringement.

12.3 FOREIGN PATENTS

An inventor who wishes to protect an invention in a foreign country must apply for a patent in that country.[37] Foreign patent systems generally convey rights similar to those obtainable in the United States, but there are important differences.

Other countries award a patent to the *first person to file a patent application*, whereas the United States awards a patent to the *first person to invent.* The first-to-file system provides a far simpler way to handle issues of priority, which in the United States must be resolved by complex inquiries into conception, reduction to practice, and diligence.[38] The United States may adopt the first-to-file rule in order to make its practice consistent with that of the rest of the world.[39] Still, there is something to be said for rewarding the person who is first to invent, rather than the person who wins the "race to the Patent Office."

Many other countries allow a degree of public participation in the process of patent examination. In Japan, for example, applications are "laid open"—that is, made public—18 months after filing. Afterward members of the public, most likely competitors of the applicant, may submit prior art that bears upon the patentability of the claimed invention. If the Patent Office still determines that the patent should issue, those who disagree may oppose.

---

[33] 35 U.S.C. § 161.

[34] 35 U.S.C. § 163.

[35] One may infringe a *utility* patent by growing the patented plant variety from saved seed. *See* Monsanto Co. v. David, 516 F.3d 1009, 1014 (Fed. Cir. 2008); Monsanto Co. v. McFarling, 302 F.3d 1291, 1299 (Fed. Cir. 2002).

[36] *See* Imazio Nursery, 69 F.3d at 1569–70.

[37] Many countries, including the United States, are parties to the Patent Cooperation Treaty, which provides for a standardized patent application acceptable for filing in any of the participating countries. The patent laws of the participating countries differ, however, so an invention that is patentable in one country may be denied a patent in another.

[38] See Sections 8.9.2 and 8.9.3.

[39] See Section 12.5.

This system ensures a more rigorous examination than typically occurs in the United States, where the Patent Office deals only with the applicant. As discussed in Section 5.1, the legislation allowing publication of United States patent applications does not provide for any form of third-party opposition.

An applicant for a United States patent can take the benefit of an earlier filing date in most foreign countries, if the filing date of the foreign application is no more than 12 months before the United States filing date.[40] This earlier effective filing date does not remove any "statutory bar" problems raised by 35 U.S.C. § 102(b).[41] The foreign filing date can, however, be used to establish an earlier constructive reduction to practice,[42] possibly avoiding certain prior art references or improving the applicant's position in an interference contest.[43] Generally an inventor who files an application in a foreign country should wait no longer than 12 months before filing in the United States. Otherwise, the foreign patent, if it issues before the United States application is on file, may constitute invalidating prior art under 35 U.S.C. § 102(d).[44]

12.4 PATENTING COMPUTER PROGRAMS

One of the thorniest questions in patent law has been whether a computer program can be patented. At first blush, there seems no reason to doubt it. A program is a process—one of the categories of patentable subject matter set out in 35 U.S.C. § 101. Computer programs are *technological* in nature. Although writing a program involves a degree of personal expression, the program ultimately controls the operation of a machine. Finally, from a constitutional perspective, there is little reason to suppose that progress in the art of computer programming is less dependent on patent protection than progress in other technological arts. Why, then, have software patents met with resistance?

The chief difficulty is the kinship between a computer program and a mathematical operation, or "algorithm." The following is an example of a mathematical algorithm that begins with two quantities, a and b:

1. Raise a to the power 2, and call the result x.
2. Raise b to the power 2, and call the result y.

---

[40] *See* 35 U.S.C. § 119.

[41] "[B]ut no patent shall be granted on any application for patent for an invention which had been patented or described in a printed publication in any country more than one year before the date of the actual filing of the application in this country, or which had been in public use or on sale in this country more than one year prior to such filing." 35 U.S.C. § 119(a). The § 102(b) "statutory bar" provisions are discussed in Section 8.10.

[42] *See* In re Mulder, 716 F.2d 1542, 1544–45 (Fed. Cir. 1983). Constructive reduction to practice is discussed in Section 8.9.2.

[43] See Section 5.4.

[44] See Section 8.11.

3. Add x and y, and call the result z.
4. Take the square root of z, and call the result c.

As we have seen, a patent cannot be granted on a "principle of nature," such as a mathematical formula.[45] The truths of mathematics cannot be owned, even by their discoverers. Pythagoras, for example, could not have patented his famous theorem. When the mathematical truth expresses a relationship, as in the case of the Pythagorean theorem, the relationship also suggests a *process* by which one set of numbers can be converted, by mathematics, to another. As the reader may already have recognized, the algorithm set forth above is simply a sequence of steps, based on the relationship expressed in the Pythagorean theorem, by which one could derive the length (c) of the hypotenuse of a right triangle, given the lengths of the two sides $(a$ and $b)$.

If the formula itself cannot be patented, it seems to follow that an algorithm based on the formula cannot be patented either. If it were otherwise, only the patentee could *use* the formula, and the effect would be the same as if the patentee owned the formula itself. Hence, courts have categorized "mathematical algorithms" as unpatentable subject matter, akin to "principles of nature" and "abstract ideas."

Computers carry out their myriad functions by performing, at tremendously high speeds, a number of very fundamental mathematical and logical operations. The program controls these operations by dictating the sequence of steps that the computer is to perform. Expressed in slightly different terms, the algorithm set forth above could be a program instructing a computer to calculate, in an instant, the length of hypotenuse c. If a programmer attempted to patent such a program, the question would arise whether the program was a practical advancement in the technological art of computer programming or nothing more than an unpatentable "mathematical algorithm."

12.4.1 The Supreme Court Decisions

The Supreme Court has addressed the patentability of computer programs on three occasions. The first case, *Gottschalk v. Benson*,[46] involved a method of converting binary-coded numbers from one format to another. The method did not rely on a new kind of computer. It could be performed with any computer, then existing or yet to be invented, and it could be used in an unlimited variety of applications. The court held the applicant's claims unpatentable, finding that the method embodied an abstract idea or a mathematical truth, rather than the application of an idea to a specific technological end.

[45] See Section 4.3.
[46] 409 U.S. 64 (1972).

Regarding "process" claims in general, the court observed that "[t]rans-formation and reduction of an article 'to a different state or thing' is the clue to the patentability of a process claim that does not include particular machines."[47] If this statement is taken at face value, it would appear that no computer program would be patentable as such, since programs involve the manipulation of information, not the physical transformation of an article to "a different state or thing." Yet the court denied that it intended to bar the patentability of computer programs altogether. Instead, it focused on the preemptive effect of allowing an inventor to patent a method that is "not lim-ited to any particular art or technology, to any particular apparatus or machinery, or to any particular end use."[48] *Benson* left open the question of whether one could patent a computer program embodying a mathematical algorithm if its use were limited to a specific technological application.

That issue confronted the court in *Parker v. Flook*,[49] where the claim at issue involved a method of updating an "alarm limit." An alarm limit is a number used to indicate an abnormal, possibly dangerous condition arising during the catalytic conversion of hydrocarbons. During certain stages of the operation, the alarm limit needs to be adjusted or updated. Flook tried to patent a computer-implemented algorithm to perform that function. As in *Benson*, the court found the algorithm unpatentable. Even though Flook claimed the algorithm only in connection with a catalytic conversion process, and even though a certain amount of specific "post-solution activ-ity" followed the calculation (namely, the adjustment of the alarm limit), the court still found that patenting the process would be tantamount to patent-ing an abstract idea or phenomenon of nature. As a part of its analysis, the court adopted an odd mixture of the patentable subject matter standard of 35 U.S.C. § 101 and the standard of novelty under 35 U.S.C. § 102. The court found that if the algorithm were treated *as though it were already known*, the claim as a whole would describe no patentable invention.[50]

The last case of the "Supreme Court trilogy" was *Diamond v. Diehr*.[51] While the facts in *Diehr* are curiously similar to those in *Flook*, the result was very different. Diehr's invention involved a process for curing rubber inside a molding press. To determine the proper time to open the press and remove the finished article, Diehr's method called for constant measure-ment of the temperature inside the press. A computer used this data and the well-known Arrhenius equation to periodically recalculate the time neces-sary for the rubber to cure. When the calculated optimum and the actual curing time were the same, the computer opened the press automatically. This time, the court found the invention to be patentable subject matter.

[47] *Id.* at 70.
[48] *Id.* at 64.
[49] 437 U.S. 584 (1978).
[50] *Id.* at 594.
[51] 450 U.S. 175 (1981).

Diehr was decided not long after *Chakrabarty,*[52] and it reflects a similarly expansive interpretation of the Patent Act. The majority viewed the invention not as a mathematical algorithm per se, but as a method of curing rubber that happened to make use of a mathematical algorithm. Viewed in this light, Diehr's method was an industrial process for "transforming . . . an article . . . into a different state or thing"—the kind of process that has always been considered patentable.[53] The use of an equation and a programmed computer did not make the process as a whole unpatentable. Although *Flook* had seemingly dismissed "field of use" limitations as the key to patentability, the *Diehr* court distinguished *Flook* as a case in which the claimed method did nothing more than calculate a number, hardly mentioning the physical process steps associated with that calculation. The implication is that if the claims in *Flook* had been drafted with additional references to the catalytic conversion process, they might have been patentable, even if the only novel aspect of the process had been the use of the mathematical algorithm.

Diehr marked a significant change in the Supreme Court's attitude toward the patentability of computer software. However, since *Diehr* did not overrule the earlier cases, the lower courts, and the Federal Circuit in particular, were left with the difficult task of reconciling and applying the rules set out in *Benson, Flook,* and *Diehr.*

12.4.2 The Federal Circuit Decisions

The Federal Circuit has distinguished between patent claims drawn to mathematical algorithms in the abstract, and claims that call for application of an algorithm to a *physical* process, or claims that call for a specific *machine* to perform the algorithm. For example, the Federal Circuit rejected claims to a method of conducting an auction, where the mathematical algorithm was neither tied to specific computer hardware nor used to accomplish any physical transformation.[55] It similarly denied a patent to an algorithm for constructing a "bubble hierarchy" to define the space around an object. This algorithm could be used to keep industrial robots from colliding with fixed objects, but, significantly, the challenged claims did not refer to this specific use.[56] On the other hand, the Federal Circuit held patentable an apparatus claim reciting various physical components, one of which used an "auto-correlation" algorithm to recognize patterns in signals (e.g., for voice recognition).[57]

---

[52] See Section 4.4.
[53] *Diehr,* 450 U.S. at 184.
[54] Arrhythmia Research Tech., Inc. v. Corazonix Corp., 958 F.2d 1053, 1058 (Fed. Cir. 1992).
[55] In re Schrader, 22 F.3d 290 (Fed. Cir. 1994).
[56] In re Warmerdam, 33 F.3d 1354 (Fed. Cir. 1994).
[57] In re Iwahashi, 888 F.2d 1370 (Fed. Cir. 1989).

No computer software performs a useful function without computer hardware to run it. Hence, a claim to a computer program can always be couched in terms of apparatus—in other words, I claim not "program x,y,z" but "a *machine configured to execute* program x,y,z." The power of that idea for avoiding issues of patentable subject matter was revealed in *In re Alappat.*[58]

In *Alappat,* the Patent Office had rejected Alappat's claims to an improved oscilloscope display, which used a software algorithm to make jagged lines appear smoother. The claims called for an apparatus comprising a combination of "means" to perform the necessary functions of calculation and display.[59] On appeal, the majority of the court held the claims patentable subject matter, stressing the disclosure of specific memory and logic circuits to perform the functions recited in the claims: "This is not a disembodied mathematical concept which may be characterized as an 'abstract idea,' but rather a specific machine to produce a useful, concrete, and tangible result."[60] Two dissenting judges complained that the "apparatus" on which the majority relied was nothing more than conventional computer hardware, and the only thing that Alappat had invented was a mathematical operation. In the dissenters' view, Alappat's choice to describe the invention not as mathematics per se, but as conventional hardware to perform the mathematics, should not have determined whether the invention was patentable subject matter.

Alappat suggests that virtually any software invention can be patented, as long as it is claimed in terms of a *machine* to perform the necessary functions. This is so even if the apparatus disclosed is nothing more than what one would find in any run-of-the mill computer. In the majority's view, "[new] programming creates a new machine, because a general-purpose computer in effect becomes a special purpose computer once it is programmed to perform particular functions pursuant to instructions from program software."[61] *Alappat* also introduced the idea that software is not unpatentably abstract if it produces a "useful, concrete and tangible result."[62] The software at issue did that, by creating an improved oscilloscope display.

In *State Street Bank & Trust Co. v. Signature Financial Gp.,*[63] the court showed how far these ideas might be pushed. In *Alappat,* the applicant's invention was a technological advancement; in *State Street,* it was a method of organizing a family of mutual funds to save expenses and avoid taxes. Yet

---

[58] 33 F.3d 1526 (Fed. Cir. 1994) (*en banc*).
[59] See the discussion of "means-plus-function" claims in Section 7.7.4.
[60] *Alappat,* 33 F.3d at 1544.
[61] *Id.* at 1545.
[62] *Id.* at 1544.
[63] 149 F.3d 1368 (Fed. Cir. 1998).

the patentee claimed invention in terms of the computer "system" used to implement the business scheme. Although the hardware was nothing new, and it was depicted in the patent only in cartoon-like sketches, the court held that the invention—a statutory machine—produced the "useful, concrete and tangible result" necessary to distinguish the invention from a mathematical abstraction.[64]

State Street implied that any useful software-implemented invention could be patented, if it were claimed in the right way. However, the tide may be turning once again. In *In re Bilski*, the Federal Circuit rejected the "useful, concrete and tangible result" standard. A patentable process, the court held, must be tied to a particular machine, or it must transform an article "into a different state or thing"—a standard that calls into question the patentability of much computer software.[65] It remains to be seen whether the problem can be avoided by confining the process to a general-purpose computer (technically, a "machine") programmed to perform a novel software algorithm.[66]

12.5 PATENT REFORM

The Patent Act has lasted, with relatively minor changes, for more than half a century. Recently Congress has considered significant new legislation that would, in many respects, make the United States patent system more like that of other nations. Nothing is certain at the time of writing. Although many had predicted rapid adoption of these reform proposals, opposition

---

[64] "Today, we hold that the transformation of data, representing discrete dollar amounts, by a machine through a series of mathematical calculations into a final share price, constitutes a practical application of a mathematical algorithm, formula, or calculation, because it produces 'a useful, concrete and tangible result'—a final share price momentarily fixed for recording and reporting purposes and even accepted and relied upon by regulatory authorities and in subsequent trades." *Id.* at 1373.

[65] In re Bilski, 2008 U.S. App. LEXIS 22497, *38-42 (Fed. Cir. 2008) (*en banc*); *see also* In re Comiskey, 499 F.3d 1365, 1376 (Fed. Cir. 2007) ("a claim reciting an algorithm or abstract idea can state statutory subject matter only if, as employed in the process, it is embodied in, operates on, transforms, or otherwise involves another class of statutory subject matter, i.e., a machine, manufacture, or composition of matter").

[66] *See Bilski*, 2008 U.S. App. LEXIS 22497 at *47 ("We leave to future cases the elaboration of the precise contours of machine implementation, as well as answers to particular questions, such as whether or when recitation of a computer suffices to tie a process claim to a particular machine."). In *Comiskey*, the court observed that "[t]he routine addition of modern electronics to an otherwise unpatentable invention typically creates a prima facie case of obviousness." *Comiskey*, 499 F.3d at 1379. Here the court seems to be conflating patentable subject matter and novelty in the manner of *Flook*, subsequently disapproved in *Diehr*. If a mathematical algorithm was non-obvious (whether or not it was patentable subject matter on its own), combining that algorithm with obvious electronics could not, logically, make obvious the invention *as a whole*.

from some U.S. industries has slowed the process. If reform does occur, these are among its more likely components:

- *Introduction of a first-to-file system for determining priority.* Currently if more than one person has invented the same thing, the right to secure a patent belongs to the person who invented first.[67] In other countries, the right belongs to the first person to file a patent application. A change to the first-to-file system would encourage the prompt submission of applications and it would greatly simplify the resolution of priority issues, now burdened by difficult issues of proof.
- *Publication of all patent applications.* Currently many patent applications are published, but applicants can avoid publication by filing only in the United States.[68] Reform proposals would require that all patent applications be published 18 months after filing.
- *Expanded opportunities for public participation.* Currently third parties have very limited opportunities to bring to the attention of the patent examiner reasons that a published patent application should be rejected.[69] They cannot, for example, explain why certain prior art is relevant to the application. Reform proposals would expand those opportunities, making U.S. procedures more like those of other nations.
- *Elimination of the "best mode" requirement.* Currently patent applications must disclose the *best* method known to the applicant for making and using the claimed invention.[70] Reform proposals would eliminate the "best mode" defense to infringement, which is said to invite complex inquiry into highly subjective matters. The "enablement" requirement[71] would still demand disclosure of information sufficient to make and use the invention.
- *Invalidating patents based on pre–filing date disclosures.* Currently public disclosure of the invention more than *one year* before the filing date may invalidate a patent.[72] Reform proposals would limit that one-year "grace period" to disclosures made by the applicant. Third-party disclosures would invalidate a patent if made at any time prior to the filing date.
- *Limiting "reasonable royalty" damages to some portion of the value of the infringing product.* Currently courts often award a "reasonable royalty" for infringement based upon the "entire market value" of the infringing product.[73] Although the amount of the royalty may take into account the importance of the patented invention to consumer demand for the entire product, some reform proposals would allow courts to apportion more explicitly in order to avoid over-compensating patentees whose inventions are relatively minor aspects of the infringing product. Whether this would really change anything is debatable.

[67] See Section 8.9.1.3.
[68] See Section 5.1.
[69] See *id.*
[70] See Section 8.7.
[71] See Section 8.6.
[72] See Section 8.10.
[73] See Section 11.8.1.

- *Changes to the standard of willful infringement.* Damages for patent infringement may be increased if the defendant "willfully" infringed."[74] Reform
  proposals would confine willful infringement to limited circumstances—
  including where the infringer ignored a written notice from the patentee,
  where the infringer deliberately copied from the patentee, or where the
  infringer continued to infringe after an adverse decision by a court.

[74] See Section 11.8.2.

Note on Sources

In any area of the law, there is no substitute for the original sources. In the specific case of patent law, the primary source is Title 35 of the United States Code, known as the Patent Act. Several one-volume references reproduce the Patent Act and other selected legislation concerning copyright and trademark law. A good example is *Selected Statutes and International Agreements on Unfair Competition, Trademark, Copyright and Patent*, edited by Paul Goldstein and Edmund W. Kitch and published by Foundation Press. Rules and regulations specifically relating to patent applications and prosecution can be found in Title 37 of the Code of Federal Regulations, published by the Office of the Federal Register, National Archives and Records, and the Manual of Patent Examining Procedure (or MPEP), published by the Department of Commerce. All of these materials can now be conveniently located online at the PTO website, http://www.uspto.gov/main/patents.htm.

Judicial opinions cited in this book can be found in any good law library or through electronic resources like Lexis or Westlaw. Supreme Court decisions are found in the *United States Reports* (abbreviated in case citations as U.S.), published by West Publishing Co. Published decisions of the Federal Circuit Court of Appeals are found in West's *Federal Reporter* (abbreviated as F.2d or F.3d). District Court opinions are found in West's *Federal Supplement* (F. Supp. or F. Supp. 2d) or in BNA's *United States Patent Quarterly* (U.S.P.Q. or U.S.P.Q.2d).

Several multi-volume treatises provide very detailed surveys of United States patent law, including its historical development. The one the author turns to most frequently is Professor Donald S. Chisum's *Chisum on Patents*, published by Matthew Bender. Ernest Bainbridge Lipscomb's *Lipscomb's*

Walker on Patents, published by Clark Boardman Callaghan, is also a valuable resource. Robert L. Harmon's *Patents and the Federal Circuit*, published by BNA Books, is a work that concentrates on the development of the law in the Federal Circuit Court of Appeals. Any of these works will serve as a useful supplement to this book when greater detail is required.

Sample Utility Patents

United States Patent [19]

Oviatt

[11] Patent Number: 5,502,918

[45] Date of Patent: Apr. 2, 1996

US005502918A

[54] **MOUSETRAP FOR CATCHING MICE LIVE**

[76] Inventor: **Bill Oviatt**, 1375 Highway 71 North, Springdale, Ark. 72764

[21] Appl. No.: **347,890**

[22] Filed: **Dec. 1, 1994**

[51] Int. Cl.⁶ A01M 23/02
[52] U.S. Cl. 43/61; 43/60; 43/66
[58] Field of Search 43/66, 67, 61, 43/60, 58, 75

[56] **References Cited**

U.S. PATENT DOCUMENTS

944,926 12/1909 Turnbo 43/66
1,226,641 5/1917 Cushing 43/60
4,768,305 9/1988 Sackett 43/61

Primary Examiner—Kurt Rowan
Attorney, Agent, or Firm—Rick Martin

[57] **ABSTRACT**

A "Y" shaped mousetrap lures a mouse into an open end of the "Y" by means of smelly bait located at a closed end of the bottom of the "Y". The "Y" is pivotally supported horizontally by a stand. As the mouse walks past the pivot point, a ping pong ball rolls from the opposite short "Y" tube member and down to the entrance of the open ended tube member. The mouse is trapped alive and can be drowned by immersing the mousetrap.

8 Claims, 3 Drawing Sheets

FIG. 1

FIG. 2

FIG. 3

FIG. 4

FIG. 6

FIG. 7

FIG. 5

FIG. 8

FIG. 9

1

MOUSETRAP FOR CATCHING MICE LIVE

FIELD OF INVENTION

The present invention relates to a better mousetrap.

BACKGROUND OF THE INVENTION

Mice can be a nuisance and/or a health menace. Traditional mousetraps are comprised of either a mechanical or chemical killing means. When a mouse is killed in a household, many health problems can arise. These health problems include the release of body fluids containing viruses inside the household. Parasites including worms or lice can be released. Decomposition bacteria will cause odors and cause injury to pets or children who ingest them.

The present invention eliminates these hazards by catching the mouse alive. A simple, cylindrical, teeter-totter contains bait at a closed end of the cylinder. The mouse enters the open end of the cylinder and walks toward the bait. As the mouse passes a fulcrum the cylinder tilts the bait end of the cylinder downward. The mouse becomes trapped by a downward rolling ping pong ball. The trap containing the trapped mouse can be brought outside where the entire trap can be thrown in a bucket to drown the mouse.

SUMMARY OF THE INVENTION

The main object of the present invention is to trap a mouse alive.

Another object of the present invention is to provide an inexpensive trap.

Yet another object of the present invention is to allow the trap to be easily dropped into a bucket of water to drown the mouse.

Still yet another object of the present invention is to reuse the trap.

Other objects of this invention will appear from the following description and appended claims, reference being had to the accompanying drawings forming a part of this specification wherein like reference characters designate corresponding parts in the several views.

BRIEF DESCRIPTION OF THE DRAWINGS

FIG. 1 is a top perspective view of the preferred embodiment.

FIG. 2 is a front plan view of the preferred embodiment shown in FIG. 1.

FIG. 3 is a longitudinal sectional view taken along line 3—3 of FIG. 2.

FIG. 4 is a side plan view with a partial cut-away showing the mouse of FIG. 3 trapped.

FIG. 5 is a top perspective view of an alternate embodiment.

FIG. 6 is a front plan view of the retaining ring of FIG. 5.

FIG. 7 is a front plan view of the pivot stand of FIG. 5.

FIG. 8 is a longitudinal partial sectional view of the embodiment of FIG. 5 in the process of trapping a mouse.

FIG. 9 is a partial cut-away of the embodiment shown in FIG. 8 having caught the mouse.

Before explaining the disclosed embodiment of the present invention in detail, it is to be understood that the invention is not limited in its application to the details of the particular arrangement shown, since the invention is capable

2

of other embodiments. Also, the terminology used herein is for the purpose of description and not of limitation.

DESCRIPTION OF THE PREFERRED EMBODIMENT

Referring first to FIG. 1 the trap 1 is comprised of a support stand 2 preferably made of wire. Support stand 2 has wire ends 3, 4 which form a fulcrum for the main tube 5. Main tube 5 preferably is a plastic cylinder having holes 6, 60, 61. Holes 60, 61 removably attach to the wire ends 3, 4 thereby permitting the main tube 5 to teeter-totter around the fulcrum F. Holes 6 also provide an entrance for water when the trap 1 is immersed to kill a mouse.

A pair of removable end caps 7, 8 seal the ends of main tube 5. Before the end caps 7, 8 are secured to main tube 5, the bait 10 and the ping pong ball 9 are inserted as shown at bait end 100 and ball end 90.

An entrance tube 11 forms a "Y" with the main tube 5. Entrance tube 11 depends downward from main tube 5 and points away from the bait end 100.

FIG. 2 shows a mouse eye view of the trap 1. The lure of the bait 10 emanates from entrance E. In FIG. 3 the mouse M is entering entrance E of entrance tube 11. The main tube 5 is in the loaded position which is horizontal. Thus, the ping pong ball 9 rests at ball end 90.

Referring next to FIG. 4 the mouse M has had it. He's eating the bait 10. But as he walked past the fulcrum F his weight caused the main tube 5 to pivot around fulcrum F so that the bait end 100 fell down in direction D and the ball end 90 rose up in direction U. The ping pong ball 9 urged by gravity rolled in path C to close the entrance E. A rim 13 prevents the ping pong ball 9 from rolling past the entrance E.

When finished eating mouse M will turn around and walk past fulcrum F. Main tube 5 will teeter back to a horizontal position. However, ping pong ball 9 will prevent the egress of mouse M out of entrance E. All mouse M can do is travel back and forth in main tube 5 and entrance tube 11, thereby causing the trap 1 to teeter-totter around fulcrum F. Trap 1 can then be immersed in water to drown mouse M or opened at end caps 7, 8 to release mouse M. Of course, in an alternate use one could kill mouse M with poison bait and trap him in the same manner.

Referring next to FIGS. 5, 6, 7a trap 50 is shown. FIG. 5 shows the trap 50 in the horizontal loaded position. In this alternate embodiment a main tube 51 teeter-totters around fulcrum FF. Preferably a plastic ring 70 has a flat base 71 which acts as fulcrum FF. The entrance EE is at the entrance end 610 of the main tube 51. A removable cap 52 seals the bait end 609 of the main tube 51. Holes 66 can allow water to enter main tube 51 during immersion.

The trapping mechanism is comprised of a retaining tube 59 forming a "Y" with the main tube 51. Retaining tube 59 rises obliquely from main tube 51 away from the bait end 609 of the main tube 51. The ping pong ball 53 is held up in the load position by retaining prong 57 of swivel ring 56.

Referring last to FIGS. 8, 9 mouse M is first entering in FIG. 8 entrance EE. The swivel ring 56 is resting on the ground in the cocked position. The retaining prong 57 is pivotally supported in hole 67. Retaining prong 57 is holding up the ping pong ball 53.

When the mouse M passes the fulcrum FF he becomes trapped. The main tube 51 teeters so that the bait end 609 falls in direction D, and the entrance end 610 rises in direction U. The swivel ring **56** pivots in direction T because the prong **57** is urged downward by ping pong ball **53**. Hole **67** acts as a fulcrum. The ping pong ball **53** is restrained from exiting entrance EE by rim **54**. End caps **52**, **55** prevent the mouse's egress.

Although the present invention has been described with reference to preferred embodiments, numerous modifications and variations can be made and still the result will come within the scope of the invention. No limitation with respect to the specific embodiments disclosed herein is intended or should be inferred.

I claim:

1. A mousetrap comprising:

a main tube having a central fulcrum means, a bait end, and a ball end;

a base stand having a means to support the main tube at the fulcrum;

said bait end further comprising mouse bait and a main tube closure;

said ball end further comprising a ball and a main tube closure;

an entrance tube depending down from the main tube at the central fulcrum means, and angled toward the ball end;

said entrance tube having a mouse entrance adjacent a supporting surface for the base stand; and

said main tube having a horizontal load position wherein said ball rests at the ball end, wherein a mouse enters the mouse entrance, walks toward the bait up the entrance tube, and passes the fulcrum means, thereby causing the main tube to teeter down at the bait end, and cause the ball to roll down the main tube then down the entrance tube, functioning to block an egress of the mouse out the mouse entrance.

2. The mousetrap of claim **1** wherein said central fulcrum means further comprise holes in the main tube.

3. The mousetrap of claim **2** wherein said means to support further comprises a pair of prong ends fittingly engaged in the holes in the main tube.

4. The mousetrap of claim **1** wherein the ball further comprises a ping pong ball.

5. The mousetrap of claim **3** wherein said central fulcrum means further comprises a support stand depending from the main tube.

6. A mousetrap comprising:

a main tube having a closed bait end, a mouse entrance end, and a central fulcrum means supporting the main tube on a support surface;

a ball tube angularly rising from the main tube;

said ball tube further comprising a closure, a ball, and a ball support means, functioning to hold the ball against the closure when the main tube is teetered in a cocked position;

a bait in the bait end, functioning to lure a mouse into the mouse entrance, past the central fulcrum means, thereby causing the main tube to teeter downward at the bait end, and causing the ball support means to release the ball to roll into the main tube and thereby block an egress of the mouse out the mouse entrance.

7. The mousetrap of claim **5** wherein said ball support means further comprises a swivel ring suspended from a hole in the ball tube by a prong, wherein said prong swings away from the ball, thereby releasing it when the main tube is teetered downward at the bait end.

8. A mousetrap comprising:

a "Y" shaped tube pivotally supported at a center point by a stand;

said "Y" shaped tube having a straight tube closed at both ends, and having a bait at one end, and a ball at an opposing ball end, said ball end being adjacent to an open tube member;

said open tube member depending from the straight tube so as to form a mouse entrance when the straight tube is suspended horizontally, whereby a mouse attracted by a bait at the bait end passes the center point and causes the straight tube to teeter with the bait end down, thereby causing the ball to travel to the open tube member, thus trapping the mouse.

*   *   *   *   *

United States Patent [19]

Fisher

[11] Patent Number: 4,662,101

[45] Date of Patent: May 5, 1987

[54] **RAT OR MOUSE TRAP**

[76] Inventor: **Harry L. Fisher,** 9336 S. 208th St., Kent, Wash. 98031

[21] Appl. No.: **880,285**

[22] Filed: **Jun. 30, 1986**

[51] Int. Cl.⁴ A01M 23/04

[52] U.S. Cl. 43/69

[58] Field of Search 43/69

[56] **References Cited**

U.S. PATENT DOCUMENTS

121,608	12/1871	Francisco	43/69
290,580	12/1883	Harwell	43/69
1,208,206	12/1916	Poynter	43/69
1,525,349	2/1925	Yamasaki	43/69

FOREIGN PATENT DOCUMENTS

81327 8/1934 Sweden 43/69

Primary Examiner—Gene P. Crosby
Attorney, Agent, or Firm—Bruce A. Kaser

[57] **ABSTRACT**

A mousetrap (10) is made of a pivoting platform (12) suspended over a pitfall (14). The platform (12) is balanced in a manner such that it normally assumes a horizontal position, thus giving a mouse an appearance of a stable bridge over the pitfall. When the mouse (42) steps onto the platform (12) for the purpose of obtaining bait placed thereon, however, the platform (12) spins and dumps the mouse into the pitfall thereby trapping it.

1 Claim, 5 Drawing Figures

*Fig.*1

Fig. 2

Fig.3

Fig.4

Fig.5

1

RAT OR MOUSE TRAP

TECHNICAL FIELD

This invention relates to animal traps, and in particular, traps for rats, mice and/or similar vermin.

BACKGROUND ART

The damage caused by rats and mice to agricultural products is well known. Every year these pests cause incalculable damage to crops, whether they be in the field or stored, and other foodstuffs of a similar nature. Further, the problems associated with rat or mice infestation of domestic household environments are well known.

Man has continuously engaged in war with these pests and has engaged in various attempts at eradicating and/or controlling them. The present invention provides yet another attempt which has certain advantages over previous ones. As will become apparent, the present invention is, quite literally, the better mousetrap.

DISCLOSURE OF THE INVENTION

The present invention provides a trap for rats, mice and similar vermin. This invention employs a pit or pitfall into which these pests fall and are trapped. Once there, they may be either killed or maintained in a live condition.

A platform is suitably supported over the pitfall in a manner such that the platform can freely turn or pivot about a center line axis. The platform is balanced in a manner such that it normally assumes a horizontal position thereby giving a vermin an appearance of providing a secure supporting surface over the pitfall. The vermin can access the platform from the edge of the pitfall, and when the vermin moves onto the platform, the vermin's weight causes the platform to become unbalanced and turn, thus causing the vermin to fall into the pitfall. Of course, the vermin would be enticed onto the platform by a suitable bait placed on the platform but out of reach from the edge of the pitfall's opening.

Preferably, the pitfall is made of a bucket or another suitable container of like nature. The platform is supported over the bucket's opening by a pair of supporting members hooked to the bucket's rim. One supporting member is positioned directly across the bucket's opening from the other.

The platform comprises a generally rectangular sheet of material which spans the distance between the supporting members, with each end of the platform being pivotally connected to the end's respective adjacent supporting member. These connections are symmetrical, that is, the mid-point of each end of the rectangular platform is pivotally connected to a supporting member. This makes a pair of pivot points which define the center line axis, such axis extending generally horizontally across the bucket or pitfall's opening and about which the platform is free to turn.

The rectangular platform is curved sufficiently that its center of gravity is offset from the center line axis. Since the platform can freely turn, this causes the platform to normally assume the above-mentioned horizontal position. After the weight of a mouse or rat on the platform unbalances it, causing it to turn, the platform naturally turns back to the horizontal position after the mouse or rat falls off.

Each supporting member may have an inwardly projecting ledge from the rim or edge of the bucket or

2

pitfall which provides vermin-access onto the platform. Swivel members are provided for making the pivotal connection between each ledge and the ends of the platform.

An advantage to the present invention is that it is effective in controlling vermin without using poison. Poison, of course, has been known to be one of the most effective methods of controlling vermin. However, it is undesirable to use poison in situations where the poison may get mixed into foodstuffs that are eventually to be consumed by humans. This invention is ideally suited for use in these kinds of situations.

Another advantage to the present invention is that it may be used as a live trap, or otherwise, if so desired. The bottom of the bucket may be filled with a few inches of water into which a mouse or rat will fall after being dumped by the platform. Eventually, the mouse or rat drowns. However, by leaving the bucket empty, they may be trapped alive.

BRIEF DESCRIPTION OF THE DRAWINGS

In the drawings, like reference numerals and letters refer to like parts throughout the various views, and wherein:

FIG. 1 is a pictorial view of a preferred embodiment of the invention, and shows a curved rectangular platform pivotally supported over the opening of a bucket;

FIG. 2 is an enlarged fragmentary pictorial view showing a swivel member which connects the platform shown in FIG. 1 to a supporting member connected to the rim of the bucket;

FIG. 3 is a side elevational view of the platform shown in FIG. 1;

FIG. 4 is a view like FIG. 3 but shows the platform in a pivoting or turned condition; and

FIG. 5 is a view like FIG. 2 but shows an alternative embodiment for connecting the rectangular platform in FIGS. 1, 3 and 4 to a supporting member on the bucket's rim.

BEST MODE FOR CARRYING OUT THE INVENTION

Referring now to the drawings, and first to FIG. 1, therein is shown at 10 a preferred embodiment of the invention. The invention includes a rectangular platform 12 which is suspended over the upwardly directed opening of a bucket 14. The platform 12 is attached to the bucket 14 by a pair of supporting members 16, 18. Each supporting member has a hook portion 20 that is attached to the bucket's rim 22. Further, each member 16, 18 has an inwardly projecting ledge portion 24 that provides vermin-access from the edge of the bucket 22 onto the platform 12.

The platform 12 is pivotally connected at each of its ends 27, 29 to respective adjacent supporting members 16, 18 as shown at 26, 28. These connections are better illustrated in FIG. 2 which shows a swivel member 30 interconnecting a first member 32 and a second member 34. The swivel member 30 is connected to the two members 32, 34 by rivets 36, 38, or other suitable means, and permits the first member 32 to pivot relative to the second member 34.

Referring back to FIG. 3, each swivel member 26, 28 connects the approximate center point of the platform's ends 27, 29 to the supporting members 16, 18. The swivel members 26, 28 thus define two points through which a horizontal center line axis 40 passes. The plat-

3

form 12 is free to turn about this axis 40 and is curved slightly so that its center of gravity is offset from the axis. This offset causes the platform 12 to be normally balanced in the horizontal position shown in FIGS. 1 and 3.

Referring again to FIG. 1, therein is shown a mouse 42 poised on the rim 22 of the bucket 14. A suitable bait 44 is positioned on the center of the platform 12 and attracts the mouse 42. It should be understood that a suitable ramp or similar structure would be provided to permit the mouse 42 to access the bucket's rim 22. This is not shown in the drawings, however. The bait 44 would, of course, be positioned on the center of the platform 12 so that its weight would not unbalance the platform.

The horizontal position of the platform 12 gives the mouse 42 the appearance that the platform provides a bridge across the opening of the bucket 14. However, when the mouse 14 steps onto the platform 12, in its desire to obtain the bait 44, the mouse's weight unbalances the platform, causing it to turn as shown in FIG. 4, and thus dumps the mouse 42 into the bucket 14. The offset center of gravity of the platform 12 then causes the platform to return to the horizontal position after the mouse falls therefrom.

It should be appreciated that the above-described curved platform 12 could be replaced by a straight platform having a suitable counterweight attached thereto. This would not be a preferred embodiment, however.

The bottom of the bucket 14 may be filled with a few inches of water as indicated by the dashed lines 46. The mouse 42 may be able to swim in the water for a certain period of time but will eventually become tired and drown as shown at 48.

FIG. 5 shows an alternative embodiment of the swivel member 30 shown in FIG. 2. This embodiment may be used if it is desired to adapt the platform 12 to a bucket or other container having a different diameter. In this embodiment, the swivel member 30 comprises a plurality of swivel links as indicated at 50a, 50b, and 50c. The length of this alternative swivel member 30 is therefore adjustable by catching and releasing the links

4

50a, 50b, 50c from a link-catch 52 which is suitably connected to member 32.

The above description is presented for exemplary purposes only. This description is not meant to limit patent protection insofar as it is understood that certain departures may be taken from the above-described embodiments without departing from the overall spirit and scope of the invention. With regard to patent protection, the invention is to be limited not by the above description but only by the subjoined patent claims, in accordance with the well-established legal doctrines of patent claim interpretation.

What is claimed is:

1. A trap for mice, rats or vermin of a similar nature, and for use in connection with a pitfall having an upwardly directed opening, comprising:

a generally rectangular platform having a top surface and a bottom surface, and having a thin cross section;

a pair of platform supporting members, each of which is connected to the edge of said pitfall's opening, wherein one of said supporting members is positioned across said opening from the other, and wherein said platform substantially spans the distance between said supporting members, with a first end of said rectangular platform being pivotally connected to one of said members, and with a second end of said platform being pivotally connected to the other of said members, wherein such connections generally define a pair of points through which a center line axis extends across said pitfall's opening, said center line axis being an axis of symmetry for said platform and said platform being freely pivotally about said center line axis, and wherein

said platform's cross section is curved so that said top surface is concave and said bottom surface is convex, to cause said platform's center of gravity to be slightly offset from said center line axis, and to cause said platform to normally pivot into a position where said center of gravity is positioned below said center line axis, so that said platform is balanced in a manner that said platform's top surface provides said vermin with an appearance of a bridge across said pitfall.

* * * * *

United States Patent [19]

Fodor

[11] Patent Number: **4,819,368**

[45] **Date of Patent:** **Apr. 11, 1989**

[54] **DISPOSABLE MOUSETRAP**

[76] Inventor: John Fodor, 13 Village Park Cir., Morgantown, W. Va. 26505

[21] Appl. No.: 552,153

[22] Filed: Nov. 14, 1983

[51] Int. Cl.⁴ A01M 23/18; A01M 23/02
[52] U.S. Cl. 43/61
[58] Field of Search 43/61, 60, 62, 67, 70

[56] **References Cited**

U.S. PATENT DOCUMENTS

2,573,228	10/1951	Slauth	43/61
2,598,007	5/1952	McCormick	43/61
3,729,852	5/1973	Holmes	43/61
3,823,504	7/1974	Dosch	43/61
4,142,320	3/1979	Marcolina	43/61
4,231,180	11/1980	Bare	43/61
4,232,472	11/1980	Muelling	43/61
4,238,902	12/1980	Holl et al.	43/61

Primary Examiner—Kurt Rowan
Attorney, Agent, or Firm—Mason, Fenwick & Lawrence

[57] **ABSTRACT**

A disposable rodent trap is formed of an aluminum beverage can comprising an internal chamber, a bottom end wall with an opposite end wall including an entry opening therein of sufficient size to permit a rodent to pass into the internal chamber. A door member in the form of a can end is positioned externally of said end wall and movable into a closed position covering and blocking the entry opening by a rubber band. A latch means normally holds the door open by engagement with an edge surface of the entry opening but is movable by rodent contact inside the chamber to unlatched position to permit the rubber band to move the door member to its closed position to trap the rodent in said internal chamber.

15 Claims, 2 Drawing Sheets

229

FIG. 1

FIG. 2

230

FIG. 3

FIG. 4

FIG. 7

FIG. 5

FIG. 6

DISPOSABLE MOUSETRAP

BACKGROUND OF THE INVENTION

The present invention is in the field of animal trapping devices and is more specifically directed to a unique disposable rodent trap of particular value for capturing mice.

Numerous devices have evolved over the years for either capturing or killing mice. Many of the known devices have suffered from a number of shortcomings such as failing to operate properly and being overly expensive to fabricate. The most relevant prior known U.S. Patents comprise U.S. Pat. Nos. 100,986; 924,237; 1,261,189; 1,326,662; 1,372,663; 1,415,093; 1,861,478; 2,087,646; 2,434,031; 2,437,020; 2,573,228; 2,608,018; 3,426,470; 3,729,852; 3,733,735; 3,992,802. The present invention overcomes the shortcomings of the foregoing patents in providing a fool-proof functionally operational device that is quick and effective for capturing mice or other rodents and which is economical to fabricate and assemble due to the use of well-known widely available materials many of which are presently thrown away as scrap. It is consequently possible to simply dispose of the subject invention following the capture of a mouse or other rodent.

Therefore, it is the primary object of the present invention to provide a new and improved rodent trap which is functionally more effective than prior known rodent traps and is also economical to fabricate and assemble.

SUMMARY OF THE INVENTION

Achievement of the foregoing objects is enabled by the preferred embodiment of the invention in a remarkably effective manner. More specifically, the preferred embodiment of the invention comprises a container in the form of an aluminum beverage can of the type normally used for beer, soft drinks or the like. Such cans comprise a cylindrical wall member having a bottom end wall and a dispensing end wall with the dispensing end wall of the can used in the present invention including an elongated transverse entry opening of sufficient size to permit the passage of a rodent into the interior of the can.

A movable door is positioned adjacent the dispensing end wall of the can and is connected to an elongated latch member comprising an elongated tubular rod which extends into the interior of the can. Also, a rubber band extends from the bottom wall of the can through the length of the can outwardly through an opening provided in the dispensing end wall and is connected to the movable door member so as to urge the movable door member toward a closed position in which it overlies the entry opening and completely blocks same. The latch member includes a transverse surface engagable with a catch surface adjacent the edge of the entry opening so as to hold the door member in an open position against the urging of the elastic rubber band member. A tubular metal sheath encloses the rubber band member across the span between the dispensing end wall and the bottom end wall of the can so as to prevent any captured rodent from gnawing through the rubber band to permit the door to then open.

The inner end of the tubular latch member is provided with means for retaining bait on the inner end of the latch member for the purpose of attracting mice or

other rodents so as to cause them to enter the interior of the can. When such a mouse has entered the can, he will attempt to eat the bait and will dislodge the tubular latch member from engagement with the catch surface so that the elastic rubber band member immediately snaps the door closed and the rodent is consequently entrapped within the confines of the can. Additionally, the latch member is also provided with a lock latch surface which engages a second catch surface along the inside edge of the entry opening upon closure of the door member so as to lock the door member in closed position. Thus, the operation of the elongated elastic rubber band member and the lock surface provides a dual locking function to preclude escape of a captured rodent. In one embodiment of the invention the latch tube receives the bait member in an open-ended recess adjacent the end of the latch member with a transverse bore opening being provided on opposite sides of the opening so as to permit impalement of the bait by a retaining pin extended therethrough. In a second embodiment the bait is retained on the end of the latch member by a wire clip or the like extending through openings provided in a flattened end of the latch member.

BRIEF DESCRIPTION OF THE DRAWING

FIG. 1 is a perspective view of the preferred embodiment of the invention illustrating the door member in open position;

FIG. 2 is an exploded perspective view of the embodiment of FIG. 1;

FIG. 3 is a sectional view taken along lines 3—3 of FIG. 1 and illustrating the door in an opened condition;

FIG. 4 is a sectional view similar to FIG. 3 but illustrating the door in the closed position for imprisoning a rodent;

FIG. 5 is a sectional view taken along lines 5—5 of FIG. 3;

FIG. 6 is a side elevation view of a second embodiment with portions removed for the sake of illustration; and

FIG. 7 is a perspective view of a second embodiment of tubular latch means employed in the invention.

DESCRIPTION OF THE PREFERRED EMBODIMENTS

The preferred embodiment of the invention as illustrated in FIGS. 1 etc. comprises a disposable rodent trap including a container 10 in the form of a disposable aluminum beverage container having a cylindrical body wall 12, a bottom end wall 14 and a dispensing end wall 16. It should be observed that the bottom end wall 14 is normally the "bottom" wall when the beverage can is used for its original purpose whereas the dispensing end wall 16 is the end from which the beverage contained within the container is dispensed. Dispensing end wall 16 includes an opening 17 of sufficient size to permit the passage of a rodent therethrough so as to enter the interior of the container can 10 and also includes a peripheral flange 19. A stabilizer tab 18 extends through slots 20 provided in the cylindrical body wall 12 as best shown in FIG. 2. Stabilizer tab 18 prevents the can from rolling on a supporting surface in an obvious manner.

A floating door 22 comprising an end wall from a similar can is positioned adjacent and in contact with the dispensing end wall 16. Floating door 22 is provided with an upper circular opening 24 and a lower slot 26.

The upper circular opening 24 is in general alignment with an opening 28 in the dispensing end wall 16. The bottom end wall 14 is provided with an opening 30 in alignment with the opening 28 of the dispensing end wall. Biasing means in the form of an elastic rubber band member 32 extends through the openings 28 and 30 with the end of the biasing elastic rubber band member 32 adjacent the bottom wall 14 being anchored by a tubular anchor lug 34 while the opposite end of the rubber band member which extends through openings 28 and 24 is anchored by a similar lug 36. The lug members 34 and 36 can for example be formed of rolled pieces of aluminum scrap or the like. Thus it will be seen that the tension in rubber band 32 tends to move the floating door member 22 toward a closed position. A protective sheath 38 formed of metal in the form of aluminum or the like extends between the bottom wall 14 and the dispensing end wall 16 to fully enclose the rubber band 32 to prevent any rodent on the interior of the can from gnawing or eating through the band so as to cause its failure.

An elongated tubular latch member 40 is provided internally of the container can 10 and includes a flat outer end 42 which extends through the slot 26 and is held in position by an outer keeper pin 44 and an inner keeper pin 46 which are respectively on opposite sides of the floating door member 22. The inner end of the elongated tubular latch member 40 is provided with a pair of openings 48 through which a bait retention loop or wire or the like 50 extends so as to permit the attachment of bait 52 to the end of the latch member. Latch member 40 includes a first transverse latch surface 54 and a second transverse oppositely facing lock surface 56.

When the floating door 22 is in its open position the latch surface 54 is engaged with an upper external catch surface 60 extending along entry opening 17 in the dispensing end wall 16. Thus, the latch member retains the floating door in its open position. A mouse or other rodent can enter the opening 17 and upon attempting to eat the bait 52 will effect dislodging of the latch surface 54 from the catch surface 60 to immediately result in a rapid and quick movement of the door member 22 from the open position of FIG. 3 to the closed position of FIG. 4. The rodent on the interior of the container will consequently be imprisoned. Moreover, movement of the floating door 22 to the closed position immediately results in the lock surface 56 becoming engaged with a lower catch inside surface 62 as shown in FIG. 4. Thus, the floating door member 22 will be held in closed position by operation of the lock surface 56 as well as the elastic urgings of the rubber band 32.

FIG. 6 illustrates a slightly simplified embodiment in which the protective sheath 38 is dispensed with and the bare rubber band extends between the bottom wall 14 and the dispensing wall 16. The advantage of this embodiment is that it is slightly easier to manufacture. Additionally, the embodiment of FIG. 6 is illustrated with a second embodiment latch member 40' which is basically identical to the first latch member with the exception of the manner in which the bait 52 is connected to the inner end of the latch member. More specifically, the inner end of the latch member 40' includes an open end chamber or cavity 70 through which diametric openings 72 extend with the chamber or cavity 70 being of sufficient size to receive the bait 52. A retention pin 75 extends through the opening 72 and the bait 52 to retain the bait 52 in the end of the

latch member in the manner shown in FIG. 6. Otherwise, the second embodiment operates in exactly the same manner as the first embodiment.

It should be understood that, while preferred embodiments of the invention are illustrated herein, numerous modifications of the disclosed embodiments will undoubtedly occur to those of skill in the art. For example, practice of the invention is not limited to the use of beverage cans and other type cans or containers of larger sizes could be employed. In fact, it would even be possible to practice the present invention by the use of such large containers as oil drums or the like for use in capturing larger animals. Consequently, the use of the term "rodent" as discussed herein and as set forth in the claims should be broadly interpreted to include other types of animals. For these reasons, the spirit and scope of the invention should be broadly interpreted.

I claim:

1. A disposable rodent trap comprising a container defining an internal chamber, an end wall having an entry opening therein of sufficient size to permit a rodent to pass therethrough so as to enter said internal chamber, a door member provided externally of said end wall and movable from an open position toward said end wall into a closed position covering and blocking said entry opening, biasing means comprising a rubber band for urging said door member toward its closed position, latch means having a portion inside said chamber and extending between said door member and a catch surface on, and forming part of, said end wall comprising an edge surface adjacent said entry opening for normally holding said door member in its open position but being movable by rodent contact inside said chamber out of contact with said catch surface to permit said biasing means to move said door member to its closed position to entrap the rodent in said internal chamber and wherein said container is a disposable beverage can having a cylindrical body wall, a bottom end wall and a dispensing end wall with said entry opening being provided in said dispensing end wall which comprises a wall from which beverage would normally be dispensed during usage of said beverage container for its original purpose.

2. The invention of claim 1 wherein said latch member comprises an elongated tube connected at one end to said door member and having a transverse latch surface medially of its length for engaging said catch surface adjacent one edge of said entry opening and further including a lock latch surface extending transversely of said tubular member at a location near the door member for engaging an inner edge surface of said entry opening for latching said door member in said closed position.

3. A rodent trap as recited in claim 2 additionally including a tubular sheath extending between said bottom end wall and said opening in said dispensing end wall for enclosing said rubber band portion inside said internal chamber for preventing any rodent in said chamber from chewing on said rubber band.

4. A disposable rodent trap as recited in claim 3 wherein said door member comprises a can end from a similar can which has one end engaged with said dispensing end wall, said dispensing end wall including a peripheral flange surface which retains said door member in position.

5. A rodent trap as recited in claim 4 wherein said latch member includes means on its end opposite its end connected to said door member for retaining rodent attracting means thereon.

6. A rodent trap as recited in claim **5** additionally including transversely extending means connected to said body wall and engagable with a supporting surface for said rodent trap for maintaining said rodent trap in fixed position on said supporting surface.

7. A rodent trap as recited in claim **6** wherein said bottom end wall is provided with an aperture through which one end of said rubber band extends to provide an external loop of said rubber band and wherein said rubber band is connected to said wall by an elongated anchor lug passed through said loop.

8. A rodent trap as recited in claim **7** wherein said door member is provided with an opening through which a loop of said rubber band extends and further includes an anchor lug extending through said loop for retaining said loop externally of said door member.

9. A rodent trap as recited in claim **8** wherein said door member includes a slot through which one end of said latch member extends and said latch member includes keeper pins extending transversely through said latch member on opposite sides of said door member so as to retain said latch member in said slot.

10. A rodent trap as recited in claim **4** wherein said latch member has an open-ended bait receiving cavity on its end opposite its connection to said door member.

11. A disposable rodent trap comprising a container defining an internal chamber, an end wall having an entry opening therein of sufficient size to permit a rodent to pass therethrough so as to enter said internal chamber, a door member provided externally of said end wall and movable from an open position toward said end wall into a closed position covering and blocking said entry opening, biasing means for urging said door member toward its closed position, latch means having a portion inside said chamber and extending between said door member and a catch surface on, and forming part of, said end wall for normally holding said door member in its open position but being movable by rodent contact inside said chamber out of contact with said catch surface to permit said biasing means to move

said door member to its closed position to entrap the rodent in said internal chamber and wherein said container is a disposable beverage can having a cylindrical body wall, a bottom end wall and a dispensing end wall with said entry opening being provided in said dispensing end wall which comprises a wall from which beverage would normally be dispensed during usage of said beverage container for its original purpose and wherein said biasing means comprises an elastic band having one end secured to said bottom end wall, said second end wall includes a small opening spaced from said entry opening and the opposite end of said elastic band extends through said small opening and is secured to said door member by retainer pin means.

12. The invention of claim **11** wherein said latch member comprises an elongated metal tube connected at one end to said door member and having a transverse latch surface medially of its length for engaging said catch surface and further including a lock latch surface extending transversely of said tubular member at a location near the door member for engaging an inner edge surface of said entry opening for latching said door member in said closed position.

13. A rodent trap as recited in claim **12** additionally including a tubular sheath extending between said bottom end wall and said opening in said dispensing end wall for enclosing said elastic band portion inside said internal chamber for preventing any rodent in said chamber from chewing on said rubber band.

14. A disposable rodent trap as recited in claim **13** wherein said door member comprises a can end from a similar can which has one end engaged with said dispensing end wall, said dispensing end wall including a peripheral flange surface which retains said door member in position.

15. A rodent trap as recited in claim **14** wherein said latch member includes attachment means on its end opposite its end connected to said door member for retaining rodent attracting means thereon.

* * * * *

45

50

55

60

65

Sample Design Patents

US00D463046S

(12) **United States Design Patent** (10) Patent No.: **US D463,046 S**
 Kumar (45) Date of Patent: ✱✱ **Sep. 17, 2002**

(54) **GLASS PUMPKIN CAULDRON VOTIVE HOLDER**

(75) Inventor: **Sanjeev Kumar**, Munster, IN (US)

(73) Assignee: **Hosley International Trading Corporation**, Lynwood, IL (US)

(**) Term: **14 Years**

(21) Appl. No.: **29/149,517**

(22) Filed: **Oct. 11, 2001**

(51) LOC (7) Cl. **26-01**
(52) U.S. Cl. **D26/11; D26/16**
(58) Field of Search D26/9, 10, 11,
 D26/16; 431/125, 291; D11/125; D7/612,
 628

(56) **References Cited**

U.S. PATENT DOCUMENTS

D128,373 S * 7/1941 Heisey D26/9
D337,614 S * 7/1993 Turner D26/9
D412,369 S * 7/1999 Kumar D26/16
D422,720 S * 4/2000 Hardy D26/11

* cited by examiner

Primary Examiner—Robin V. Taylor
(74) Attorney, Agent, or Firm—Olson & Hierl, Ltd.

(57) **CLAIM**

The ornamental design for a glass pumpkin cauldron votive holder, as shown and described.

DESCRIPTION

FIG. 1 is a perspective view of a glass pumpkin cauldron votive holder of the present invention;

FIG. 2 is a right side elevational view of the glass pumpkin cauldron votive holder;

FIG. 3 is an opposite side elevational view of the glass pumpkin cauldron votive holder;

FIG. 4 is a top plan view of the glass pumpkin cauldron votive holder;

FIG. 5 is a bottom plan view of the glass pumpkin cauldron votive holder;

FIG. 6 is a front elevational view of the glass pumpkin cauldron votive holder; and,

FIG. 7 is a rear elevational view of the glass pumpkin cauldron votive holder.

1 Claim, 2 Drawing Sheets

FIG. 1

FIG. 2

FIG. 3

FIG. 4

FIG. 5

FIG. 6

FIG. 7

(12) **United States Design Patent**   (10) Patent No.:   **US D463,007 S**

Lord   (45) Date of Patent: ** Sep. 17, 2002

(54) **FAUCET**

(75) Inventor: **Judd A. Lord,** Carmel, IN (US)

(73) Assignee: **Masco Corporation of Indiana,** Indianapolis, IN (US)

(**) Term: **14 Years**

(21) Appl. No.: **29/136,756**

(22) Filed: **Feb. 7, 2001**

(51) **LOC** (7) **Cl.** **23-01**
(52) **U.S. Cl.** **D23/241;** D23/238; D23/242
(58) **Field of Search** D23/238–257; 4/675–678; 137/801

(56) **References Cited**

U.S. PATENT DOCUMENTS

D287,395 S	* 12/1986	Piesco	D23/255
D318,099 S	* 7/1991	Reid et al.	D23/255
D375,345 S	* 11/1996	Warshawsky	D23/241
D377,516 S	* 1/1997	Doughty et al.	D23/241
D407,466 S	* 3/1999	Hundley et al.	D23/252
D433,106 S	10/2000	Spangler	
D433,735 S	11/2000	Lord	
D434,118 S	11/2000	Lord	
D436,397 S	1/2001	Lord	
D438,292 S	* 2/2001	Lord	D23/249
D439,954 S	4/2001	Spangler	
D439,955 S	4/2001	Spangler	
D448,456 S	* 9/2001	Lord	D23/249

OTHER PUBLICATIONS

U.S. patent application Ser. No. 29/136,750 filed Feb. 7, 2001.
U.S. patent application Ser. No. 29/136,845 filed Feb. 7, 2001.
U.S. patent application Ser. No. 29/136,836 filed Feb. 7, 2001.
U.S. patent application Ser. No. 29/136,760 filed Feb. 7, 2001.
U.S. patent application Ser. No. 29/136,804 filed Feb. 7, 2001.

U.S. patent application Ser. No. 29/136,839 filed Feb. 7, 2001.
U.S. patent application Ser. No. 29/136,833 filed Feb. 7, 2001.
U.S. patent application Ser. No. 29/136,752 filed Feb. 7, 2001.
U.S. patent application Ser. No. 29/136,765 filed Feb. 7, 2001.
U.S. patent application Ser. No. 29/136,769 filed Feb. 7, 2001.
U.S. patent application Ser. No. 29/136,805 filed Feb. 7, 2001.
U.S. patent application Ser. No. 29/136,782 filed Feb. 7, 2001.
U.S. patent application Ser. No. 29/136,761 filed Feb. 7, 2001.
U.S. patent application Ser. No. 29/136,766 filed Feb. 7, 2001.

(List continued on next page.)

Primary Examiner—Louis S. Zarfas
Assistant Examiner—Gregory Andoll
(74) *Attorney, Agent, or Firm*—Myron B. Kapustij; Lloyd D. Doigan

(57)   **CLAIM**

The ornamental design for a faucet, as shown and described.

DESCRIPTION

FIG. 1 is a front perspective view of the faucet showing my new design;
FIG. 2 is a rear perspective view thereof;
FIG. 3 is a front elevational view thereof;
FIG. 4 is a left side elevational view thereof, the right side being a mirror image;
FIG. 5 is a rear elevational view thereof;
FIG. 6 is a top plan view thereof; and,
FIG. 7 is a bottom plan view thereof.
The broken line showing of the apertures in FIG. **7** are for purposes of illustration only and form no part of the claimed design.

1 Claim, 7 Drawing Sheets

239

OTHER PUBLICATIONS

U.S. patent application Ser. No. 29/136,763 filed Feb. 7, 2001.

U.S. patent application Ser. No. 29/136,773 filed Feb. 7, 2001.

* cited by examiner

Figure - 1

Figure - 2

Figure - 3

243

Figure - 4

244

Figure - 5

245

Figure - 6

Figure - 7

247

(12) **United States Design Patent** (10) Patent No.: **US D460,410 S**
Thrasher et al. (45) **Date of Patent:** ✶✶ **Jul. 16, 2002**

(54) **SIDEWALLS OF A TIRE**

(75) Inventors: **Danny Austin Thrasher**, Anderson; **Sylvain Leynaert**, Greer; **Joseph George Hoover**, Simpsonville, all of SC (US)

(73) Assignee: **Michelin Recherche et Technique S.A.** (CH)

(✶✶) Term: **14 Years**

(21) Appl. No.: **29/152,417**

(22) Filed: **Dec. 18, 2001**

(51) LOC (7) Cl. **12-15**
(52) U.S. Cl. **D12/605**
(58) Field of Search D12/531, 579, D12/588, 594, 595, 600, 601, 605, 900, 901; 152/209.1, 209.12, 209.16, 209.17, 209.25, 523, 524

(56) **References Cited**

U.S. PATENT DOCUMENTS

D59,717	S	✶ 11/1921	Coats	D12/605
D120,687	S	✶ 5/1940	Moonan	D12/605
2,745,459	A	✶ 5/1956	Pennock	152/153
D260,872	S	✶ 9/1981	Wright et al.	D12/596
4,915,150	A	✶ 4/1990	Takusagawa et al. ..	152/209.16
D313,777	S	✶ 1/1991	Yamashita	D12/596
D319,994	S	9/1991	Manestar	D12/147
5,849,118	A	✶ 12/1998	Matsumoto	152/209.11
D442,128	S	5/2001	Allison	D12/605
D444,742	S	7/2001	Dunlap	D12/147
D447,449	S	✶ 9/2001	Guspodin	D12/605

OTHER PUBLICATIONS

Tread Design Guide, 2000, p. 79, BFGoodrich Radial Mud–Terrain T/A.
Tread Design Guide, 2000, p. 85, Dayton Daytona Stag XT.
Tread Design Guide, 2000, p. 103, Mickey Thompson Baja Claw Radial.
Tread Design Guide, 2000, p. 103, Mickey Thompson Baja Claw.
Tread Design Guide, 2000, p. 103, Mickey Thompson Baja King.
Tread Design Guide, 2000, p. 103, Monarch Highliner Premium Hwy. Traction ND.
Tread Design Guide, 2000, p. 106, National Durango M/T.

* cited by examiner

Primary Examiner—Robert M. Spear
(74) *Attorney, Agent, or Firm*—Martin Farrell; Robert R. Reed; Alan A. Csontos

(57) **CLAIM**

The ornamental design for sidewalls of a tire, as shown and described.

DESCRIPTION

FIG. 1 is a perspective view of sidewalls of a tire showing our new design, it being undestood that the surface pattern repeats circumferentially throughout the side portion of the tire, the opposite side perspective view being identical thereto;

FIG. 2 is an enlarged fragmentary front elevation view of a tire showing portions of the surface pattern of the tire sidewalls of FIG. 1; and,

FIG. 3 is an enlarged fragmentary side elevation view of one tire sidewall thereof, the surface pattern being repeated throughout the sidewall area, the opposite side elevation view being identical thereto.

The broken line disclosure of the tire tread and inner bead is for illustrative purposes only and forms no part of the claimed design.

1 Claim, 3 Drawing Sheets

Fig. 1

249

Fig. 2

$$Fig. 3$$

Index

About the Author

ALAN L. DURHAM is Professor of Law at the University of Alabama School of Law, where he teaches in the areas of intellectual property, antitrust, and torts. A native of California's Silicon Valley, he practiced law there from 1989 to 1998, primarily in the field of high-technology patent litigation. He has a J.D. from the University of California, Berkeley.